KELLY JAMES CLARK, Editor

Abraham's Children

LIBERTY AND TOLERANCE IN AN AGE

OF RELIGIOUS CONFLICT

Yale UNIVERSITY PRESS
New Haven &
London

Published with assistance from the John Templeton Foundation.

Yale University Press books may be purchased in quantity for educational, business, or promotional use. For information, please e-mail sales.press@yale .edu (U.S. office) or sales@yaleup.co.uk (U.K. office).

Set in Sabon type by Westchester Book Group
Printed in the United States of America

Library of Congress Cataloging-in-Publication Data

Abraham's children : liberty and tolerance in an age of religious conflict / edited by Kelly James Clark.
        p. cm.
    Includes bibliographical references and index.
    ISBN 978-0-300-17937-8 (pbk. : alk. paper)   1. Freedom of religion.
2. Religious tolerance.   3. Abrahamic religions.   4. Religions—Relations.
I. Clark, Kelly James, 1956–
    BL640.A27 2012
    201'.5—dc23

                                                            2011044936

A catalogue record for this book is available from the British Library.

This paper meets the requirements of ANSI/NISO Z39.48-1992 (Permanence of Paper).

10 9 8 7 6 5 4 3 2

Abraham's Children

To Stewart Shapiro
who prodded/inspired me/this project

Peace

When will you ever, Peace, wild wooddove, shy wings shut,
Your round me roaming end, and under be my boughs?
When, when, Peace, will you, Peace? I'll not play hypocrite
To own my heart: I yield you do come sometimes; but
That piecemeal peace is poor peace. What pure peace allows
Alarms of wars, the daunting wars, the death of it?

O surely, reaving Peace, my Lord should leave in lieu
Some good! And so he does leave Patience exquisite,
That plumes to Peace thereafter. And when Peace here does house
He comes with work to do, he does not come to coo,
He comes to brood and sit.

—Gerard Manley Hopkins

Contents

Acknowledgments

About two years ago, I started inviting prominent Muslims, Christians, and Jews to defend religious liberty and tolerance from within their own faith traditions. Not that it was a race, but former president Jimmy Carter, arguably the most famous and unarguably the oldest contributor, finished first. Kudos to President Carter! The last to finish, He Who Will Not Be Named, gave me a few gray hairs as the deadline passed.

There is no end of books in defense of liberty and tolerance written from a Western, liberal, enlightenment perspective. But those preach only or mainly to the Western or Western-influenced choir. For more conservative Muslim, Christian, and Jewish choirs, music in their own theological language is required. The authors of these essays were asked to refer and defer to their own Holy Writ, theological reflection, and tradition. Moreover, they were asked to appeal to a wide audience and so to include stories but avoid scholarly pedantry (lo, that last phrase is pedantic; I thus repent). In short, they were asked to be persuasive.

Each essay is, of course, intended to be persuasive to those who share their tradition. But there is also the hope that each essay will prove persuasive to those outside each author's own tradition—that readers from various traditions will sympathetically understand practitioners of other religions. Perhaps, even, outsiders will "see themselves" in the formative faith and fundamental practices of those in other traditions. Sympathetic understanding makes it a lot harder to restrict the liberty of others.

Some will look over the list of contributors and think (and others will say and some will even write), "Why wasn't so-and-so included?" where so-and-so is the "obviously best" Muslim, Christian, or Jewish thinker on the topic of religious liberty and tolerance. Suffice it to say that so-and-so may have been invited but refused the invitation. Although tempted, I will not name those who lacked the good sense to participate in this project. And some will think, say, or write, "Why wasn't this or that view or theological position represented?" Again, suffice it to say that I asked countless people for advice about whom and what to include. I did my best to be inclusive of people, genders, and positions. We got what we got. And it's pretty darn good.

I did not dictate or even suggest what anyone would write. Each author was given a free hand. And so although each author is committed to peace, liberty, and justice, there is a great deal of disagreement about the causes of injustice and intolerance and, hence, any possible solutions. So be it. It's a messy world we live in.

Finally, a note about the essays by the presidents. Much of Jimmy Carter's essay is excerpted, with his permission, from previously published works. From his books and speeches we excerpted various of his writings on the topic of this volume. President Carter then carefully read the essay over, added something here and there, and then returned it to us with permission to publish. We do credit, at the end of his essay, every publisher from which we excerpted portions of his essay. With regard to President Abdurrahman Wahid's essay, we are grateful to his good friend C. Holland Taylor—with whom President Wahid established LibForAll Foundation and its International Institute of Qur'anic Studies—for kindly granting us permission to include it in this volume. LibForAll's Kyai Haji Hodri Ariev provided valuable editorial assistance in preparing the essay for publication.

This sort of collaborative project requires the work of many hands. I wish to thank my research assistants, Emmalon Davis and Dan Hooley, for their invaluable insights and excellent work. Thanks also to my lovely daughter, Emily, and Grace Hardy for help in preparing the manuscript for publication. I'm grateful to the Calvin College Philosophy Department Colloquium for suggestions on improving my essay. And, most of all, I wish to express my gratitude to my administrative assistant, Donna Romanowski, for her indefatigable work and good cheer at every stage of this project.

Abraham's Children

Calling Abraham's Children

KELLY JAMES CLARK

History is full of religious wars; but, we must take care to observe, it was not the multiplicity of religions that produced these wars, it was the intolerating spirit which animated that one which thought she had the power of governing.

—Baron de Montesquieu

Caricatures of Religious Intolerance

There is a familiar narrative of religiously motivated violence. It claims a long and unbroken chain from antiquity to the present of the intolerance on the part of religious groups, especially the Abrahamic religions, toward members of other religious groups. It is a narrative of violence, oppression, torture, and war. This highly selective narrative omits any of the goods that religions have brought to the world and is deeply caricatured. Many of its claims are blatantly false. Sadly, because of its influence, it needs to be retold, reconsidered, and reevaluated.

Caricature #1. The early Hebrews, under strict orders from their God, razed villages devoted to competing gods, destroying men, women, and children alike. Their subsequent oppression by virtually every other religious group and their forced sojourn from their home is well known. And the Holocaust is surely one of the worst atrocities in all of human history. But since their return to Israel, the oppressed have become the oppressors—the Palestinians were forcibly rejected from their homeland of more than 2,000 years and are treated as second-class citizens or worse. Any non-Jew who dares question Israeli policies is an enemy of Israel and an anti-Semite; Jews who dare question Israeli policies are self-loathing and self-hating.

Caricature #2. Although the Christian scriptures teach that love has no bounds, Christians throughout history have set narrow limits to their love. They have betrayed their own deepest commitments, often in the name of God and against practitioners of other religions. The institutionalization of Christianity by the Roman Empire set an apparently pacifistic religion on a path of violence. The Crusades sought unsuccessfully but at great human expense to rid the holy lands of Muslim "infidels." The atrocities and religious wars of the Reformation, committed and waged by all sides, caused the river Seine to run red with blood. Native Americans have been exploited and destroyed under the banner of God. Christopher Columbus brought the gospel and germs to the New World, taking back slaves and gold. In our own day we have witnessed the excesses of religious fundamentalists who kill in the name of God or in defense of fetuses. And American leaders have used Christian commitments to inspire the nation to new holy wars in Iraq and Afghanistan with careless disregard for human welfare.

Caricature #3 (especially fashionable since 9/11). Islam is, by its very nature, a conquering religion. Although the Prophet Muhammad demanded hospitality to strangers inside one's tent, outside the tent plunder and pillage ruled the land. Islam spread by the sword from the tiny oasis of Medina to all of the Middle East, North Africa, and Spain, to create a huge earthly empire. Post-9/11, the term "Muslim" has become synonymous with "terrorist." Israeli Jews fear that their Muslim neighbors cannot be trusted and are plotting their destruction as a nation. The frequent missile strikes from the Gaza Strip into nearby Israel are not reassuring.

There is much to dispute in these highly selective and tendentious narratives. Jewish, Muslim, and Christian beliefs have motivated deep and lasting good, maybe much more good than evil (we will come to that later). But they have, indeed, been implicated in deep and disturbing evil—evil that is hard to explain given their commitment to an All-Merciful God. But, some charge, religiously motivated violence is not so hard to explain when one fully understands the faith of Abraham's children.

The New Atheist Challenge

In his documentary "The Root of All Evil?" Oxford biologist Richard Dawkins proclaims (in spite of the question mark) that religion is the root of (nearly) all evil. Apparently sacred, benign, and even peaceful religious faith sets the young and committed believer on the sure path to stonings and suicide bombings. According to Dawkins, the paradigm believer is not, as one might expect, Gandhi, St. Francis, or Mother Teresa, but rather the fundamentalist terrorist who has followed his or her religious belief to its logical conclusion—unquestionably assisting an angry God in the just eradication of false beliefs and practices (by persecuting the impious and destroying their idols). He charges that religions themselves are the cause of most of the violence and intolerance that we find in the world. He also claims that religiously motivated violence and intolerance are inevitable given the essential characteristics of the children of Abraham—Jews, Christians, and Muslims: "To fill a world with . . . religions of the Abrahamic kind," writes Dawkins, "is like littering the streets with loaded guns. Do not be surprised if they are used."[1] To paraphrase the famous Christian hymn: "Onward Christian, Muslim, and Jewish soldiers."

Dawkins is not alone in his claim that religion especially tempts human beings to violence and intolerance. Frequently called the "New Atheists," a group of influential writers has charged that all religions are inherently intolerant and lead inevitably to religious persecution and violence. According to Christopher Hitchens, "People of faith are in their different ways planning your and my destruction. Religion poisons everything."[2] Striking a similar chord, Sam Harris writes that those who are adherents of theistic religions seem to all agree on one thing: that respect for other faiths and for the views of unbelievers is not something endorsed by God. He writes:

> While all faiths have been touched, here and there, by the spirit of ecumenicalism, the central tenet of every religious tradition is that all others are mere repositories of error or, at best, dangerously incomplete. Intolerance is thus intrinsic to every creed. Once a person believes—really believes—that certain ideas can lead to eternal happiness, or to its antithesis, he cannot tolerate the possibility that the people he loves might be led astray by the blandishments of unbelievers.[3]

These writers contend that promoting secular defenses of religious tolerance will not solve the problems of religious violence and intolerance. As they see it, the problem is religion itself.

Dawkins commenced his critique of religion after the 9/11 attacks on the World Trade Center. These attacks were, for Dawkins, the final straw: "My last vestige of 'hands off religion' respect disappeared in the smoke and choking dust of September 11th, 2001, followed by the 'National Day of Prayer,' when prelates and pastors did their tremulous Martin Luther King impersonations and urged people of mutually incompatible faiths to hold hands, united in homage to the very force that caused the problem in the first place."[4] So what caused this irresistible force in the first place? According to Dawkins, unthinking faith and misguided devotion to a particular sort of delusion—an egomaniacal and zealous deity; of Yahweh, he writes, "The God of the Old Testament is arguably the most unpleasant character in all fiction: jealous and proud of it; a petty, unjust, unforgiving control-freak; a vindictive, bloodthirsty ethnic cleanser; a misogynistic, homophobic, racist, infanticidal, genocidal, filicidal, pestilential, megalomaniacal, sadomasochistic, capriciously malevolent bully."[5] Little wonder, if that is his nature, that Yahweh incites his faithful to inflict extraordinary and horrific suffering.

Amongst these writers, two important claims emerge. Religion is a force not for good, but for violence and intolerance. The exclusive claims of religions, particularly beliefs about salvation and the afterlife, motivate, even necessitate, intolerant behavior. Again, a few days after 9/11, we find Dawkins arguing the following:

> If death is final, a rational agent can be expected to value his life highly and be reluctant to risk it. This makes the world a safer place, just as a plane is safer if its hijacker wants to survive. At the other extreme, if a significant number of people convince themselves, or are convinced by their priests, that a martyr's death is equivalent to pressing the hyperspace button and zooming through a wormhole to another universe, it can make the world a very dangerous place. Especially if they also believe that that other universe is a paradisiacal escape from the tribulations of the real world. Top it off with sincerely believed, if ludicrous and degrading to women, sexual promises, and is it any wonder that naïve and frustrated young men are clamouring to be selected for suicide missions?[6]

According to Hitchens, religion "does not have the confidence in its own various preachings even to allow coexistence between different faiths."[7]

A second charge goes beyond the claim that the fundamental beliefs of religion inspire intolerant and harmful behavior. Although there certainly are religious extremists, most religious believers are just your average neighbor and citizen, who show in their lives respect and tolerance for the views of others. But their religious beliefs are not, as one might think, the source of their respect and tolerance. "Religious moderation," Sam Harris writes, "is the product of *secular* knowledge and religious *ignorance*."[8] So the second claim is that religious moderation arises not from religious belief but from the believer's secularization. According to Harris, religious moderation "has nothing underwriting it other than the unacknowledged neglect of the letter of the divine law."[9] If one paid heed to divine law, one would be out killing infidels. So one can be a religious moderate only by ignoring much that is in the sacred texts of one's faith. Thus, taking one's uncompromising Abrahamic faith seriously is unlikely to lead to tolerance or respect for other faiths. Moderation can be achieved only through secularization, not through religion properly understood and followed.

Because Harris thinks moderation can be achieved only by embracing secular humanism, he argues that the religious moderate has no basis from which to argue against the religious fundamentalist. "From the perspective of those seeking to live by the letter of the texts, the religious moderate is nothing more than a failed fundamentalist. We cannot say that fundamentalists are crazy, because they are merely practicing their freedom of belief; we cannot even say that they are mistaken in religious terms, because their knowledge of scripture is generally unrivaled."[10] In the words of Hitchens, religious moderation and tolerance "is a compliment to humanism, not to religion."[11] He claims that only secular humanism, not divine revelation, can motivate tolerance and respect for other religions.

The path to peace, then, calls not for the promotion of tolerance and respect for other religions, but rather for the dissolution of religious belief itself. Peace can be achieved only if we convince individuals to abandon their religious beliefs. To end the religious intolerance and violence that we find in the world today requires that people abandon their mistaken and exclusive views and adopt in their stead a secular humanist viewpoint. For the future of humanity, religious belief—especially the monotheism of Abraham's children—must be abandoned.

Religion: A Force for Good or Ill?

The New Atheists claim that in spite of its pretensions to love and peace, religion is really a force for evil in the world. Religious groups may have established the odd hospital or orphanage, and believers may have visited the occasional prisoner and widow (although the New Atheists concede little, if any, of religion's goods). But, so the New Atheist claim goes, overall religion is more likely to produce or enflame—and, indeed, has produced and enflamed—bigotry, hatred, persecution, violence, and death. The result is that there is more religiously motivated wickedness than religiously inspired goodness.

How does one determine if religion is an overall force for good and evil in the world? How does one count the religiously motivated good and then subtract the religiously motivated bad? How does one determine if it was religion, after all, that motivated, say, the Crusades or the Inquisition or 9/11 and not the nonreligious desire for earthly power, prestige, or wealth? We cannot peer into the human heart, so we cannot know for sure if violence is motivated by faith in a heavenly God or by mundane human selfishness (in the guise of religion). According to Chris Hedges, a veteran *New York Times* foreign combat correspondent, it is a myth that religions are the source of war:

> The ethnic conflicts and insurgencies of our time, whether between Serbs and Muslims or Hutus and Tutsis, are not religious wars. They are not clashes between cultures or civilizations, nor are they the result of ancient ethnic hatreds. They are manufactured wars, born out of the collapse of civil societies, perpetuated by fear, greed, and paranoia, and they are run by gangsters, who rise up from the bottom of their own societies and terrorize all, including those they purport to protect.[12]

Although religion is not the cause of war, religion may be the solution. According to Hedges, only the self-giving, other-regarding charity and kindness made possible by deep religious commitment can counter the native human impulses to war.

Recent research has shown that religious conviction is superior to nonreligious motivations to morality and is empirically verified as better at motivating moral behavior. Although religious beliefs sometimes channel intolerance and violence, they are more likely to tame our vicious and selfish nature than any secular alternatives. The health and longevity benefits of being part of a religious community have long been known, but the moral benefits of religion are just as well attested. Arthur Brooks, the Louis A. Bantle Professor of Government Policy at the Maxwell School of Citizenship and Public Affairs at Syracuse University, concludes that active religious believers are considerably more generous than nonbelievers.[13] In *Who Really Cares*, Brooks presents the striking moral difference between religious and secular Americans: the religious believer is vastly more likely than the secular person to, among many other things, volunteer, give blood, and loan money to friends and family (and to do so more generously). On nearly any metric of generosity, the religious person trumps the secular person. Brooks concludes: "Religious people are more charitable in every measurable non-religious way—including secular donations, informal giving, and even acts of kindness and honesty—than secularists."[14]

The New Atheists, who trot out horrific anecdotes such as the 9/11 terrorist attacks and female genital mutilation, ignore the goods delivered by religion. In addition to generosity and honesty, religious belief has produced many other great goods. What about religious involvement in the eradication of infanticide, gladiatorial games, and slavery? Or religiously motivated poverty and famine relief, or the general kindness shown by the believer to her children, her neighbor, or even strangers (not to mention widows, orphans, and prisoners)? Many helping institutions, such as hospitals, universities, and orphanages, owe their origins to religious believers. Natural and equal rights, and, hence, democracy, arose within cultures that affirmed the equality of all children of God. Human dignity originated from the doctrine of creation in the divine image.

Moreover, to make their case against religion and for secularism, the New Atheists ignore or try to explain away secular atrocities. In our century alone, the Holocaust, the killing fields of Cambodia, and the Communist pogrom dwarf the collective religious atrocities throughout all of human history. Even if we take the highest estimates of deaths caused by the Crusades and the Inquisition—150,000 and 50,000, respectively—these religious atrocities are mere fractions of the millions, perhaps more than a hundred million, killed by Josef Stalin and Mao Zedong. If we were to add Hitler's death camps and World War II, and Pol Pot's murderous regime in Cambodia, the difference would be even greater (even if, on the other side, we add the more than 3,000 killed in the 9/11 terrorist attacks and every other religious murder). In the atheist evil versus religious evil contest, atheistically motivated evil is the easy winner.

Winning this contest affords no great prize. Although the Abrahamic faiths may beat secularism in the good/evil contest, it is nonetheless undeniable that a great deal of violence has been done in the name of religion (even if it is disputable that such violence was motivated by genuine faith) and possibly even by sincere believers moved by their faith. A quick look at many global hotspots where we find chronic and seemingly intractable conflict reveals all too often that religious intolerance is part of the problem, adding fuel to the flames of conflict. Israel and Palestine, Northern Ireland, the Sudan, the Balkans, Kashmir, Pakistan, India, Sri Lanka, and the Caucasus (just to name a few) all provide examples of persistent conflict that is at least partly exacerbated, if not caused by, religious belief.

The urgent need for greater religious tolerance and for the protection of religious liberty for all is by no means limited to areas of chronic conflict or the developing world. As increasing numbers of immigrants have moved to Great Britain and Western Europe, the continent has seen a backlash against its Muslim immigrants and even its Muslim citizens. The summer of 2010 saw many expressions of this anti-Muslim fervor and anxiety; several European countries considered legal measures targeting the religious expression of their Muslim citizens. Belgium became the first European country to ban the wearing of the burqa in public. A few months later, France passed a similar ban, adding to previous legislation that had banned the headscarf and other religious symbols in schools. A similar ban was narrowly defeated in Spain. Some parts of Germany, Belgium, and the Netherlands have previously banned schoolteachers from wearing the headscarf. And just a year earlier, in 2009, Switzerland passed a nationwide ban on the construction of minarets (the prayer towers of mosques). Demographers project that Muslim populations will grow twice as fast as non-Muslim populations over the next twenty years, and so the percentage of Muslims in European countries will increase dramatically. Fear of the Islamization of Europe is palpable. Fear of Islamization likely drove the 2011 massacre of civilians in Norway.[15]

Anxiety and fear of Muslims is on the rise in the United States as well. This, too, became apparent in the summer of 2010 when efforts to build an Islamic community center two blocks from ground zero—the former site of the World Trade Center—drew national coverage. Widely portrayed in the media and by right-wing political pundits as "the mosque at ground zero," it was, ironically, neither a mosque nor at ground zero. One of the leaders of the efforts to build the center, Feisal Abdul Rauf, was portrayed in some media as connected to radical terrorist groups. These unjustified claims gained credence by being widely repeated. All this was despite the fact that Rauf was chosen by the U.S. State Department, under both the Bush and Obama administrations, to tour the Middle East speaking about religious tolerance and the need for interfaith dialogue. Following the national coverage, fueled by anti-Islamic anger, a torrent of anti-Muslim sentiment ensued, along with a wave of vandalism directed at Muslims. A Muslim cab driver in New York was repeatedly stabbed after the perpetrator asked the man if he was Muslim, and a Florida preacher threatened to have his congregation burn copies of the Qur'an.

If religious believers have access to divinely ordained, transformational processes—through divinely inspired writings, divine grace, divine rituals, or divine assistance—then we should expect to find transformed behavior. "Faith-based intolerance" seems a contradiction in terms. Because of the corrosive effects of sin, we do not expect perfection, of course, but moral and spiritual improvement surely. So there remains a disturbing tension between the Abrahamic command to show mercy to the stranger and the religiously motivated intolerance and violence that we see in our contemporary world and throughout history.

Faith-Based Tolerance

I conceived of *Abraham's Children* after I had completed a draft of my book *Explaining God Away?* written in response to Dawkins and the New Atheists. In that book, I address their philosophical arguments against rational religious belief. I only briefly consider their claims regarding religious intolerance because these claims are irrelevant to the philosophical discussion that concerned me. But their insistent recitations of religious intolerance and violence deeply troubled me. Not their insistent recitations, though: religiously motivated intolerance and violence deeply trouble me.

I embraced the New Atheists' allegations as a challenge to religious believers to do everything in their power to prevent the New Atheists' claims from coming true. That is: religious believers should do everything in their divinely motivated power to effect religion as a force for good. Believers should make it so that genuine faith in God inspires kindness, compassion, and liberty but not intolerance, hatred, and violence. So I invited prominent political figures, as well as those deeply involved in peace and justice movements, to defend religious liberty and tolerance from the perspective of their own faith tradition. If religious believers don't work hard and together, religiously inspired evil may eventually win out over religiously motivated good. Without religious believers doing everything in their power to bring peace and reconciliation to our broken world, religion could be the death of us all.

Instead of the usual Western, universal legitimations of tolerance grounded in impartial reason, I invited religiously particular defenses of tolerance that begin with the sacred writings and beliefs of the various major Abrahamic religions. Each writer was asked to write persuasively, passionately, and winsomely from within his or her own religious tradition. Instead of denigrating tradition in deference to "pure reason," we celebrate tradition and seek defenses of tolerance from within these Abrahamic theological traditions. The authors were asked to use holy writ, theology, and narrative to understand and ground liberty and tolerance. Given the diversity of personal experiences and religious beliefs of each author and the differing narratives they accept, sometimes to account for or explain the same historical facts, the reader can expect to encounter a diversity of opinions in this book. Each essay is its own unique mixture of experiential, philosophical, and political opinion, making the collection as a whole occasionally contradictory or paradoxical.

I completed the outline for *Abraham's Children* while attending a seminar at Oxford University on the psychological origins of religious belief. We are, so it seems, naturally disposed to religious belief; religious belief is in our bones and brains. So in spite of the New Atheist hope, religious belief is unlikely to go away. And if religion is not likely to go away, pinning liberty and toler-ance on irreligious humanism seems futile. Moreover, Western, secular, lib-eral, rationalistic justifications of liberty and tolerance are unlikely to appeal to serious, conservative religious believers. Such believers do not take Western ("imperialistic," "rationalistic," "atheistic," "colonizing," "immoral," and so on) culture and values as their source of authority. They take only their own holy writ and their own religious tradition as authoritative. Calling such be-lievers "ignorant" unless they accede to Western secular, liberal arguments is unlikely to do more than make the name-caller feel superior to "benighted" religious believers and to cause such religious believers to dig in their righ-teous heels. All this seems counterproductive to liberty and tolerance.

Suppose the New Atheists are right: religion, especially of the Abrahamic variety, encourages intolerance and even violence. Let me state clearly that I am not conceding that they are right—human beings as such are tempted to intolerance and violence. Intolerance is a fundamental human problem; it is not the special vice of the religious. It can find a wide variety of manifestations—race, color, nationality, socioeconomic status, geographical and political affili-ation, and sometimes religion. Humans, as humans, have a hard time tolerating those others who are not us, those who are not part of our own kin or group. It is as simple as that. But suppose also that religion is not going away. How then can religious believers resist the religious temptation toward intolerance and find their way to mutual peace, uncompromised liberty, and principled tolerance?

What Is Tolerance?

We have been speaking roughly of tolerance and intolerance, yet we have not carefully understood these terms. Let us pause to do so. Although people with deep and sincere moral or religious convictions are often intoler-ant, deep and sincere moral or religious convictions can provide the pre-conditions of tolerance. Without a robust sense of rightness with respect to religious beliefs or moral practices, tolerance is simply not possible. Toler-ance comes from the Latin *tolerare*, "to bear or endure"; it connotes putting up with a weight or a burden. Tolerance is, at first glance, the disposition to endure or bear beliefs and practices that one takes to be either false or im-moral. Tolerance assumes that some beliefs and practices are true or right and that others are false or wrong. The beliefs and practices that one finds true and right are not burdensome, but there must be, for tolerance to be possible at all, some beliefs or practices that are burdensome. Only when

I am in firm possession of my own moral and religious judgments can I tolerate people with differing beliefs and practices.

Disagreement alone, however, is not an adequate precondition of tolerance. People routinely disagree about matters they take to be trivial or unimportant; this sort of disagreement does not require tolerance. I prefer vanilla ice cream and you prefer chocolate. I do not tolerate your chocolate preference because I do not care about your ice cream preferences. Tolerance requires, in addition to disagreement, an element of caring that is usually rooted in a deep commitment to the belief or practice in question. The sort of caring relevant to tolerance must be deep enough to create a burden, which is why tolerance usually arises in connection with matters of fundamental human concern. We may not care about ice cream preferences, but we do care, very deeply, about our moral and religious beliefs and practices.

Because of the depth of care about matters of fundamental human concern, it is easy to see why human beings seem naturally inclined toward intolerance. We invest ourselves in the things we care about, and those who disagree with us deny that our concerns are worthy of such care and investment. When we find that what others care about is a burden to us, we naturally wish to preserve our own cares and investments. This often leads to dismissing, alienating, or even persecuting those with different practices and beliefs.

In tolerance, one devalues the other person's beliefs or practices without devaluing the *person* who holds those beliefs. The tolerant person chooses to treat the person with significantly different beliefs and practices as intrinsically valuable, in spite of that person's rejection of her fundamental human concerns. Tolerance is the disposition to subdue our natural inclination to distance, reject, or persecute others whose beliefs and practices differ from our own. The tolerant person is, rather, disposed to respect the other in spite of these differences. The tolerant person says, in effect, "Our fundamental disagreement does not diminish my estimation of your worth as a human being, and, therefore, though I disagree with your beliefs or practices, still I will endure them." Intolerance, by contrast, acceding to the natural inclination to devalue the other, encourages the rejection of the person (which can then issue forth in harm). Tolerance, then, is a virtue that must be cultivated to tame our natural disposition to reject and disrespect those who are different from us.

In contemporary America, tolerance is sometimes viewed as more of a vice than a virtue. No one wants to be tolerated—they want to be respected, esteemed, valued; they do not want others to hold their noses while putting up with their stinky beliefs and repulsive behaviors. This betrays a deep misunderstanding about tolerance: we do not tolerate *people*, we respect, esteem, and value people; we tolerate behaviors and beliefs. Moreover, although tolerance has such negative connotations (who, after all, wants to be endured?), it would be a dramatic improvement in most other parts of the world. In places where those who convert are killed, Jews are forbidden, Christian churches or mosques cannot be built, believers are imprisoned, and people are not permitted religious or much other self-determination, religious believers are begging to be endured. Where the current option is murder, persecution, discrimination, and shunning, being endured would be a very positive step forward. So although those in the West sometimes denigrate tolerance, it is precisely the step that needs to be taken where some are currently intolerant of others' religious beliefs and practices (that is, everywhere).

And yet bearing or enduring is not the essence of the virtue of tolerance. In the Judeo-Christian-Muslim tradition, tolerance should be grounded in respect, and this respect is grounded in the dignity and worth of all human beings, which is, in turn, grounded in the image of God.

Religious persecution and intolerance might be as old as religion itself, and the threat of religiously motivated, shaped, or focused violence is not likely to fade away any time soon. In fact, tensions between different religious groups appear likely to increase as the world becomes more interconnected and it becomes easier to export intolerance and violence around the world. Globalization brings increased awareness of and contact with moral and religious differences, as well as all the fears, anger, and frustration that that instills. If we wish to avoid misunderstanding and violence, tolerance and respect are increasingly valuable commodities. Let us hope and pray they are not scarce commodities.

Religious Defenses of Tolerance

Although tolerance is a desperately needed virtue, many religious believers are skeptical of liberal defenses of religious tolerance that either ignore or dismiss their religious convictions. For them, "impartial," liberal defenses of religious tolerance are unappealing and lacking authority. Whether good or bad, many religious believers reject secular, Western, liberal reason. Religious believers must, then, find within their own traditions the essential ingredients of tolerance and liberty. Religious leaders and thinkers, then, must speak up and show why and how tolerance is defensible from within their own tradition. This perspective is crucially needed, moreover, as some religious extremists passionately cite holy writ in defense of intolerance and violence.[16]

The Abrahamic faith traditions (Judaism, Christianity, and Islam) claim that their particular beliefs and practices are essential for personal salvation. Given these exclusivist claims, the New Atheists argue, these religions foster an antagonism toward the unbeliever and create an environment conducive to religious violence and oppression. As the beliefs and practices of religious believers are held to be of supreme importance and as they think that they are in possession of the one and only Truth, it follows (so the charge goes) that sincere religious believers are incapable of dialogue and respect. The problem, as the New Atheists see it, is that the religious believers' unwavering faith in their own beliefs, their unfettered confidence, precludes valuing the beliefs of other individuals. Moreover, those individuals who hold contrary beliefs are neither respected nor valued: they are viewed not as simply and sadly mistaken but as idolatrous, impious, and even immoral; religious believers take the slight step from viewing other believers as wrong to viewing them as infidel. It is no surprise, then, that intolerance ensues. Infidels attack nothing less than God himself and it is the true believer's solemn and sometimes final task to protect God's honor.

This charge—that exclusive religious claims lead to intolerance—is an important claim that must be addressed. It merits attention in part because it is claimed to be the direct and inevitable result of religion fully grasped.

The essays in this book offer various responses to this charge. Writing from within the three Abrahamic traditions, the authors illustrate how a Muslim, Christian, or Jew can retain their distinctive religious identity, beliefs, and practices while fostering tolerance and respect for those of different faiths. Each of the essays in this book comes from a believer in one of the Abrahamic faiths. And each particular faith has its own tradition, its own sacred texts, and its own unique resources that can be put forward to motivate and call for religious tolerance.

Shared Grounds for Liberty and Tolerance

Although distinct, the Abrahamic traditions share some fundamental beliefs that are foundational to tolerance and respect of other faiths and other people. These beliefs not only can but also should motivate tolerance and respect for believers of other faiths. Shared understandings of divine justice and love also support religious tolerance. Finding that there is shared ground would be a very good thing. We tend to focus on the differences between our own beliefs and those of other religions (and they are undeniable, substantial, and sometimes irreconcilable). This often leads to thinking of other believers as faithless, disobedient, and maybe even not fully human. As they are denigrated and disrespected, they are then easier to ignore, persecute, and even kill.

Abrahamic faith at its most confident should create humility and mercy rather than the arrogance and hatred so evident in purveyors of intolerance. The faith of Abraham is the faith that a merciful God is in control and that submission to God's providential will is the path of human righteousness. Abraham's attempts at self-assertion—his strayings—were disastrous. The Muslim saying "There is no god apart from God" should preclude any mere human from making god-like assertions concerning life and death. Complete submission to the will of God (*Islam* means "submission") should preclude blind submission to the vicious orders of contemporary "prophets." The Jewish Sabbath is a weekly reminder that we are but creatures wholly subject to the one true God.

What other beliefs do children of Abraham share that can prevent intolerance? First and foremost is the belief that all humans are created in the image of God. This understanding of the human person, shared by Judaism, Christianity, and Islam alike, undergirds a conception of the human person as a bearer of intrinsic and immeasurable value. This robust understanding of human value supports a healthy sense of respect for other persons, even when they disagree with you regarding matters of fundamental importance. This divinely instilled value grounds the respect for persons that is required for tolerance.

Believers of the Abrahamic faiths also affirm the creatureliness of human persons. That is, they recognize humans as finite, frail, and fallible beings. There is one God and we are not him. Given this belief, we can expect all humans, including ourselves, to err in some of our beliefs and practices. Thus, the religious believer approaches her own beliefs and those of others with a healthy dose of creaturely humility. Recognition of the inevitability of error provides a motive for real and substantive respect for people with whom we disagree.

I do not mean to suggest that religious believers are required to doubt the most fundamental beliefs of their faith—for it is precisely those fundamentals that ground mercy and respect. And mercy and respect thusly grounded can overcome our natural tendency to distance ourselves from others with differing beliefs and practices.

Creaturely humility should also instill both a sense of fallibility with respect to the nonessentials of our faiths and allow for liberty on matters that are neither fundamental nor clearly conceived within our holy writ. Christians, for example, have shamefully persecuted other Christians based on differing understandings of the proper age for baptism, the exact relationship of the

Father, the Son, and the Holy Spirit, and various roles of faith and works. Yet all the while, such Christians shared the deep belief that Christ bore their sins. That belief should powerfully unite Christians who are so easily disposed to divide over peripheral beliefs. I have no doubt that Muslims and Jews could easily fix the heart of their own faith and then, based on the heart of their faith, find a way to tolerate those practices and beliefs that are neither as essential to nor as clearly taught as the heart of their faith.

Taking these beliefs together we can begin to see how religious belief need not entail dogmatism and intolerance. Merely having confidence in a belief that we take to be important does not mean we will ignore or alienate or persecute those with whom we disagree. Although this is an all too common human tendency, it is by no means exclusive to religious matters (consider, for example, the type of dialogue we find when it comes to matters of politics). However, the religious believer has good reason to recognize and then resist this tendency: humans, after all, are fallen creatures and are prone to error. This belief, joined with the belief that all humans are immensely valuable, precludes persecuting or alienating others for their religious beliefs. The religious believer respects the other, even when they disagree. Moreover, she understands she might have something to learn from those of different faiths.

One might think that I have just offered a Western, liberal, irreligious defense of tolerance. After all, one might think that there is nothing especially Abrahamic or even religious about human dignity, respect, and fallibility. This sort of objection fails to recognize the deep religious roots of these concepts and values. The enlightenment values have deep religious roots—they did not spring into the minds of English and French thinkers *ex nihilo*. They arose from within Christian-Jewish-Muslim cultures after centuries of theological reflection on, say, creation in the image of God and the priesthood of all believers. Indeed, most of the so-called secular enlightenment figures were deeply religious, mining their own religious traditions for the doctrines that would come to support liberty and tolerance. John Locke did not think it was even possible for an atheist to be tolerant! Contemporary secular philosopher Richard Rorty concedes the hundreds of years of religious influences that turned these extraordinary and revolutionary ideas—human dignity, human rights, human equality, natural law, and so on—into common sense.[17] These doctrines find their roots within religion.

We have looked at some beliefs that are shared in the Abrahamic traditions. Are there religiously particular defenses of tolerance? Let me briefly explore that from within my own tradition.

A Christian Defense of Tolerance?

This Christian defense of tolerance is a Christian defense in two senses—it was offered by a Christian clergyman, Roger Williams, and it draws on Christian beliefs. Moreover, it draws on the unlikeliest of Christian beliefs—early American Puritanism. "Puritanism" and "intolerance" are practically synonymous in contemporary parlance. Williams (ca. 1604–1684), the American founder of the colony of Rhode Island, was a Protestant Christian. Growing up a persecuted religious minority in England, Williams was on the receiving end of religious intolerance. He lamented the blood shed during centuries of wars and persecution by those professing allegiance to Jesus Christ the Prince of Peace. Williams, in his plea for religious liberty, defended liberty not only for his fellow Christians, but also for pagans, "anti-Christians," Jews, and Turks (Muslims). Christian belief was not thereby diminished nor were Christians precluded from defending their confidently held beliefs— however, Williams claimed that Christians should persuade only by God's word, not by the human sword. Religious coercion at the tip of the sword was nothing more than a "ravishing of conscience." It is morally and spiritually wrong, and of the highest order of wrong, to "molest any person" for their religious beliefs.

For Williams, the need to tolerate and respect the religious belief of others is grounded in the inherent dignity and value of each individual's conscience, something Williams took to be infinitely valuable and precious. Williams thought that many of the Christians living around him in the new American colonies were seriously mistaken about their religious beliefs. However, like all good Protestants (those who protested against the authority and hegemony of the Roman Catholic Church to mediate between God and humanity), he believed that each individual's conscience must consider and decide religious matters on their own; this is the essence of faith. Williams's Protestantism, therefore, grounded his radical individualism. So Williams's belief that his version of Protestant Christianity was the absolute truth (and that deviations from this belief would damn a person's soul to hell) was not in opposition to his belief that each individual's conscience and personal choice are infinitely valuable and so worthy of respect and liberty.

Williams considered religious persecution "soul rape," making clear his theological and spiritual condemnation of intolerance. Williams's beliefs in support of religious toleration do not stray far from his theological convictions. In fact, his religious beliefs explicitly support his beliefs about conscience and free choice.

Conclusion

The threat of religious intolerance looms large in our world today. Yet amidst this threat there is opportunity. Against the charge of the New Atheists that religions foster only intolerance and hatred toward other faiths, religious believers can and must defend the contributions their religious traditions have made to tolerance, and they must continue to work toward building a more tolerant and respectful climate for people of all faiths. And frequently we can find religious believers responding to this call.

In the United States, in the months of debate and attention that surrounded the building of a community center ("the mosque at ground zero"), many religious believers and religious organizations voiced their support for the mosque and for Muslims citizens and spoke out against the defamations and lies being spoken about Muslims. One of the strongest defenses of the mosque came from the Jewish mayor of New York City, Michael Bloomberg. In several speeches, Bloomberg forcefully defended the construction of the center and, according to aides close to the mayor, his passionate defense was motivated to a large extent by the prejudice his own family faced growing up.

There is, however, a flip side to this opportunity. Although the religious persecution and religious intolerance in our world today gives religious believers a chance to reclaim the true nature of their faith and put into practice the tolerance and respect that their God demands, it also leaves open the possibility that believers will fail to respond.

Our hope in writing this book is that children of Abraham will seize the opportunity, embracing tolerance and respect. The God of Abraham calls us to show mercy to the stranger. And Abraham's children understand humans as created in the image of God. Both mercy and the *imago dei* are theologically specific groundings of tolerance toward those outside our own circle of faith. We offer these theological defenses of the mercy, respect, and humility necessary to both understand and respect those who hold fundamentally different beliefs and practices; this would, in turn, create safe space for practitioners of other religions. We are seeking within our own traditions precisely what is already there—a theology that motivates mercy and embraces both human dignity and human creatureliness. Recognition of these theological truths can ground kindness, humility, compassion, hospitality, and so on toward the stranger (without fear or anger). The essays that follow illustrate and draw upon the religious basis for tolerance and respect for other faiths that is found in the Abrahamic traditions. In doing this, we hope not only to reinforce these traditions' contributions to religious tolerance, but also to show to religious believers that taking their faith seriously can create a freer and more tolerant future.

Notes

1. Richard Dawkins, "Religion's Misguided Missiles," *The Guardian,* September 15, 2001.

2. Christopher Hitchens, *God Is Not Great: How Religion Poisons Everything* (Boston: Twelve Books, 2009), 13 (emphasis in original).

3. Sam Harris, *The End of Faith: Religion, Terror, and the Future of Reason* (New York: W. W. Norton, 2005), 13.

4. Richard Dawkins, *The God Delusion* (New York: Mariner Books, 2006), 157.

5. Dawkins, *The God Delusion,* 31.

6. Dawkins, "Religion's Misguided Missiles."

7. Hitchens, *God Is Not Great,* 17.

8. Harris, *The End of Faith,* 21 (emphasis in original).

9. Ibid., 18.

10. Ibid., 20.

11. Hitchens, *God Is Not Great,* 27.

12. Chris Hedges, *War Is a Force That Gives Us Meaning* (New York: PublicAffairs, 2002), 20.

13. Drawing upon data from the 2005 National Bureau of Economic Research, the 2000 Social Capital Community Benchmark Survey, the 1996–2004 General Social Survey, the 1998–2001 International Social Survey Programme, and many others.

14. Arthur Brooks, *Who Really Cares: The Surprising Truth About Compassionate Conservatism* (New York: Basic Books, 2006), 38.

15. Not Christian belief, as was widely but erroneously reported. The killer was a self-confessed atheist.

16. These citations are often highly contentious and foisted upon those who do not have direct access to the texts.

17. Richard Rorty writes: "Many responsibilities begin in dreams, and many transfigurations of the tradition begin in private fantasies. Think, for example, of Plato's or St. Paul's private fantasies—fantasies so original and utopian that they become the common sense of later times." From "Is Derrida a Transcendental Philosopher?" in his *Essays on Heidegger and Others* (Cambridge: Cambridge University Press, 1991), 121.

Abraham's Jewish Children

2

The Peoples of the Earth and the Tents of Jacob: Humanity in the Image of God

EINAT RAMON

Dr. Einat Ramon teaches modern Jewish thought, literature, and feminism at the Schechter Institute of Jewish Studies. A former dean of Schechter Rabbinical Seminary, Ramon received ordination from the Jewish Theological Seminary in New York in 1989, becoming Israel's first woman rabbi. She received her PhD from Stanford University and is the author of many published articles and the recent book A New Life: Religion, Motherhood, and Supreme Love in the Works of Aharon David Gordon. *Since 2006, Dr. Ramon has been active in the clinical pastoral care movement in Israel. She has been involved in setting up the first clinical pastoral education unit in Israel, participating in the network of spiritual caregivers as the writer of the professional standards for training chaplains. Recently she set up an academic program specializing in Jewish spiritual care at the Schechter Institute. Ramon considers herself currently a nondenominational observant Jew, she lives in Jerusalem with her husband, Rabbi Arik Ascherman, and their two children.*

Humanity Through the Jewish Prism: Diversity, Particularism, and Human Solidarity

The Ramon (Weissberg)-Alpern family, from which I come and whose members live today in various locations in Israel, has always considered Zionism, Judaism, and human solidarity to be deeply intertwined. Zionism provided us with the framework for hope that we, as Jews, would live a life of dignity, together, in our own land after 2,000 years of exile, enduring contempt in various countries and under various regimes—Christian, Muslim, and secular (Communist). And though engraved in our minds were the memories of "righteous gentiles" (non-Jews who were our grandparents' friends from the old countries and non-Jews who had sometimes helped Jews), the generation that emigrated from Europe did not want to return to their home countries (Poland, Russia, and the Ukraine). They were happy with their move to their ancestors' homeland, eager to build homes, families, and communities—happy to be part of the Jewish tradition coming to life in its own birthplace, as promised by our prophets (Ezekiel 37).

Today my husband and I, with our children, live in Jerusalem among Jews who "ascended" (that is, who emigrated to the Land of Israel) from Islamic countries in the 1950s. Our neighbors fled anti-Jewish violence in the Middle East, Asia, and North Africa.[1] Despite relatively long periods of Jewish-Muslim coexistence in some of those countries (where the Jews have silently accepted their fate as second-class citizens—called *dhimmi*—according to Islam and where Islam has been forced on some of them[2]), Arab nationalist revolutions came about in the 1950s or later. During these uprisings, and later during the Islamic revolution in Iran in the 1980s, Jews in Islamic countries had to flee and leave most of their belongings. About a million Jewish refugees from Islamic countries emigrated to Israel during the first years following the establishment of the state. Luckily, the state of Israel existed and could absorb them, unlike when Jews fled the Holocaust during the years prior to the establishment of the state of Israel.

Despite the pain of being uprooted, my grandparents as well as my neighbors have avoided any vengeance or envy. Though we mourn for our dead, for the exile from our land (beginning with the Roman Empire), and for the violent loss of the culturally rich Jewish communities liquidated by premodern pagans, the Crusades, the Spanish Inquisition,[3] and totalitarian ideologies (nazism, fascism, communism),[4] we hold no resentment toward those who have persecuted us, whether in the West or in Islamic countries. Instead, we focus on building our lives here, as Jews, in Israel. We remember the humiliation and the persecutions, but we do not dwell on them. We are dedicated to the future of our people in our land, which, as we believe, provides hope and sets an example, not only for ourselves but also for endangered peoples and ancient cultures around the world.

Our optimistic worldview stems from the Torah—the Hebrew Bible, which we believe was given to us in written and oral form by God (written later as the Talmud between A.D. 500 and 800) at Mount Sinai. Yet its deeper meaning still unfolds through dedicated and accurate interpretation and through our lives lived in accordance with it. The Torah highlights the importance of our religiously and culturally unique tradition, which we believe is necessary for the survival of humanity. The Jewish traditional ethos calls for a balance between particularistic and universalistic perspectives and commitments. Thus, Judaism is anti-imperialistic in its essence, as it advocates finding one's life's meaning and purpose only within a particular family tradition. Finally, Judaism is not a missionary religion. It strives for the clarification of Divine Truth and Divine Will through the very delicate channel of dialectic reasoning, stemming from the need to understand the text of the Torah. It envisions a constructive collaboration between the Jews as a separate people (open to those who wish to take upon themselves the yoke of 613 commandments) and "all the families of the earth" (Gen. 12:3).

In light of these initial remarks, I will present the Jewish understanding of humanity and its destiny, then share my family's personal spiritual history. Next, I will portray the model of tolerance founded by the ancient rabbis— our primary interpreters and carriers of the Torah. Finally, I will share my perspective on the current conflict in Israel and the Middle East.

Israel Among the Nations

The first twelve chapters of the book of Genesis in the Torah reveal to us the moral evolution of humanity as understood by Jews and later adopted by the other monotheistic religions, Christianity and Islam. According to the Torah, we humans all have common ancestors: a man and a woman, Adam and Eve, who were both created together in the image of God and were commanded to procreate together and "rule" over the animals together (Gen. 1:26–28). Thus Judaism, as the first monotheistic religion, claims that all humans were created in the image of God, though we regard that statement as defining a task—a goal for which we must strive—not simply a moral fact.[5]

Following the appearance of radical evil in the good world of God's creation (symbolized by the serpent) and the invasive feelings of envy, revenge, and hatred (Gen. 3), the first murder happened (Gen. 4), and it evolved into a dangerous mania in the next generation, setting the ideological stage for mass murders (Gen. 4:23). Eventually, when "the earth became corrupt before God, as it was . . . filled with lawlessness" (Gen. 6:11), God destroyed humanity in the flood, then re-created humanity through the righteous man, Noah, and his family (Gen. 7). God then gave humanity a set of natural laws—which we in Judaism call the seven Noahide commandments—hoping the disaster of a destructive immorality would not happen again (Gen. 9:1–17).[6] The laws, later outlined by the rabbis, refer to the sanctity of life and, as a result, the sanctity of the traditional family structure and restrained sexual relations.

Yet a little later, states the Torah, human arrogance returned in full force when "everyone on earth had the same language and the same words . . . and built a tower with its top in the sky, to make a name for themselves" (Gen. 11:1, 4). This time God, the creator of the heavens and the earth, deeply concerned with humanity's dangerous ability to unite for the purpose of controlling (and thereby destroying) the world, confounded their speech. God thus created various languages and cultures and "scattered them over the face of the whole earth," declaring, in that sense, that humanity thrives when, in addition to following the seven Noahide commandments, it cultivates small, intimate communities and different tribal/national and cultural traditions. It is assumed in the Torah that without those particular affiliations—each one with its own boundaries and unique interpretations for the human condition—our endless egotistic and totalitarian desires could easily destroy humanity and the earth.[7]

Mordecai M. Kaplan, an American Jewish theologian (1881–1983), explained why humans thrive in small, homogeneous groups (families, communities, and nations) when he explained the need for public worship. When we "find ourselves in the fellowship of others who have similar interests, acknowledge similar responsibilities, and respond appreciatively to similar values, we feel a sustaining power, we feel God's presence, we feel at home in the world, we are aware of a supporting and sustaining power outside our individual selves, enabling us to observe in nature and in humanity the presence of God."[8] Small communities, as well as national, creative, rich symbols and life cycles, provide us with context and meaning in life; they guarantee that we know our leaders and have a direct connection to them. Thus, nations, communities, and families ensure both our freedom and our human dignity (Lev. 25:39–46).

It is not accidental that cruel empires throughout history have enslaved people, have tried to erase particular identities, and have exiled people from their homelands into foreign lands, where they lost their human dignity and could no longer continue their family traditions and legacy. Thus, states the

Torah, the threat of idolatry—that is, humans' tendency to worship themselves and their power and, as a result, to enslave others—remains a dangerous threat for the existence of the world (Ezek. 19:3).

God, according to the Jews' perception of the world, chose Abraham and Sarah to build a family that would stop the world from deteriorating into idolatry. God elected a family that would set an example of how to protect human freedom in the difficult contexts of human existence, overcoming our vulnerabilities and tendencies to enslave ourselves and others. "Who, then, is free?" asked Abraham Joshua Heschel, a twentieth-century American Jewish theologian (1907–1972): "The creative man who is not carried away by the streams of necessity, who is not enchained by processes, who is not enslaved to circumstances."[9] This is what the stand for human freedom means in its deeper sense, with the help of the Torah, that was given to the world on Mount Sinai to guide us, the descendants of Abraham and Sarah, in that task.

The task that Jews loyal to their tradition have taken up—to fight idolatry—was not without its complexity: the demand to eradicate idolatrous humanity and the essential Jewish value of the sanctity of life seem at odds with one another. The Hebrew Bible speaks without mercy about idolatrous peoples and it commands us to rid the world of idolatry and its degrading moral features (Deut. 12, 13). However, the commandments to eradicate idolatrous people, especially those living in the ancient Land of Israel, would involve bloodshed that could lead Jews down a murderous slippery slope. As archaeology and the Bible teach us, the demand to eradicate the seven idolatrous peoples of ancient Israel was never implemented. The Hebrews in antiquity conquered the Land of Israel but continued to coexist with the pagan peoples and pagan cultures until they, too, were exiled by the empires of that time. The harsh readings in the Torah commanding us to eradicate those cultures would come to acquire a symbolic meaning teaching us how dangerous idolatry could affect us and the world.[10]

Our fight against idolatry and against foreign ideologies and religions being forced on us turned into a quietist battle of sanctifying God's name through our daily actions and being committed to the Torah. Those of us attached to our religion do everything we can to continue our life as Jews, despite the constant threats to our being. If we had to choose between dying or leaving our religion, those of us loyal to our people would prefer to die (or continue our observance in secret) rather than abandon our ancestors' way of life. Moses Mendelssohn (1729–1786), the founder of the Jewish enlightenment who brought philosophical thinking to the modern Jewish world, became concerned that under the guise of tolerance Jews in Western countries would be subtly pushed or seduced to abandon their religion for the sake of secular or syncretistic ideals that are regarded as "higher" by Western society. In 1784 he wrote to a colleague: "This tolerance is a sham. . . . In this case, it would be even more necessary for the small band of those who do not wish to convert others or be converted themselves to keep together and close ranks."[11] Realizing the potential intolerance of secularism and atheism to try to impose secular dogmas on Jews and thus "confine the human mind," Mendelssohn warned, "Let us not pretend that conformity exists where diversity is obviously the plan and goal of Providence."[12] He called upon the Jews, who were and still are a minority in the world to "adopt the mores and constitution of the country in which you find yourself but be steadfast as well in upholding the religion of your fathers, too."

The belief in not wanting to be converted and not wishing to convert is rooted in the ancient Jewish belief that "the righteous of all gentiles have a share in the blessed world to come" (Tosefta, Sanhedrin, 13). There is no need for gentiles to be converted to Judaism; they simply must be good and honest people, follow the seven Noahide commandments, and respect the special mission that the Jews have taken upon themselves. Through this biblical vision of humanity, constituted by different nations, signified by their particular languages and holidays, linked to their particular lands, carrying their particular tasks, respecting, in that context, their unique histories, the Jewish people uphold, and expect other nations to uphold, the Jews' own unique historical attachment to the Land of Israel, to each other, and to the Torah. Although all of these attachments are challenged by modern, universalistic ideologies, traditional Judaism regards them as essential for human survival and responsibility. A commitment to one's family and, above all, to one's mother, father, people, and homeland from which stem a deep sense of responsibility for a common human morality are regarded as the most cherished channels to God and to living a full, meaningful life.

From Persecution to Independence: My Family's Journey

My own family's histories may demonstrate how these great biblical and rabbinic ideas influenced a small East European–Israeli Jewish family. I was born in 1959 in Jerusalem, the city most holy to the Jews throughout our 3,000 years of history. During the formative years of my life, the city was divided between Israel, then a young and struggling state (barely twenty years old), and the Jordanian-Hashemite kingdom (formed by the British Empire as a separate, Arab kingdom in order to solve the Jewish-Arab conflict).[13] While living in a divided city (until age seven), I longed to pray at the Western Wall and other holy Jewish sites, which we could not visit because they were under Jordanian rule. Nonetheless, we have always felt that it was a privilege to live in Jerusalem. My mother, herself a "native Jerusalemite," still lives with my father in the house built by her grandfather in the 1920s, and she will never move from it. In my childhood, she often told me and my sisters stories about the old city of Jerusalem, describing the Western Wall and the beautiful synagogue, the Hurva (the Ruin), in the Jewish section. The Hurva synagogue (recently renovated and reopened) was destroyed by the Jordanians in the 1948 war, when all the Jews were forced out of the Jewish Quarter. On certain nights, living in West Jerusalem, we had to seek shelter in the corridor of our small apartment because Arab soldiers from East Jerusalem were shooting at us. Yet even the children knew, without really being told, that to live in Jerusalem following 2,000 years of exile from our land was a very special gift. Although we were not a very religious family, deep in our hearts we believed in God, in a morality sanctioned by God, in the brother-hood/sisterhood of all peoples, and in the special destiny and role of the Jewish people.

My great-grandparents were traditional East European Jewish families living at the "Pale of Settlement," the only area where the Jews were allowed to live for many generations in Eastern Europe, located between Russia and Poland.[14] With the opening of more educational and professional opportunities in Russia and Poland at the end of the nineteenth century and with the rise of secular socialist and communist ideologies, my great-grandparents began to leave the traditional lifestyle of their parents. Although my grandparents attended secular Russian and Polish schools, in their homes they strictly kept the traditional Jewish Sabbath and holidays, as well as Jewish dietary laws. It is a mystery to me how most of my great-grandparents (though attracted by the ideas of the enlightenment and seeking secular education for their children) were drawn to Zionism at a time when most liberal and Orthodox Jews showed no interest in that idea. At that time, there were perhaps a few hundred or a few thousand Jews who were passionate about the Jews' return to Israel, yet my great-grandparents were among those few. My great-grandparents were simple laypeople—not leaders, not scholars—yet they realized, as a result of the rise of modern anti-Semitism, that they had no future in Eastern Europe before (or after) World War II. They, almost silently, showed the Zionist direction to my grandparents, who were quite young at the time.

The story of each of my grandparents' families is different, yet they all share common tragedies and beliefs. Around 1915, my paternal grandfather's family was attacked by a Ukrainian mob in their hometown of Proskurov; this mob was led by a Ukrainian national revolutionary named Petlura.[15] My family was miraculously saved by hiding behind a closed door at their store.

Following this traumatic event, they moved from Ukraine to Warsaw—one of the most thriving Jewish communities at the time—only to find death two decades later in the Warsaw Ghetto and Auschwitz, leaving no trace of where and how their lives ended. Soon after their move to Warsaw, two of their sons—my grandfather and his brother—moved to Israel to build a kibbutz and to build Tel Aviv, the first Hebrew-speaking city in the world.[16]

My paternal grandmother, who lived in the city of Lvov of the former Poland/Soviet Union, immigrated to Israel with three of her siblings, leaving behind four siblings who eventually perished in the Holocaust. My maternal family was spared the horrors of the Holocaust, yet was severely affected by the communist killings and the totalitarian enforcement of secularization, so they hid their Jewish identity for two generations. In the Soviet Union, the practice of any religion was illegal (religion was considered unscientific). One of my mother's uncles was killed at a camp set up by Josef Stalin for those who deviated from the mainstream Communist Party line. My maternal grandmother's family emigrated to Israel following the Communist Revolution. They consciously chose to come to Jerusalem rather than go to the United States because of their Zionist aspirations and involvement.

My maternal grandfather, who had a tremendous spiritual influence on me, was one of the few Jewish officers in the tsar's Russian army. He left his family in Russia and literally crossed Russia by foot in order to serve with the British army, which eventually stationed him in Israel. He arrived in Israel in 1919 at age twenty-one, with the blessing of his mother, who never saw him again. From the moment of his arrival, he dedicated his life to building the new Jewish state. My grandfather, who had become secular because of the spirit of his time, returned to Jewish learning in his later years. I was drawn to traditional Jewish texts partly because of his renewed interest in Jewish thought and mysticism.

My parents, who were born before World War II, were among the first generation of "Sabras"—Israeli-born Jews. In that sense, they were similar to children of the "Old Yishuv"—the Jews who had lived in the Land of Israel for hundreds (or thousands) of years, especially in the ancient cities of Jerusalem, Hebron, Zefat, and Tiberius.[17] My parents met in the Zionist-Socialist youth movement and established their home in Jerusalem, next to my mother's family. We lived very close to aunts, uncles, and cousins, meeting together often during the week; on Friday night, our Shabbat meal was the one very special occasion where we all gathered for a meal at my grandparents' home and where guests often joined us.

My immediate family welcomed, befriended, and gave support to any person who respected us as humans and as Jews, regardless of their opinions, political affiliation, religion, and religious observance. My ancestors sought out people who shared the values of truth and friendship. In Israel, people live in small, particular, cultural communities, so our very close friends and acquaintances were mostly of East European Jewish origin like us. Some were secular people like us; others, in more distant social circles, were Orthodox. Some had right-wing political views. Others, like my own grandparents, were left-wing Zionists. They all freely debated each other, often raising their voices, and even screaming loudly at each other—sometimes on a weekday at the kitchen table when they dropped by to say hello, sometimes on Shabbat. Yet they loved each other and supported one another in times of distress and need. They were all refugees, but they never regarded themselves as such because they were delighted to be in their national homeland.

Growing up in such an ideologically diverse environment made me wonder, in later days, what the subconscious conceptual framework was that allowed such pluralism to evolve and express itself at our Shabbat table. How could right-wing and left-wing religious and nonreligious Jews (and sometimes even non-Jews) maintain a sense of human solidarity despite heated discussions and ideological disagreements? This personal experience of tolerance, which I try to pass on to my children at our Shabbat table, caused me to further explore how we Jews survived when facing the dark parts of human history, the times when moral fetters were broken.

As I became more religiously observant, I was also drawn to exploring features of Jewish secularism. Jewish secularism, as I have learned, had for a few generations neglected the synagogue, but because the Jewish people are so connected to each other and to their Torah, Zionist secular Jews never became (and never could become) totally secular. Through my research, I have discovered the theological roots of Jewish pluralism and humanism, of which I was only intuitively aware in my own upbringing.[18] I have learned about the ancient wisdom of traditional Judaism, which always strives to balance opposing opinions. What I witnessed at my parents' and grandparents' secular Shabbat table (in addition to lighting Shabbat candles and reciting blessings over the wine) was an outcome of an ancient Jewish culture that revolved around learning the Torah through debating its meaning. "Three who dine at a table and exchange words of Torah are considered as having eaten at God's table" (Mishna Avot 3:4). Although extrapolating meaning from the Torah is a difficult task, it is said in our rabbinic sources: "Study it and review it: You will find everything in it" (Mishna Avot 5:24). The drive to study and review Torah, and thus all matters of human life, manifested itself in my family and in many other Jewish homes. Everything was open for discussion and clarification. Although one's own opinions were slowly formed after hearing different perspectives, we all assumed the blessing of living a Jewish life in the Land of Israel.

Our historical commitment to the Torah and our desire throughout history to clarify problems and dilemmas as accurately as possible have enabled Judaism to be a minority religion that coexists with majority religions and at times a majority religion respecting those different faiths that live under a Jewish sovereign political entity, as is the case today. Muslims living under Israeli sovereignty enjoy full religious autonomy and religious freedom limited only by contextual security concerns. Israeli Jewish students learn Arabic as a requirement in all Israeli public schools; they also learn about the rise of Islam and its contributions to the Middle East and to world science and philosophy during the Middle Ages. And although I believe that we should deepen our respectful knowledge of Islamic culture and Arabic, our education does not even come close to the ignorance and anti-Jewish sentiment that filter through education in Arab states, including the Palestinian Authority. This is very different from the situation of Jews living under Muslim rule today. (In fact, very few Jews live under Muslim rule now, as the Jews have all escaped.) In some Arab countries—even those countries that have diplomatic relations with Israel such as Jordan and Egypt—Jews cannot build synagogues or schools.

My return to Jewish observance was motivated by understanding that it is only through observant Judaism that we can reestablish our Jewish identity, reestablish our human solidarity (broken by the mass murders of the twentieth century), and build our connection with other nations. I fear that ideologies that glorify "science" (interpreted as human self-sufficiency masking an underlying arrogance while not respecting traditions and civilization) could, God forbid, lead once again to mass murders. The Holocaust, the Communist mass murders, and other cruel wars and revolutions that colored the twentieth century created a precedent that humanity must stop. And yet our memories continue to haunt us: How could humankind neglect so many aspects of human civilization over such a short period? The American Jewish thinker Abraham Joshua Heschel has expressed this concern more eloquently:

> We live in an age where most of us have ceased to be shocked by the increasing breakdown in moral inhibitions. The decay of conscience fills the air with a pungent smell. Good and evil, which were once distinguishable as day and night, have become a blurred mist. But that mist is man-made. God is not silent. He has been silenced.[19]

I have much faith in our religious traditions (interpreted through the intellectual tools that our responsible sages have left us), which contain a sense of responsibility for the continuity of humanity, a continuity that is being challenged today for the first time in human history. Our various religions (as long as they abide by a common, natural law and respect the differences between them) could, I believe, save us from the terrible fate of modern versions of idolatry.

The Tents of Jacob: Models for Jewish Pluralism

Looking back at my childhood, I realize that my ancestors subconsciously followed a long tradition of having an open house and creating hospitality that invites the discussion of different positions. Today, I try to emulate that atmosphere and pass it on to my own children. Consider the following story from the Talmud, which in my mind reflects the atmosphere at our Shabbat table:

> R. Yannai was taking a walk, and he saw a man very neatly dressed [as a student]. Rabbi Yannai said to him, "Will the Rabbi be pleased to be our guest?" He said, "Yes." So R. Yannai took him to his house. . . . Then R. Yannai said, "What merit do you have . . . that you should eat at my table?" The man said, "I never heard an unkind word and returned it to its speaker, and I never saw two men quarreling without making peace between them."[20]

Sitting around my Shabbat table as a child, I saw how my grandparents and parents found a grain of truth in almost every school of thought. Thus they were open to conversation with every person and were eager to learn from everyone, even from people with whom they severely disagreed. There is an important saying in the Mishna (our holy book that is the foundation for all of our rabbinic thought): "Who is wise? One who learns from all persons, as it is written, 'From all my teachers have I gained understanding'" (Ps. 119:99, Mishna Avot 4:1). In order to guarantee a diversity of opinions, we must allow different groups, representing different schools of thought, to develop their own perspective. When different spiritual homes are allowed to set up their different cultural boundaries in order to maintain their opinions and when different spiritual homes create dialogues with one another, a better social agreement is formed and a more accurate clarification of complex problems comes about.

This is how the Jewish people kept their ethnic and intellectual diversity throughout the generations. Fundamentals of Jewish law were considered the common denominator that held us together—family law, the holiness of the Hebrew language, the strict observance of the Sabbath, our unbreakable relationship to the Land of Israel, and our sense of peoplehood. Abraham Joshua Heschel summarized our sense of peoplehood as follows: "Jewish existence is not only the adherence to particular doctrines and observances, but primarily the living in the spiritual order of the Jewish people, the living in the Jews of the past and with the Jews of the present."[21]

Whenever we do not respect the need to make concessions with one another and learn from one another, we forfeit our role as part of the spiritual discipline of the Jewish people and, as a result, forfeit our contribution to humanity. This explains the reality of my maternal grandfather's two close friends (regarded by us, his children and grandchildren, almost as family members): one was a Communist Jew, the other a right-wing Jew. My grandfather had helped save the life of each of them (in different ways and in different circumstances) and hosted them regularly. But that did not prevent him from telling each of them, with no shame, that he thought they were wrong on certain issues. The debate was fruitful for all sides because, looking back, each of them, including my grandfather, changed his mind over the years as a result of learning from each other and continuing the debates.

This experience follows not only the model of hospitality but also the intellectual model of different academies in ancient Judaism. In the Land of Israel, people dedicated to the learning of Torah regularly reached different conclusions on issues. I refer to the two rabbinic schools of thought: the House of Shammai and the House of Hillel. (Hillel and Shammai were both rabbis living in Israel early in the first century, who spontaneously formed places of learning and interpreting Torah.) Their followers formed academies that ruled differently and debated on a variety of minor legal issues while agreeing on the fundamentals of Jewish interpretations and boundaries.[22] Their disagreements were documented and viewed positively by the Jewish tradition, which considered differences devoid of ego struggles an expression of God's will.

> A difference of opinion (machloket) for Heaven's sake will have lasting value, but a difference of opinion (machloket) not for Heaven's sake will not endure. What is the example of a difference of opinion for Heaven's sake? The debates of Hillel and Shammai. (Mishna Avot 5:19)

The model that students of the ancient academies of the Bet Shammai and the Bet Hillel presented in the following rabbinic source teaches us that Jewish men and women from the two different schools also married into each other's families, even in the midst of very serious controversies between political and religious camps. "Even though these prohibit and these permit, these declare ineligible and these declare eligible, Bet Shammai did not refrain from marrying women of Bet Hillel, nor Bet Hillel from Bet Shammai" (Babylonian Talmud Yevamot 1:4).

It is important to note that following many years of painful disagreements between the two houses (Jerusalemite Talmud Shabbat 1:4), a final decision was made to follow the rulings of the House of Hillel. Certain exceptions were made to follow the rulings according to the House of Shammai. Furthermore, it was decided that in the "world to come," in the messianic future, the rulings of the House of Shammai would be followed, thus communicating to future generations that the House of Shammai was equally smart and holy. Shammai's students' reasoning was accurate from God's point of view, but we, the people, must follow one set of laws. In most cases, we follow that of the students of Hillel while we remember and learn about the students of Shammai, keeping their school of thought with us (Babylonian Talmud Eruvin 13:B).[23]

This model could be applied to today's Jewish state. Pluralism does not mean that everything is permitted, nor does it mean that an ideological community has no right to define and defend its boundaries and rules. It is important to emphasize that boundaries are the vehicles by which the Jewish people and their different spiritual communities define themselves. One of the major tasks of rabbis/scholars, teachers, and leaders is to draw the lines for the definition of our Jewish spiritual homes. Within our contemporary spiritual homes—a family, a community, or an ideological movement—our unique set of beliefs and observances can be deepened and celebrated. At the same time, we must maintain a common sense of Jewish peoplehood through direct or indirect dialogue between different groups of Jews.

Largely because of Zionism's dominance throughout the middle to late twentieth century, it is understood that the first step taken in one's Jewish identity is to be in solidarity with the Jewish community. Spiritual homes are important as long as we hold on to the overriding spiritual framework: the Jewish people. That framework in and of itself weakens the concept of "heresy" in Judaism as claimed in the Talmud: "A Jew (an Israelite) even though he had sinned is still a Jew" (Sanhedrin 44a). It means that the Jewish community (or the people) will continue to do everything to enfold those of Jewish ancestry, even if they have deviated from Jewish law, so long as they keep the basic boundaries of the Jewish people and Jewish law.

In our generation, we have seen how challenges presented by one school of thought toward the other have been taken seriously and eventually have created change. For example, Orthodox Jews have recently embraced aspects of religious feminism, whereas the Reform movement has shifted away from anti-Zionism. And yet many disputes remain unresolved, including disputes concerning the Hebrew language, Jewish law, Shabbat observance, Zionism, and intermarriage.

Some of today's most heated discussions in the Jewish world concern issues of gender. Should we continue the traditional definition of marriage as a union between a man and a woman? Is it within the boundaries of our tradition to ordain women? Jews on the liberal side of the debate tend to have definite and rigid feminist ideologies to which, they believe, all Jews must immediately and fully comply. As a reaction, Jews on the traditional side tend to object to feminist ideas whether within or without the boundaries of the historical Jewish law.

Because of this liberal rigidity and absence of complexity and nuance, I have decided to leave my liberal denomination and define myself as a non-denominational, observant Jew. Although I still believe that empowering women (and men) and their relationships is one of the major spiritual and moral challenges today, I no longer view traditional Judaism as the side that must inevitably be abandoned. There is much spiritual power and inspiration for women within the traditional frameworks of family life as wives and mothers. Yet women, I believe, should also contribute to our understanding of Torah, through learning, teaching, and more actively participating in religious communities. At the same time, women can be abused within liberal, academic, and progressive circles as a result of sexual promiscuity, lack of respect, and exploitation of women at home and in workplaces, including ignoring mothers' special needs and perspectives. Jewish leaders today, on both sides of these debates, tend to see flaws only in the other camp. Very few see merit in the coming together of all Jews and in the necessity to make concessions for each other based on our historical legacy. And yet in Israel, I think the norm among the people and among the leaders that represent most of the people is that they want to come together. I believe that all denominations have erred in understanding the Torah, yet all have contributed to the advancement of the Jewish people and their contribution to humanity, but in different ways. The most important thing is to learn from each other.

How do we resolve these tensions by using the models that we have inherited from the Bible and rabbinic thought? Because different Jews have different moral and hermeneutical perspectives on such topics, a better image than "one big tent" would be that of many tents that share the same Jewish "camp," that is, the spiritual path of belonging to the Jewish people of the past and the present. When we think of the Jewish people as a cluster of various schools of thought and tribes cultivating their own perspectives on Torah yet committed to each other and to Jewish peoplehood, we can see the road for the future of our people as one people, centered in Israel, continuing our learning of the Hebrew Bible and its rabbinic interpretations. The idea of a camp full of "small, spiritual tents" indicates that we may continue to disagree and make concessions toward one another, thus keeping the boundaries of the Jewish people in order to keep our common camp. The metaphor, "a camp of many tents," is inspired by the verse that we recite in our morning prayers as we enter the synagogue:

> How fair are your tents, O Jacob
> Your dwellings, Oh Israel. (Num. 24:5)

The Jewish State of Israel and the Muslim Middle East

In conclusion, I wish to argue that the same philosophical-political models of pluralism and human solidarity that apply within Judaism also apply to our relationship with our neighbors—Muslim and Christian Arabs living in the state of Israel (and outside it), some who have lived in the Land of Israel prior to our return. I would like to repeat the claim I made two decades ago, which has been stated very eloquently by all of Israel's prime ministers from the very beginning of Zionism: we, the Jews, are not colonialists; we were thrown out of our homeland and have returned.[24] Yet Israel has always been willing to make painful sacrifices and split the land into two states, even withdraw from areas and settlements to which we are historically attached—for example, the city of Hebron and the area near Shechem (Gen. 23, 37:12–13).[25] In the city of Hebron there has been a continuous Jewish settlement over a period of hundreds of years. We cannot, however, risk our lives and withdraw from areas necessary for our security; neither can there be peace with people who refuse to recognize our history as a people in our land, our right to self-determination, and our unique contribution to this region and to the world.[26]

The conflict itself is very complicated; Israel's government has repeatedly declared that it is willing to withdraw from territories in order to allow for a demilitarized Palestinian state as long as Palestine will recognize the legitimacy of a Jewish state and the history of the Jews in their land. So far, the Palestinian leadership has refused to do so. Although the status quo is currently imperfect and there is much concern about voices questioning the Camp David Accords (even in Egypt after the latest revolution), the situation here in Israel is much better than a situation in which an agreement is imposed on us by outside forces.

While we wait (and we may need much patience) for that change to come, I would like to point out that the daily lives of Jews and Arabs in the Land of Israel include relatively few clashes and a lot of collaboration. It seems to me that we all prefer to live in separate communities. As a Jewish-Israeli mother and teacher, I am not even aware of our positive daily encounters because they seem so natural. Whether it is hiring an Arab babysitter (who is now a lawyer), or approaching her uncle, a well-known (Arab) surgeon, to consult on a medical problem of my son's, or seeing my neighbor purchase vegetables from an Arab woman who comes to our house regularly, coexistence of Jews and Arabs in Israel is natural despite the fact that we strongly disagree with each other ideologically. The mainstream media, which thrives on conflicts, never documents these positive interactions.

And finally, I would like to add another argument, a theological one. I see our local conflict as one of the many manifestations of the conflict between Islam and the West. Many have commented that the Arab-Israeli conflict is but one slice of the bigger conflict between Islam and Western secular culture, a debate that revolves to a great extent around gender issues. Many Western leaders blame Islamic culture for discrimination against women and demand that the relationship between men and women common in the West be applied to Islamic countries. Many Muslims object; they wish to keep their traditional family structures. Their tribal affiliation protects them and their identities, just as religious affiliations do for traditional Jews and traditional Christians. Will the West allow them to do so? I doubt that. While we blame "radical Islamists" for being intolerant, we ignore our own dogmatic thinking as Westerners. As Mendelssohn pointed out, there has been an element of arrogant totalitarianism in our modern secular culture from its very beginning in the eighteenth century. Many Muslims object to our presence in Israel not just because we are Jews but because we embody and symbolize the West's imposition of its secular cultural norms, which the Arabs perceive as harmful to them. Surely, there are behaviors that all cultures and all religions (in the East and in the West) must consider unenlightened: rape, sexual harassment, domestic violence, exploitation, depriving women of education, and so on. Yet has the West done its soul-searching regarding the culture's relationship to women, the growing alienation between men and women, and the benefits and losses of feminism? As a woman who grew up in Western secular culture saturated by the sexual revolution of the 1960s and identifying with the call to empower women through feminism, I now wonder whether the Western model has achieved the goals it set to achieve through feminism. Surely opening the doors of education and professional training in every field has benefited women, but sexual promiscuity and the collapse of the traditional institution of marriage has been damaging.

One way to help resolve our conflict would be to soften the part of it that concerns issues of gender. Are we willing to listen to our "enemies" and consider what they have to say to us regarding family and relationships between men and women? Are we prepared to see the "grain of truth" in the camp of our current enemies (who we hope will one day be our good neighbors and allies)? It seems that in no age as this one, intimacy and respectful friendship and partnership between men and women could contribute to peace in the world.

To conclude then, my current view is that there is much more coexistence, brotherhood, sisterhood, faith, and joy in daily life in Israel among Jews, and between Jews and Arabs, than we are willing to admit. Perhaps one way to improve the situation is to focus on these joys and to increase them until the day when Jerusalem will glorify God, bless her children within her (Ps. 147:12), and all those who are on earth would praise God, (Ps. 148:7), "Young men and women alike old and young together" (Ps. 148:12).

Notes

1. See B. D. Yemini, "The Jewish Nakba: Expulsions, Massacres, and Forced Conversions," May 20, 2009, www.solomonia.com/blog/archive/2009/05/ben-dror-yemini-the-jewish-nakba-expulsi/.

2. See B. Lewis, *The Jews of Islam* (Princeton, NJ: Princeton University Press, 1984).

3. On the impact of the Crusades on the Jews, see www.crusades-encyclopedia.com/jews.html.

4. Hannah Arendt, *The Origins of Totalitarianism* (New York: Schocken Books, 1951).

5. See P. Trible, *God and the Rhetoric of Sexuality* (Philadelphia: Fortress Press, 1978), 17, 21–22.

6. On the Noahide commandments, see www.noahide.org/article.asp?Level=540&Parent=342.

7. D. Gordis, "The Tower of Babel and Birth of Nationhood," *Azure* 40 (2010), 19–36.

8. Mordecai M. Kaplan, *The Meaning of God in Modern Jewish Religion* (New York: Reconstructionist Press, 1962), 246–248.

9. A. J. Heschel, *God in Search of Man: A Philosophy of Judaism* (New York: Farrar, Straus, and Giroux, 1955), 410.

10. For that reason our medieval sages have pointed out that the seven peoples of Canaan no longer exist. Maimonides, Mishneh Torah, Hilkhot Issurey Bi'ah 12:25.

11. Moses Mendelssohn, *Jerusalem and Other Jewish Writings*, trans. and ed. Alfred Jospe (New York: Schocken Books, 1969), 109, 147. He referred to the "desire to establish a systematic union of faiths" and move the Jews into that union.

12. Ibid., 109.

13. On the history of Jordan in the context of Middle Eastern history, see E. Ramon, "Jerusalem After 40 Years," *The Jerusalem Post*, May 14, 2007, www.jpost.com/Features/Article.aspx?id=61295.

14. "From 1791 until 1915, the majority of Jews living in Eastern Europe were confined by the Czars of Russia—starting with Catherine the Great—to an area known as the 'Pale of Settlement' (meaning 'borders of settlement'). The Pale consisted of 25 provinces that included Ukraine, Lithuania, Belorussia, Crimea, and part of Poland (which had been partitioned between Russia, Prussia, and Austria in 1772). The western side of what had formally been Poland was absorbed into the Austro-Hungarian Empire. This western half of Poland (which contained important Jewish communities such as those located in Galicia) contained a smaller, but not insignificant, number of Jews. The physical and economic situation of these Jews of the eastern Austro-Hungarian Empire was generally much better than their fellow Jews living in the western end of Czarist Russia. The Jews of Russia were specifically expelled from Moscow and St. Petersburg and forced into the Pale. Later they were also expelled from rural areas within the Pale and forced to live only in shtetls." www.simpletoremember.com/articles/a/pale_of_settlement/.

15. Jewish Virtual Library, "Pogroms," www.jewishvirtuallibrary.org/jsource/judaica/ejud_0002_0016_0_15895.html.

16. On the history of the kibbutz movement, see Daniel Gavron, *The Kibbutz: Awakening from Utopia* (Lanham, MD: Rowman & Littlefield Publishers, 2000).

17. See "Yishuv," www.answers.com/topic/yishuv.

18. On the dialectics of Jewish secularism, see my book, E. Ramon, *A New Life: Religion, Motherhood and Supreme Love in the Works of Aharon David Gordon* (Jerusalem: Carmel, 2007, Hebrew). Sections of this book were published in English: see E. Ramon, "'A Woman-Human': A. D. Gordon's Approach to Women's Equality and His Influence on Second Aliya Feminists," in *Jewish Women in Pre-State Israel: Life History, Politics and Culture*, ed. Ruth Kark, Margalit Shilo, and Galit Hazan-Rokem (Waltham, MA: Brandeis University Press, 2008), 111–121; E. Ramon, "Equality and Ambivalence: The Political Repercussions of A. D. Gordon's Maternal Ethics," *Nashim: A Journal of Women's Studies and Judaism* 3 (Spring–Summer 5760/2000): 74–105. On pluralism and Jewish secularism, see E. Ramon, "Jewish Secularism as a Challenge for Modern Jewish Theologians: The Case of David Hartman's Thought," in *JISMOR: Journal of the Interdisciplinary Study of Monotheistic Religions* 3 (2007): 18–40. The following study is a fundamental work on the sources and features of Jewish secularism: E. Luz, *Parallels Meet: Religion and Nationalism in the Early Zionist Movement (1882–1904)*, trans. Len J. Schramm (Philadelphia: Jewish Publication Society, 1988).

19. A. J. Heschel, *Man Is Not Alone: A Philosophy of Religion* (New York: Farrar, Straus, and Giroux, 1951), 152.

20. Leviticus Rabba, Tzav quoted in C. G. Montefiore and H. Loewe, *A Rabbinic Anthology* (New York: Schocken Books, 1974), 277–278.

21. A. J. Heschel, *God in Search of Man: A Philosophy of Judaism* (New York: Farrar, Straus, and Giroux, 1955), 423.

22. On the two schools of Shammai and Hillel, see Marcus Jastrow and S. Mendelsohn, "Bet Hillel and Bet Shammai," http://www.jewishencyclopedia.com/articles/3190-bet-hillel-and-bet-shammai.

23. Ibid.

24. E. Ramon, "The Ethics of Ruling a Jewish State with a Large Non-Jewish Minority," in *Jewish Ethics: A Reader*, ed. Elliot Dorff and Louis Newman (Oxford: Oxford University Press, 1995), 441–453.

25. For further information about Israel's official position, shared by most Israeli Jews and Jews around the world, see www.nrg.co.il/online/1/ART2/243/844.html?hp=1 &cat=404&ap=1&from_art=2244812&to_art=2243844 (in Hebrew) and the May 24, 2011, speech by Prime Minister Benjamin Netanyahu to a joint meeting of the U.S. Congress, reproduced at www.facebook.com/notes/the-prime-minister-of-israel/speech -by-prime-minister-benjamin-netanyahu-to-a-joint-meeting-of-the-united-sta /148067348598197.

26. B. D. Yemini, "Israeli Pride Parade," May 17, 2008, http://www.mideasttruth.com /forum/viewtopic.php?p=19926.

3

Dance of the Spirit: The Land of Israel and the Jewish Soul

DOV BERKOVITS

Rabbi Dov Berkovits studied at the University of Chicago. He holds degrees in sociology, philosophy, and Jewish history from Yeshiva University and received rabbinic ordination there. He went to Israel in 1970 and lives today with his family in Shilo. He studied in Israel at Yeshivat Merkaz HaRav and at the Shalom Hartman Institute until becoming chairman of the faculty at the Pardes Institute for Jewish Studies, a position he held for fifteen years. In 2001, Rabbi Berkovits founded Bet Av-Center for Creativity and Renewal in Torah. He has published three books, most recently The Temple of Life: Family Relationships and the Sanctity of Life. *His teaching has inspired thousands of students from all sectors of Israeli society. Rabbi Berkovits has written widely on Judaism and the arts and on Jewish environmental thought. He writes a weekly column for an Israeli newspaper on the Talmud and issues of contemporary concern.*

The Mystery of Makom

I grew up in Boston and in the suburbs of Chicago savoring the sweet tastes of America—the then twenty-eight ice cream flavors of Howard Johnson's, a baseball doubleheader on Sunday afternoon at Fenway Park, bike rides in the forest preserves outside Chicago, the never-ending horizons of the Great Plains, family trips to Jamestown and Washington, and the dream of a life of freedom and opportunity.

My parents were thrown out of Nazi Germany in late 1938. Thank God. As presiding rabbi of a synagogue in Berlin, where he had obtained rabbinic ordination and a PhD in philosophy, my father spoke of the eternal people of Israel. They would outlast the "2,000-year Reich" that, as he taught, would soon be in the refuse heap of history, just like all the other "empires" that attempted to annihilate the Jews.

He escaped from Nazi Germany with a few suitcases, one of which he used to salvage the writings of his teacher rather than save personal belongings. My parents and brothers survived the German bombing, the "blitzkrieg," in London. My uncle, my mother's brother, did not.

I was born in Leeds, and soon afterward we immigrated to Australia in order to procure visas for my father's few remaining relatives left in Europe after the Holocaust. I learned to walk on the ship as it rounded the Cape of Good Hope. This has always seemed to me to be the symbol of being born an Ashkenazic[1] Jew in the middle of the twentieth century: learning to walk with no ground under your feet–with no *makom* to give life to one's soul.

The Hebrew word *makom* has a number of meanings. It can denote "place" or "space" and is often used in the Bible as the "place where God's name dwells," namely the Temple. In Talmudic literature the word *makom* came to be a preferred name of God, the "nexus of all creation." These various connotations suggest a sense of permanence or existence. In that sense every person requires their *makom* to grow and flourish.

I grew up with one grandfather and no grandmothers. My grandfather and my only surviving uncles and aunts lived thousands of miles away. Before I was six years old, I had lived on three continents. By the time I was fourteen, in seven different homes. All this for no other reason than that I was born a Jew, son of a young rabbi from Hungary, who met a young woman from Poland in Berlin and who, by the grace of God, was miraculously given life by a Gestapo agent, a friend from university days—born in passage to freedom.

On Thanksgiving Day we would dress for a festive meal and read Psalms thanking God for America and celebrating the salvation of being alive as a Jew despite the Holocaust.

Unexpectedly, something deep in the hidden rhythms of my life was altered. Our family had a profound connection to music. Traditional poems sung at the Sabbath table, my brother's harmonies while doing the dishes, Bach and Beethoven on long-play 33-1/3 RPM records. Suddenly, there was something totally different—songs from Israel. Nothing extraordinary, just the music that Israelis were listening to in the late 1950s—"A Caravan in the Desert," "A Wandering Minstrel," "Uziyahu, the King Built Towers in Jerusalem," and others. I had never taken a liking to the pop music of that period in America, or to the new rock and roll that could be heard everywhere. But I felt an uncontrollable welling up of the spirit every time I would listen to the popular Israeli songs.

How old was I? What does it mean to talk of the "welling up of the spirit" of a preteen whose major interest in life seemed to be baseball? I could hardly understand the words. But the music, oh the music, moved me deeply. I felt, without knowing, that I had seen the landscape that had inspired the music. Something deep within was revealed about my personal *makom*, as if a door had been opened to an unknown chamber. I knew without understanding and yet without a shadow of a doubt: "I am from there, not from here."

A Meditation on Makom

The spirit is ever evolving, the dynamic source of energy that pushes life itself ever onward, in search of knowledge and wisdom, aspiring for fulfillment, dreaming of the final realization of the good in human society. Philosophers and theologians have spoken of this. From Heraclitus who spoke of the ever-changing river of time to Hegel who wrote of the "spirit of history," from the shamans of early nature religions to the sophisticated meditations of mystics moved by the various forms of monotheism—the human mind has sensed from within and from without, the pulse of a life-thriving and divine reality that underlies all things.

At the center of Jewish existence stands the Torah, given by God to Moses at Mount Sinai and during the years of wandering in the desert. Traditionally, Jews have accepted the ultimate authority of the Torah as it was given and passed down through the generations as the word of God—eternal and unchanging.

Yet even a superficial encounter with Jewish learning and literature reveals that the word is ever evolving. The book is never closed. Through various forms of interpretation and exegesis, of legal argumentation and creative religious imagination, the five books of Moses have become a rich, ever-deepening discussion of the generations, of communities cast to the ends of the earth.

This library and the creative life experience to which it gives expression is one of the most dramatic and life-affirming human endeavors, a continuous encounter of the eternal and the human.

During the darkest days of the Holocaust, rebuilding his family in England while fully aware of the systematic attempt to wipe out European Jewry, my father, may his memory be a blessing, wrote, perhaps in protest, perhaps as commentary to what he perceived as the link between nazism and the perception of the Jew as a bane in history for many Christians:

> Judaism is in love with life, for it knows that life is God's great question to mankind; and the way a man lives, what he is doing with his life, the meaning he is able to implant in it, is man's all-important reply. Actual life is the great partner to the spirit, without the one the other is meaningless.
>
> The teachings of the Torah can therefore reveal their real sense only when there is a concrete reality to which they can be applied. On the one hand we have Torah, trying to give shape to that raw lump of life which is so reluctant and evasive; on the other hand, each bit of Torah-shaped life—in social institutions, in economic arrangements, in the relations between man and his neighbors, in the street and in the market as well as in the places of worship— living Torah reacting on the very intentions of Sinai. For just as Torah shapes life, so does Torah-shaped life, in its turn, direct and thus unfold Torah. It is as if Torah was using its own experiences to determine its next new phase. And in each new phase it strives again to re-fashion our lives, which, newly fashioned, will again affect the meaning of the teaching as revealed during its preceding phase in history.
>
> And so on to eternity; Torah leading life, and Torah-led life unfolding Torah. This is the inner meaning of the partnership between Torah and prosaic, every-day existence; and out of this partnership emerges a Judaism capable of unlimited development. It is the spirit developing life, and that new life with its new necessities challenging the spirit to unfold new meanings. The eternity of the Torah lies in being able to accept the challenge and to reveal new meaning from among those latent in the original Sinaitic tradition.
>
> But this is only possible as long as the partnership exists, as long as there is a corporate Jewish existence controlled by a group of people who are prepared to realize Torah in everyday life.
>
> The great spiritual tragedy of the Galut [exile] consists in the breach between Torah and Life, for Galut means the loss of Jewish-controlled environment.[2]

This passage is not only a profound rabbinic teaching. It is the testimony of life of a Jew, not radically different from the testimony of millions—perhaps more expressive, more elegant and eloquent, but no different. It is the testimony of those who lived among the nations and yet separate from them. Not because of a belief in national or religious supremacy but because of a deeply felt need to preserve spiritual integrity while scattered in exile among the nations. The passage describes a commitment to human life that does not deny body because of spirit, but uses the spirit to sanctify the bodily. Not some hallowed spirit that dwells separate from the exigencies of life, but a spirit that dwells in homes and communities, in the uplifting of commercial activity, and yes, in hallowed sexuality—to become the Temple of Life, a place wherein God himself dwells, by sanctifying life itself.

In life's ever-changing encounter with Torah, through the unique life experiences of individuals and communities, the word of God is in ever-deepening revelation to the world.

Jewish history, however, all too often saw life's brutal defilement at the hands of murderous "civilizations." And so, the living testimony of the Jew was of a dreamer in exile. The exile was not only ghettoization and oppression and suffering and death, but also the exile of Torah from life. Without "the total life of a people in their land" there could not be the fulfillment of the Torah. Without fashioning the ethical norms of a vibrant and fair society, without social services that alleviated pain and suffering, without bearing the burden of questions of life and death in medicine and in the military, without the opportunity to develop an indigenous creative culture: without living with and in a people in their land, the Torah itself was in exile.

We, the Torah-led people of Israel, have recently entered our land for the third time in history. The first time, in approximately 1400 B.C.E., after 210 years of Egyptian enslavement and forty years in the desert, we crossed the Jordan River to fulfill the covenant made with God at Mount Sinai. More than 400 years passed before David and Solomon made Jerusalem the capital of the kingdom and built the Temple of Hashem[3] to the God of Israel; God's presence dwelt above the ark in the inner chamber of the temple. But in the year 586 B.C.E., the Babylonians destroyed Jerusalem and its temple. They exiled the indigenous population, uprooting home and economic base and denying a sense of place and peoplehood.

But the God of Israel is also named *Makom*: place. This the rabbis explain: "The creation is not the *makom* of God; God is the *makom* of creation."[4] So the Jews in exile understood that the God of Israel is not only in the land itself, but also in every *makom*.

If God is in every *makom*, if God is omnipresent, why a land, a temple—a fixed *makom*? The links between God, the creator of the universe, beyond space and time, and the land, Jerusalem, and the temple, are paradoxical. The book of Samuel 1 says that the elders of Israel brought the Holy Ark to the battlefield because on the one hand, they believed that it embodies the divine presence that will defeat Israel's enemies.[5] In doing so, they turned the ark into nothing but wood and gold: an idol. On the other hand, during that same period, because they believed that Hashem dwells in heaven above and beyond in eternal holiness, they accepted lesser gods, mediators between heaven and earth, as go-betweens. This, as well, involved the worship of idols.

The people of Israel were then exiled to Babylon because they could not see past the idols and perceive how a sanctified bounded space could be a vessel for the unbounded noncorporeal Presence. In exile, separated from their sanctified space, they were "liberated" from their spiritual shackles—the seduction of a fruitful land that had generated the nature religions that surrounded them and the physical symbols of the Temple of God that created a mistaken sense of the corporeality of God's presence and prideful sense of easy access to its power.

In Babylon they discovered what they were meant to experience while in the Land of Israel: Dwell in physicality, do not deny it. Experience the vitality of life; understand that the source of life is in the unbounded spirit, that spirit sanctifies body, and that body sanctified gives physical vitality to the spirit. Perceive physicality as an image, a projection, a representation, of that which is not physical in both the union of soul and body, and in the seeming impossibility of an unbounded Presence that dwells in Creation.

And so, when the people of Israel reentered the land for the second time during the fifth century B.C.E., they had separated themselves from idols to become the people of the book. In a very real sense, the book had become their *makom*. They then fashioned a new form of spiritual speech: Talmud.[6]

Divisiveness and the Redeeming Deed

After graduating high school in 1962, I made my first trip to Israel, by boat. Two weeks in the "ship dormitory" below the engines. When we docked for the night in Marseille and the engines were turned off, none of our group could sleep for lack of the noise we had gotten used to.

Three nights later we didn't sleep again. Like many Jews before the advent of regular international airline flights, we didn't want to miss the first sight of Mount Carmel at dawn. Unlike Jews of many generations, two weeks out of high school we kept ourselves awake playing the card game Hearts. What made my real heart miss a beat? Not a loved one or a moment of professional success, but catching a view of a land known for years within my soul, but never seen with my eyes.

Most of the year spent in Israel before returning to study physics at the University of Chicago, I carried irrigation pipes across the cotton fields of a kibbutz in the south. The young Israeli who slogged on with me on many a hot day was Menachem Kahane, who became a close friend. Menachem later left the kibbutz to become a central figure, a prize-winning scholar, in the Talmud department at Hebrew University in Jerusalem. Little did we realize then that in our friendship lay the seeds of as yet unknown aspirations.

As Menachem would leave the kibbutz for a life dedicated to the best of academic Talmud scholarship, I would soon give up on following my brothers into science as a profession and, through the study of sociology, philosophy, Jewish history, and Jewish text, seek to discover my own destiny.

However, the chimes of history do not always ring when you are ready. For days everyone at Yeshiva University had been glued to their radios listening to the dramatic events taking place in the Middle East in the early days of June 1967. Threatened by the amassed armies of Egypt, Jordan, and Syria, the possibility of a new Holocaust was very real. Thousands of graves were prepared in Israel for the war that was certain to come. But what could we do in New York? We were at JFK Airport helping load gas masks onto planes headed to Israel, because of reports that Egypt had used mustard gas in Yemen.

During the first few days of the war, reports of stunning Israeli victories seemed as unreal as Arab claims of the destruction of Israeli cities. And then, while I was showering in the university dormitory, a radio hanging on the clothes hook, a report came in that the Israeli Defense Force had removed the Jordanian army from the Old City of Jerusalem—the place where Solomon had built the Temple of Hashem (where it was rebuilt after the Babylonian exile and where it stood in total for 830 years) had been taken back. Journalists both inside and outside Israel were caught up in the tide of the astonishing events and their historic implications. Instead of reporting about the battle that had taken place, they focused on the drama of the return of the Jewish people to their center; they spoke of the powerful and moving experience of the restoration of their place, of their home.

Standing in the shower, unable to control my emotions, I wept and wept. Countless tears were flowing uncontrollably down my face. The tears of my father, shed for the one and a half million Jewish children slaughtered without mercy in the Holocaust. The tears of my grandfather, who suffered a heart attack days before the Nazis entered the town of Oradea, Romania, where he taught Torah. The tears of my grandmother and my aunts and uncles who sang "I believe in the coming of the Messiah" as they were taken to Auschwitz. The tears of generations, dreaming of the land they would never see, who sang at the most hallowed of times: "Next Year in Jerusalem."

So clear to me at that moment was the profound sense of return, when the encounter of the divine and the human is not only an aspiration or a mere possibility but an actual moment within time and within space—a moment of redemption in history.

How could I not weep uncontrollably, thinking of all those generations at such a moment, even while standing in the shower?

Three years later I returned to Israel, this time for good, to study philosophy at Hebrew University and to pursue advanced Torah study at the seminary founded by the first Chief Rabbi in modern-day Israel, Rabbi Avraham Isaac Kook. I spent many hours wandering the streets of Jerusalem in a dance of the spirit while touching the old and the new in Jerusalem. On one such walk, while soloing my way in the Old City, I came upon the Western Wall. The Wall is part of the imposing rampart that surrounds the Temple Mount, built by King Herod and strengthened by a Turkish sultan. In the years to come, I would pray and dance at the Wall, feeling an intimacy with a Presence unlike anything I had felt before.

Years passed. I married a young Israeli woman whose family had lived in Jerusalem for seven generations, many in the Old city itself. With two young children and nine months pregnant, caught up in the vibrant rhythms of a young and idealistic society, we sought to join other couples to build new life, new communities.

Although we did not share the ideology of building new settlements in Judea and Samaria (in the so-called Occupied Territories), to our surprise we felt at home with the wonderful young couples we met in Shilo, an Israeli community in the hills of Samaria, and we moved there in 1980. In 1989 I was elected to the community council. Three months later the intifada began. Many Shilo residents were injured by stones and Molotov cocktails on the road to and from work and in terrorist attacks in Jerusalem. We visited the local sheik but were told that he had no control over the youth who wanted the throw off the yoke of Israel's occupation.

When we first arrived at Shilo, there seemed to be real hope of creating a constructive and mutually beneficial relationship between our community and the three Arab villages in the area. Our leadership helped their counterparts in the villages procure electricity and running water—something the Jordanian authorities who controlled the area until 1967 had failed to provide. Our telephone exchange was situated in one of the villages and the Arab operators knew all of us by first name; fruits and vegetables were sold to us by residents of the villages.

As the years passed, my wife and I asked ourselves a series of questions regarding our relationship to the Arabs in the nearby villages. Was our presence legitimate? Was it moral? At what price would we be willing to leave our home for conciliation with the Arabs? Was real peace possible?

The Wall surrounding the Temple Mount has become a symbol for me of both redemption and conflict. Praying at the Western Wall had been a dream of Jews for generations—to touch its weathered stone was redemptive. Yet the powerful urge to pray at the Wall and to touch its stone created a deep inner conflict. I felt the Wall beckoning inward, to the Temple Mount itself. Could the dream of generations be realized without God's Presence in the Temple of Hashem? A massive stone structure cut me off from worshiping on the Temple Mount itself. Jews prayed at the Wall, I came to understand, because it allowed them to experience the Presence *beyond* the Wall.

Yet for generations the Wall has also been a symbol of redemption, of the realization of Torah in the world. But if "the Torah's ways are ways of pleasantness, and all her paths are peace,"[7] how could the Wall incite divisiveness and conflict? The Temple Mount was given by the government of Israel to Muslim religious authorities to control as an important place of Muslim worship. Should Israel remove them because of our vision of redemption? I think not. Although Jews had waited generations to return to Israel, we will have to wait still longer to return to the place we turn to three times daily to pray.

Not only is the specter of conflict and violence with the Arabs reflected in the struggle for Jerusalem, but also these hallowed places are points of divisiveness within Israel itself. What is Israel's ultimate vision: peace or land, prosperity for all in the Middle East or never-ending conflict, humanistic values of democracy and freedom or the aspirations of generations of Jews for the realization of national redemption at the expense of the basic rights of the "stranger"?

I never believed that these polarities would be helpful in clarifying the national debate and in moving us forward or that they even reflected the reality in Israel. The Temple Mount, the Wall, and Jerusalem are at the center of the present standoff between Israel and the Palestinians. My perspective on the issue of land, place, and peace as a moral dilemma in the political context had become very simple.

If the Arabs put down arms, recognized Israel, and sued for peace, what would happen? There would be real peace and the vast majority of Israelis, myself included, would be willing to make concessions regarding the most hallowed of our national possessions for the sake of reducing bloodshed and celebrating the sanctity of life.

And what would happen if Israel put down its arms in pursuit of peace? It would, very likely, be destroyed by Arabs. Israel faces a coalition of powerful Arab interests, including Palestinians of most stripes that refuse to recognize Israel's right to exist as the homeland of the people of Israel.

And when will the Temple of Hashem be rebuilt on the Temple Mount? No one knows. But certainly not by conquest! Taking the Temple Mount by force would counter the fundamental universal message of the Third Temple of Hashem: to be a light to all nations. Perhaps the Temple of Hashem will be rebuilt only when the world's spiritual cultures turn to the people of Israel and say: "We need the Torah, the Word of God, as taught in Israel through Talmud, for our lives. Build the Temple of Hashem so that God's word can be revealed to all."[8]

While waiting—and hoping—for a shift in the winds that blow across the Middle East, there is a fundamental moral commandment to defend ourselves and to protect our families.

A fundamental tenet in the biblical and Talmudic concept of moral behavior is that greater power obligates greater kindness; accumulation of power requires greater commitment to use that power to fulfill God's will. The state of Israel today is a significant power in the Middle East and on the international scene. That position obligates Israel to create the conditions for all people of the Middle East to live in peace with the blessings of life. And Israel must go as far as possible to allow Palestinians to achieve those goals under their own autonomous rule.

However, the gift of power does not on its own make the powerful guilty. Unfortunately, in the Middle East today the gift of power is a basic condition for our survival. Israel faces threats to its existence from Arab states such as Syria and Iran who speak of our destruction and support the Hezbollah on our northern border and the Hamas on our southern border. Many Palestinians identify with these forces and with their clearly stated vision of the disappearance of the Jewish state.

So the moral commandment to protect ourselves is clear. Until Palestinian leadership offers a plainly stated recognition of Israel's right to exist as a Jewish state, we must maintain communities in Judea and Samaria for self-protection. Right now such communities prevent the creation of a Palestinian state that would in all likelihood join those forces seeking the destruction of the Israel. Since peace requires reciprocity, denying the right of the Jewish people to their *makom* in Israel means denying the right to *makom* for those alongside.

And of the Temple Mount we continue to pray and dream, as Jews have done for many centuries while allowing Muslims and Christians freedom of worship everywhere within our jurisdiction.

Beyond Prophecy

Rabbi Kook, who founded the Torah seminary in which I studied, saw the third entry of the Jewish people into Israel as a providential redemptive event. His vision of the renewal of the national life of the people of Israel as the fulfillment of the words of the prophets inspired many in Israel and in the Diaspora. He saw the return to Israel as the fulfillment of the universal aspiration for the moral good in human society, which he understood in mystical terms to be embedded in the very dynamics of Creation.

One of those attracted to the poetry and pathos of Rabbi Kook's writings was Rabbi David Cohen. When, as a student, he heard that the famous Jerusalem rabbi would be visiting Switzerland, he traveled to meet him and spent an evening with him discussing philosophy and theology. Lying in bed the following morning, he heard Rabbi Kook devoutly praying. So moved by the power of his prayer, he exclaimed: "I have found myself my spiritual mentor!"[9] Years later, a few months after arriving in Israel in the early autumn of 1922 to become a disciple of Rabbi Kook, Rabbi Cohen wrote in his diary:

> I went for a walk around the holy city to awaken my spirit in the holy mountains that surround me, and lo, my spirit lives. With great bitterness I sat opposite Avshalom's monument, took out my pocket Bible and read of Avshalom's rebellion against his father David as described in Samuel II. Everything I read came alive before my eyes. There, in the Valley of the Kings my spirit lives, and my soul was elevated by the amazing view that lay before me where the holy prophets once walked. And my spirit filled with hope and anticipation that prophecy would be revealed. And my heart filled with anticipation regarding the "Great Yeshiva" (seminary) and study hall that would be built there. The Yeshiva for which I fashioned a curriculum and which I showed to our teacher the Rabbi, may he live many days, and in which the first words were: "the revival of the spirit of prophecy."[10]

Rabbi Cohen believed that the time was spiritually and intellectually ripe for the renewal of prophecy. The vision of the prophets walking those paths made this far-reaching aspiration—the integration of the spiritual imagination with Talmudic legalism—seem attainable.

Will there soon be a renewal of the prophetic vision in the Land of Israel, on the holy mountains that surround Jerusalem? Rabbi Kook saw the renewal of prophecy in the renewed encounter between the eternal and the human in the rebuilding of the Land of Israel. For him the encounter between the eternal word of God and evolving human consciousness is reflected in the three periods during which the people of Israel dwelt in their land: the biblical (or prophetic), the Talmudic, and the modern (the unification of the prophetic and Talmudic). The word of God is manifest in human life in radically different modes in each of these periods.

Rabbi Kook developed a model of history in which Divine revelation itself is described as an ever-evolving phenomenon moving human consciousness in the people of Israel forward—in a manner that has dramatic universal implications:

Prophecy saw the great evil of idolatry in ancient Israel, and protested against it with all its might; it envisioned the majesty and delight associated with the belief in one God, and portrayed it in all its radiance. It saw the corruption in moral depravity, the oppression of the poor, murder, adultery and robbery, and it was infused with the spirit of God to offer help and to rectify these conditions through lofty and holy exhortations.[11]

Rabbi Kook perceived the "radiance" of the belief in one God as reflected in the ongoing struggle to remove violence and moral corruption from human society. The prophets exhorted Israel and the nations to change their ways and to fashion civilization in justice and loving kindness.

In a similar vein, Maimonides, one of the central figures in medieval Jewish history, wrote of the impact of the prophetic protest against idolatry and barbarism. Maimonides describes how the early civilization of Israel, through the power of the prophets and the five books of Moses, became the foundation of the two great religions that fashioned Western civilization, Christianity and Islam. In a sweeping vision of the history of civilization, Maimonides describes the defeat of idolatry as part of the development of a human moral consciousness based on the belief in the one God that would lead to the Messiah. He believed that the prophecy of Israel entered the bloodstream of human culture as an expression of the grace of God embedded in human history.[12]

Prophecy was the hallmark of Israel's first entry into the land to build the Temple of Hashem. But the temple in Jerusalem was destroyed by the Babylonians in 586 B.C.E. However, the paths of God's grace are gradual; the evolution of the spirit in history requires human vessels to indwell in the physical world. It would take another 600 years for the vision of the prophets to begin to assume a role in fashioning civilization on a broad scale outside Israel.

During this period Israel entered the land again to rebuild the Temple of Hashem. The word of God remained the ultimate authority, but the mode of its revelation changed, evolved, deepened. Prophets were no more, replaced by the sages and by the development of the Talmud.

Though Rabbi Kook longed for the renewal of prophecy, he focused on a well-known aphorism in the Talmud, "The sage is more important than the prophet":

> But the little lapses out of which was forged the gross body of sin—these remained hidden from the eye of every prophet and seer. Similarly it was not within the sphere of prophecy to grasp how the habituated performance and the study of commandments will, after a span of time, release their hidden

inner graces, and a wholly divine influence will decisively vanquish the darkness of idolatry. Nor could it grasp how the slow negligence, which dispar-
ages the performance of the commandments, with their inferences and
elaborations, will start a process of erosion, destroying the vessels in which
is stored the exalted spirit. . . .

It was, therefore, necessary to assign the enunciation of general principles
to the prophets and of the particulars to the sages; and, as the Talmud declares, "the sage is more important than the prophet."[13] And what prophecy
with its impassioned and fiery exhortations could not accomplish in purging
the Jewish people of idolatry and in uprooting the basic causes of the most
degrading forms of oppression and violence, of burden, sexual perversity
and bribery, was accomplished by the sages through the expanded development of the Torah, by raising many disciples and by the assiduous study of
the particular laws and their derivative applications.[14]

One of the most basic Jewish claims regarding the human endeavor to fash-
ion the redemptive deed is the sanctification of the particular. In that regard
Talmudic discussion in all its complexity is not religious obscurantism, as
Christendom often characterized it; rather it is the wellspring of life.

It is not enough to know the essence of the good and the right, or even to
recognize it as the word of God. The human dilemma is how to induce people
to act effectively in accord with their obligations. Judaism assumes that there
is an "appetite for goodness" in everyone. However, mind and good faith
alone are not enough to bring about ethical action. In order to achieve ethical
conduct, our emotional forces, often uncontrolled by faith and mind alone,
must submit to a discipline that is required for moral action.[15]

This was the goal of Talmud as a tool for the formation of character and,
by virtue of that, the dedication of human creativity to the moral good in the
fashioning of culture. "The assiduous study of the particular laws and their
derivative applications," as Rabbi Kook describes the language of Talmud, has
been going on in every Jewish community across the globe for 2,500 years. Its
goal is not sainthood, but hallowed "humanhood"—the fulfillment of the
hope of being created "in the image of God," living fully in the vitality of
the physical yet sanctified by the words of God in the Torah.

Rabbi Kook believed that in the revelation of God's word during the third
entry of Israel into the land, the law of the Torah will be infused with the
vitality and vision of the prophets; the light of prophecy will begin to have its
revival as we are promised: "I shall pour out My spirit on all flesh" (Joel 3:1).
The radiance of prophecy will reemerge from hiding and reveal itself as the
first fruits full of vitality and life. At that time we will embrace the vision of

unity expressed by the psalmist: "Mercy and truth have met, justice and peace have kissed, truth will rise out of the earth and mercy will show itself from heaven; the Lord will also bestow what is good and our earth will bring forth its bounty" (Ps. 85:11).[16]

Talmud for the Whole World

As a student of Rabbi Kook's writing, I too yearn for a radical union of prophetic pathos and Talmudic rigor. And, like every good student in the tradition of the Talmudic study hall, I want to add a thought of my own.

Just as prophecy, the language of the spirit during the period of the First Temple of Hashem, became the source of inspiration for many nations and cultures, the third entry of Israel into the land marks the beginning of the epoch of Talmud for all of human civilization. A blessed wind of renewed life has swept across many nations in modern times, an aspiration for a redeemed human existence—less corruption, less war, less depravity. Freedom and democracy are key in the renewal of the human spirit. Yet they are insufficient. There is need for a fundamental transformation so that the word of God can pass from spirit to daily deed, from faith to ethical obligation—for every human in daily life.

The tool for human consciousness to effect such a transformation is God's law as understood and formulated by human Talmud. This is a gift that God has given to all humans through the experience of the Jew in exile across the globe.

One of central formulations of Talmudic logic is, "these and those are the words of the Living God."[17] This aphorism makes an astonishing theological claim: that the word of God has many facets and that those facets are revealed through different committed and believing human souls. The Talmudic study hall at the time that this aphorism was formulated consisted of the students and scholars of the Houses of Shammai and Hillel, the main schools that formulated Jewish law and belief in the Mishnaic period. They differed on many issues of law and belief. In the spirit of the diverse search for truth in open debate and argumentation, we affirm the vision of committed and believing human souls from many nations and cultures all "talking Talmud."

One of the greatest sages of the Talmud, Rabbi Elazar ben Azaria, who presided for a time as president of the Sanhedrin just after the destruction of the Second Temple of Hashem, phrased this principle in a Midrash based on the image of young and vital saplings grouped together as described in chapter twelve of the book of Ecclesiastes. He taught that the image represents the students of Talmud who sit together in groups studying the Torah. Some decide in favor of defilement, some in favor of purity. Some are stringent and prohibit, some are lenient and permit. Some disallow and some decide in favor of "Kosher." Lest the student exclaim: "And how can I study the Torah now (faced with such diversity within the understanding of God's word)?" Thus teaches the words of the Torah itself—all the opinions were given by one shepherd, one leader proclaimed them from the mouth of the ruler of all creation, may he be blessed, as it is written: "And God commanded these words" (Exodus 20:1, introducing the Ten Commandments). You too (continues Rabbi Elazar ben Azaria as if turning to the questioning student), open your ear like a funnel, acquire a heart that perceives and penetrates, and listen carefully to the words of those who decide in favor of defilement.[18]

Dissension, conflict, even excommunication were not unknown in the halls in which Rabbi Elazar presided and taught. Well aware of the dangers inherent in disagreement and dissent, he reaffirmed the will of God to create the people of Israel as twelve separate tribes—each with its unique spiritual character and vitality.

One can formulate these teachings in the following way. Every human soul was created by God and yearns for the good. God spoke through the prophets of Israel in order to offer humankind the tools that would effectively fashion civilization committed to moral conduct. In that spirit the sages of the generations created the language of Talmudic debate to transform the human ego and its creative capacities for the preservation of life.

In more philosophical terms this intuition can be formulated in terms of truth. For most of Western civilization, "truth" has been considered absolute. This often led differing cultural and spiritual groups to claim: "My truth denies your truth"; and with no less vehemence: "Your truth denies my truth." Talmudic logic, by contrast, posits the nature of truth in a radically different mode. Truth in Jewish law and in the speech of Talmud is multiple—"these and those are the words of the Living God." Truth also emerges from differing views regarding even the most basic laws and beliefs as long as participants in truth accept the authority of the Torah.[19]

Can this Talmudic concept of truth become a universal principle of discussion and debate among cultures and religions that have differing assumptions about the most basic issues of human life and belief? A world of tolerance, liberty, and peace is a dream common to most of humankind. Yet despite many an aspiration and countless attempts to turn utopian visions into reality, we have been unable to achieve this goal. Belief and ideology create divides that invite both misunderstanding and conflict.

Can we overcome those divides? The encounter of the Torah as the word of God combined with Talmud as human speech fashioning the Torah, in an ever-changing and evolving reality, can be the Jewish gift to civilization. Herein lies the dimension of universal meaning in the third entry of Israel to the land. Imagine the light of life redeemed, that of the wisdom inherent in the word of God as revealed by myriad souls talking Talmud. Every human soul can discern and penetrate the language of Talmud and learn to speak it and by doing so can become a vessel for the revelation of God's word in life.

Returning Home

An evening on a hot midsummer's day. A cool breeze from the Mediterranean ruffles the pages of prayer books and small paper booklets. Spread across the bare ground are many of the families of Shilo, from grandparents to babies cradled in their mother's arms, sitting together in the dark.

It is the eve of the ninth day of the month of Av, the day on which, for countless generations, Jews in every community across the earth mourn the exile and the destruction of the Temple of Hashem built by Solomon as well as the destruction of the Second Temple of Hashem. Amazingly, the destruction of the First Temple by the Babylonians in 586 B.C.E. and of the Second Temple by the Romans more than 650 years later took place on exactly the same day as marked on the Jewish calendar, seemingly a providential act of God.

To commemorate these tragic events, the community reads the book of Lamentations, written by the prophet Jeremiah, who prophesied and witnessed the destruction of the First Temple. The usual custom—for hundreds, maybe thousands of years—was to do the reading by candlelight while seated on the floor, like mourners, in the synagogue. Yet many of the residents of Shilo, young and old, Israeli born or not, come together to read Lamentations at the base of Tel Shilo.

The biblical city of Shilo became the religious capital of Israel when the people of Israel entered the land for the first time. According to the Bible, Joshua set up the Tabernacle, the Tent of Meeting that the people of Israel carried with them through the desert, in Shilo.[20] The Tent of Meeting stood at Shilo for 369 years, serving as the Temple of Hashem before David and Solomon built the temple in Jerusalem. Many Christian and Jewish groups come to visit and pray at the Tel.

The Talmud remarks that the Tent of Meeting was placed on a stone foundation, symbolizing that the Promised Land was a reality. The desert was now the past, the stone represented the new, solid reality. However, the Temple of

Hashem remained in a tent, symbol of the nomadic life. Only when the Holy Ark came to rest in Jerusalem would the Torah be revealed in its fullest.

Now, thousands of years later, the men and women of Shilo reading the words of Jeremiah seated physically close to the place of the Tent of Meeting feel, even more deeply, the loss of the temple. But our mourning mingles with hope: the experience of loss and incompleteness is sweetened by expectation. The earth itself on which we lie, the breeze that comes across the hills, the stones that mark the gate to the biblical town of Shilo turn the chant of Lamentations into living testimony to the third entry into the Land of Israel.

Redemption? Not yet. Exile? No more. The families assembled at the reading include a family whose four living generations live in Shilo and families from all continents except Antarctica. The eve of the Ninth of Av, at the base of Tel Shilo, is a moment when the glimmering flashlights and gas lamps used to follow the reading are the sparks of countless communities and generations gathered here to witness the meeting of Jeremiah and the new community of Shilo.

For 369 years, the Tent of Meeting stood at Shilo, until it was destroyed by the Philistines. The period was one of divisiveness and conflict. The tribes of Israel vied with each other for power. Neighboring rulers made war with Israel for control of the land and sources of water, for booty, and for taxation. It was a period when many in Israel were enticed by foreign cultures. The hope of an indigenous and unique spiritual creativity binding the word of God to the new experience in the Land of Israel was left unheeded. All this is told in the book of Judges.

Israel, once again, seems to be in a period of transition from exile to redeemed national existence. We lack a common spiritual language, and self-interest has replaced the national cohesion of the early years of the state of Israel. Foreign cultures, especially the most superficial and showy aspects of modern America, once again entice us.

Yet the third entry of Israel into the land is creating its own language of revelation of God's word. Once there was God's word in prophecy; then there was God's word in the Talmudic discussions of the sages based on the words of Moses and the prophets. Today there is a spiritual adventure taking place. Young Israelis have created a broad-based movement for a more just and compassionate society. Creative artists are exploring new forms of expression in music, poetry, theater, and the visual arts that give expression to the spirit. The study of Talmud itself is undergoing reevaluation to give age-old discussions personal meaning for young people born in a dynamic and creative modern society. Continually, in a myriad of schools, homes, and communities, in aspects of private and public endeavor, many groups are studying and discussing the Torah, dealing with questions and concerns that were never part of the living reality of previous generations.

How will Torah fashion life in modern Israel? How will it be a vessel for the renewed revelation of Torah? How will life fashion Torah? We are working at it, and when it happens, the Temple of Hashem will be the beacon for a new face of God in the world.

Wholly Other?

Jacob was named "Israel" by an unnamed angel of God—in struggle. Who was the divine figure who refused to reveal his name to Jacob?[21] Early Jewish tradition claims that the angel with whom Jacob struggled in the darkness was the spirit of Esau, Jacob's twin brother. Although close brothers can share compassion and understanding, there is no hatred and cruelty like that between brothers whose jealousy has turned to uncontrollable rage. If brothers can wrestle so mightily for the love of a human father, how much more intense will the fighting be if the struggle is for the love of Father in heaven? Who are the chosen people? And how much blood has been shed, mostly Jewish blood, over that question?

Secular thinkers claim that the only solution is the denial of religion. But is the notion of a "chosen people" really the source of all evil in human civilization?

Jacob's identity as Israel was made known to him during his struggle with the Godly as revealed in his brother, Esau; ever since he has been seeking to find the key to reconciliation with him. Can we recognize the Godly in others and, in so doing, find the key to reconciliation with them?

There have always been two faces to the Jewish encounter with the "other"—on the one hand, a deep sense of common humanity and of shared responsibility, and on the other hand, a profound sense of fear of a brother's animosity.

When Jews have felt secure in their home and in the synagogue, secure from marauding Mongols and crusading Christians, from Ukrainian nationalist zeal and from the venomous pogroms of neighbors and friends, Jewish communities—while diligently preserving their own identity—have consistently sought reconciliation with their brothers, Esau and Yishmael (the ancestor of Islam). Returning to Israel for the third time provides renewed opportunity for the people of Israel to pursue their destiny among nations, perhaps to be understood for the first time. Central to the realization of Israel's identity and destiny is the manner in which the state of Israel treats the "other," which must include two foundational ideas:

Axiom #1: There is no wholly other, there are only the children of Esau and Yishmael, our brothers.

The commitment to strengthen the state of Israel as an expression of our uniqueness among the nations must not become a tool for the demeaning and mistreatment of others. The destiny of Israel can only be realized in the betterment of the condition of all those who dwell amongst us and those who are our neighbors.

Axiom #2: Those who do not recognize our basic right to exist and to build our life in this land are our enemies.

And if the state of Israel means anything, it means the end of "the curse of the Jew," which says that Jews are the Satan of history who can be persecuted and murdered at will.

But there are others who lived here when the third return began. What needs to be done to ensure that they do not become "wholly others" in our eyes?

Who are the Palestinians? When did they enter Israel? Have they been here for 2,000 years as they claim or are they immigrants who came from Syria in the nineteenth century as many in Israel see them? In the end, what does it matter? We are both here—sharing this beautiful, but impossibly small piece of land between the Jordan River and the Mediterranean Sea. We are like Jacob and the angel, intertwined and inseparable. Each of our names is being shaped in this struggle. What are we to do?

If a solution can be found, it will emerge only from mutual trust. Only mutual trust can turn a "wholly other" into a "holy brother." But can mutual trust be created in the Middle East? It can happen only when each side is willing to recognize the violence that comes from within, to admit that there is a festering of spirit gone bad somewhere in one's own culture and society, in one's own religion.

The Bible commands:

> If one be found slain in the land which the Lord thy God gives thee to possess it, lying in the open field, and it be not known who has slain him: then the elders and judges shall come out, and they shall measure to the cities which are round him that is slain; and it shall be that the elders of the city which is nearest to the slain man shall . . . wash their hands on the sacrifice that is brought and they shall say in responsive declaration. "Our hands have not shed this blood, nor have our eyes seen it done. Be merciful O Lord to thy people Yisrael, whom thou hast redeemed, and lay not the spilling of innocent blood to the charge of thy people Yisrael." And the blood shall be

forgiven them. So shalt thou put away the spilling of innocent blood from among you, when thou shalt do what is right in the sight of the Lord.[22]

The Talmud asks: Is it possible that the "elders" are guilty of murder? No—but was the slain man given food and lodging in the city? Why was he sent off alone, not accompanied by someone?[23] The Talmud means to say that when there is violence and the innocent are murdered, the elders must step forward and bear responsibility for the social norms that allow it to happen. And so:

Axiom #3: The leaders of each society must be self-critical and assume responsibility for acts of violence stemming from its society.

The Jewish penchant to be self-critical often reaches the point of self-hatred. Some claim that we Jews are responsible for all of the Arab-Israeli violence. We must take responsibility where appropriate. But we are not responsible for all of the problems in the Middle East. Muslim leaders contribute to the conditions of violence when they fail to speak out against the traditions within their religion that justify violence. And few Arab voices publicly reject the exhortations of those who encourage violence and terrorism. And when will a Palestinian openly criticize the way Israelis are portrayed in their textbooks?

There can be mutual trust only when the spiritual and communal leadership of both sides are willing to publicly question themselves and their society and then to proclaim in truth, "Our hands have not shed this blood and our eyes have not seen what was done." (Deut. 21:7). Only then will we begin to see ourselves as brothers; only then can there be a chance for peace in the Middle East.

Notes

1. In Hebrew the literal meaning of the word *Ashkenazi* is "Germanic." However, since the beginning of the Middle Ages, following the great divide of Jewish communities and their traditions across Europe and North Africa, the word has come to mean all Jews who lived in communities in eastern and northern Europe. Jews from southern Europe and North Africa were called "sephardim" after the Hebrew word for Spain, *Sepharad.*

2. Eliezer Berkovits, *Towards Historic Judaism* (Oxford: The East and West Library, 1943), 32–33. The term "the Torah" refers to the written text of the Bible, specifically to the five books of Moses accepted by Jewish tradition to be the authoritative text revealed to Moses by God. The more general term "Torah" refers to God's living word which infuses the written Torah with wisdom and imperative relevant to all generations. For a similar use of these terms, see "Revelation and Tradition as Religious Categories in Judaism" by Gershom Scolem in *The Messianic Idea in Judaism* (New York: Schocken,

1971). I use similar terminology to distinguish between *Talmud* as a rhetoric that shapes cultural consciousness and *the Talmud* which refers to specific texts. See note 7.

3. *Hashem*, which means "The Name," is a term used by Jews to refer to God in common parlance.

4. Midrash Rabba, Genesis, 68, 9.

5. Samuel 1, 4:3–4.

6. I use the term "Talmud" throughout this essay as it is used in the classic texts of Torah to refer to a form of human speech, a finely tuned rhetoric developed to discuss the fundamental values that shape society and culture. Talmud in its original and constitutive form is an oral project, in principle. I use the term "the Talmud" to refer to a specific text—for instance, the Babylonian or Jerusalem Talmud. The Talmud as text is an example of edited protocol of Talmud as oral culture, composed in response to the growing need for centralization of authority and community coherence in times of calamity and dispersal in exile. Talmud as a culture of the written word expanded over time, but never replaced the original sense of Talmud as the nexus of spiritual and intellectual activity for scholars and for laypeople in the community at large.

7. Proverbs 3:17.

8. Is this formulation simply sublimated religious nationalism? I think not. Is it a sincere, but unrealistic aspiration? A messianic dream? Probably. But remember this: the return of the people of Israel seemed for many generations to be just that—a messianic and improbable dream.

9. David Cohen, *Introduction to the Lights of Holiness by Rabbi Avraham Isaac Kook: Mossad Harav Kook* (Jerusalem: 1969), 17–18.

10. David Cohen, *Nazir Echav (The Nazirite of his Brothers)* (Jerusalem: Committee for the Publication of Rabbi David Cohen's Writings, 1977), 281.

11. Rabbi Avraham Isaac Kook, *The Classics of Western Spirituality*, translated by Ben Zion Bokser (New York: Paulist Press, 1978), 253.

12. Maimonides, *Mishneh Torah, Laws of the Kings*, chapter 12:1.

13. Babylonian Talmud, Tractate Bava Batra, folio page 12a.

14. Kook, *Classics of Western Spirituality*, 253–254.

15. Based on Eliezer Berkovits, *God, Man, and History* (New York: Jonathan David Publishers, 1959), 108–109.

16. Rabbi Kook is clearly responding to important spiritual movements in modern Jewry, one of which was the socialist, secular idealism he knew well and deeply respected that moved the early pioneers in Israel who wished to leave the "particulars" behind in their vision of a redeemed Jew in Israel.

17. Babylonian Talmud, Tractate Eruvin, folio page 13b.

18. Ibid., Tractate Hagigah, folio page 3b.

19. My good friend and hevruta Rabbi Tzuriel Wiener formulated this idea. I add this to his thought. The postmodern attempt to neutralize the seeds of conflict embedded in the position that there exists "one absolute truth" was to formulate the popular disclaimer: "There is no Truth; there are only differing narratives." This, of course, has not helped anyone "open their ears like a funnel and acquire a heart that perceives and penetrates and listens carefully." At most it has allowed for a certain tolerance, but not

an ability to appreciate, understand, and identify with the "truth" that underlies value assumptions that differ from our own.

20. Joshua 18:1.

21. Genesis 32:30.

22. Deuteronomy 21:1–3, 6–9.

23. Babylonian Talmud, Tractate Sotah, folio page 48b.

$$4$$

Revisiting the Holy Rebellion

LEAH SHAKDIEL

In 1988, Leah Shakdiel, Israeli peace activist, became Israel's first female member of a local Religious Council, following a successful struggle that ended with a landmark Supreme Court decision. Through teaching and continued activist work with Israeli Human Rights NGOs like Machsom Watch, Mirkam Azori, Darom4Peace, and Rabbis for Human Rights, Shakdiel works to bring the values of peace, equality, human rights, and social justice to the next generation of Israelis.

Introduction: My Background

When my father died, my oldest sister composed the following text for his tombstone:

R. Moshe-Tzvi, of blessed memory,
Son of R. Aharon-Yossef
Shakdiel (Mandelboym).
Torah scholar and pure of heart
Dedicated his life with endless love
For the establishment of a faithful generation
An honest servant of the public

Persistent at helping all people in modesty
While still in Exile, converted many to Zionism
And all his years on the Land he spent working for National-Religious
    schooling.
Born in Poland 1905
Came up to the Land with the Pioneers 1934
Took his leave in Jerusalem 1957.
May his soul be gathered in the Wreath of Life.

I was five years old and was not taken to the funeral. But I know this text by heart; it is like a mantra to me. "Torah scholar and pure of heart . . . converted many to Zionism . . . years on the Land he spent working for National-Religious schooling."

When my mother died years later, she was laid to rest next to him, and her tombstone's inscription states that she, too, came from Poland to the Land of Israel with the pioneers in 1934. My parents had met in Poland and married soon after their arrival here, turning their backs on their families who had not supported their choices. Earlier, my mother had run away from home to the city of Krakow to join a "kibbutz" (an agricultural commune of pioneers preparing for emigration to Palestine) because her parents had not believed that it was possible to become a Zionist and remain religiously observant. She proved them wrong. But when they realized their error, it was already too late. My four grandparents and almost all our relatives in Europe were murdered by the Nazis. My parents became the mainstay of the few survivors who ended up in Israel.[1] On my mother's tombstone, we added a memorial plaque for our grandparents (the Mandelboyms, the Hochhausers, the Koralls, and the Sattlers) and all their descendants who were murdered by the Nazis and who have no grave.

In 1937, my father traded his Yiddish last name, Mandelboym, for its Hebrew translation, Shakdiel, upon receiving his citizenship of the British Mandate for Palestine, which he proudly considered "our new birthland." If he had not changed his name then, he likely would not have abandoned the name Mandelboym after the Sho'ah. After all, Mandelboym is a beautiful name—it means "almond tree," which is reminiscent of the longed-for Land of Israel.[2] "May God work diligently for me and for our people, for the good, amen," he wrote. He was part of the generation of Jews who emigrated to Palestine because they believed there was no future for their people in Europe, and they lived to see their prediction come true in an ironic horrible historical twist.[3]

How Victimhood Breeds Conquest

I choose to introduce myself in this way because it provides an insight into Israeli society today. Two, and even three, biological generations later, we are still a "generation" of guilt-ridden Sho'ah survivors. I am using the term *generation* here in the sense coined in 1927 by sociologist Karl Manheim—he defines it as a distinct grouping of people whose actions, politics, output, and discourse are best explained by a foundational, earth-shaking experience they share, an experience so engulfing that it overrides all their differences and preferences. In Manheim's Germany of the 1920s, their generation's foundational, earth-shaking experience was the Great War (later known as World War I). For Israel, it was—and still is—the Sho'ah.

Today, the majority of Israeli Jews, as well as the majority of Israel-identified Jews outside Israel, still suffer from untreated post-traumatic stress—no matter how many years after the Sho'ah they were born, no matter how far away their grandparents lived during the Sho'ah, no matter how good their actual lives have been since then, no matter who else suffers around them and to what degree, and—I must admit painfully—no matter if those other sufferers are victims of our very own wrongdoings. We Jews carry with us the marks of "ultimate victims," and, therefore we tell the world, "Do not mess with us; never try to compete with us in our suffering." In this sense, it is amazing to note that even Israeli Jews who come from non-European cultures (about half the population of Israeli Jews) have also internalized the Christian image of the homeless, haunted, Jewish ghost, cursed with eternal suffering, as an essential aspect of mainstream Jewish identity in this "generation."

I am a teacher. Wherever I can, I show my students Eyal Sivan's 1991 documentary, *Yizkor: Slaves of Memory*, about the Israeli state school system's all-encompassing focus in the spring on three historical dates: the ancient holiday of Pesach (Passover), which commemorates the exodus from Egypt; Memorial Day for the Sho'ah; and Memorial Day for the Fallen Soldiers with the adjoined Independence Day celebration. The film shows how, during this month, the entire school system, from kindergarten to grade twelve, is one continuous, educational manipulation, replete with emotional ceremonies and classroom teachings that fit perfectly with other public ceremonies in Israel's "civil religion."[4]

Like many other Israeli thinkers today, I have adopted the use of this new analytical tool —civil religion—because it seems like a good way of explaining an apparent contradiction: the majority of Israelis identify themselves as nonreligious, yet they display a devotion to the Jewish aspects of public life in Israel. They cherish their freedoms from the clerical establishment and often get angry at the political gains that the establishment makes, but they never doubt the centrality of that same clerical establishment to the survival of Jewish identity everywhere, including Israel. They even lean on that clerical establishment to safeguard their Jewishness while they live their lives as they please. I believe this is typical in societies (including Islamic societies) that do not separate conceptually between state and church—many people opt to be nonreligious, religious sinners in their own eyes, a peculiar mental twist that breeds some negative feelings, describing themselves with such statements as: "I cannot define myself with positive content, I can only say that I am a Jew who does *not* keep the Sabbath, who does *not* keep kosher." "I know I am a sinner, I practice some Judaism sometimes but cannot defend my choices." "Of course I believe in God, I am not an atheist, and don't you dare tell me that I am less of a good Jew than anyone." These nonreligious Jews make up for the discomfort and ambiguity of this mindset with a display of devotion to the collective, without even noticing how much of that devotion looks like a new religion, a hybrid of ancient God-given rituals with human-made ceremonies that bind the nation together. Thus they allow the Israeli army to hold training ceremonies in religious sites such as the Western Wall plaza and more recently the Ancestral Burial site in Hebron, with a national flag that takes its two blue stripes from the Jewish prayer shawl (tallit), a gun, and a Jewish Bible on which the soldiers swear their allegiance to the state of Israel. The sites, the gun, the flag, and the Bible become signifiers of a new kind of holiness, the sanctified taboos of Israel's civil religion. It is the sweeping consensus around the centrality of such sites and rituals of loyalty to the collective that caused some of us adopt the term *civil religion* to describe it; most Israeli Jews are not religious in the accepted sense of this term, but they are rather dogmatically devout in the national, Jewishly ethnic civil religion, which they share with religion-practicing (religious in the accepted sense) Israeli Jews like me.

I screen the film *Yizkor* in three parts, each part problematizing one of the three dates. The documented scenes are self-explanatory, but Sivan adds a running commentary, his interview with the late maverick iconoclast Professor Yeshayahu Leibovitz (1901–1994), which he scatters throughout the film in small digestible pieces. I have the students meticulously read the written text of this interview, and I tell them that the value of watching this film lies in seeing and hearing the person I consider the most important interpreter of this generation's Jewish condition, our angry prophet, the Jeremiah of our times. Jeremiah spelled out the necessary outcomes of the sins in his time— the destruction of the temple, of Jerusalem, and of the land—if the people fail to repent; likewise, Leibovitz was the first public figure to warn, from every podium, that the state of Israel, the internationally recognized state of the Jewish people, had impregnated itself with the sin of hubris because of its post-1967 policies[5] and that if we do not repent, we are doomed to experience a tragic fall. Leibovitz's critique was different from everyone else's in the Israeli Left because his discourse did not revolve around any of the popular concepts of peace, coexistence, or even human rights. He campaigned to end the conquest immediately and unilaterally, not for the sake of the Palestinians but for the sake of Israel.

A favorite slogan of the peace activists in Israel is *dai la-kibbush*; the accepted English translation of this is "end the occupation." But I claim that the word *kibbush* is used in the Bible only in the context of dominating other creatures (as in Gen. 1) and enslaving human beings who are considered naturally given to us to dominate them (for example, the king's subjects in Sam. 1:13 and women in Esther 1). In short, *kibbush* is about dehumanizing humans and treating them like animals, which we domesticate so that they can better serve us—like a natural resource that we keep and guard so we can benefit from it. We need to end the occupation not because we occupy a space on the land that we should not, but because we occupy the space by an active conquest of the Palestinians living in this space. And we need to end the occupation by treating Palestinians as fully human, not as animals that require domination and domestication. The unique nature of humans among other creatures is at the root of two ethical dogmas—the advantage they have over all other creatures means that they alone have the responsibility to sustain and guard the world; and that advantage and responsibility is the property of all humans without exception. Like Leibovitz I maintain that the European humanists who laid the foundation to modernity, including the secular and even atheist versions of modernity, not only preserved this biblical view of the centrality of humans in the world, but also lent it extra moral power by building upon it the faith in universal human rights and the political regimes of democracy grounded in it.

In the 1970s, Israeli official language referred to the Territories as merely "occupied" (*muhzakim*), pending a lasting political solution to the periodic outbreaks of violence between Israel and its neighbors. But the occupation soon became a conquest: Jewish citizens of Israel have been allowed and even encouraged to settle in those Territories, carrying with them all their rights as citizens, whereas none of these rights have ever been conferred on the Palestinian Arabs there; the Palestinians of the enlarged Jerusalem metropolitan area are barely tolerated and only as municipal residents, not as full citizens of Israel; local resources, such as land and water, are systematically diverted for the use of the state and its citizenry and away from the Palestinians;

and security as the basis for the harassment of Palestinians has become the securing of Israel's "way of life," including a half million Jewish settlers in the Territories.[6]

The Identity of the Israeli Jew

Leibovitz forces us to look in the mirror and face what has become since 1967 "the Israeli way of life," which we are called to defend and shed blood for, much in the same way U.S. citizens are periodically called to defend and even shed blood for "the American way of life," because there is a connection between the way we live and the way we justify morally the wars in which we are engaged. In answer to Sivan's questions, Leibovitz claims that our suffering at the abusive hands of others throughout history (the pharaohs, the Nazis, the Arabs) is the one and only foundational value we inculcate in the young. This suffering, he claims, poses no problem for us. But it poses a moral, ethical, and spiritual problem for the non-Jews who inflicted this suffering on us. Because we dwell on our own suffering so vigorously, we neglect our moral, ethical, and spiritual challenges: the reality of that which we do to others. We prefer to dwell on what was done to us because we are not responsible for it. So we believe we can dominate and abuse others because that which was done to us was even worse. Leibovitz says that the immediate aftermath of the Six Days War in 1967 was a turning point for us because this is when we switched from the moral task of establishing a nation-state that protects the Jewish people to an immoral colonial state, an empire ruling over others. In his words, we used nationalism as a stepping stone from humanism to bestiality.

Many Israeli Jewish patriots rejected Leibovitz because he went so far as to claim that Jews are not immune from Nazi-like criminal behaviors; they ignore the fact that he said it as a devout Zionist committed to national independence as a recognized basic human right since the nineteenth century. Israel, he said, could slide from humanistic nationalism to bestial nationalism, in the same way that his generation lived to see Germany slide from Schiller's "Ode to Joy" in the end of Beethoven's Ninth Symphony to Nazi barbarism. Nazism cannot cancel German culture and identity, nor can it cancel the basic right of the German people to a sovereign state, but it had to be overcome and eradicated so that Germans could be proud Germans again. Likewise, claimed Leibovitz, Israeli patriotism must undo the criminal reality of the conquest of Palestinians, a prerequisite to regaining its moral stature among other sovereign nations.

Leibovitz sees the self-justifying manipulation of our traumas into violent patriotic soldiering as the centerpiece of education, simply because no other

Jewish value is taught. Having worked as a Jewish studies teacher for many years (at both the high school and university levels), I concur: our curriculum, in the past generation, leaves less and less time for less and less content in the humanities and in social studies because of the societal and political pressures to train students to not just survive, but succeed in what is perceived as a competitive global economy—more high-tech and computer literacy at the expense of a well-rounded liberal education. But I do not think the turning point was in 1967; I think it was the 1973 war, itself a direct result of 1967—that is, the unwillingness to resolve the territorial occupation by a political settlement that would secure the state of Israel. The 1973 war exposed the old serving elites, the nonreligious socialist-Zionists with their formerly vibrant, dynamic, interpretation of Zionism as Judaism, as tired, dysfunctional, and conceding to the culture of economic success and daily comforts. Humanistic liberal education became superfluous, while the religious schools continued to regard the study of Torah as indispensible. The old masters, such as Ahad Ha'am, A. D. Gordon, David Ben-Gurion, and Yitzhak Ben-Zvi,[7] must be turning in their graves with this disappointing agony: they were Jewish through and through, dedicated to lifelong study of Jewish texts, not as a religious obligation but as the cultural canon of the people.

We live in a time when many Israelis claim to be universalists of the liberal democracy brand rather than self-identified Jews. They envy media images of efficient schools in Japan or Finland that produce successful individuals committed to self-fulfillment in a raceless, nationless, neutral world, like John Lennon's "Imagine." They are committed to "the Israeli way of life" as described above, but no thought is given to its Jewish content. They choose a bourgeois lifestyle in a rather successful modern state that is among the top eighteen in the world. Leibovitz was right: they are Jews only by virtue of their perpetuated identity as Nazi victims and, therefore, are patriotic in the worst sense of the term—"my country, right or wrong; we were interred in Auschwitz, and therefore we are justified even when we drop a one-ton bomb on Gaza." Any contrary opinion is anti-Semitic, especially when it comes from "self-hating" Jews such as Judge Richard Goldstone (the ardent Zionist who headed the UN inquiry into the military actions in Gaza in 2008 and 2009) or human rights activists involved in organizations like Machsom Watch (women who monitor the behavior of soldiers and police at checkpoints in and around the Occupied Territories) to which I proudly belong. They live with the self-image of liberals who vote for equality because it sounds progressive, advanced, and future oriented and at the same time allows the Jew in them to remain uneducated, instinctive, triggered thoughtlessly by the untreated post-Sho'ah fear. The humanists, religious or secular, understood the need to embed every individual in two circles of collective identity—the particular and the universal—and therefore educated the young to be well versed in both areas. The impoverished current state of liberal education means that people are ill prepared to hold fast to the humanistic agenda because they are uneducated on both levels. They know little about the philosophies, literatures, histories, struggles, sacrifices, and role models that have personified and embodied abstract moral principles in the real lives of people.

I am particularly bothered by those liberal democrats who are committed to the human rights agenda yet insist on turning their backs on Judaism—for example, those insisting on dialogue between Israelis and Palestinians. When the self-appellation "Israeli" replaces the more accurate "Israeli Jews," no room is left in Israel for the 20 percent of the Israeli citizenry who are Palestinians. And turning our backs on our Jewishness is futile. We are Israeli because we are Jews; we came back to this land where we belong as Jews, and the state we established here is called Israel. If we deny the fundamental link between our Jewishness, religious or secular, and our Israeliness, then we are nothing but another colonialist power that is here to disown and displace the indigenous Palestinians. We thereby lose the moral standing of Zionism as a universally recognized liberation movement of a distinct people who deserve to have a safe home, a sovereign state, in its historical land. Jewishness, Jewish identity, Jewish peoplehood—all these terms signify a reality bigger than either religion alone ("Judaism," I am a Jew because God told me to be a Jew and even told me how to be a Jew), or victimhood alone (I am a Jew because Hitler said so, because the non-Jew does not allow me to assimilate). But there can be no humanistic Jewish identity without an informed consciousness of Jewish culture—it is learned, not given, not born.

Leibovitz was right. However, to all the nonreligious Israeli Jews who swallow his politics but leave out his Jewish message, I say: "You must return to the study of Judaism as an essential part of your national, many-layered culture; Jewish values should nurture your identity as individuals and as a society." The repossession of Jewish culture will enable Sho'ah-centered panic-stricken Israelis to place the bitter historical memories of persecution and massacre on the shelf of "that which was done to us against our will, and therefore we are not responsible for," so that we can move on to "that for which we are responsible."[8]

Palestinians Mirror the Same Identity Problems

One of the participants in an Israeli-Palestinian, three-faiths clergy group I attend is Sheikh Bilal Zreinah from Beit Jala in the West Bank.[9]

I have recently heard him retell an old Israeli parable: a man's apartment is on fire, so he jumps to the sidewalk to save his life, thereby killing a passerby. Europe is on fire, so the Jews flee and throw themselves on the Palestinians, who now become the victims of victims and therefore the winners in the World Victimhood Championship.

This parable fails to account for the complexity of the history of either side, and I do not quote it here for the sake of its original purpose. I use it to demonstrate how victimhood becomes a dominant aspect of national identity among Palestinians, too, as if they caught this "cognitive virus" from us Israeli Jews. They too will gain nothing by perpetuating an identity based on victimhood alone, on their Naqbah[10] as the mirror of our Sho'ah. They must likewise take responsibility for their legacy, culture, future, and how they treat others.[11] Both sides should stop manipulating their own *historia lacrimosa* (tearful history)—as well as the complementary denial of any suffering of the other side—and invest in developing a collective identity based on the humanistic values of respect and justice.[12]

Create Space for the Other's Narrative

I can read Arabic only in translation.[13] Thus, I was deeply affected by the discovery in 1992 of the Hebrew translation of the diaries of Khalil el-Sakakini (1878–1853), the leader (and some say founder) of the Palestinian national movement during the British Mandate for Palestine (1918–1948). Sakakini was a great humanist with a huge library in several languages, and he dedicated his life to (among other things) setting up a countrywide network of schools because he knew that education was the key to both modernity and nationalism. He had an acute sense of urgency: there was a rival national movement in the same land (Zionism), and time was running out. He took great pride in his European cultural identity, from ancient Greece to contemporary modernism, and dedicated his life to the creation of a modern schooling system for all of Palestine. But one element of this modernism was particularly central to his work—the making of all Arabs in the land into a coherent nation (*sha'ab*). He understood that it was important to have substantial achievements in all aspects of collective life (conferences and institutions, dictionaries and school textbooks, public services in the villages and in the cities) and ahead of the Zionists. When the Palestinian Authority made the city of Ramallah its capital in 1993, it named the cultural center after Sakakini, and it seems that the current Palestinian prime minister, Salim Fi'ad, is at work on the task of national development along these lines: international political gains will take root only if people's daily lives are improved and empowered.

Like other middle-class Christian Palestinians in Jerusalem in the 1930s, Sakakini built a house in the new Arab neighborhood of Katamon. I had been brought up on the story of that hill as it figures in the Jewish narrative: in April 1948, after months of bitter fighting, the Jews conquered the neighborhood and found it deserted; here as elsewhere, the Palestinian refugees were never allowed to return. But this prior historical knowledge did not prepare me for the unexpected burst of the Palestinian narrative into the Jewish one: a footnote supplied by the Hebrew translator of Sakakini's diary identified the location of his house with the current address, which I recognized immediately—it was right around the corner from my childhood home (a beautiful Arab house that harbors some of my best memories). I realized for the first time that the Palestinian Naqbah was an economic breakthrough for my family: my father bought our house in 1953, when the government of Israel had completed the official takeover of property declared "deserted by missing persons" and then sold the valuable houses cheaply. By purchasing this house, my parents had finally entered the middle class. My next visit to the neighborhood of my childhood was an eye opener for me because the familiar houses were not the same any more: it drove home the nature of 1948 as a Janus mask— rebirth of a nation on one side, catastrophe and exile on the other side.[14]

Later I bought a book by Sakakini's daughter, Hala, and to my amazement it included family photographs from the middle-class Katamon neighborhood in the 1940s. Their photographs looked exactly like my family photographs from a decade later: a daughter playing the piano, the family posing formally on the front steps of the house, the family holiday at the beach, the father in hat and suit. In the book I found the neighborhood map she had drawn from memory with a tailor's shop at the corner of what are now Bilu and Cheil Nashim streets; this shop became the grocery store of Sho'ah survivors Ignatz and Adela, of my childhood.

Although contemporaries, living and working in the same city, my father and Sakakini never knew of each other, but they shared many things.[15] They were both humanistic patriots committed to their respective nations, and neither harbored a hatred for the other side, just a sense of urgency to get there first. So they both left us with an important (albeit lacking) legacy: love your side, take pride in it, get on with the unfinished work for it. But as to the other side: ignore it; it may as well remain a faceless abstraction, practically unknown, uninteresting, and invisible behind fortified state borders, bars, and other obstacles.

My father's and Sakakini's legacy is part of the foundation we need to build on ("love your side"), but we need to add to it. We need to change our national movements; we need to intentionally create a space in our national movements for the existence of the other side. Zionism, and its mirror image the Palestinian national movement, were born in a world of one truth that excluded all other claims to truth: it is our task to take it to the next stage, which is holding on to our own truth while making room for the narratives, and fully human existence, of other people.[16]

A few years after discovering the diaries of Sakakini, I was asked to speak at an annual Jerusalem Day celebration marking the "liberation" (occupation, conquest) of East Jerusalem in 1967. It was an alternative ceremony planned by a number of Jewish and Palestinian groups. A spiritual message was sought, but it was decided not to invite clergy to speak, since it was impossible to include adequate representation of all the Christian churches. So the planners asked me—a female, Orthodox Israeli Jew who was not a rabbi—to speak for the Jews. I was honored. In that outdoor gathering near the walls of the Old City, I spoke about the similarities between my father and Sakakini and about the difference between the task of their generation as they saw it and the task of our generation (as explained above). I have since had many opportunities to shock Jewish audiences with this story. I have also, on occasion, upset Israeli Arab students by being a Zionist Jew who introduces them to Sakakini, their own unknown national hero—unknown to them for two reasons: first, because their parents were too devastated by the Naqbah as experienced locally to understand much about the whole picture of Palestinian politics, and second, because their schools are not allowed to teach them their own national history.

The Danger of Applied Messianism

I feel an additional responsibility to include here a specific message for my own community—the religious flank of Zionism. This flank started out in 1902 as a political party within the Zionist movement, the Mizrahi—rabbis and other religious Jews (like my parents) who supported the pragmatism of secular Zionism as a national liberation movement. Apocalyptic versions of supernatural Jewish messianism were set aside in favor of more modest albeit tangible achievements—political recognition, de facto coalition with secular Jews, agricultural settlements, defense forces, and the mechanisms of a sovereign state. Over the years, however, most of the Religious Zionists have turned away from this pragmatic approach and have even come to view it in retrospect as a compromise of Torah-observant Judaism. Instead, they are increasingly embracing irrational, kabbalistically based ideas of Jewish supremacy over non-Jews, especially Muslims, Arabs, and Palestinians.

Thus, one hears claims that Arabs are like the biblical Amalek and the seven nations of Canaan whom the ancient Israelites were ordered to annihilate. Moreover, one hears that Jewish peaceniks are like the mixed race (*erev rav*) that infiltrated the Israelite camp as it made its exodus from Egypt, with the sole purpose of destroying the people from within. These claims are based on a peculiar application of certain mystical writings and go completely against the grain of accepted interpretation of Jewish law (*halacha*).

None of these ideas would have occurred to my father or his colleagues. Quite the contrary—their generation was close enough to the vivid memories of life as a minority, dependent on the goodwill of the ruling majority. In biblical terms, their generation remembered what it was like to live as temporary, rootless foreigners (*guerim*) in Egypt.[17] Religious Zionists in my father's generation were outspoken about the need to abolish the death sentence that Israel inherited from the British[18] on the grounds that already in the second century the Mishna emphasizes that a mistaken death sentence is irreparable.[19] These same leaders were the first to denounce the massacre committed in the Palestinian village of Qibia in 1953 (as retribution for the murder of Jewish Israeli civilians by Palestinian terrorists) at the time when Ben-Gurion was pretending he had no knowledge of this. In my father's generation, Religious Zionism could both attack the militaristic zeal of the ruling socialist-Zionist elites as "un-Jewish" and feel at one with the leader of the parliamentary opposition, Menachem Begin, whose Jewish warmth was duly fortified by his humanistic conscience. Unfortunately, this is no longer so. When leaders mistakenly assess a historical circumstance as ripe for messianic outburst, when they become falsely inspired by supposed prophetic zeal and ignore the necessary compromises that arise from our human condition, usually nothing but destruction ensues.

The zealous spirit of the Zionist pioneers was a "holy rebellion" against the misfortunes of Jewish life in exile. But it took two separate false turns that ironically need each other, enable each other, reinforce each other. Religious Jews in Israel distort religion into national chauvinism, and even racism, in a way too similar to certain contemporary abuses of Islam. At the same time, nonreligious Jews in Israel neglect Jewish culture and leave the national spirit to its post-Sho'ah addiction to military power.[20] It is high time to revisit this holy rebellion, correct it, and pursue its next phase.

Zionism as a Holy Rebellion, Then and Now

Rabbi Shmu'el Chaim Landoy (1892–1928), one of the most charismatic leaders of Religious Zionism, coined the phrase "the holy rebellion." He was an avid student of Chassidism, and his experiences in political leadership were as a Chassidic *rebbe*.[21] In a public gathering in Jerusalem, celebrating the consecration of a Torah scroll for a new synagogue for ha-Po'el ha-Mizrahi (the socialist Religious Zionist faction), and later in a letter to youth in Europe, he quoted the Chassidic *rebbe* Mendel of Kotzk (1787–1859), a fiery enigmatic man: "Give me ten chassidim, dressed in rags but eager to go to the rooftops and scream, 'God is our Lord!' A few men motivated by "azut de'kedushah" (audacity of holiness), which helps them transcend human enslavement to the smallness of everyday life, can hasten the coming of the Messiah!"

Landoy then went on to name the zealous spirit of the Zionist pioneers "mered kadosh," a holy rebellion, obviously tailored after the spiritual revolution his predecessor envisioned, but in a totally different context. It was paramount that his revolutionary followers know that their new actions were only a reinterpretation of a sanctified tradition. Landoy thus helps us to preserve a sense of the prophetic aspect of Torah Judaism—a never-ending revolution, one holy rebellion after another, led by iconoclasts. So the paradoxical, intentional oxymoron "holy rebellion" remains a slogan that should safeguard us against stagnation on the one hand and rootlessness on the other.[22]

But the gates of innovative reinterpretation[23] must never close. So what follows is my version—my reinterpretation—of the holy rebellion in which I am engaged: stand up against all forms of dehumanization you detect around you and rehumanize society, culture, and politics wherever you can.

In the area of religion, do not give in to the erroneous notion that oppression lies in "a lot of religion" and freedom is secured when this load is lightened. It is not an issue of quantity, it is an issue of quality. Expose exclusive, egocentric, chauvinistic versions of religion as racist, show how they override all other content of faith and practice and text, show how these versions of religion lead to crimes committed in the name of the Almighty, how His name is borne in falsehood and desecrated in public. Teach the humanistic versions of religion, all religions. Teach critical readings of holy texts. Challenge dangerous readings of texts and dangerous religious leaders. Train a different kind of religious leadership. Create new religious texts, remember that these novelties must not remain marginalized in your tradition and in your community, and work to legitimate them and mainstream them.

In the area of civil religion, resist the identification of "nonreligious" with "universal cultural identity only." To be fully human is to nurture all layers of one's identity, individual as well as tribal, national as well as universal. Do not allow anti-Semitism to define your Jewishness for you because this breeds a neurotic fear of victimhood that is calmed down only by a show of power over permanent enemies. Make sure your identification with the collective of Jews in Israel is based on a shared knowledge of Jewish culture of all ages. Teach the humanistic content of patriotism, of every national history. Uncover humanistic role models from the past, and create new ones. Uncover traditions, rituals, holidays, texts, oral myths. Create new materials in all these categories.

I believe that only action on these two fronts simultaneously will create the necessary solidarity among different Jews and Palestinians. All groups should feel empowered toward responsible action on all levels, intercommunal and intracommunal. Both religion and patriotism can and should create a mindset that cannot tolerate the sacrifice of some to benefit others.

Fleshing out the details of this holy rebellion would take volumes. The one act of my life that constitutes for me the choice of this road is my decision in 1978 to leave Jerusalem and position myself ever after in Yeruham, where I made my home. This is a small Israeli town—fewer than 10,000 people—in the Negev desert. Yeruham has a diversified, almost all-Jewish population and is a neighbor to a Bedouin village that is (so far) unrecognized by the government. My parents chose to "come up" to the land of Israel (*make aliya*, in Hebrew), and I chose to "come up" to Yeruham, as a way of centering a life of family and work and politics and Torah study around my reinterpreted holy rebellion. I moved there in 1978 with a small group of like-minded Jews—we believed it was more important to work with the residents of an economically depressed town in the desert, toward empowerment and equal opportunity on all levels, than to create more Jewish settlements among Palestinians in the Occupied Territories. I started teaching children and adults and had to relearn my profession before I could take pride in the success of my students in class and in life. I married psychologist Moshe Landsman, a member of our group. We bought the house we still live in, had children and raised them in the local school system. We also fostered children from broken homes for several years, which evolved as an extension of our life with the people around us. But our choice to become "engaged intellectuals," in the words of some Marxists, led us to political action, in the microcosm of the town as well as in Israel in general. I became the first woman to serve on Yeruham's town council and then the first woman in Israel to serve on a municipal religious council that provides and monitors religious services for the town. I fight for social justice for peripheral populations, Yeruham-ites, and neighboring Bedouins, Palestinians in the Territories, and women everywhere—and I bring these messages to my synagogue and to the public at large.

Abraham's Example—and His Sin

I would like to close this chapter by identifying myself as a child of Abraham. Abraham was el-Khalil—a friend of the one God—and the idols he broke were not just useless figurines. By partitioning the land to settle the animosities between his shepherds and Lot's shepherds,[24] he broke the idol-ization of the Promised Land and the idea that a child of God must possess the Promised Land entirely, exclusively, and immediately.

The biblical concept of *covenant*, which means "cut" in Hebrew, is reflected in the accompanying ritual of circumcision, the setting aside or cutting of ani-mals, and the establishment of an actual border (for example, Gen. 31:44–53). The purpose of the covenant, which is always literally cut between unequal partners, is to establish mutual respect of boundaries and sovereignty as a pre-requisite to mutual trust, cooperation, peace, and even love. With this in mind, we can draw from the Torah the idea that sharing the land to resolve a serious conflict is sometimes more important than taking possession of a God-promised inheritance:

> And there arose strife between the shepherds of Abram's cattle and the shep-herds of Lot's cattle. . . . And Abram said to Lot: "Let there be no strife be-tween you and me and between my shepherds and yours, for we are close relatives. Is not the whole land before you? Please separate from me, if you go left, I will go to the right, and if you go to the right, I will go to the left." . . . And they separated from each other. (Gen. 13:7–11)

We need to reappropriate these and other texts and traditions that are con-ducive to life and liberty. Not enough thought has been invested in drafting alternative modes of relating to Arabs based on our tradition. If we come to the task of peacemaking with all the richness of our tradition, we will be bet-ter equipped to create inspiring solutions. In particular, at this juncture, we need to creatively interpret our tradition and holy texts to emphasize the val-ues of life, justice, and peace, over the value of the Land of Israel. We are told repeatedly that our religious duty is to settle in parts of our historic home-land contested by its Arab inhabitants, and this to our detriment. So we must state that we disagree with such views. We also must learn to create innova-tive perspectives with our Palestinian partners to make room for them.

Abraham does not wait for instructions from God when he decides to partition the land with Lot. However, there is another episode in his life that I want to explore here, when he seems to follow God's word to the letter—or does he? I would like to uphold the Jewish tradition of learning not only from the virtues of our biblical role models but also from their faults and failures: they erred and sinned, too, because only God is infallible. When Abraham prepared to sacrifice his son to God, I believe he missed the point entirely, and, in doing so, sinned.[25]

Abraham wrongly believed that God actually demanded that he make a human sacrifice; he believed that this lesson—taught through him but useful for all humanity—would show that faith requires a leap beyond human reasoning. He believed that this was God's will and that he must submit to the instruction he heard; he believed that he must be faithful through unquestioned obedience while overriding both his emotions and ethical instinct.

The text is unambiguous: God really did tell Abraham to sacrifice his son; this is no figment of Abraham's imagination. I claim that the text shows that God was testing Abraham by telling him to do this. I believe God expected Abraham to argue with him, the way he argued with him before the destruction of Sodom in Genesis 18. In fact, the situation here with Isaac calls for arguing with God even more so than did the situation with Sodom. With Sodom, God was going to do the killing, whereas in this situation, a human would kill another human for no reason. Abraham was supposed to understand that this was a trial, but he missed the point—and continued to miss the point—until, at the very last moment, God sent an angel to stop his slaughtering hand. God was forced to save Isaac because Abraham was too eager to do the right thing, so he ignored the obvious dissonance between God's words and God's laws as he knew them. He decided to obey the words he heard, rather than conclude that these words were only a trial.

Indeed, just as Abraham suspected, God did intend to make a lasting example of him, but the message was not that God demands human sacrifice. The message was even stronger than the earlier message sent through Noah. Noah had been taught the difference between beasts and humans: only humans are made in the image of God. Therefore, permission to shed the blood of an animal in order to eat its meat is explicitly juxtaposed to the killing of humans. The shedding of human blood is defined as a capital crime deserving of capital punishment[26] because it decreases God's representation on Earth. Abraham's trial has an additional dimension: the killing of humans is criminal even when believed to be a sacrifice to God, even when you hear God ordering you to do it for him. Even under those circumstances, you are supposed to stick to God's constitutional "natural law" and understand that the present command is "unconstitutional" in God's world, therefore must be only a trial.

I am well aware that by suggesting that Abraham sinned, I go against almost all Jewish readings of this text,[27] as well as against readings in Islamic and Christian traditions. But I think that there is a reason this episode in Genesis 22 ends with the news Abraham receives about his brother's eight sons; one of these sons will become the father of Rebekah who will become the wife of Isaac. Abraham's light is going out; the time has come for his son to take his place. God does not speak to Abraham ever again.

As a child of Abraham, I say: no more human bloodshed, which our religions, as well as our civil religions, have ritualized. We must reject this pointless practice, in Israel and Palestine as anywhere else.

Notes

1. I was named after my murdered maternal grandmother; two of my children are named after other family members who were killed.

2. Some Mandelbaums preserved the myth of an eighteenth-century ancestor who had bribed Habsburg officials for the right to adorn himself with this name. *Shakdiel* in Hebrew means "almond," plus God's name, "el."

3. The Hebrew root *sh.k.d.* means "to apply oneself diligently to a task." The almond tree is named "shaked" because it is the first fruit tree to bloom in the spring in this land. My father was thinking of Zionism as Jewish renewal in terms of the almonds (sh'kedim) on the flowering rod of Aharon (Num. 17:23), but the Sho'ah was more like the torn almond branch God shows the prophet Jeremiah (1:12) when he tells him, "I shall apply myself (shoked) to make my word come true" to destroy Israel because of their sins.

4. This concept was introduced in 1983 by Israeli sociologists Charles Liebman and Eliezer Don-Yihye, following U.S. scholar Robert N. Bellah's "Biblical Religion and Civil Religion in America," *Journal of the American Academy of Arts and Sciences*, "Religion in America," Winter 1967, Vol. 96, No. 1, pp. 1–21.

5. According to this view, the very establishment of the state of Israel in 1948 is not disputed, as it follows the United Nations' 1947 decision to divide the land into two states, one "Jewish" (that is, for Jews) and one "Arab" (that is, for Arabs, which at the time were not yet recognized as a separate Palestinian people, not even by other Arab states). Moreover, this critique is not aimed at the results of the 1967 Six Days War— the military victory itself, the saving of Israel from the attacks of the Arabs on it—but at the ongoing policy of continued occupation and conquest of the parts of the land outside the 1949 armistice borders, known as "the Territories."

6. The state of Israel fully annexed after 1967 only areas that had been ethnically cleansed (by transfer, not massacre) of unwanted Arab citizens (the Syrian Golan Heights where only the Druze were allowed to stay, and the Latrun enclave on the Jerusalem–Tel Aviv highway).

7. Ahad Ha'am (1856–1927), the pen name of Asher Zvi Hirsch Ginsberg; Aaron David Gordon (1856–1922), thinker and role model for the pioneers; David Ben-

Gurion (1886–1973), the first prime minister of Israel; Yitzhak Ben-Zvi (1884–1963), the second president of Israel.

8. As the years pass, I become more and more aware of the importance of Leibovitz for me. But to set the record straight, he was very much a loner in the Religious-Zionist camp I was brought up in. I acknowledge the urgency of the angry prophecy of Jeremiah chapter 1 but need my father's tireless optimism. Yes, God smote the Jewish people with one hand, but He also nurtured with the other hand the young Zionist movement into a real State we have many reasons to rejoice in.

9. As an Orthodox Jew and a woman, I cannot (yet) be ordained in my denomination, but I am proud to be invited to forums to speak from a rabbinical point of view.

10. *Naqbah* in Arabic means "catastrophe," the literal equivalent of the Hebrew word *Sho'ah*, and not by coincidence. The term refers to the catastrophe suffered by the Palestinians during the war of 1947–1949: loss of lives, land, and property and the yet unresolved issue of the refugees. It is marked on May 15, the date of the expiration of the British Mandate in Palestine in 1948. The Jews at the time accepted the UN plan of partitioning Palestine into two states and declared the establishment of the Jewish state of Israel on the eve of that date, that is, May 14. The Arabs rejected the UN plan and thought they would eventually get the whole land. Unfortunately they lost the war, and even the parts of the land that remained outside Israel in 1949 did not become a Palestinian state.

11. For this analysis, I credit Ilan Gur-Ze'ev, professor of education, University of Haifa.

12. In Buberian terms, if your "I" is deficient and neurotic, there is no room for "Thou" in your world, only an objectified "It."

13. This is my alibi: The religious state high school I attended, Zeitlin in Tel Aviv, had separate classes for boys and girls. The boys studied Arabic as a second foreign language, and the school produced many top academic scholars of Arabic as well as top intelligence officers. The girls studied French instead, an interesting version of gendered socialization and acculturation in a beleaguered nation-state. As feminist scholar Nitza Berkovitz puts it: men's soldiering is in the army, women's soldiering is in wifehood and motherhood, and because this is the desirable middle class, all of this socialization is spiced with Westernized professionalism, which is gendered as well.

14. Dalia Landau opened this venue for me—she had written up the more dramatic story of her childhood ex-Arabic house in Ramla.

15. There is, however, a striking difference between these two men, which sheds light on one 1948 phenomenon: most of the Palestinian middle class, like Sakakini, fled the war-torn land and left the poor with virtually no leadership and no means to flee. My father, by contrast, refused to leave the besieged, starved, waterless, and bombarded Jewish Jerusalem, though he was already ill, and even undertook more public responsibilities.

16. I now think of this necessary change in this land as compatible with the generational zeitgeist change from modernism to postmodernism, but whereas many Israeli Jews in the peace movement speak of Post-Zionism, I insist I am a Zionist, albeit a postmodernist Zionist, looking for postmodernist Palestinian liberationists to live and work with. This academic discourse, though, goes beyond the scope of the present essay.

17. For a discussion of Jewish biblical commands on how to treat *guerim*, see Nurit Peled-Elhanan's essay in this collection. [Editor's Note]

18. This law excepted the Nazis and their assistants, which is why the convicted Adolf Eichmann was hanged in 1962.

19. See Sanhedrin chapter 4, which is partially quoted in the Qur'an sura 5 aya 32.

20. The third problem I see is the undoing of Israel as a welfare state with built-in mechanisms of social solidarity. This is a result of the charms of hypercapitalism and globalized economy that benefit some and disempower many others. The ensuing social-Darwinist spirit emphasizes competition in a win/lose world, in geopolitics as well as in other areas: if we are to win, then the Palestinians must lose. The analysis of this third problem goes beyond the scope of the present essay. It should be noted, though, that all three problems have plagued Israel simultaneously since 1973 and are interrelated.

21. A spiritual Jewish movement from the eighteenth century on, founded in Eastern Europe, Chassidism is based on popularized versions of Jewish mysticism. The leader of a group of Chassidim is called "*rebbe*," which means "rabbi" in Yiddish.

22. I learned early on from my parents what the holy rebellion was all about. On my mother's eightieth birthday, I spoke of her three heroic acts (the age of eighty is termed "heroic acts," *gevurot*, in the Mishna): the audacity to disobey her parents and their rabbis, the humility to stay away from self-righteousness and pass on to us paradoxically the greatness of that same Torah world she disobeyed, and the courage to pull her family through hardships and widowhood into brilliant lives for all four of her daughters.

23. *Ishtihad* in Islam.

24. See Genesis 13.

25. In Hebrew, "to miss the point" (*lahato*) and "to sin" (*lehahti*) share the same root.

26. Genesis 9:6 is a portion of God's covenant with Noah where God says, "Whoever sheds the blood of man, by man shall his blood be shed; for in the image of God has God made man."

27. One of the exceptions is Shulamit Har-Even, an Israeli Jewish writer and essayist. Some also read a similar message in *The Guide to the Perplexed* by Maimonides (twelfth century).

5

Does Judaism Teach Universal Human Rights?

ARIK ASCHERMAN

Rabbi Arik Ascherman was the executive director of Rabbis for Human Rights for fifteen years. Rabbis for Human Rights is an organization that gives voice to the Jewish religious tradition of human rights for Israelis, Palestinians, and foreign workers alike. He currently develops special projects for the organization. In 2009, he was the co-recipient of the Leibowitz Prize, awarded by the Israeli human rights group Yesh GVUL. Ascherman lives in Jerusalem with his wife, Einat Ramon, and their two children. On July 7, 2010, he was featured in an article in the New York Times.[1]

Introduction

I have a confession to make. There are days when I wake up and think to myself, "Maybe John Lennon was right. Maybe the world really would be a better place without countries or religion." When one thinks of all the blood spilled in the name of religion and nationalism, it is easy to dream of a world without borders in which we all speak Esperanto.

For some of us, though, faith is not something we can turn off like a light switch. It is the core of our being. It is what nourishes and sustains us. Furthermore, from everything that I know about human psychology, were we to eliminate all the differences between people tomorrow, we would in all likelihood create new differences the day after. Of course, I do not simply feel that I am a believing and practicing Jew because I do not have any other option. My faith nourishes and sustains me because it provides me a positive vision of the world God would have us help create and urges me to do my part in making that vision a reality.

For those of us who are painfully aware of the evils that our traditions have wrought, who believe that our traditions could and should be a force to make our world a better place, and for whom abandoning our particular religious tradition is not an option, the remaining possibility is to fight for the soul of our religion. This is all the more true when we consider the power of religion in the Middle East and around the globe.

Hiding Behind Religion

A few years ago at an Amnesty International conference in Morocco, I had the privilege of being one of a handful of Jews and Christians at a conference composed primarily of Muslim scholars. I taught a series of texts included in *Life, Liberty, and Equality in the Jewish Tradition*, a book edited by Rabbi Dr. Noam Zohar on behalf of Rabbis for Human Rights (RHR), which I directed from 1995 to 2010 and continue to serve.[2] The book outlines the struggles within Judaism as to how we treat other humans. The Mishna (the first codex of Jewish law after the Torah, edited around A.D. 200) teaches that when an ox owned by a Jew gores an ox owned by a non-Jew, the penalty is much less than when an ox of a non-Jew gores the ox of a Jew (Mishna Baba Kama 4:3). However, the generation of rabbis that came after the generation who wrote the Mishna was troubled by this. The Gemorrah (a discussion of the Mishna, which together with the Mishna makes up the Talmud) shows their conflict over this kind of discrimination. They ultimately justified the discrimination in the Mishna by stating that the non-Jews of the time did not observe the seven Noahide commandments, and therefore Jews did not need to consider these people *re'im*. *Rei'ah* (singular of *re'im*) is usually translated "neighbor," as in "Love your neighbor as yourself," but is perhaps better translated as "the one like you." The Noahide commandments are something like natural laws in the Jewish tradition and include prohibitions against idolatry, murder, theft, and sexual immorality. Although our tradition does not expect all people to observe the many commandments incumbent on Jews, we are not relativists. We believe that all humanity should observe these seven fundamental principles. The rabbis writing the Gemorrah concluded that because the people were not our *re'im*, discrimination was permissible (Talmud Baba Kama 38a).

In the Middle Ages, HaMeiri, an important Talmudic scholar and adjudicator of Jewish law, argued that in his generation the people of the earth had adopted "the culture of religion" (interestingly, he does not claim that everybody is religious), and therefore, according to the logic of the Talmudic rabbis themselves, the discrimination they justified should be cancelled. HaMeiri neither steps outside the Jewish tradition nor blindly accepts it. He argues from within. Using the tradition itself, he turns it on its head (Beit HaBekhira to Baba Kama 38a and elsewhere). As I explained to participants in the conference, HaMeiri is an example of somebody who neither stepped outside our tradition, nor accepted the tradition blindly. He did not reject the Talmud, but neither did he hide behind it and say, "I have no choice but to believe in discrimination toward non-Jews because that is what the Talmud teaches." He applied principles within the Talmudic text in the context of a different reality to achieve a different conclusion. Whether it be canon law or sharia law, synod decisions or certain interpretations of the Bible, each of our faith traditions has something we can hide behind if we wish. However, we can struggle within our traditions, letting our personal faith interact with our ancient texts.

In a similar example, according to the Talmud, one of the factors for determining the amount of compensation owed an injured person is the level of humiliation he or she has suffered. A mentally handicapped person was once deemed not to have feelings and so could not feel humiliation. Therefore, such a person received less compensation for an injury than a mentally able person. Today, of course, we know that this assumption is false. I learned from Rabbi Avi Novis-Deutsch[3] that some modern Jewish legal authorities have changed Jewish law in this matter, remaining true to the Talmudic principle that the level of humiliation one feels is a factor in determining compensation, but applying our modern knowledge regarding the feelings of the mentally handicapped.

Speaking from Within Religion

Some people have stepped outside the traditions they grew up with. Just as Abraham smashed the idols his father built, their private faith has led them to radically reject the assumptions of previous generations. However, in order to inspire and influence members of my own faith tradition, I must speak from within, as "a member of the club." I, and those like me, may challenge others by speaking from the outermost boundary of our respective traditions, but we need to speak the language that gives us authenticity if we want to engage these members and bring about change.

This is not easy. The act of engaging, as opposed to the act of breaking away, can rattle us to our spiritual core. On those days when I wake and question my own beliefs, my questioning often starts with the radical difference between the Judaism I grew up with and the dominant voices of religious Judaism in Israel today. Given the Judaism I was brought up with, it was and is self-evident that Judaism demands us to actively pursue universal human rights and social justice; this is what I learned from my parents, my rabbis, my teachers, and my community. I was shocked to discover that in Israel the dominant voices of Judaism are so different. Those voices are extremely particularistic, viewing Jewish teachings on how to treat fellow humans as only applying to fellow Jews or even to one's own insular community within the wider Jewish community. There have been moments when I have asked myself if those voices were right. Challenged to my very essence, I return to our shared tradition, looking at the texts that we all regard as holy, and confirm that the Judaism I was taught is every bit as authentic and textually based as the version of Judaism that has become dominant here.

Judaism is an ancient and multilayered tradition based on debate. I cannot say that my understanding of the Jewish tradition is more authentic than those who disagree with me. The Talmud is a record of the debates and arguments between our sages. We are taught that when we argue "for the sake of heaven," then *Elu v'elu d'varim Elohm khayim*, "These words are each the words of the living God." The Midrash (a form of rabbinic commentary on the Bible; the oldest collections of midrash were codified by our sages almost 2,000 years ago) records on one page seemingly contradictory interpretations of the same biblical verse. We come to learn that each interpretation teaches something true about life. This is what I call "Midrashic truth," as opposed to "Greek rational truth." Given this multiplicity of Jewish voices, a warning light should go off in our heads whenever we hear a claim that begins with "Judaism says." Unfortunately, this means that those with whom I so passionately disagree can also quote from our tradition and cite proof texts. Neither they nor I can decisively "win" the debate between us.

I cannot "win" the debate, yet I have no intention of giving up. So I continue to struggle from within for the soul of my people. I do this with humility, respecting differing opinions, and knowing that when I truly engage, I too may be changed. I must try to engage authentically so that I have a chance of winning hearts and minds of my people while not betraying God's Still Small

Voice speaking to me from within. A basic Jewish understanding is that we can all do *teshuvah*. That is, we can all answer God's Call and return to our true and highest selves. Even when we find ourselves in sharp and painful disagreement, the Image of God in our fellow Jews means that *teshuvah* is possible.

Recently, the members of a focus group that I observed, composed of average Israelis, all wanted good things for Palestinians (with one exception). However, they all also felt that our security came first, trumping any other moral or ethical considerations. I think that many of my fellow Israelis have an insufficient understanding of Palestinians and the realities of occupation. Therefore, they do not fully appreciate the hard choices they will be forced to make or the price they will pay for peace. They often create false dichotomies between security on the one hand and peace and human rights on the other. Many believe that anything is legitimate in the interest of security. However, they also want us to be a moral nation. While they maintain their understanding of our situation by sticking their heads in the sand or believing we have no options, their narrative is that we are a tiny nation of survivors acting as morally as possible, given that we are surrounded by enemies seeking our destruction, backed by a hostile world. And they believe our army is the most moral army in the world. (Although I do not believe that our army is even close to being the most immoral army in the world, it was painful for me to realize that I no longer believed that our army is more moral than others.)

I have faith not only in God, but also in my fellow Jews and Israelis, in the Jewish tradition, and in our ability to let our history of oppression strengthen our resolve to fight all oppression. It is this faith that allows me to enter into the struggle for the soul of my tradition and ask my fellow Israelis to view Palestinians with spiritual insight. Although there are parts of my tradition that do not support my understanding of God or my worldview, my beliefs are firmly supported by what I see as the core of our tradition as well as my personal experience of God.

I engage my fellow Israelis as a firmly committed Jew, rabbi, Israeli, and Zionist. Zionism holds that the solution to centuries of Jewish persecution is the return to our ancient homeland to take control of our own destiny. When I am accused of being "anti-Israel" or "a traitor," this makes no sense to me. We all know that there is no military solution to our conflict. We are either going to learn to live here together or we are going to die together. I prefer living together.

Two Jewish Principles of Universal Human Rights

On some days, as I am hurrying to leave the house, I waste much time looking for my keys. Often, after a long search, I find them just where I should have looked in the first place. We are taught in the Torah, "Surely, this Instruction which I enjoin upon you this day is not baffling for you, nor is it beyond reach. It is not in the heavens, that you should say, 'Who among us can go up to the heavens and get it for us and impart it to us, that we may observe it?' Neither is it beyond the sea, that you should say, 'Who among us can cross to the other side of the sea and get it for us and impart it to us, that we may observe it?' No the thing is very close to you, in your mouth and in your heart, to observe it" (Deut. 30:12–14).

For years I searched for the ultimate Jewish text explaining the connection between justice and universal human rights. To be sure, there are many important and inspiring words uttered by our sages throughout the centuries, but, just as I so many times found my keys exactly where I should have looked in the first place, I realized that the answer I was looking for was right there "In the beginning" of the Torah, in the very first verses of the book of Genesis. There we find two principles that would bring about a world very different from the one we have today if we were to truly assimilate them into our life and deeds. These two principles are also the basis of the entire Midrash, which guides my life and says that we are to be partners with God in *tikun olam* ("repairing the world"), participating in the healing, sanctification, and ongoing creation of the world.[4] We are God's eyes and hands in this world.

The first principle: Observing the Sabbath. "In the Beginning God created heaven and earth" (Gen. 1:1). And then God rested from all his work; and God blessed the seventh day and made it holy (Gen. 2:2–3). Rabbi Abraham Joshua Heschel says that one of the problems of modern civilization that leads to wars and injustice is the human tendency to think of ourselves as the pinnacle of existence. If there is nothing above us, why shouldn't we rape the earth and kill to get what we want? Therefore, he wrote, the Sabbath is necessary. One day each week we cease using everything we have created to manipulate our world to feed our desires; Sabbath, in turn, teaches us that we are not only creators, but also created. Call it "God," call it the truth built into the very fabric of the universe, or call it something else. There is something above us and something more important than our human desires and impulses. Rabbi Heschel says:

> Technical civilization is the product of labor, of humankind's exertion of power for the sake of gain, for the sake of producing goods. It begins when humans, dissatisfied with what is available in nature, become engaged in a

struggle with the forces of nature in order to enhance their safety and increase their comfort. To use the language of the Bible, the task of civilization is to subdue the earth, to have dominion over the beast.

To set apart one day a week for freedom, a day on which we do not use the instruments which have been so easily turned into weapons of destruction, a day for being with ourselves, a day of detachment from the vulgar, a day independent of external obligations, a day on which we stop worshipping the idols of technical civilization, a day on which we use no money, a day of armistice in the economic struggle with fellow humans and the forces of nature—is there an institution that holds out a greater hope for man's progress than the Sabbath?

On the Sabbath we live, as it were, independent of technical civilization: we abstain primarily from any activity that aims at remaking or reshaping the things of space. Man's royal privilege to conquer nature is suspended on the seventh day.[5]

In our Friday night prayers we call the Sabbath "A reminder of the Act of Creation." It reminds us of the first principle, that, with all of the importance that Judaism accords to humanity, there is something greater than us and our sometimes harmful and destructive desires. Were we all to put ourselves and our desires in the proper perspective, the world would be a better place.

The second principle: Recognizing and respecting the Image of God. In Genesis 1:27 we are taught, "And God created humanity in God's Image, in the Image of God, God created him. Male and female God created them." In the Midrash Mekhilta D'Rabi Ishmael, our sages explained that if we picture the Ten Commandments on the two stone tablets, the first commandment (as we count them in the Jewish tradition), "I am Adonai your God," parallels the sixth commandment, "Do not murder." Our sages compare the defacing of statues, pictures, and coins depicting earthly rulers with murder: murder defaces the Image of the Sovereign of the Universe. As Rabbi Heschel pointed out when speaking against modern racism, even though Judaism rejects any depiction of God, we believe that there is an Image of God in this world. It is the human: "And yet there is something in the world that the Bible does regard as a symbol of God. It is not a temple or a tree, it is not a statue or a star. The symbol of God is man, every man."[6] So the ancient Midrash teaches us that when we harm a fellow human, we are attacking God and diminishing God's Image in the world.

These two principles are the basis of what we are taught over and over again in the Torah: "Don't turn away" (Deut. 20:3), and "Don't stand idly by while your neighbor bleeds" (Lev. 19:15). The idea that we are created in God's Image is the basis for what we call *mitzvot beyn adam l'khavero*, the interpersonal commandments instructing us how to treat fellow humans. However, if respect for God's Image leads to Hillel the Elder's version of the Golden Rule, "What is hateful to you, do not do unto others," when asked to teach "the entire Torah on one foot," we need to heed his subsequent advice: "Now, go and learn" (Talmud Shabbat 31a).

Spiritual Insight

Perhaps the most important debate in Judaism for me today is between those who see our Jewish tradition as primarily teaching us how to treat our fellow Jews (or maybe not even all Jews, but just those who think as we do) and those of us who see our tradition as telling us that Genesis 1:27 does not say that only Jews are created in God's Image, but that all people, Jew and gentile alike, are created in God's Image. Rich and poor are created in God's Image. The text particularly emphasizes that both men and women are created in God's Image. This debate is not unique to Judaism, and it certainly is not a new debate. Mishna Sanhedrin 4:5 teaches us: "One who destroys a single life, it is as if he or she has destroyed an entire world. One who saves a single life, it is as if he or she has saved an entire world." In the Middle Ages, however, the verse was changed to read, "One who destroys/saves a single Jewish life. . . ."[7] Apparently somebody did not feel comfortable with the universalistic implications of the original text.

Ultimately, universal care is a matter of spiritual insight. But as my teacher, Rabbi Leonard Kravitz, used to tell us, there is nothing like "getting klopped on the head" to impair spiritual vision. He showed us that the most universalistic Jewish teachings were promulgated when the Jewish people lived in welcoming societies, and the most particularistic texts were written when we were most oppressed. We have had so many head kloppings, so many "good reasons" to hate, fear, and mistrust. For the Jewish people, centuries of oppression, along with the current Israeli experience of feeling that we are constantly fighting for our survival, have taken their toll. The Jewish collective consciousness of suffering, combined with the fact that we do have real enemies today, can lead us to suspect every non-Jew as an enemy. And then we act out of anger because of past injustice.[8] Psychologists tell us that those who are beaten as children are more likely to beat their own children. The outside world's criticisms of our actions as Israelis are perceived as further examples of hostility and bias by those who did not lift a finger to stop the Holocaust. (And sometimes it is hostility and bias, although by no means always.) It therefore requires extraordinary spiritual insight to detect God's Image in every human, even in those who are our enemies.

Although it is difficult to see the Image of God in others after being "klopped on the head," we do make choices. We cannot change the past, but we can determine what we do with it. I have known Holocaust survivors who felt that because the world did not help Jews, the world now "owed them" and had no right to judge them if they wished to look out for themselves first and foremost. Other survivors, however, have helped to draft international human rights and humanitarian law.

My sympathetic understanding of the reasons that lead to human rights violations cannot deter me from the need to prevent human suffering and injustice. At the same time, I must always be looking, humbly and compassionately, for ways to help and inspire my fellow Israelis to perceive and act upon God's Image in the "other." My mission therefore is to do everything I can to prevent or redress human rights abuses in Israel, regardless of whose rights are being abused: Israeli Jews, Israeli Arabs, Palestinians in the Occupied Territories, guest workers, African refugees.

Jewish tradition offers several important principles to help us attain this spiritual insight: *Gerim Hayitem*—Let our history guide us to identify with the oppressed; *Ba'asher Hu Sham*—Not every non-Jew is our enemy or responsible for the wrongs of the past or present; *Hamashkhit S'bhem Gufa*—We can be both a victim and a victimizer at the same time; *HaKherev Ba L'Olam*—Injustice only further endangers us; *Eizehu Gibur M'ha'giburim?*—Regarding those who truly are our enemies we are taught, "Who is truly mighty? . . . There are those who say, 'The one who turns an enemy into a friend' " (Pirke Avot D'Rabbi Natan 23:1). And when we have a true and irreconcilable conflict between human rights and self-defense: *Mi yaymar d'dama sisakh sumac t'fai?*—Even when it comes to security, there are clear lines defining what is acceptable and what is not.

Let us consider each of these principles.

GERIM HAYITEM B'ERETZ MITZRAYIM

"Identify with the oppressed." Exodus 22:20 states: "You shall not wrong a stranger or oppress him/her, for you were strangers in the land of Egypt." So we are *commanded to love the stranger, because we were once strangers ourselves*. The most repeated commandment in the Torah is to love the *ger* (stranger), and not to oppress him or her. Many argue that this refers only to the *ger tzedek*—the convert to Judaism. However, the justification for this oft-repeated commandment is that we were strangers in the land of Egypt. Unless Jews had converted to the Egyptian religion, the *ger toshav* is the "other" in our midst who agrees to abide by the basic rules of our society. Grounding this command in our experience of slavery means that God demands that our own history of oppression sensitize us to those suffering oppression, rather than embitter us.

As a college student in the late 1970s and early 1980s, I was active in the anti-apartheid movement. Often campus ministers would speak at demonstrations, and I asked that my campus rabbi, Rabbi Ben Zion Gold, be invited to speak at one. It was agreed, and on the appointed day the master of ceremonies said, "And now Rabbi Gold will give a blessing." Rabbi Gold said, "I will give a blessing, but I have something to say first. When I exited the gates of Auschwitz, leaving my first family behind in the ashes, I made two promises to myself. First, to dedicate my life to the Jewish people. That is why I am a rabbi today. Second, to do everything in my power to make sure that no people should suffer injustice and oppression. That is why I am here today." Israel's former prime minister, Menachem Begin, exhibited both of these characteristics. Although he greatly increased the pace of settlement of the Occupied Territories, arguing that the world had no right to criticize Israeli actions, one of his first acts upon becoming prime minister was to take in Vietnamese boat people being ignored by most other nations. He argued that we who had faced closed borders in our time of need could not stand idly by as the boat people were stranded in rickety boats in the middle of the ocean.

The medieval Torah commentator Ibn Ezra claims that *ger* in the Torah refers to the non-Jew living among a Jewish majority, one of the powerless groups in society. In his commentary on Deuteronomy 27:19, "Cursed be the one who subverts the judgment of the stranger, the orphan and the widow," he argues, "for they have no power [in some versions, 'no helper']. The Torah speaks of the stranger, the orphan, and the widow because if a judge subverts the judgment of others they will appeal and will make the matter known. However, the stranger, the orphan, and the widow have no ability to do so."

Rabbi Samson Rafael Hirsch, from the late nineteenth century, says that our treatment of the *ger* must be connected to lessons learned from our own history of oppression. He writes in his commentary to the Torah:

> Exodus 22:20 states: "You shall not wrong a stranger or oppress him/her, for you were strangers in the land of Egypt." . . . The verse emphasizes the central principle, oft-repeated in the Torah in many places: It is neither race, nor descent, nor birth, nor country, nor property, nor anything else external, nor due to chance, or anything other than the simple and pure inner essential essence of a human, which gives him or her human and civil rights. [These rights] are dependent only on the spiritual and moral value of one's humanity. And the special explanation, "for you were strangers in the land of Egypt," is given in order to prevent this principle from being compromised

in any way. Your whole misfortune in Egypt was that you were "foreigners" and "aliens" there. As such, according to the views of other nations, you had no right to be there, had no claim to rights of settlement, home, or land. They could do with you whatever they wished. As aliens you were without any rights in Egypt. This was the root of our slavery and the wretchedness that was imposed on you. Therefore beware, so runs the warning, from making rights in our own state conditional on anything other than on basic humanity, which dwells in every human by virtue of being human. With any suppression of these human rights the gate is opened to the brazen mistreatment of other humans. This is the root of the Egyptian horror.[9]

We see our suffering as unique and we rightfully get upset when every form of oppression is compared to the Holocaust. Yet, without making comparisons, Rabbi Gold's experience as a survivor made him sympathetic to victims of other forms of injustice. Rabbi Hirsch understood that the Torah commands us to be on our guard because our own experiences do not make us immune to Pharaoh residing in our hearts. Even though every experience of suffering is unique, we can draw the connections between our suffering and the suffering of others.

In 2005, twenty-two homes were demolished in the tiny village of Khirbat Tana and only one home was left standing. I observed the Tisha B'Av fast on a hot summer day while helping to rebuild those homes. The Tisha B'Av fast commemorates the destruction of the two Jewish temples that once stood in Jerusalem. And, as we read on the Yom Kippur fast, "Is this not the fast I desire: To unlock the fetters of wickedness, and untie the cords of the yoke. To let the oppressed go free; to break off every yoke. It is to share your bread with the hungry, and to take the wretched poor into your home. When you see the naked, clothe him, and not to ignore your own kin" (Isa. 58:6–7). Several years earlier, one of the first houses that Rabbis for Human Rights helped rebuild was the Shawamreh home in Anata (*Anata* is the Arabic version of "Anatot," the hometown of the prophet Jeremiah).[10] We rebuilt the home over the three days leading up to Tisha B'Av.

The demolition of a single home, or even an entire village, is scarcely comparable to the bloodshed and destruction accompanying the siege of Jerusalem, the demolition of the Second Temple by the Romans, the end of Jewish sovereignty, and the exile of the Jewish people from their homeland. However, the destruction of a home demolishes the family that was living in it. For that family, the demolition is every bit as much of a tragedy as the tragedy we mourn on Tisha B'Av. That the one is personal and the other is national is unimportant. Part of the spiritual ability to see God's Image in others is to be able to make the emotional connection between their oppression and ours, without feeling that making the connection negates the unique aspects of our personal and collective experiences.

BA'ASHER HU SHAM

"Not every non-Jew is our enemy." Even though we are in the midst of a conflict that sometimes involves Palestinian terrorists, not every Palestinian is a terrorist or a *rodef* (a "pursuer," someone who has forfeited some of his or her humanity and human rights because of his or her actions to harm others). Once a man, who had lost his daughter in a terror attack, pointed at a Palestinian friend of mine and said that he had every right to kill my friend. He believed that because some Palestinians have blood on their hands, every Palestinian is guilty; everything they own, even their lives, are *hefker* (for the taking). Although his feeling was understandable, the Jewish tradition commands us to distinguish between the guilty and the innocent.

I have witnessed similar feelings among Israeli security forces. One of our major Palestinian human rights projects is our Olive Tree Campaign. We have replanted thousands of trees that have been uprooted by vigilantes and by the Israeli security forces. Since 2002 we have sent volunteers to act as human shields to protect Palestinian farmers from violent settlers when the farmers attempt to plow, plant, and harvest their olives (the general principle applies: not all settlers are violent religious fanatics). As a result of our work, our engaging Israeli security forces, and a major victory in the Israeli High Court in 2006, many farmers are now accessing lands they had been unable to access for up to fifteen years. The Israeli security forces for the most part now fulfill their obligation to protect Palestinian farmers. However, some soldiers, who may have lost a loved one or an army buddy, are angry and resentful and ask, "I've lost a loved one to these Palestinians and now I have to protect them?" The task is emotionally difficult, yet that is what we must do.

In Genesis 21:9–21, Hagar and Ishmael are banished to the desert and are dying of thirst until God prepares a well and saves them. In one of the *midrashim* written by our sages so long ago, the angels come to God before God prepares the well and demand that God let Hagar and Ishmael die because of the future suffering the children of Ishmael will cause the children of Israel. God refuses their request and says, *"Ba'asher hu sham"* (right now in front of me is an innocent child). We, who are created in God's Image, are therefore commanded to be as God-like as humanly possible (Talmud Sotah 14a). So we must honor God's Image both in others and in ourselves by distinguishing between the Palestinian terrorist coming to murder my family and the Palestinian family that simply wants to harvest their olives.

HAMASHKHIT S'BHEM GUFA

"We can be both a victim and a victimizer." When I speak with my fellow Israelis about injustices and human rights violations we have committed, their responses are: "But look at what the Palestinians have done to us." Or "Look what the Americans do in Afghanistan" or "Syrians and Libyans sit on the UN Human Rights Committee." Israel is far from the worst human rights violator in the world, and there is a large measure of hypocrisy in those countries that lecture Israel about human rights. But we should not be relieved because other countries are worse. As my mother told me, "Two wrongs don't make a right."

Rather than compare ourselves with others, we must be true to our own highest values. RHR founder Rabbi David Forman would often say, "There is no ethical shopping mall." We cannot do "comparative shopping" and pick and choose our values as we like (and at the cheapest price). What are the values that a Jew must live by? The late Israeli author Yizhar Smilanski once wrote a newspaper article titled "The Secret of Jewish Existence," which serves as both inspiration and accusation:

> The argument today is not about the territory, even though it is about territory; and not about security, even though it is about security; and not about peace, even though it is about peace. What is the argument about?
>
> The fundamental argument of today is about the Jew. Whether there are things in the world that are forbidden for the Jew to do. Because he is a Jew.
>
> Because for the Jew to be a Jew is not devoid of meaning, an empty phrase. A Jew has limits and prohibitions. And there are things which differentiate a Jew from others, not necessarily things that give pleasure or make things easier, or comfortable, or simple—actually just the opposite: they make things harder, curb comfort, and make the easy more difficult while complicating the simple.
>
> For instance, everything that touches on injustice and justice.
>
> For instance, everything connected to the use of force and the conquest of force.
>
> For instance, "the poor man's lamb." For instance, "both to murder and to inherit."
>
> And for instance, "Justice justice you shall pursue."
>
> And so why, then, actually be a Jew?
>
> Really, just like the ground beneath the feet.
>
> To exist, to survive, not to be destroyed, yes, certainly. There is no question.

But the struggle for existence, also in the struggle for existence—there are things that for the Jew it is forbidden to do and that the Jew cannot do. Because of being a Jew. Even when it is difficult.

For instance, to inherit what is not one's own.

For instance, to ignore the tears of the oppressed.

For instance, to expel one's neighbors.

For instance, to suppress that in others what we hate that others suppress in us.

If [you are] a Jew—then there are things that you cannot do. The religious commandments, for example, you can do or not do in any place in the world.

But here, on this Land, the test of the Jew is in the morality of self-restraint, in the obligation of self-restraint.

And this obligation, apparently, is the secret of Jewish existence.[11]

The late-nineteenth-/early-twentieth-century rabbi Aaron Shmuel Tamerat explained that the reason God commanded the children of Israel to stay in their homes when the angel of death passed over Egypt is because even when your cause is just, any contact with violence can awaken the angel of death within us all and make us oppressors ourselves. The difference between being a victim and a victimizer is less than a hair's breadth. We are so convinced that we are the victims, that we are furious should anybody dare to suggest that we are victimizers. We must always be on our guard because we can be victim and victimizer at the same time.

HAKHEREV BA L'OLAM

"Injustice only further endangers us." Israelis are understandably obsessed with security. However, one of the ironies is that we often end up endangering ourselves more when we justify acting unjustly in the name of security. During the Second Intifada, the Israeli army reinstituted a policy of demolishing the homes of terrorists or those suspected of having carried out terrorist acts. The belief was that a potential terrorist would be deterred by the suffering he or she would cause his or her family. The army eventually stopped that policy because they realized the hatred and anger generated by this sort of punishment was generating more terror than it was stopping. Sadly, however, there are still reverberations from the policy of demolishing Palestinian homes. Landowners are unable to obtain building permits, which are nearly impossible to come by.

To this day, there is a debate among Israel's military intelligence agencies as to whether the Second Intifada was planned or spontaneous. Those of us working in the field predicted the Second Intifada a year and a half before it happened. Just as many Israelis became disillusioned with the Oslo peace process because the Palestinian Authority was unwilling (or unable) to stop terror, we heard more and more Palestinians saying, "This is not a peace process." Land expropriations, tree uprootings, and other things were taking place at the same pace after Oslo as before. The message communicated to the average Palestinian by these ongoing human rights violations was that this was not truly a peace process. Perhaps if the Palestinians had continued to negotiate, they would have gotten everything back. We will never know. However, we must concede that these human rights violations made Palestinian society ripe for intifada.

A Palestinian once told me of buying a bicycle for his seven-year-old son. Shortly thereafter, the army raided their apartment, irreparably damaging the bicycle. The son refused to throw the bicycle away. Moreover, every time he went to a toy store after that, he only wanted to buy toy guns. A Palestinian colleague says that all the things he teaches his children about coexistence come undone when the police burst into his home and arrest him at four in the morning or when his children see their neighbors' homes demolished. While we do not condone or excuse violence, the insight from our Jewish tradition is accurate, "*HaKherev Ba L'olam*—The sword comes into the world because of justice delayed and justice denied" (Pirke Avot 5:11).

EIZEHU GIBUR M'HA'GIBURIM

"Who is truly mighty? . . . Some say, 'The one who turns an enemy into a friend.' " Just as injustice brings the sword to the world, acts of justice and solidarity can achieve the opposite. Here are a few examples I have experienced personally.

Empower Palestinian parents. When I have helped to rebuild a Palestinian home destroyed for the lack of a permit (which, again, are nearly impossible to obtain), Palestinian parents often insist that their children meet me. Time after time I hear the same refrain, "My ten-year-old son has just seen his home demolished in front of his eyes and his parents humiliated. What do we say to him when he says, 'I want to be a terrorist when I grow up'? We want him to know that not every Israeli comes with a gun to destroy our home. Some Israelis stand shoulder-to-shoulder with us to rebuild our homes." While we (justifiably) get upset about propaganda being taught about Israelis in Palestinian schools, we need to do all that we can do to empower Palestinian parents who want their children to experience something different.

Light the first candle. I recall one day picking olives with farmers from Beit Furik, near Nablus. I was a bit surprised to discover that the young man who was harvesting the tree with me was a member of Yasser Arafat's presidential guard. If I was a bit surprised, he was ten times more surprised to discover that he was working with an Israeli rabbi. He asked me why I was there. It made no sense to him. I told him about the Jewish tradition of peace and human rights, *tikun olam*, and justice. He responded, "For us Palestinians there is no justice." Although we were still a few months away from Hanukkah, the holiday at the darkest time of the year when we light an increasing number of candles for eight nights, my answer was a basic teaching of Hanukkah: "When all is dark, you must begin by lighting that first candle." He got excited and repeated this to his family.

I am not naïve. I do not know what the young man has done since or what he may do the next time he is confronted with an ethical choice. Many members of Palestinian security forces have engaged in terrorist acts. However, I am certain that this young man is more likely to choose the path of nonviolence having had that encounter, than had he not.

Come to the rescue. On April 15, 2004, at the end of a demonstration along the route of the Separation Barrier, I was asked to come quickly to where a thirteen-year-old boy had been caught by the border police and was being beaten. Two other Israelis and I started making our way the few hundred meters to the jeeps. The border police shot tear gas at us. The other two Israelis turned back; I was the only one stupid enough to go forward. The commanding officer beckoned me forward. Then he grabbed my throat, shook me violently, head-butted me, and screamed that I was under arrest. The boy was strapped to the windshield of a jeep. Two others and I were handcuffed and forced to stand in front of other jeeps. Palestinian youth began to throw stones, hitting the jeeps we were "protecting." For several hours, we were forced to act as human shields. My demands not to use us as human shields and to look after the boy were met with threats and laughter.

I learned that the boy woke with nightmares every night for at least a month. Who knows what psychological scars he will have for the rest of his life. Who knows what he might be thinking about all Israelis, perhaps even all Jews. However, when he gave an affidavit to our fellow human rights organization, B'tselem, he concluded his story by saying, "And then a tall Jewish man in a *kippah* [a Jewish religious head covering] came to my rescue and told me not to be afraid."

"I'm with them." Of all of the risky actions I have taken over the years, one more than any other leads me to ask, "Did I really do that?" A settler was shooting at the feet of an older Palestinian man, and I stepped between them. When the army finally arrived and began to separate Israelis from Palestinians, I looked like one more settler with my beard and *kippah*, and they wanted me to move to where the settlers were standing. However, I pointed to the Palestinians and said, "I'm with them." This was simply a statement of fact on my part. However, one of the Palestinians who was present reminded me of this later and would tell this story in my presence to other Palestinians for years.

The statement "I'm with them" had huge implications in his eyes. The truth is that, rather than being seen as "with the Israelis" or "with the Palestinians," I see myself as "with humans." What was intended as a simple statement of fact on my part was heard as an unusual declaration of our common humanity. There is an incredible need for solidarity, which can only happen when enemies become friends.

These stories do more than demonstrate my ability to respect God's Image in Palestinians. In each of these cases, I was able to help Palestinians see God's Image in me and in my fellow Israelis. Sometimes I think that this is more important than the human rights violations we have succeeded in preventing or redressing. We humans must break down the stereotypes that so many Palestinians have of Israelis and Israelis of Palestinians, stereotypes that dehumanize and prevent each of us from seeing the Divine Image in the other. Only then, can we work together in faith to create a coalition of hope for the sake of both our societies.

One tragedy of our current situation is that although Israeli activists can break down Palestinian stereotypes of Israelis, Palestinians have fewer opportunities to break down the stereotypes Israelis hold. Once, I was paying a condolence visit to a family whose son had been killed by the Israeli army under suspicious circumstances. I (perhaps insensitively) asked those who were gathered to imagine what similarly bereaved Jews in Tel Aviv were saying about Palestinians. Most of the people, given their anger and bitterness, were unable to hear what I was saying. However, one man said to me, "I wish I could go and pay a condolence call to bereaved Israelis the way that you are visiting us. However, you are able to come here, whereas I cannot get a permit to go to Tel Aviv and visit that family."

I wish that more Israelis would meet Palestinians who are members of Combatants for Peace, a group of Israelis and Palestinians who were once part of the armed conflict but who have decided to lay down their arms and seek peace. I wish they could meet Noaf Tzuf, who spent thirteen years in Israeli prisons for being part of the armed resistance. Because he had no blood on his hands, he was released after the Oslo Accords were signed. Thirteen years gave him time to think, and he came out totally committed to Israeli-Palestinian nonviolent resistance to the occupation. Noaf almost singlehandedly aided or helped found many initiatives for Israel-Palestinian nonviolent cooperation. I have seen Noaf stop a stone thrower's arm midthrow, and we have had talks late into the night about what he would do to ensure that his children did not make his mistakes. He has told me that, if his efforts were initially met with suspicion, the accomplishments on behalf of Palestinian rights he achieved cooperatively with RHR and other Israelis eventually won people over at the highest levels of Palestinian society. His beliefs were tested when his brother was paralyzed by an Israeli bullet as he tried to bring children inside during an army raid in their village. However, his commitment to nonviolence remained firm.

Again, "Who is truly mighty? The one who turns an enemy into a friend" (Pirke Avot D'Rabbi Natan 23:1). With bombs having gone off not far from my home, I believe that glimpsing God's Image in my enemies is the beginning of the best thing I can do to protect my children.

MI YAYMAR D'DAMA SISAKH SUMAC T'FAI?

"Even when it comes to security, there are clear lines defining what is acceptable and what is not." Generally, human rights violations increase hatred and endanger our security, whereas acts of justice can improve our security. However, at times there is a real conflict between human rights and security. I sometimes do a little exercise with Israelis. Every Israeli schoolchild can quote from the Talmud, "If somebody is coming to kill you, get up earlier and kill them first" (Talmud Sanhedrin 72a). However, I get blank stares when I ask, "What comes afterward?" We are taught that if somebody is chasing after another person to kill them, you must kill the pursuer. However, even though you were trying to save a human life, you are guilty of murder if you could have stopped the pursuer by injuring him instead of killing him (Talmud Sanhedrin 73a–74a). This is the doctrine of minimum necessary force.

Then another story: a man comes to Raba, one of the Talmudic rabbis, and explains that the village strong man will kill him if he does not kill an innocent third person. Raba would have had no hesitation if the question had been, "Can I defend myself?" However, regarding the innocent person, Raba says, "Let yourself be killed, rather than kill. Who says that your blood is redder than his?" (Talmud Sanhedrin 74a). Can humans live by this standard? How many of us are willing to sacrifice our own lives in order to protect innocents? This was once part of an Israeli army doctrine called Purity of Arms.

The Jewish tradition has a series of tests to apply every time we have a conflict between security and human rights. We need to ask ourselves:

1. Will the action we take be effective? As opposed as I am to home demolitions or collective punishment, if demolishing the homes of terrorists would really save human lives, I would grit my teeth and remember the Jewish

tradition of *pikuakh nefesh*, which says that almost any law can be violated in order to save human life. However, we learned quickly that the home demolition policy was not saving lives.

2. What is the minimum necessary force? Just as the Talmud teaches that one is guilty of murder if one could have stopped a potential murderer without killing him, the army should not have demolished homes if there were less harmful ways to achieve their goal. And if it is true that Hamas was willing to extend the June 2008 ceasefire were Israel to keep its promise to ease up on the blockade of Gaza, it would have been better to ease the blockade rather than go to war because Hamas had resumed rocket fire.

3. Will we harm civilians if we defend ourselves against aggressors?

In the First Lebanon War, Rabbi Forman was a soldier, and one day his commander pointed to a nearby banana grove, where there were Palestinians aiming rocket-propelled grenades at them. His commander said that they could not shoot because the Palestinians were holding civilians in front of them. Rabbi Forman and the Israelis did not shoot. Tragically, two of his army buddies were killed.[12]

Hassidic Tales

There is a Hassidic tale about a man lost for days in a forest. He comes across a second man and asks him if he knows the way out. "No," he replies, "but if we compare the directions each of us has already tried and work together, there is a greater chance that we both will discover the path." Like those lost in the forest, we all know where we need to get to but cannot seem to find the way to get there. However, if those Palestinians and Israelis who share a dream for a better future support each other in a "coalition of hope," we have a much better chance of finding our way out of the forest. If we can talk and listen—Jew to Jew, Jew to Palestinian—and compare our wrong paths, we might be able to work together to find the right path.

The spiritual work we need to do to achieve spiritual insight is not simple. The rabbis asked, "Who is the mysterious being Jacob wrestles with in Genesis 32:25–32, the night before he is to meet his brother Esau after so many years?" Afterward, Jacob is renamed Israel, "the one who wrestles with God," for as he was told by the mysterious being, "You have wrestled with God and humans and have prevailed." Jacob/Israel calls the place Peniel ("the face of God"), saying that he has seen a divine being face-to-face. When he meets his brother the next day, he also says, "To see your face is like seeing the face of God." I believe that the previous night, Jacob had wrestled with the part of himself that had tricked and cheated Esau; Jacob recognized that he was not the person he wanted to be. Having painfully acknowledged in himself that which he had denied for so long, he was a changed man and was able to meet his brother. In that moment of encounter and reconciliation with the other who was also himself, God's Image was present. We Jews need to recognize that we, like Jacob, have not always been the people we want to be, the people we are called by God to be. Only when we acknowledge our own shortcomings and take responsibility can we authentically come together and have true reconciliation with our brothers and sisters in Palestine. (Palestinians must do their own soul-searching as well.) However, if we can use the spiritual tools Judaism provides to wrestle with our tradition and with those aspects of ourselves we would rather project onto others, we will be blessed with the spiritual insight to find God in holy reconciliation with the "other." In spite of all of the spiritual pain involved in this process, those moments in which a Palestinian boy can say "And then a tall Jewish man in a *kippah* came to my rescue and told me not to be afraid" are the moments when God is present. I believe this is the only way to ensure a better future for my children, as well as for the children of that boy.

Notes

1. Nicholas D. Kristof, "In Israel, the Noble vs. The Ugly," *New York Times*, July 7, 2010, http://www.nytimes.com/2010/07/08/opinion/08kristof.html.

2. Noam Zohar, ed., *Life, Liberty, and Equality in the Jewish Tradition* (Jerusalem: Rabbis for Human Rights, 1991 [English translation, 2006]).

3. A former head of an RHR yeshiva.

4. These two principles together are the basis of what Rabbi Akiva calls the metaprinciple (*Klal Gadol*) of the Torah ("Love your neighbor as yourself" [Leviticus 19:8; Jerusalem Talmud Nedarim 41:3]) and what Hillel the Elder calls "Torah on One Foot" ("Do not do unto others what is hateful to you" [Shabbat 31:1]).

5. Abraham Joshua Heschel, *The Sabbath* (New York: Noonday Press and Farrar, Straus, and Giroux, 1961), 27–29.

6. Abraham Joshua Heschel, "Religion and Race," in *The Insecurity of Freedom: Essays on Human Existence* (New York: Farrar, Straus and Giroux, 1966), 85–100.

7. Noam Zohar, page 17, citing Efraim Urbach, *M'Olamam Shel Khakhamim* (Jerusalem, 1988), 561–577. Efraim Urbach traces how the verse was changed.

8. Of course, it is not only the Jewish people who have suffered in our region. There is hardly an Israeli Arab or a Palestinian who hasn't been affected by the conflict in a very personal way. Almost all of us have had loved ones killed or injured or know those who have.

9. Samson Rafael Hirsch, *Five Books of Moses with the Interpretation of Rabbi Hirsch*, trans. from German to Hebrew by Mordechai ben Samson Breuer, ed. Mordechai ben Yitzhak Breuer (Jerusalem: Machon Breuer, 1989).

10. Rabbis for Human Rights was a founding member of the Israeli Committee Against House Demolitions.

11. Yizhar Smilanski, "The Secret of Jewish Existence,"(Hebrew) *Davar*, January 29, 1988.

12. Rabbi Forman said he was never sure if they had done the right thing. How could he have shot and killed innocent civilians? But how could he look the Israeli widows in their eyes and tell them that their husbands were dead because they hadn't shot back?

6

The Intolerance of Israeli Education

NURIT PELED-ELHANAN

This essay is dedicated to Smadari—the nascent fruit that was nipped in the bud, a little girl who was killed just because she was born Israeli by a young man who was oppressed and desperate to the point of murder and suicide just because he was born Palestinian.

And to Abir Aramin who was shot at the age of nine by an Israeli soldier just because she was Palestinian.

Since the death of her thirteen-year-old daughter, Smadar, in a suicide bombing in Jerusalem, Israeli peace activist Nurit Peled-Elhanan has worked to promote dialogue between Israelis and Palestinians. In 2001, she was one of the laureates of the Sakharov Prize for Human Rights and Freedom of Speech awarded by the European Parliament. She is the author of Palestine in Israeli School Books: Ideology and Propaganda in Education.

Abir

On a Tuesday afternoon, January 16, 2007, an Israeli soldier shot nine-year-old Abir Aramin in the head as she was buying a lollipop after school in Anata, a neighborhood north of Jerusalem. She was killed by a rubber bullet that was allegedly fired from the rifle of a member of the Israeli border police who was allegedly sitting in an armored jeep, allegedly thrust the barrel of his rifle through the opening that was allegedly designed for that purpose, and allegedly aimed and fired at the head of the girl who was standing beside her sister at a kiosk, allegedly buying candy. The army did not conduct an inquiry into Abir's death. The official "investigation" was defined by the High Court of Justice as a travesty. No one was questioned except for Abir's sister, eleven-year-old Areen, who held her sister's hand as she fell.

According to the Israeli Defense Force, the shooting never happened. Their official account of Abir's death states that she "might have" been hit by a stone thrown "at our forces" by one of her classmates. A senior pathologist who examined her body at the family's request contradicted this account.

Stones thrown by ten-year-olds do not blow brains out. Moreover, Israeli jeeps routinely circle Palestinian children on their way to and from school in Anata, greeting them with stun bombs, rubber bullets, and riot control gas.

I saw Abir at Hadassah Hospital, where she slept quietly in a huge hospital bed. Her face was white, her eyes were closed. By then, she was already brain dead, and the doctors decided to allow the rest of her to die as well. I could see that she had been shot from behind, but the doctors at Hadassah would not disclose the cause of her death.

Abir Aramin entered into the Holy Land's ever-growing underground kingdom of dead children. She will be welcomed by my own little girl, Smadari, who was killed at age thirteen in 1997 by a suicide bomber.

Visiting Abir at Hadassah Hospital, I sat with Salwa, Abir's mother, and tried to say, "We are all victims of occupation," although I know that her hell is worse than mine. My daughter's murderer had the decency to kill himself and spare us any thoughts regarding his presence in the world. The murderer of Abir likely spent that very evening in a bar, and will continue to spend many more evenings in many more bars, while Abir's parents seek justice. If Smadari's killer had survived, he would have been sent to prison for his crime, and his family's home would have been demolished.

Abir's father, Bassam Aramin, co-founded Combatants for Peace along with my son, Elik, who served as an Israeli soldier before becoming a "refuser." On Wednesday, October 14, 2009, I attended—along with members of Combatants for Peace, Women of Machsom Watch (*machsom* is Hebrew for "checkpoint"), and Bereaved Families for Peace—the hearing at the High Court of Justice on the closing of the investigatory file on the killing of nine-year-old Abir Aramin, due to lack of evidence.

Although Salwa and Bassam Aramin are neither Jewish nor Israeli, they live under Israeli military occupation and have no choice but to seek justice in an Israeli court and demand that the truth come to light in a court of the occupiers. The perfect crime, Jean-François Lyotard wrote in his book *The Differend* (1988), is not only the killing but also the suppression of the testimony and the silencing of the voices of the victims. And the greatest injustice is to compel the victims to seek justice in the court of their tormentors.

Journalists were running around in the High Court corridors, asking lots of questions before the trial: Who died? A little girl? Really? Excuse me, sir, did your daughter die? Yes. Then you are Bassam Aramin? No, I am Rami El-hanan. Oh, sorry. So where's that Aramin? And who are you? What are you doing here? I am a friend. Of those Palestinians? Yes. How come? Did you too have a daughter who died? Really? When? How? What was her name? And after that, you are still on their side? Can I interview you?

But, in the end, no Israeli journalists reported anything.

Bassam Aramin, a former member of the Fatah (the Movement for the National Liberation of Palestine), spent seven years in an Israeli jail for trying to throw an old Israeli grenade onto an Israeli army Jeep. Once a warrior who fought the occupation, Bassam Aramin now fights against violence and for a peaceful future for his remaining five children. Bassam, as a Muslim, believes he must pass a test; as a man of honor, he must neither seek revenge nor give up. And he must not stop the struggle for dignity and peace on his own land. Bassam made his eldest son, Arab, swear an oath on the Koran that he would never use violence in his struggle against the occupation.[1]

My son Yigal was seventeen years old at the time of the trial. He sat in the courtroom all day with a shocked expression on his face. That night he departed for Auschwitz with his classmates, to commemorate the Holocaust. For his sake, I hoped, I prayed, I implored, I nearly shouted at the drowsy female judges to find a spark of humanity, of motherly feeling, within themselves and to look into the eyes of Salwa, who never stopped crying, and at Bassam's ashen face and to say: "The High Court of Justice sympathizes with you over the death of little Abir." They didn't.

On Sunday, July 10, 2011, 8 Tammuz, the Israel High Court of Justice ruled that the child Abir Aramin, age nine, was struck by a bullet that came from an unknown rifle fired by unknown people. The projectile that was found under her small body has found no home, and it might as well stop searching. In other words: the High Court has authorized the shedding of the blood of little Palestinian girls and sent a clear message to the soldiers/police of the Israeli Occupation Forces—the murder of little Palestinian girls, especially those who buy candy at a kiosk next to their school at nine in the morning, is not a crime. No one has been punished and no one will be punished. The allegations of the prosecution—that is, of the parents—the eyewitnesses, the Yesh Din organization, the proof, and the evidence did not make their way into the ears of the judges.

"The Claim to Memory and the Call for Justice Can Become a Call to Murder" (Pierre Nora)

On the International Memorial day of the Holocaust, Israeli "leaders"—the men who occupy the highest posts of government—flew to Europe to ask the world to recognize "our" pain and remember the evil "we" were subjected to, although more than half of the Israeli citizens of today came from Arab countries, where there was no Holocaust, and where leaders—such as the king of Morocco—protected them from Hitler.[2] Nonetheless, Israeli children learn at school that "we" have always suffered from "them"—the non-Jews—and are still suffering and will suffer even more if "we" don't arm ourselves to the teeth and control "them" day and night. The trauma of the Holocaust has become the essential ingredient of Israeli education and identity and the ultimate excuse for aggression against Palestinians. Auschwitz has become the core of our being, the center point of our existence—not the *lesson to be learned* from Auschwitz, but only the trauma, which is re-created and reproduced in Israeli education in order to enhance the sense of victimhood and revenge. As one Ethiopian student, talking about her identity, said: "I wanted to become Israeli, so I went to Auschwitz."

According to Daniel Bar-Tal and Rafi Nets-Zehngut, political psychologists, the "Israeli Jewish consciousness is characterized by a sense of victimization, a siege mentality, blind patriotism, belligerence, self-righteousness, dehumanization of the Palestinians, and insensitivity to their suffering."[3] The present essay argues that this consciousness is the product of Israeli education. How else can one explain the way Israeli boys and girls in uniform treat Palestinians every day and every hour?

Jewish Tolerance

When asked by a new convert to Judaism to teach him the whole Torah "on one foot," Hillel the Elder, one of the most prominent Jewish sages of the second century, answered: "That which is hated upon you, don't do to thy friend. That is the whole teaching of the Bible. All the rest is commentary. Go and learn!"[4] It is believed that this was Hillel's interpretation of the famous verse that is known as a fundamental principle of the Bible: "Love thy friend as thyself."[5] Hillel goes much further than regarding this commandment as a fundamental principle of the Torah. He says that the whole Bible, with all of its 613 commandments and its stories and teachings, is condensed into this one commandment. Hillel claims that instead of the commonly accepted view of the Bible—that it speaks mainly of our relationship with God—it actually speaks primarily of our relationships with one another.

Two questions arise: First, how can this be the whole teaching of the Bible when the Bible is known for having so much information and so many commandments in it? Second, what does Hillel mean?

Hillel's saying, summarizing the Bible's essence in this manner, is radical. It goes much further than vague notions of personal affection. Hillel contends that the Bible's goal is down-to-earth deeds that are obligatory for us as humans toward our fellow-humans. What matters in the end is how we relate to, treat, and act toward each other.

Hillel's saying is well known to Jews in Israel—religious and secular alike—and is advertised on school walls everywhere. But Israeli children are taught to believe it applies only to how we treat other Jews. However, Hillel's explanation is addressed to a "guer," an outsider and a non-Jew, who asks to be taught the whole Torah—the Bible's instruction—in a nutshell.

Guerim ("Strangers")

The Bible repeatedly commands the way we should relate to and treat the *guerim* (strangers)—people who have left their homes and lands to find a sanctuary in ours, as well as new converts.[6] There is no exact definition of the word *guer*, but its root in the Hebrew language is the same root as that of the verbs "to live" and "to fear" (*lagur*). These three actions—to convert, to live, to fear—are connected associatively by the esoteric interpretation of the Zohar[7] to the Bible's phrase: "And Yaakov (Jacob) sat in אר־ימגורי אביו the land in which his father had sojourned."[8] The Zohar, making the correlation between fear in the land of temporary residence expressed in the word גָר (*gar*) and מגורים (*megurim*, which means "residence"), contrasts it with the word נחלה (*nahala*, which means "permanent place of living,") and להתבחל (*Lehitnahel*, which means "to settle down"). *Nahala* usually applies to the land one owns, on which one builds his home, in contrast to the dwelling or residence one lives or sojourns in. The Zohar thus forms a link between fear and being a stranger who is a temporary resident amongst owners of lands and homes. Thus the word גר (*guer*, which means "stranger, newcomer, or religious convert") is linked in the Bible with the feeling of fear and being unsafe, with feeling not-at-home, and, maybe most of all, with being dependent on the goodwill of those permanent owners amongst whom one resides. This triple link between a temporary residence, a stranger or new convert, and fear makes clear the importance the Bible attaches to the attitude toward *guerim*—strangers living among the children of Israel.

Consider some of the biblical commandments concerning the relation to the *guerim* (all quotes are from the Jerusalem Bible)[9]:

> Thou shalt neither vex a stranger nor oppress him for you were strangers in the land of Mitzrayim.[10]
> You shall have one ordinance, both for the stranger and for him who was born on the land.[11]
> For the Lord our God . . . loves the stranger, giving him food and raiment. Love therefore the stranger for you were strangers in the land of Mitzrayim.[12]
> If you oppress not the stranger, the fatherless and the widow and shed not innocent blood in this place . . . then will I cause you to dwell in this place.[13]
> And if a stranger sojourn with thee in your land, you shall not wrong him. But the stranger that dwells with you shall be to you as one born among you, and thou shalt love him as thyself.[14]

Zionist Jews, though they see themselves as the returning indigenous people of the Land of Israel, are in fact *guerim*, foreigners, or rather invaders: people who arrived about a hundred years ago, driven by a myth of a glorious past and majestic ancestry to live on the land where Palestinians have always lived, claiming it as their own, and using the Bible as their justification.[15] The establishment of the state of Israel has turned the indigenous Palestinian people into *guerim*. Yet the state of Israel continually disobeys the commandments regarding the *guerim* in spite of its 1948 Declaration of Independence, which explicitly commands respect for all the other inhabitants of the land and grants them full civil and cultural rights. Israel's political and religious leaders, as well as its cultural and educational institutions, have followed neither the Torah nor the Declaration of Independence in their attitudes and practices regarding the Palestinians who were turned, by force, into *guerim* on and in their own land.

Palestinians in Israeli Textbooks

Hillel's command was, "Go and learn." What, then, do Israeli children learn regarding their Palestinian neighbors and co-citizens? Israeli education, which literally brackets the 2,000 years of Jewish life in the Diaspora and preaches its denial, all but conceals the 1,300 years of Palestinian life on the land. The Zionist creed "Know your homeland" means forgetting 2,000 years of civilization on this land and seeing present Jewish life in Israel as a direct continuation of the biblical kingdom of Judea.[16] So we find in the elementary school textbook *The Mediterranean Countries*: "Jerusalem has always been the capital of the Jewish people (except for the 2,000 years we were not here)."[17]

This perception serves what the French historian Pierre Nora termed the "cult of continuity," typical of national narratives.[18] According to the cult of continuity, the land, too, was in exile; historian Gabriel Piterberg states that according to Zionism, the land "lacked any meaningful or authentic history, awaiting redemption with the return of the Jews."[19] Piterberg contends that the Zionist slogan "a land without a people to a people without a land" does not mean the land was literally empty, but that it was empty of its proper custodians and populated by insignificant intruders.[20]

The Classification of "Others"

The classification of people is often demeaning, especially when they are referred to "in terms of the major categories by means of which a given society or institution differentiates between classes: age, gender, provenance, class, wealth, race, ethnicity, religion, sexual orientation etc."[21] The classification of Palestinians is part of what critical discourse analyst Teun van Dijk terms the language of self-presentation and other-presentation.[22]

The language of self-presentation and other-presentation is evident in Israeli schoolbooks[23] that differentiate Israeli Jews and non-Jews (that is, Arabs).[24] Even in matters that do not touch upon national or ethnic matters, such as industry, agriculture, the professions, official documents, textbooks, and even maps, the life-world in Israel is divided ethnically into Jewish and non-Jewish. The distinction between Jews and non-Jews helps to establish the Jews as the dominant group and as more real—for it has a distinct name—and to marginalize Palestinian citizens as the "others."

The name those of the Palestinian national movement chose for their land at the beginning of the twentieth century is Falastin but Israeli discourse does not respect this name. The label "Palestinian" is seldom used in political or educational discourse to name the Palestinian occupied territories or the Palestinian people. In most schoolbooks, it is synonymous with "terrorist," and the Palestinian Liberation Organization (PLO) is presented as a terrorist organization. Schoolbooks often claim that Palestinians constantly inflame and escalate all the conflicts in the region and portray refugees as a source of trouble in the countries in which they dwell, such as Lebanon and Jordan.[25]

Both Palestinian citizens, called "Israel's Arabs," and Palestinian noncitizens, called "Philistinians" (*Pales(h)tinaiim*), are often lumped into the category "Arabs." This label enhances the idea that the Palestinians are not a nation in their own right but belong to another, much bigger nation outside Israel—the Arab nation. As "Arabs," then, they could and should settle in any of the twenty-one different Arab states. Writing about Palestinian nationality, schoolbooks emphasize that Palestinian refugees yearn for *our* land, Israel, not for *their* land, Palestine.[26]

The label "Arab" also depicts other indigenous "minorities." A geography textbook refers to all indigenous non-Jews, regardless of their origin and faith, as Arabs:

> The Arab Population: Within this group there are several religious groups and several ethnic groups: Muslims, Christians, Druze, Bedouins, and Circassians. *But since most of them are Arab they shall be referred to henceforth as Arabs.*[27]

"Arabs" are always depicted stereotypically, as nomads, terrorists, refugees, or primitive farmers; the men have mustaches, wear galabias (traditional loose-fitting outer garment) and kaffiyehs (traditional Arab headdress), and ride or are followed by camels, and the women wear traditional dress and are usually depicted crouching on the ground. Such false representations are possible because of the mental and material barriers Israel has built between Jews and Palestinians. Israeli children often live their lives without ever meeting a Palestinian face-to-face, let alone talking to one. The last two generations of Israeli Jews grew up knowing almost nothing of the neighbors who live just a few kilometers from them, the people that their fathers and their fathers' fathers turned into refugees or second-class citizens. Israeli education teaches nothing about those neighbors except for their being demographic, security, and developmental threats. The "Palestinian problem," one book explains, which "matured in the poverty and inaction that were the lot of Palestinians in their pitiful camps,"[28] must be "solved," for it has "poisoned for more than a generation the relationships of Israel with the Arab world and with the international community."[29] Labeling a nation "a problem" is considered racist[30] and is quite disturbing when it is used in a Jewish textbook only sixty years after the Jews were called "the Jewish problem."

Since Israeli education instills in the students the utmost importance of a Jewish state with a Jewish majority, the solution to the Palestinian problem requires that they be diminished or even eliminated. Armed with this conviction, Israelis drove about 700,000 people away from their homes and lands in 1948 and about 350,000 more in the 1967 war. When the refugees wanted to return to their homes, their villages, and their crops, which Israel had erased and overtaken, they were denied this right (contrary to both Israel's promise and international decisions) and were called dangerous infiltrators and terrorists. Many of those who stayed or managed to return were legally labeled "present absentees"—which means little more than "unrecognized human beings"—people who are subjected, by law, to a permanent "state of exception" and who are denied all social and legal status.[31]

The need to eliminate the Palestinian "problem" is reflected in norms and regulations that permit the demolition of whole villages,[32] collective punishments, excessive use of force (whether with bullets or tear gas) in rallies, and extrajudicial assassinations of Palestinians. Such conduct is not conceivable in relation to Jewish citizens, or even to Jewish terrorists, nor does it match norms of appropriate behavior or justice in other democratic states.

Israeli schoolbooks convey the notion that an Arab-free country is a blessing for Israel. In one book, we read of the "miracle" of the Palestinian exodus: "In the eyes of the Israelis the flight of the Arabs solved a horrifying demographic problem and even a moderate person such as [the first president] Weitzman spoke about it as 'a miracle.' And indeed, very soon it became obvious that Israel was not going to allow the return of the refugees."[33] In another book, we read the advantages of this exodus for Israel:

- It strengthened the military power of the Jewish community.
- It created a [Jewish] territorial sequence as a "strategic asset."
- It had positive effects at the diplomatic level for it convinced the Americans and the Russians that the Jewish community is strong militarily and can fend for itself.[34]

That same book goes on to claim that "the Arabs brought it upon themselves for they fought the Jews to perdition."[35] This book states that when the United Nations decided that some 60,000 refugees must be allowed to return, "Time was against them. The villages were razed to the ground and Jewish immigrants were relegated to the abandoned areas."[36] Lodging Jewish immigrants on abandoned Palestinian lands was made possible by laws that state that the refugees are not allowed to return to their homes, to reclaim their property, or even to seek compensation.[37]

Israeli children have always been told that because the "Arabs" freely abandoned their land, they did not deserve to get it back. Since abandoning the land contradicts the Palestinian norm of *Sumud*, which means clinging to the soil of the homeland at all costs, by using verbs such as "abandon," "desert," and "escape" Israeli education tries to convince young Palestinians as well that their parents or grandparents have forsaken the land and, therefore, have lost the right to return.[38]

Racist Representations

Of sixteen mainstream textbooks I studied,[39] none describe, either in text or images, any positive cultural or social aspect of Palestinian life, be it literature, poetry, history, agriculture, art, architecture, customs, or traditions.

Schoolbooks use a number of strategies to represent Palestinians as "others."[40] The most widespread strategy is not to show them at all, to ignore these people and the contexts in which they live and work among us and to conceal the very existence of a Palestinian territory. This is apparent in maps where Palestinian cities, villages, universities, and other cultural sites are simply absent, both within and without the borders of the state. For example, in the geography schoolbook *The Mediterranean Countries*, in the chapter "One Sea with Many Names," instead of finding all the names given to the Mediterranean Sea by the people living along its coast, we find the following biblical phrases:

> And thou shalt spread abroad to the west, and to the east, and to the north, and to the south.[41]
>
> And I will set thy bounds from the sea of Suf [the Red Sea] even to the sea of the Pelishtim [the southern shores of the Mediterranean], and from the desert to the river.[42]
>
> Every place whereon the sole of your foot shall tread shall be yours. . . . From the river, the river Prath [Syria and Iraq] to the uttermost sea shall be your border.[43]
>
> From the wilderness and this Lebanon as far as the great sea . . . towards the going down of the sun, shall be your border.[44]

The only verse that is interpreted in modern Hebrew regards the "spreading": "The interpretation of the verse: In the future your country will expand to the west, and to the east, to the north and to the south."[45] The verses are displayed alongside a map of greater Israel that includes Palestine, parts of Jordan, Syria, and Lebanon. Religion, then, serves Israel's secular goals in forming a collective narrative that legitimates the occupation of Palestine.

Palestinians are also represented in the following ways:

> As parasites: "The Arab society is traditional and objects to changes by its nature, reluctant to adopt novelties. Modernization seems dangerous to them. They are unwilling to give anything up for the general good. . . . In the Jewish sector there is no objection to allocate some of the private lands for public building. In the Arab sector there is an expectation that all public services and needs be provided from the land reservoir of the state."[46]

As outlaws: "Most of illegal Arab houses are built on municipal land and agricultural lands that belong by the Israeli law to the state. Illegal building is also a result of wishing to evade payment for license."[47]

As thieves: "The struggle for water: The Palestinian authority steals water from Israel in Ramallah."[48]

As the enemy within: Israel must "preserve the national land and protect it from illegal invasion by the non-Jewish population, to acquire land for development in order to prevent a territorial sequence of non-Jewish settlements, for fear that an Arab sequence would cause the detachment of Galilee from the state of Israel."[49]

As inferior and subservient: "Some of the foreign workers are Palestinians who come from areas controlled by the Palestinian Authority. They are employed in unprofessional jobs and their wages are lower than that of the Israeli citizens who do the same jobs. This is characteristic of all developed countries."[50]

In the history, geography, and civics books I studied, as well as in books for the general public, Palestinians are always mentioned as a collective, either "The Arabs are . . ." or "The Arab is . . ." The impression created by these kinds of references is that Palestinians are all alike and exist only in packs or masses, like cattle. Even their deaths in massacres or wars are reported like the deaths of animals—in approximate numbers or quantities. In several reports about the Dier Yassin massacre we find the following:

The number of casualties is not clear and it ranges between 100 and 254.[51]

In the course of the battle that developed on the ground, between 100 and 250 persons were killed, including women and children.[52]

In summing up the consequences of the 1948 war, a history book (which is not a schoolbook) that may be considered progressive because it presents both Israeli and Palestinian narratives side-by-side provides exact figures of Israeli losses during the 1948 war: 6,000 killed (4,500 soldiers and 1,500 civilians) and more than 30,000 wounded. However, the book provides only estimated quantities for Palestinians: "There were many casualties, many villages were destroyed, and hundreds of thousands Palestinians became refugees."[53] In some textbooks Palestinian dead are labeled "corpses," which aligns with Israeli media discourse that never labels Palestinian casualties "victims": "245 corpses were counted in the village—men, women and children."[54]

Viewing all Palestinians as quantities or masses prevents the reader from seeing them as individual human beings and considering their elimination a human catastrophe. These types of factual, uncommitted, and unengaging reports, which never include photographs of normal or suffering Palestinians, preclude generating any empathy on the part of the reader about the death of "our enemies."[55]

This stance also dominates the negotiations between Israel and the Palestinian Authority regarding the exchange of prisoners, which transforms the Palestinian captives—both adults and minors—into a faceless "price" Israel has to pay in return for one particular Israeli soldier (labeled "a child") who has a name, a face, a family, and a biography.

The "Arabs" never receive any positive attributes or affective or cognitive verbs, which implies that these people never feel anything or think rationally. As a rule, Arabs and Palestinians rarely do anything in Israeli schoolbooks except lurk, attack, and multiply.[56] In some books, "the Arabs" are downright demonized: in the books of Professor Bar-Navi, praised by researchers for their progressiveness and political correctness, we find comparisons of Palestinians with Nazis and the devil: "The Prime Minister saw in Arafat the embodiment of Hitler."[57] "Arafat was considered as the personification of Satan, and the PLO as a clan of murderers."[58] "The action in Lebanon seemed to [Prime Minister Begin] as a salvation war that would save Israel from a second Auschwitz."[59] These comparisons are presented as quotes from authoritative leaders of the state and, therefore, are invested with the aura of truth. They are never contradicted by the authors of textbooks.

Such representations prevent Israelis from perceiving Palestinians as PLU ("people like us"): "rational and educated, possessing the positive characteristics Israeli students tend to associate with their own collectives, a rational, well spoken, responsible Arab—a civilized, stereotype-busting native, with a jacket, a degree and an understanding smile."[60] And if "the Arabs" are not people like us, they are not worthy of the most basic human respect, dignity, and rights.

Visual Racism

People can be categorized visually, as well as verbally, in terms of negative cultural or biological stereotypes. Usually these characteristics, connoting negative or positive values and associations—especially in cartoons or caricatures—are exaggerated. "Biological" categorization of people implies that these characteristics are "in the blood."[61] For example, in one geography textbook, next to a cartoon of the "traditional Arab"—that is, with a moustache, Ali Baba–type dress, pointed clown shoes, a kaffiyeh, and a camel—we read that "the Arab society is traditional and objects to changes *by its nature,* reluctant to adopt novelties . . . unwilling to give anything up for the general good,"⁶² suggesting that the "Arabs" possess, by their very biological nature, these unfavorable but unchangeable traits. Though the cartoon does not represent any living Arab in Israel or Palestine, it symbolizes all Arabs as seen through Israeli eyes.

Writing about Palestinians' suffering with what Dominick LaCapra has termed "empathic unsettlement," or showing Palestinians as people like us, who look into our eyes, is dangerous from the Israeli point of view because such representation may engage us emotionally and even "demand" something of us.⁶³ *A World of Changes* is the only book that presents a photograph where one can look into the eyes of a Palestinian. The photograph shows a class of Palestinian refugee children in Jordan. One girl looks directly into the camera and hence into our eyes. Her gaze leaves us shaken and uncomfortable and makes one think of her circumstances and their cause. This schoolbook, published in 1999 when the Ministry of Education was led by the Labour Party, was pulped by the right-wing ministry that followed, for not being Zionist enough.⁶⁴

A World of Changes is also the only book that shows a map with the escape routes that the Palestinians used when they were expelled in 1948 and that calls the conflict the Zionist-Palestinian conflict instead of the Jewish-Arab conflict. In this book one can also find the original names of Palestinian cities and villages before they were changed into Hebrew names.

Legitimation of Massacres

The conflict between Israel and the Palestinians is presented in most Israeli schoolbooks as the struggle between good and evil. Whereas Israeli actions are usually presented as morally right according to both universal and Jewish norms, Palestinian actions are presented as arbitrary and vicious. Israel "reacts to Arab hostility" and executes "punitive deterring actions" against Palestinian terror. "Arabs" murder Israelis, commit terrorist actions against Israel, and take revenge.

Although Israeli schoolbooks still use the expressions "panic-stricken flight," "abandon," "exit," "desert," and so on for the expulsion of the Palestinians in 1948 (also known as the Naqba), some schoolbooks concede the massacres. However, the massacres are written about in a digestible way that shows them to be "the founding crimes" of the nation in a way that exonerates the Israeli perpetrators. The legitimation of the massacres of Palestinians is usually conveyed through stories that unfold in such a way that the negative act is counterbalanced by positive consequences, such as victory or rescue; the conflict between evil and good always results in the victory of good, that is, in positive consequences for Israel. Consider some examples.

The Dier Yassin massacre of 1948, involving the slaughter of friendly Palestinians that had signed a nonaggression agreement with the Hagana in a village west of Jerusalem, is portrayed in the books that I reviewed as the accelerator of the flight of other Palestinians, which enabled the (miracle of) the establishment of a Jewish state. The Kibya massacre of 1953, involving the slaughter of sixty-nine Palestinians in their homes, is credited with instilling Jewish confidence and restoring morale and dignity to the Israeli Defense Force.[65] The overall claim of these narratives is that a positive outcome (for us) outweighs the evil (done to them).

Legitimation is also achieved by *moral evaluation*,[66] for example, by calling the massacre an appropriate reaction to terror or by calling it a punitive action, deterrence, or retaliation. The killers are often portrayed as role models. One textbook claims that the soldiers of the notorious Unit 101, which committed the Kibya massacre by demolishing sixty-nine houses on top of their residents as revenge for the murder of a Jewish woman and her two children in the cleansed Palestinian town of Yahud, were endowed with "extraordinary courage, improvisation, perseverance in the hardest conditions, tenacity and loyalty to wounded friends [and] became the myth of the combatant soldier in the IDF [Israeli Defense Forces]."[67]

This praise is repeated in other books next to photographs of the warriors of Unit 101, headed by Ariel Sharon, with chief of staff Moshe Dayan, who came to congratulate them after a successful "operation." The soldiers in the photographs, all handsome and manly, wear the "object signs" that connote excellence and heroism in Israel: red military berets, dark khaki combat garb, parachutist wings, and red parachutist boots. These photographs are more than an elaboration of the text. They do not just reveal who the Unit 101 soldiers were, but they constitute a legitimizing device, for they show the men—such as Ariel Sharon, Rafael Eitan, and others—who set the high standards of the Israeli army and who later rose to the highest political positions. Such heroes could not have done unjustified wrong.[68] This visual and textual glorification propagates the myth of the beautiful and just killers.

The Bible Tells Me So

Another strategy of legitimation is by reference to the authority of the Bible, or the authority of tradition, custom, and Jewish law. Thus, massacres may be presented as compatible with such "biblical" norms as "kill whosoever sets out to kill you." This biblical norm, allied with "an eye for an eye" justice, which originally does not encourage revenge but rather making amends, has a modern twist in defense of deterrence and retaliation, which serve regularly as rationale for Israeli violence against Palestinians. For example, on September 20, 2007, Yuval Steinitz, Member of Parliament and head of the Knesset Committee for Security and Foreign Affairs and the current Minister of Finance, declared on Israeli radio that he supported shooting civilians in areas from which Kassam missiles are launched. Answering the legal advisor to the government who had warned against committing war crimes against civilians, he said: "Israel's deterrent capacity rests upon the principle of fire for fire and horror for horror and those who denounce that forsake the security of Israeli citizens."[69]

Following killings at the religious college Merkaz Harav in Jerusalem, and in support of the decision of Israeli defense minister Ehud Barak to demolish the home of the killer's family, Rabbi Elyahu, ex–chief rabbi of Israel, said: "The Gemara says that if the gentiles take silver from Israel they should return gold; anything they take they should return double. But in this case it cannot be because 1,000 Arabs are not worth one Jewish student."[70]

The controversial book *Torat Hamelech* (*The King's Torah*),[71] written by influential rabbis and distributed among soldiers, justifies the killing of non-Jewish children. My own sons, who were soldiers at the time of their sister's murder by a Palestinian suicide bomber from the West Bank in 1997, were egged on by their commanders to avenge her death by committing "reprisals" in Lebanon. They refused.[72]

Intolerance Toward Jewish Guerim

Though the practices of discrimination may be different, Israeli attitudes of intolerance, superiority, and contempt are also manifest in the relationships between the state of Israel and Jewish and other *guerim*. These *guerim* include Jewish immigrants who were brought in for demographic purposes after the establishment of the state, especially from Arab countries and, later on, from the former Soviet Union and Ethiopia, refugees, and foreign workers from war-torn and poverty-stricken countries. In principle, the state of Israel welcomes and aims to bring all Jews to Israel, granting them instant citizenship. However, these immigrant Jews are not encouraged to preserve their culture, their traditions, or their way of life. Jewish languages such as Yiddish, Ladino, Jewerish, and Amharic and other languages are crushed by the Hebrew state. Jewish traditions that vary from the official Israeli ones are declared "non-Jewish."

Consider Ethiopian Jews. When they come to Israel, they are recircumcised; they have to pass difficult examinations (that few Israelis could pass), including demonstrating an understanding of Jewish Halacha (the collective body of Jewish law, including biblical laws—the 613 *mitzvot* ("commandments"), Talmudic and rabbinic law, customs, and traditions); upon arrival, they are given Hebrew names to replace their Jewish-Ethiopian ones; and they are taught to be Jewish "the Israeli way." Adapting to the modern Israeli way of life is hard for Ethiopians because many of them arrive illiterate from villages that had no electricity or running water. Upon their arrival, they are lodged in caravans in "Absorption Centres" that are little more than slums. Many Ethiopian families are stuck there for years, segregated from their white neighbors, dependent on charity, encountering difficulties in finding work and improving their situation. In Mevaseret Zion near Jerusalem, there is a large Absorption Centre where I volunteer tutoring children. Every day, at about a quarter to seven in the morning, yellow buses transport all of the black children to schools in villages far away from mostly white Jerusalem. Even there, they may be segregated. As one of their principals admitted: "We care for them so much that we separate them not only during classes but also during breaks."

Why can't these children study where they live? The answers vary, but the truth, very likely, is that the residents of white Jewish neighborhoods don't want their children mingling with "third-world" kids even though these "newcomers" were brought over by the state with the promise of living a more dignified Jewish life than the one they had in Ethiopia.

The children in this Absorption Centre, brilliant, gifted, ambitious, just like other children—even more so because they know their future and their families' future may depend on their education—quickly learn that they are the "others." One of the girls I tutored, Sintayho (meaning "how much I've seen"), when asked why she was crying on the way to the swimming pool, replied between sobs: "Remember last week, the coach in the swimming pool said it was stinking? I looked around and I was the only Ethiopian." Sintayho also told me that white children (called "Faranji" by Ethiopians) at school don't want to be photographed next to Ethiopians because "they stink like garbage." When I asked what her teacher said to these students, she replied, "Nothing. She probably thinks the same thing. They all say our color is sad." Another child, Yimsrach, told me very naturally that only the Faranji children were taken on Tree Day to plant trees. The Ethiopian children stayed behind. A teacher who used the Jewish Halacha in order to justify her attitude toward Ethiopian children said she avoids these kids because they are profane. This teacher was not evil. She was ignorant. And as Albert

Memmi explained in his book *Racism*,[73] ignorance breeds fear and fear breeds racism.

Here is what an Ethiopian university student wrote as an epilogue to his award-winning BA thesis about the integration of the Ethiopian Jews. Refusing to reconvert, this boy could not get a job in his profession, was rejected by the army, and was not entitled to any sort of financial help. He soon found himself in jail, where he completed his studies:

> I could never stand the attitude of the religious people towards us. . . . Sometimes I felt like telling them I don't give a damn about them. Only God knows what is in my heart and only He can decide whether to bring me to Jerusalem or not. . . . In the absorption centre they kept stalking us. Every now and again a rabbi called Rabbi V., would come, gather all the students and ask some really hard questions about the Jewish religion. I always knew the answers and always got a prize, but after all that I am not Jewish enough. I am foreign labor force. I refuse to re-convert, I have no reason to be converted. I am Jewish, an original Jew. I was born Jewish and am Jewish. I don't care what they think of me. If they don't let me get married or be buried in a Jewish cemetery [as they often do not] they cannot harm me more than that.
>
> We have always dreamt of Jerusalem, but Jerusalem only wants us as slaves, road sweepers, cleaners, gardeners in their schools—a life without a shred of dignity. All our lives we have yearned for Jerusalem, and She received us as thieves, as burglars. Why? Because we came from a poor country? Have we come to rob her of her gold? Jerusalem humiliated us, disappointed us, and spilled our blood.[74]

Teachers in Israel are required to turn their Jewish immigrant students into "Israelis" as quickly as possible. Immigrant students must relearn how to be Jewish, but, this time, Israeli-style. When asked if she was aware that by teaching her Ethiopian pupils her version of Judaism she disconnects them from centuries-old traditions and from their parents, one teacher answered, in a missionary style: "I do, you are right; but I do it with love."

Teachers in Israel are not required—nor are they taught—to appreciate the diversity in their classes. On the contrary, they are instructed to erase it, to homogenize the class, or, as the Hebrew expression goes, to "consolidate." A teacher may be reprimanded if her class is not "consolidated." Therefore, immigrant children often sit apart from the others, in the corner, with the hyperactive, the dyslexic, and other "marked" children who "spoil" consolidation. In one class I visited, the Russian child was drilling Hebrew grammar while the other children wrote the traditional Friday letter to their parents. When asked why he wasn't writing to his parents, the teacher answered, "Because he still has difficulties in Hebrew."

However, there are some teachers who welcome and treat immigrant children appropriately, as *guerim* should be treated; these teachers enjoy the extra value one can gain from getting to know another language or culture. Susi, a kindergarten teacher (herself an immigrant from dictatorial Argentina), received a five-year-old child, Benjamin, who was diagnosed as having "communication problems." Benjamin would come to school every morning and spend five hours crouching under a table. Susi refused to hand him over to special education, saying, "He is Russian and has never been to an Israeli kindergarten. Of course he has communication problems." She then devised a solution. One day, she announced to the class: "I am going to open a Russian club. Who wants to learn Russian?" All the kids raised their hands. "But," said Susi, "I have a problem. I can't find a teacher." Upon these words, little Benjamin crawled out from under the table. From then on, every Wednesday, he gave a Russian lesson to the class. Four months after Benjamin started his Russian club, just before Passover, I visited this kindergarten and received from Benjamin a very scholarly lecture about the pyramids—in Hebrew.

Segregation and marginalization receive their official stamp in schoolbooks. In the textbook series *Living Together in Israel: A Textbook in Homeland Studies, Society, and Civics for Years 2–4*, Palestinian, Jewish-Ethiopian, Bedouin, and Druze living in Israel are excluded from the main texts and from the primary visuals depicting "Israeli Life."[75] They are, rather, confined to pages of different colors; being presented in separate pages decontextualizes and marks them as specimens of Israeli "minorities" or "ethnicities," to be observed and scrutinized, represented anthropologically as "other types" of human beings with no connection to the rest of the population and with no share in the culture represented in the book. The booklets teach the reader, both verbally and visually, that these children, framed hermetically in their special pages, are marginal, excluded, and marked off. On the cover of every booklet, there is a colorful drawing of people of all ages (who apparently represent the Israeli population). None of these people are Arab or black. In each of the booklets, we meet a "gang" of children, drawn as comic-strip figures, who act as guides and take the reader on a trip in Israel to meet the people and become acquainted with places and customs and who greet the Jewish newcomers. In this gang, except for one blond child called Sasha (hinting at the successful absorption of Russian Jews), all of the children are Israeli-born and are white.

From the age of seven, then, Israeli Jewish children learn to marginalize Palestinian, Druze, and Bedouin citizens and Ethiopian Jews and to exclude them from mainstream life in the state of Israel.

The Danger of National Narratives

Verbal indoctrination and negative representations of "others" can encourage people to resort to physical violence quite easily, because "the victim group has long been typed, [and] people have begun to lose the power to think of the members of the out-group as individuals"[76] and only treat them as threatening masses.

Besides serving as a tool for instilling discriminatory ideas and racist attitudes, the narrative inculcated in Israeli schools enhances ignorance. Assuming that school students do not run to libraries to verify the facts and that most teachers were brought up on similar narratives, one must conclude that the past three generations of Israelis are, for the most part, unaware of the geopolitical or social realities of their country. This deliberate ignorance is achieved partly through poems, songs, and stories glorifying the Zionist project and the "Judaization" of the land, but especially through the authority of the "scientific" discourse of textbooks, which is considered neutral, objective, unbiased, and therefore representative of truth. Israel's national narrative has become what Nora termed, "a form of closure, a ground for exclusion, and an instrument of war."[77]

Some years ago, in a preface to his term paper about the Israeli national narrative reproduced in schoolbooks, Tal Sela, a university student of mine, reflected on his military service:

> How could I be so gullible and let myself be duped? How can I explain that a man of peace exposes himself to such a morbid experience of his own free will? Today, I saw an officer put tight handcuffs on a taxi driver because he failed to obey the soldiers' order to park here and not there. "We told him a thousand times," the soldiers said. The man was lying on the ground in the worst heat of the summer, thirsty, for hours on end. . . .
>
> What pushes these young Israeli boys to play the role of supreme judges until they lose all judgment? In my opinion, it is the Grand Zionist Narrative which serves, explicitly as well as implicitly, as a collective conscience to the whole Israeli society. This grand narrative is the system of values that makes us belong to this particular collective.

Paul Ricoeur contends that the prime danger of national narratives lies in the handling of authorized, imposed, official "history" that conceals the "other drama." "When higher powers take over and impose a canonical narrative, the resource of narrative becomes a trap, and a devious form of forgetting is at work here . . . not without complicity, which makes forgetting semi-passive semi-active behaviour . . . in short by a wanting-not-to-know."[78] The fear of knowing is expressed, for example, in the law endorsed by the

Israeli Knesset on March 23, 2011, to withdraw budgets from municipalities that allow the commemoration of the Palestinian catastrophe in 1948 (the Naqba).

But the "wanting-not-to-know," instilled in Israeli youth through education, is, in fact, a "wanting not to teach." The state of Israel encourages neither "peace education" nor the mixing of Jewish and Palestinian students.[79] Since reconciliation, peace, and mutual understanding depend on contact and information, depriving children of contact and information regarding their neighbors perpetuates their portrayal as enemies and precludes understanding and empathy. Not only with the help of concrete walls but also with the powerful means of education, the state marks the boundaries between "us" and "them" and categorizes "them" as inferior, vile, subservient, and dangerous. Once acquired, these categories—as the history of anti-Semitism shows—tend to resist change.[80]

Such teaching contradicts the persistent Israeli claim that "Palestinians teach their children to hate us and we teach 'Love thy neighbor.' "[81]

"Take Off Your Shoes"

Both concrete walls and mental barriers make sure that another commandment of Hillel will not be obeyed: "Do not judge your friend until you have reached his place."[82] Fixed racist ideas about the "other" prevent picturing oneself as reaching the other's place, or rather walking in the other's shoes. Using the methods of the Cabbalists, we can make a correlation between the word *shoes* and the act of locking. In Hebrew, the verb *to lock* and the verb for putting on shoes are the same: לנעול (*linol*). Metaphorically speaking, being locked in "one's own shoes" means being locked within subjective stories and perspectives. Thus, wearing our shoes means that we are locked in our personal affective states and attitudes. In such a state it is difficult to see, and more so, to feel the other.

The revelation of God to Moses provides an example of unlocking one's shoes. Standing on Mount Horeb, staring with awe and wonder at a burning bush—סנה (*sneh*)—that is not extinguished by the fire, Moses hears a voice telling him to take off his shoes, as the place he is standing on is holy.[83] By taking off his shoes, he is transformed cognitively, psychically, and existentially so that he can accept that which is as it is, that which will be as it will be. Only by taking off his shoes can Moses "see" the God who defines himself: אהיה אשר אהיה (Eheye asher eheye: "I shall be that which I shall be").[84] It is solely from this holy place, accessible to Moses once he's taken off his shoes, that Hillel's saying may be understood.

Only by getting out of our personal or national story and subjective or ethnocentric construal of reality, in which we are locked and imprisoned, can we see the other, step into the other's shoes, and treat her with empathy. The question is: is this possible for a people who for nearly 2,000 years have been praying every morning: "Bless You God, Our Lord, King of the World, who did not make me a Gentile (non-Jew)"?

Conclusion

Israeli education is not unique in inculcating racist values and justifying discriminatory practices. Studies in the United States, the United Kingdom, Australia, Holland, and Sweden, among others, show similar findings regarding the representation of "others." Therefore, the entire "enlightened" Western world needs to take off its shoes and implement Hillel the Elder's sayings; to redefine the ideologically loaded word "we," not according to race or religion but according to the values of compassion, tolerance, and empathy prescribed by Hillel. For Israelis that would mean not to stand aside when little girls are murdered by soldiers, not to blame the victims for all the atrocities we inflict on them, not to fear little girls with scarves on their heads and boys in kaffiyehs, not to see people in need as invading masses that should be driven back and destroyed. Not to educate children to see nothing wrong in killing other children "before they grow."

Without this change of spirit, there will be nothing left to say or write or listen to on this land except for the silent cry of mourning and the muted voices of dead children.

Notes

I thank Dr. Dvorah Gamlieli for her valuable contribution to this paper regarding Jewish thought.

1. I failed to make my own sons take the same oath. They had to learn by experience that being a soldier in the Israeli army means joining Abir's murderers and encouraging Smadar's murderers.

2. The Holocaust did reach Tunisia. See, for instance, www.ushmm.org/wlc/article .php?lang=en&ModuleId=10007311.

3. Daniel Bar-Tal and Rafi Nets-Zehngut, "Emotions in Conflict: Correlates of Fear and Hope in the Israeli-Jewish Society," *Peace and Conflict: Journal of Peace Psychology* 14, no. 3 (2008): 233–258.

4. Babylonian Talmud Shabbat 31:A.

5. Lev. 19:18.

6. The expression in Hebrew for "converting to Judaism" is *Giyur*, and the convert is called a *guer*.

7. The Zohar (Hebrew: זהר, lit. *Splendor* or *Radiance*) is the foundational work in the literature of Jewish mystical thought known as Kabbalah. Gershom Scholem and Melila Hellner-Eshed, "Zohar," in *Encyclopaedia Judaica*, vol. 21, 2nd ed., ed. M. Berenbaum and F. Skolnik (Detroit: Macmillan Reference, 2007), 647–664.

8. Gen. 37:1.

9. Jerusalem Bible (Jerusalem: Koren publishers, 1992).

10. Exod. 22:0.

11. Num. 9:14.

12. Deut. 10:18

13. Jer. 7:6

14. Lev. 19:33–34.

15. See Shlomo Zand, *The Invention of the Jewish People* (New York: Verso, 2009).

16. As noted by literary scholar Ariel Hirschfeld in *Haaretz* (Israeli newspaper), December 27, 2008.

17. D. Vaadya, H. Ulman, and Z. Mimoni, *The Mediterranean Countries for 5th Grade* (Tel Aviv: Maalot Publishers, 1994/1996), 54.

18. Pierre Nora, *Rethinking France: Les Lieux de Mémoire,* vol. 1, *The State* (Chicago: University of Chicago Press, 1996), 12.

19. Gabriel Piterberg, "Erasures," *New Left Review* 10 (July–August 2001): 32.

20. Ibid.

21. T. Van Leeuwen, *Discourse and Practice: New Tools for Discourse Analysis*, Oxford Studies in Linguistics (Oxford: Oxford University Press, 2008), 42.

22. Teun van Dijk, *Ideology: A Multidisciplinary Approach* (London: Sage, 1997).

23. This discussion of Israeli textbooks is based on my study: *Palestine in Israeli School Books: Ideology and Propanganda in Education* (London: I.B. Tauris Publishers, 2011).

24. Non-Jews that are not Arabs are usually classified, both by the state's population registry and in geography textbooks, as "others" and are included in the Jewish group, especially in diagrams and graphs describing progress. Their privileged status is expressed in Y. Aharoni and T. Sagi, *The Geography of the Land of Israel* (Tel Aviv: Lilach, 2003), 149, where a population pyramid divides the Israeli population into "Jews and others" versus "Arabs." The book does not provide any explanation as to who these "others" are, but the impression remains that some "others" deserve to be included in the Jewish group, as long as they are not Arabs.

25. R. Firer, "The Presentation of the Israeli-Palestinian Conflict in Israeli History and Civics Textbooks," in *The Israeli-Palestinian Conflict in Israel History and Civics Textbooks of Both Nations*, ed. R. Firer and S. Adwan (Hannover: Georg Eckert Institute for International Textbook Research, 2004), 64.

26. As in E. Bar-Navi, *The 20th Century: A History of the People of Israel in the Last Generations, for Grades 10–12* (Tel Aviv: Sifrei Tel Aviv, 1998), 245.

27. T. Fine, M. Segev, and R. Lavi, *Israel—The Man and the Space: Selected Chapters in Geography* (Tel Aviv: Centre for Educational Technology, 2002), 12 (emphasis added).

28. Bar-Navi, *The 20th Century*, 195.

29. E. Bar-Navi and E. Nave, *Modern Times Part II: The History of the People of Israel, for Grades 10–12* (Tel Aviv: Sifrei Tel Aviv, 1999), 239.

30. See Van Leeuwen, *Discourse and Practice*.

31. Oren Yiftachel, "(Un)Settling Colonial Presents," *Political Geography* 26, no. 1 (2007): 43–52.

32. Today there are about a hundred unrecognized Palestinian and Bedouin villages in Israel. One of them is Al-Araqib, a Bedouin village in the Negev, demolished multiple times this year in order to plant a forest for a Christian organization called God TV that leased the land from the Jewish National Fund.

33. Bar-Navi, *The 20th Century*, 195.

34. N. Blank, *The Face of the 20th Century* (Tel Aviv: Yoel Geva, 2006), 322–323.

35. Ibid., 323.

36. Ibid.

37. An official body called the Custodian was authorized to sell absentees' land (defined in Clause 1[b] of the law) to the Development Agency, a governmental body created specifically for the acquisition of these lands. This agency then sold the land to the Jewish National Fund, which "leases" the lands to Jews only (Piterberg, "Erasures").

38. Israeli schoolbooks claim that Arab countries, not Israel, created the Palestinian problem to serve their own interests. In one book we read, not untypically, "The leaders of the Arab countries exploited the problem of Philistinian refugees for their own political needs" (Blank, *Face of the 20th Century*, 348). And another book declares: "The Arab leaders chose to use the refugees as a battering ram against Israel" (Bar-Navi, *The 20th Century*, 195). Bar-Navi quotes a UN Relief and Works Agency official who said: "[T]he Arab countries do not want to solve the refugee problem. They prefer to keep it as an open wound, as an insult against the UN and as a weapon against Israel. May the refugees live or die, what do the Arab leaders care?" (Bar-Navi, *The 20th Century*, 195).

39. Israeli schoolbooks are trade books, sold on the free market, and teachers may choose which books to use. However, they all need to be authorized by the Ministry of Education, or at least be compatible with the national curriculum. In this study only mainstream secular schoolbooks were examined. State religious books were not included.

40. Van Leeuwen offers five different strategies for representing people as "others," all of which can be found in Israeli schoolbooks (Van Leeuwen, *Discourse and Practice*, 46): (1) using exclusion, that is, not representing people at all in contexts where in reality they are present; (2) depicting people as the agents of actions that are held in low esteem or regarded as subservient, deviant, criminal, or evil; (3) showing people as homogeneous groups and thereby denying them individual characteristics and differences; (4) presenting negative cultural connotations; (5) using negative racial stereotyping.

41. Gen. 28:14.

42. Exod. 23:31.

43. Deut. 11:24.

44. Josh. 1:4.

45. Vaadya, Ulman, and Mimoni, *The Mediterranean Countries*, 60.

46. Aharoni and Sagi, *Geography of the Land of Israel*, 303. Note that the lands of the state are actually the lands that were confiscated from the Palestinian citizens in the first place; now the Palestinians are seen as trespassers on their own land.

47. Ibid., 199. For land confiscation and the ghettoization of Arabs in Israel, see Oren Yiftachel, *Ethnocracy: Land and Identity Politics in Israel/Palestine* (Philadelphia: University of Pennsylvania Press, 2006), 143, 166.

48. Aharoni and Sagi, *Geography of the Land of Israel*, 100. But Ramallah is not part of the state of Israel; it is one of the areas controlled by the Palestinian authorities.

49. Ibid., 240. This segregation is now legalized by a law that allows the Jewish National Fund to refrain from leasing land to Arab citizens and the Screening Committees Law approved March 23, 2011 (Ynet news, June 17, 2008, www.haaretz.co.il/hasite/spages/1195587.html [in Hebrew]).

50. Fine, Segev, and Lavi, *Israel—The Man and the Space*, 32.

51. K. Avieli-Tabibian, *Journey into the Past* (Tel Aviv: Centre for Educational Technologies, 2001), 284.

52. S. Inbar, *Fifty Years of Wars and Hopes* (Tel Aviv: Lilach, 2004), 180.

53. N. Hagiladi and F. Kassem, *The War of Independence/The Nakba* (Jerusalem: Van-Leer Institute and Al-Quds University, 2007), 20.

54. Bar-Navi, *The 20th Century.*

55. T. Van Leeuwen and A. Jaworski found a similar attitude in Western media reports about Palestinian or pro-Palestinian victims of Israeli aggression. They observe that "Western audiences are invited to feel the agony of Israeli [victims while] Palestinian deaths are rarely made so graphic or memorable: they are anonymous people, counted as numbers, bodies aloft among depersonalized funeral crowds" ("The Discourses of War Photography," *Journal of Language and Politics* 1, no. 2 (2002): 255–275.

56. See, for example, M. Segev and Z. Fine, *People and Settlements* (Tel Aviv: Centre for Educational Technologies, 2007).

57. Bar-Navi, *The 20th Century.* 252.

58. Ibid.

59. Ibid., 251.

60. Dan Rabinowitch, "Natives with Jackets and Degrees: Othering, Objectification, and the Role of Palestinians in the Co-existence Field in Israel," *Social Anthropology* 1, no. 9 (February 2001): 67–80.

61. T. Van Leeuwen, "Visual Racism," in *The Semiotics of Racism*, ed. M. Reisigl and R. Wodak (Vienna: Passagen Verlag, 2000), 146.

62. Aharoni and Sagi, *Geography of the Land of Israel*, 303 (emphasis added).

63. D. LaCapra, *Writing History, Writing Trauma* (Baltimore, MD: Johns Hopkins University Press, 2001), 125.

64. As reported on March 4, 2001, by the Committee for the Examination of the History Textbook *A World of Changes*, presided over by Professor Yossef Gorni. See *Haaretz*, July 13, 2001: "A few days after Limor Livnat was appointed [Israeli] minister of education, she banned a high-school history textbook called 'A World of Changes,' edited by Danny Yaakoby in consultation with seven scholars from four universities. . . . Public criticism of the book was largely political: Its critics wanted a more patriotic textbook."

65. Inbar writes: "[The massacre of Kibya and other such 'reprisals'] restored the morale and dignity to the army and helped it become a deterring vigorous army whose long arm can reach the enemy deep in its own territory" (Inbar, *Fifty Years*, 244). This effect stated as historical fact is actually a quote from an article written in the popular daily newspaper *Yediot Aharonot*, by the commander of this massacre, Ariel Sharon, thirty-nine years after the slaughter, on October 18, 1992. See also K. Avieli-Tabibian, *The Age of Horror and Hope: Chapters in History for Grades 10–12* (Tel Aviv: Centre for Educational Technologies, 2001); E. Domka, H. Urbach, and Z. Goldberg, *Nationality: Building a State in the Middle East* (Jerusalem: Zalman Shazar Center, 2009); Inbar, *50 Years*; E. Nave, N. Vered, and D. Shahar, *Nationality in Israel and the Nations: Building a State in the Middle East* (Tel Aviv: Rehes, 2009).

66. The strategies of legitimation are all taken from T. Van Leeuwen, "Legitimation in Discourse and Communication," *Discourse & Communication* 1, no. 1 (2007): 91–112.

67. Nave, Vered, and Shahar, *Nationality in Israel and the Nations*, 204.

68. Van Leeuwen adds, "The mere fact that these role models adopt a certain kind of behaviour, or believe certain things, is enough to legitimize [their actions] and the actions of their followers" (Van Leeuwen, "Legitimation in Discourse and Communication," 103).

69. As reported in YNET, September 2, 2004, http://www.ynet.co.il/articles/0,7340,L -2972117,00.html.

70. As reported in *Haaretz*, April 4, 2008. Also reported at http://news.walla.co .il/?w=/1/1260087 (in Hebrew) and http://article.wn.com/view/2008/04/02/Editorial_ HangArab_Solution/.

71. *Haaretz* published an article about the book on January 22, 2010, available at www.haaretz.com/jewish-world/news/the-king-s-torah-a-rabbinic-text-or-a-call-to -terror-1.261930.

72. The incoming head of the National Security Council, Maj. Gen. (ret.) Ya'acov Amidror, said the order to fight with caution and to try not to harm civilians is "a manifestly unlawful order." "The idea is to kill as many bastards from the other side. We should win, full stop," he said, adding that soldiers have to kill whomsoever is in their way to complete their mission (www.haaretz.co.il/hasite/spages/1218121.html [in Hebrew]). The quote translated on the English Web page is: "That's a totally illegal order. What should be said is 'kill more of the bastards on the other side, so that we'll win.' Period." See also Chaim Levinson and Mazal Mualem, "'IDF Soldiers Who Won't Fight Should Be Shot,' Says National Security Adviser Candidate," *Haaretz*, March 2, 2011. The English translation does not differentiate between illegal and unlawful, but this differentiation is crucial, as explained in the civics book *Being Citizens in Israel*, by H. Aden, V. Ashkenazi, and B. Alperson (Jerusalem: Ministry of Education/Maalot, 2001), 217–218, where one reads that soldiers are obliged to obey illegal orders (such as bursting into Palestinian houses at night without a warrant) and to disobey manifestly unlawful orders, such as slaughtering innocent people.

73. Albert Memmi, *Racism*, trans. Steve Martinot (Minneapolis: University of Minnesota Press, 2000).

74. Here he alludes to the spilling of donated Ethiopian blood with the pretext that it was contaminated with AIDS and tuberculosis.

75. Published in 2006 by the Centre for Educational Technologies, Tel Aviv.

76. G. W. Allport, *The Nature of Prejudice* (New York: Doubleday Anchor, 1958), 171.

77. Nora, *Rethinking France: Les Lieux de Mémoire*, vol. 1, *The State*, 10.

78. Paul Ricoeur, *Memory, History, Forgetting* (Chicago: University of Chicago Press, 2004), 448. See, for example, an interview with former Member of Parliament and Minister of Education Shulamit Aloni, "'Like the Germans, We Don't Want to Know': Israelis and Purposeful Ignorance to the Crimes Against Humanity Being Committed in Palestine," www.axisoflogic.com/artman/publish/article_6869.shtml.

79. See Rabinowitch, "Natives with Jackets and Degrees": "[The] plethora of opportunities notwithstanding, the topic of peace and co-existence never became part of the formal academic curriculum and never carried any academic credit in its own right" (67).

80. As Allport, *The Nature of Prejudice*, stated, "It is characteristic of the prejudiced mentality that it forms such categories in all areas of experience. The opposite tendencies seem to mark the tolerant person" (171). Yiftachel, *Ethnocracy*, states that "ethnocracies require 'the outright rejection' of all other accounts but their official one" (37).

81. Tzipi Livni, in a speech in Beer-Sheva, reported in *Inyan Merkazi*, January 1, 2009. Available at www.news-israel.net/article.asp?code=13973 (in Hebrew).

82. Ethics of our Fathers II:5 (Pirkey Avot).

83. Exod. 3:5.

84. Exod. 3:14.

Bibliography of Textbooks by Subject

Geography

Aharoni, Y., and T. Sagi. *The Geography of the Land of Israel* (for grades 11–12). Tel Aviv: Lilach, 2003.

Fine, T., M. Segev, and R. Lavi. *Israel—The Man and the Space: Selected Chapters in Geography*. Tel Aviv: Centre for Educational Technologies, 2002.

Rap, E., and T. Fine. *People in Space* (for grade 9). Tel Aviv: Centre for Educational Technologies, 1996/1998.

Rap, E., and I. Shilony-Tzvieli. *Settlements in Space: Chapters in the Geography of Settlements in the World*. Tel Aviv: Centre for Educational Technologies, 1998.

Segev, M., and Z. Fine. *People and Settlements*. Tel Aviv: Centre for Educational Technologies, 2007.

Vaadya, D., H. Ulman, and Z. Mimoni. *The Mediterranean Countries for Fifth Grade*. Tel Aviv: Maalot, 1994/1996.

History

Avieli-Tabibian, K. *Journey into the Past: Chapters in History for Grades 8–10*. Tel Aviv: Centre for Educational Technologies, 1999.

Avieli-Tabibian, K. *The Age of Horror and Hope: Chapters in History for Grades 10–12.* Tel Aviv: Centre for Educational Technologies, 2001.

Bar-Navi, E. *The 20th Century: A History of the People of Israel in the Last Generations, for Grades 10–12.* Tel Aviv: Sifrei Tel Aviv, 1998.

Bar-Navi, E., and E. Nave. *Modern Times Part II: The History of the People of Israel, for Grades10–12.* Tel Aviv: Sifrei Tel Aviv, 1999.

Blank, N. *The Face of the 20th Century.* Tel Aviv: Yoel Geva, 2006.

Domka, E., H. Urbach, and Z. Goldberg. *Nationality: Building a State in the Middle East.* Jerusalem: Zalman Shazar Centre, 2009.

Inbar, S. *50 Years of Wars and Hopes.* Tel Aviv: Lilach, 2004.

Nave, E., N. Vered, and D. Shahar. *Nationality in Israel and the Nations: Building a State in the Middle East.* Tel Aviv: Rehes, 2009.

Yaakoby, D., et al. *A World of Changes: A History Book for 9th Grade.* Tel Aviv: Ministry of Education/Maalot, 1999.

Civic Studies

Aden, H., V. Ashkenazi, and B. Alperson. *Being Citizens in Israel—A Jewish Democratic State.* Jerusalem: Ministry of Education/Maalot, 2001.

General References

Agamben, G. *Homo Sacer: Sovereign Power and Bare Life.* Meridian: Crossing Aesthetics, 1987.

Allport, G. W. *The Nature of Prejudice.* New York: Doubleday Anchor, 1958.

Bar-Gal, Y. *Moledet and Geography in a Hundred Years of Zionist Education.* Tel Aviv: Am Oved, 1993.

Bar-Tal, Daniel, and Rafi Nets-Zehngut. "Emotions in Conflict: Correlates of Fear and Hope in the Israeli-Jewish Society." *Peace and Conflict: Journal of Peace Psychology* 14, no. 3 (2008): 233–258.

Firer, R. "The Presentation of the Israeli-Palestinian Conflict in Israeli History and Civics Textbooks." In *The Israeli-Palestinian Conflict in Israeli History and Civics Textbooks of Both Nations,* ed. R. Firer and S. Adwan. Hannover, Germany: Georg Eckert Institute for International Textbook Research, 2004.

Hagiladi, N., and F. Kassem. *The War of Independence/The Nakba.* Jerusalem: Van-Leer Institute/Al-Quds University, 2007.

La Capra, D. *Writing Shoa, Writing Trauma.* Baltimore, MD: Johns Hopkins University Press, 2001.

Lyotard, J. F. *The Differend: Phrases in Dispute.* Minneapolis: University of Minnesota Press, 1988.

Nora, Pierre. *Rethinking France: Les Lieux de Mémoire,* vol. 1, *The State.* Chicago: University of Chicago Press, 1996.

Piterberg, Gabriel. "Erasures." *New Left Review* 10 (July–August 2001).

Rabinowitch, Dan. "Natives with Jackets and Degrees: Othering, Objectification, and the Role of Palestinians in the Co-existence Field in Israel." *Social Anthropology* 1, no. 9 (February 2001): 65–80.

Ricoeur, P. *Memory, History, Forgetting.* Chicago: University of Chicago Press, 2004.

Van Dijk, Teun. *Ideology: A Multidisciplinary Approach.* London. Sage, 1997.

Van Leeuwen, T. *Discourse and Practice: New Tools for Discourse Analysis,* Oxford Studies in Linguistics. Oxford: Oxford University Press, 2008.

———. "Legitimation in Discourse and Communication." *Discourse & Communication* 1, no. 1 (2007): 91–112.

———. "Representing Social Actors." In T. Van Leeuwen, *Discourse and Paractice.* Oxford: Oxford University Press, 2008, 23–75.

———. "The Schoolbook as a Multimodal Text." *International Schulbuch Forschung* 14, no. 1: 35–58. Frankfurt: Diesterweg, 1992.

———. "Visual Racism." In *The Semiotics of Racism,* ed. M. Reisigl and R. Wodak. Vienna: Passagen Verlag, 2000, 333–350.

Van Leeuwen, T., and Adam Jaworski. "The Discourses of War Photography." *Journal of Language and Politics* 1, no. 2 (2002): 255–275.

Yiftachel, Oren. "(Un)Settling Colonial Presents." *Political Geography* 26, no. 1 (2007): 43–52.

———. *Ethnocracy: Land and Identity Politics in Israel/Palestine.* Philadelphia: University of Pennsylvania Press, 2006.

Shlomo Zand. *The Invention of the Jewish People.* New York: Verso, 2009.

Abraham's Christian Children

7

Religious Tolerance

JIMMY CARTER

Jimmy Carter served as the thirty-ninth president of the United States, from 1977 to 1981, during which time he oversaw the Camp David Accords, the peace treaty between Israel and Egypt. President Carter is the author of more than twenty books, including Talking Peace: A Vision for the Next Generation, Living Faith, *and* Palestine: Peace Not Apartheid. *He is the founder of the Carter Center, which is dedicated to advancing human rights, ending human suffering, and preventing and resolving conflict worldwide. In 2002, President Carter was awarded the Nobel Peace Prize.*

Introduction

During my time in the presidency, I prayed a lot—more than ever before in my life—asking God to give me a clear mind, sound judgment, and wisdom in dealing with affairs that could affect the lives of so many people in our own country and around the world. Although I cannot claim that my decisions were always the best ones, prayer was a great help to me.

When I announced my candidacy in December 1974, I expressed a dream: "That this country set a standard within the community of nations of courage, compassion, integrity, and dedication to basic human rights and freedoms." I was familiar with the widely accepted arguments that we had to choose between idealism and realism, or between morality and the exertion of power; but I rejected those claims. To me, the demonstration of American idealism was a practical and realistic approach to foreign affairs, and moral principles were the best foundation for the exertion of American power and influence.

Upon entering White House in 1977, I had tried to express in my inaugural address as simply and clearly as possible my ambitions for America. Over a period of several weeks I had done a great deal of work on these few words, and in the process had read the inaugural addresses of the presidents who served before me. I was touched most of all by Woodrow Wilson's. Like him, I felt I was taking office at a time when Americans desired a return to first principles by their government. His call for national repentance also seemed appropriate, although I feared that a modern audience might not understand a similar call from me.

Rosalynn and I had discussed which Bible verses I would cite at the inauguration. I chose Micah 6:8: "He hath showed thee, O man, what is good; and what doth the Lord require of thee, but to do justly, and to love mercy, and to walk humbly with thy God." These words held the reminder of the need to seek God's help and guidance as we sought to improve our commitment to justice and mercy.

For each of us there are focal points for our political faith—either the resilience of our diverse peoples, the wisdom of the Constitution and its derivative laws and customs, the national spirit of hope and confidence that has shaped our history, or the unchanging religious and moral principles that have always been there to guide America on its course. Sometimes we forget, and even deviate radically from our nation's historic path. But we soon remember the advantage of compassion for the weak, ethical standards, the beauty of our land, peace and human rights, the potential quality of our children's lives, and the strength we derive from one another as free people— unfettered except for self-imposed limits. Then we are able to correct our mistakes, repair what we have damaged, and move on to better days.

Human Rights

For centuries the Middle East has been both a crossroads of trade and a center of conflict for control of the precious land surrounding the holy places of three great monotheistic religions, Judaism, Islam, and Christianity— the faiths of those who share the blood of Abraham. To understand the roots of the hatred and bloodshed that still shape the relationships among the people of the region, it is useful to go back to the Holy Scriptures of ancient times. To a remarkable degree, "the will of God" is the basis for both esoteric debates and the most vicious terrorist attacks among Jews, Muslims, and Christians. God's early promises and how they must now be implemented cause conflict some forty centuries after the patriarch Abraham fathered the Arabs and the Jews in the Holy Land, almost 3,000 years since the mighty King David's rule, nearly 2,000 years after Jesus brought his revolutionary message to the same land, and 1,350 years since the personal ministry of the Prophet Muhammad was ended. Tragically for "the People of the Book" who profess to worship the same God, the scriptures are a source of more difference than agreement, inspiring more hatred than love, more war than peace.

It is obvious that the people in every nation want an end to the bloodshed and suffering. But what prevents their leaders from even going to the negotiating table? The contending parties believe in the rightness of their cause, and some of them are willing to face death rather than change their positions or even to admit the legal existence of their adversaries. They act with absolute certainty that they are carrying out the will of God. Most of the facts are not in dispute. So how could there possibly be such sharply conflicting views among people in the same region?

In simplest terms, the Arab-Israeli conflict is a struggle between two national identities for control of territory, but there are also historic, religious, strategic, political, and psychological issues that color the confrontation and impede its amicable solution. What each wants is no less than recognition, acceptance, independence, sovereignty, and territorial identity. Neither officially recognizes the other's existence, so any testing of intentions must be done through uncertain intermediaries. Both seek worldwide approval and financial, moral, and logistical support from external allies. Each side fears total destruction or complete denial by the other, this worry being fed by a history of violence and hatred, during which each tried to delegitimize the other while propounding vigorously the unique and exclusive merits of its own cause.

Opposing forces tend to become further radicalized by the arrogance of victory and the hopelessness of defeat. In any confrontation, the most abusive statements of a few are always remembered and nurtured by those who already despise each other. Insecurity breeds paranoia and this leads to the ultimate concern that prevents any move toward mutual recognition or alleviation of hatred: the threat of extinction and the loss of identity as a people.

In order for us human beings to commit ourselves personally to the inhumanity of war, we find it necessary first to dehumanize our opponents, which is in itself a violation of the beliefs of all religions. Once we characterize our adversaries as beyond the scope of God's mercy and grace, their lives lose all value. We deny personal responsibility when we plant land mines and, days or years later, a stranger to us—often a child—is crippled or killed. From a great distance, we launch bombs or missiles with almost total impunity and never want to know the number or identity of the victims.

Indeed, the present era is a challenging and disturbing time for those whose lives are shaped by religious faith based on kindness toward each other. We have been reminded that cruel and inhuman acts can be derived from distorted theological beliefs as suicide bombers take the lives of innocent human beings, draped falsely in the cloak of God's will. With horrible brutality, neighbors have massacred neighbors in Europe, Asia, and Africa. Only by listening to the voices in each nation and by examining more closely the history of the people themselves is it possible to approach a peaceful solution.

The Bible says that when the first blood was shed among his children, God asked Cain, the slayer, "Where is Abel thy brother?" And he said, "I know not. Am I my brother's keeper?" And the Lord said, "What hast thou done? The voice of thy brother's blood crieth unto me from the ground. And now art thou cursed" (Gen. 4:9–11). The blood of Abraham, God's father of the chosen, still flows in the veins of Arab, Jew, and Christian, and too much of it has been spilled in grasping for the inheritance of the revered patriarch in the Middle East. The spilled blood in the Holy Land still cries out to God—an anguished cry for peace.

Despite theological differences, all great religions share common commitments that define our ideal secular relationships. I am convinced that Christians, Muslims, Buddhists, Hindus, Jews, and others can embrace each other in a common effort to alleviate human suffering and to espouse peace. With strong leadership, determined mediation that is trusted, a balanced role between Israel and the Palestinians, and good faith, I believe we can see peace in the Middle East in our lifetime.

Camp David Accords

After four wars, despite vast human efforts, the Holy Land does not enjoy the blessings of peace. Conscious of the grave issues which face us, we place our trust in the God of our fathers, from whom we seek wisdom and guidance. As we meet here at Camp David we ask people of all faiths to pray with us that peace and justice may result from these deliberations.

—Joint Statement issued at Camp David, September 6, 1978

As a child, I was taught by my father every Sunday about the special status of the Jewish people in the eyes of God, and when I was governor of Georgia, I went with my wife and my advisor Jody Powell to the Middle East to learn more about Israel and its relations with Arab neighbors. From the time I was a young submarine officer until I became president, I observed closely the four wars fought in the Holy Land.

When I was inaugurated into the presidency, I was determined to help resolve some of the problems in the Middle East. In 1978, I decided to invite both Israel's Prime Minister Menachem Begin and President Anwar El Sadat of Egypt to Camp David so that we could be away from routine duties for a few days. In relative isolation, I intended to act as a mediator between the two national delegations. My aim was to have Israelis and Egyptians understand and accept the compatibility of many of their goals and the advantages to both nations in resolving their differences. Some important issues to be addressed were Palestinian rights, open borders between Israel and Egypt, Israel's security, and the sensitive issues concerning sovereignty over Jerusalem and access to the holy places.

Begin and Sadat were personally incompatible, and I decided after a few unpleasant encounters that they should not attempt to negotiate with each other. Instead, I worked during the ten days and nights with each separately and with their representatives separately. On several occasions, either Begin or Sadat was ready to terminate the discussions and return home, but we finally negotiated the Camp David Accords, including the framework of a peace treaty between the two nations.

It is to be remembered that the Camp David Accords, signed by Sadat and Begin and officially ratified by both governments, reconfirmed a specific commitment to honor UN Resolutions 242 and 338, which prohibit acquisition of land by force and call for Israel's withdrawal from occupied territories. Furthermore, the accords generally recognized that continuing to treat non-Jews in the occupied territories as a substratum of society is contrary to the principles of morality and justice on which democracies are founded. In addition, the framework for an Egyptian-Israeli peace agreement was signed, calling for withdrawal of Israeli armed forces from Sinai, diplomatic relations between Israel and Egypt, borders open to trade and commerce, Israeli ships guaranteed passage through the Suez Canal, and a permanent peace treaty to confirm these agreements.

I joined Sadat and Begin in signing a peace treaty between their two nations, following four wars since the nation of Israel became a reality. These leaders had committed themselves to justice for the Palestinians, the withdrawal of Israeli military and political forces from the occupied territories, and an opportunity for Israelis and all their neighbors to live in harmony with each other. The parliaments in Cairo and Jerusalem ratified the agreements, which were overwhelmingly approved by the citizens of both countries and have never been violated. Finally, during the negotiations, good personal relationships emerged between Israel's defense minister Ezer Weizman and Sadat. Furthermore, I developed a lifelong friendship with Weizman. Until his death in 2005, he remained my closest personal friend in the Holy Land and an invaluable source of information and advice.

Religion and Women's Rights

There are clear indications that progress is being made in the secular world. We have seen women chosen as leaders in nations as diverse as India, Pakistan, Indonesia, Israel, Great Britain, Ireland, Chile, Germany, the Philippines, and Nicaragua. Their support came from citizens who are predominantly Hindu, Islamic, Jewish, and Christian and include two of the three largest democracies on Earth.

It thus is ironic that although women are now welcomed into all major professions and other positions of authority, they are branded as inferior and deprived of the equal right to serve God in positions of religious leadership. The plight of abused women is made more acceptable by the mandated subservience of women by religious leaders.

There are international agreements as well as our own Holy Scriptures that guide us. Article 2 of the Universal Declaration of Human Rights states: "Everyone is entitled to all the rights and freedoms set forth in this Declaration, without distinction of any kind, such as race, color, sex, language, religion, political or other opinion, origin . . . or other status." The Holy Bible tells us, "There is neither Jew nor Greek, there is neither bond nor free, there is neither male nor female: for ye are all one in Christ Jesus" (Gal. 3:28). Every generic religious text encourages believers to respect essential human dignity, yet some selected scriptures are interpreted to justify the derogation or inferiority of women and girls, our fellow human beings.

Most Bible scholars acknowledge that the Holy Scriptures were written when male dominance prevailed in every aspect of life. Christians can find adequate scripture to justify either side in this debate, but there is one incontrovertible fact concerning the relationship between Jesus Christ and women: he never condoned sexual discrimination or the implied subservience of women. The exaltation and later reverence for Mary, as Jesus' mother, is an even more vivid indication of the special status of women in Christian theology.

Furthermore, it is clear that during the early Christian era, women served as deacons, priests, bishops, apostles, teachers, and prophets. It wasn't until the fourth century that dominant Christian leaders, all men, twisted and distorted the Holy Scriptures to perpetuate their ascendant positions within the religious hierarchy. The truth is that male religious leaders have had—and still have—an option to interpret holy teachings either to exalt or subjugate women. They have, for their own selfish ends, overwhelmingly chosen the latter. This influence does not stop at the walls of the church, mosque, synagogue, or temple. Women are prevented from playing a full and equal role in many faiths, creating an environment in which violations against women are justified.

This continuing subjugation provides the foundation or justification for much of the pervasive persecution and abuse of women throughout the world. This is in clear violation not just of the Universal Declaration of Human Rights but also of the teachings of Jesus Christ, the Apostle Paul, Moses and the prophets, Muhammad, and founders of other great religions—all of whom have called for proper and equitable treatment of all the children of God. It is time we had the courage to challenge these views and set a new course that demands equal rights for women and men, girls and boys.

Religious Fundamentalism

There is a remarkable trend toward fundamentalism in all religions—including the different denominations of Christianity as well as Hinduism, Judaism, and Islam. Increasingly, true believers are inclined to begin a process of deciding: "Since I am aligned with God, I am superior and my beliefs should prevail and anyone who disagrees with me is inherently wrong," and the next step is "inherently inferior." The ultimate step is "subhuman," and then their lives are not significant.

That tendency has created, throughout the world, intense religious conflicts. Those Christians who resist the inclination toward fundamentalism and who truly follow the nature, actions, and words of Jesus Christ should encompass people who are different from us with care, generosity, forgiveness, compassion, and unselfish love.

It is not easy to do this. It is a natural human inclination to encapsulate ourselves in a superior fashion with people who are just like us—and to assume that we are fulfilling the mandate of our lives if we confine our love to our own family or to people who are similar and compatible. Breaking through this barrier and reaching out to others is what personifies a Christian and what emulates the perfect example that Christ set for us.

Consider the goals of a person or a denomination or a country. They are all remarkably the same: a desire for peace; a need for humility, for examining one's faults and turning away from them; a commitment to human rights in the broadest sense of the words, based on a moral society concerned with the alleviation of suffering because of deprivation or hatred or hunger or physical affliction; and a willingness, even an eagerness, to share one's ideals, one's faith with others, to translate love in a person to justice.

Bibliography

Carter, Jimmy. "To the Parliament of the World's Religions." Address, The Elder's Project, Melbourne, December 3, 2009.

———. *A Plan That Will Work: We Can Have Peace in the Holy Land.* London: Simon and Schuster, 2009.

———. *Beyond the White House.* New York: Simon and Schuster, 2007.

———. *Palestine: Peace Not Apartheid.* London: Simon and Schuster, 2007.

———. *Faith and Freedom: The Christian Challenge for the World.* New York: Simon and Schuster, 2005.

———. "Camp David Accords: Jimmy Carter Reflects 25 Years Later." At Camp David Accords 25th Anniversary, Woodrow Wilson Center, Washington, D.C., September 17, 2003.

———. "Nobel Peace Lecture." Nobel Award Ceremony, Oslo, December 10, 2002.

———. *The Blood of Abraham: Inside the Middle East.* Boston: Houghton Mifflin Company, 1985.

———. *Keeping Faith: Memoirs of a President.* New York: Bantam Books, 1982.

8

Religious Intolerance and the Wounds of God

NICHOLAS WOLTERSTORFF

Nicholas Wolterstorff is the Noah Porter Professor of Philosophy Emeritus at Yale University and a former president of both the American Philosophical Association and the Society of Christian Philosophers. Wolterstorff received his PhD in philosophy from Harvard University. Prior to teaching at Yale, Wolterstorff taught for many years at Calvin College. He is the author of many books and published articles, including Until Justice and Peace Embrace *and* Justice: Rights and Wrongs.

A Cry for Justice

They spoke of their ancestral lands being expropriated. They spoke of their ancient olive orchards being bulldozed. They spoke of their houses being dynamited after the family was given one hour to remove its belongings. They spoke of humiliating searches at airports and at checkpoints scattered around their country. They cried out for justice. And they asked why no one heard their cry.

This was my first contact with Palestinians. It happened at a conference on Palestinian rights on the west side of Chicago in May 1978. About 150 Palestinians were in attendance. The reason these evils had befallen them was that they were not Jewish. Had they been Jewish, none of it would have happened.

A year or so later I went to the Middle East; I have gone several times since. I went to the West Bank—the "occupied territory," as the Palestinians call it—and saw for myself the expropriated land, usually on the crest of hills, the crest now covered with gleaming new residences exclusively for Jews, paid for in good measure by American funds. I saw where the olive orchards had once been. I saw two families standing next to the heaps of rubble that had been their homes until the middle of the night before.

I went to Israel and talked to Jews and Palestinians. I heard from the Palestinians about the many ways in which their not being Jewish resulted in their being treated as second-class citizens. I heard progressive Israelis confirm this charge. I listened to the "spiel" of the leader of the so-called Jerusalem Embassy, an American evangelical dispensationalist organization committed to supporting the Israeli cause. He seemed either unaware that there were Christians in the Middle East or utterly indifferent to what Israel's policies and America's support of those policies were doing to them. When a question was raised afterward, it turned out that he was not unaware. These were not real Christians, he said. Nor was he indifferent. The Palestinians, Christian and Muslim alike, ought to leave. God gave this land to the Jews.

What strange turns religious intolerance takes. The patent anti-Semitism that surfaced in the famous Dreyfus case in France in the late 1800s, coming after 100 years of European enlightenment, led Theodor Herzl to conclude that Jews would never be fully accepted in Europe. The solution he proposed was that Jews establish their own state somewhere—he had no strong preference as to where that should be. The Holocaust impelled many of the surviving Jews to leave their homelands after the Second World War and emigrate to the Middle East. Their arrival was instrumental in the founding of the state of Israel—from its beginning, a Jewish state. And now this same people, who had endured so much suffering over the centuries for no other reason than that they were Jewish were seizing the ancestral lands of the Palestinian inhabitants, destroying their livelihood, dynamiting their homes, for no other reason than that they were *not* Jewish. It should be added that whereas many if not most of the founders of the state of Israel understood Jewishness more in ethnic than religious terms, that is not true of the present-day population of Israel; it is even less true of the Jewish settlers in the West Bank.[1]

A story similar to the one I have just now told about the treatment by the Jewish state of Israel of those who are not Jews could be told about the treatment by Christians of those who are not Christian, by Muslims of those who are not Muslim, by Hindus of those who are not Hindu, and so forth. From all the stories that could be told, my only reason for selecting the one I did tell is that this is the one I happened to become directly acquainted with.

In this chapter I shall present a case for religious tolerance that draws on a near-forgotten theme in the Christian theological tradition: given the assumption that religious intolerance is unjust, to be intolerant of the other person's practice of her religion is to wrong God.

This theme, of injustice as the wronging of God, does not, all by itself, constitute a full case for religious tolerance; one has to add, for example, the assumption just mentioned, that religious intolerance is unjust. So before developing the theme, let me say a bit about the nature of tolerance, identify the structure that a full case for religious tolerance would have, and pinpoint the contribution to that structure of the theme that we will be discussing.

The Nature of Tolerance and the Reasons for Practicing It

Tolerance is not indifference. It is incompatible with indifference; indifference makes tolerance impossible. If I believe that all religions are as good as my own in arriving at God, in putting us in touch with the Real, or whatever, I will not tolerate your practice of your religion; I will be indifferent as to which religion you practice. Tolerance is likewise incompatible with prizing your practice of some religion different from my own—"So interesting to have a Hindu in the neighborhood." Prizing of diversity makes tolerance impossible. When J. S. Mill urged that we prize disagreement on the ground that the clash of opinions makes the attainment of truth more likely, he was not urging tolerance of disagreement.

Some of what passes for religious tolerance in the Western world today is not tolerance but the prizing of diversity; even more of it is sheer indifference. It should be added, however, that few people are indifferent to all religions; even fewer prize all diversity. The liberal Christian who relishes having a progressive Hindu in the neighborhood is likely to be upset if a right-wing teetotaling evangelical Christian moves in. His being upset by having a right-wing evangelical Christian in the neighborhood, but not by a progressive Hindu, means that the presence of the evangelical Christian offers him an opportunity to practice tolerance whereas the presence of the progressive Hindu does not.

Tolerance and intolerance of someone's practice of their religion are alike in that both presuppose that one disapproves of that practice. One tolerates their practice of their religion if one disapproves of it but nonetheless puts up with it. Or more precisely: if one voluntarily puts up with it. If one puts up with the other person's practice of his religion only because the law compels one to do so, that is not tolerance.

Disapproval varies in intensity, as it does in what it is about the other person's practice of his or her religion that bears the brunt of one's disapproval. Perhaps what annoys me is the mere fact of a seemingly rational adult believing such silly nonsense, perhaps it is the fact that he makes me feel unsure and uneasy about my own religion, perhaps it is his unwillingness to participate in our nation's wars. Tolerance and intolerance likewise vary in intensity, and they too come in many forms. Though I may not advocate your being coerced into not practicing your religion and instead practicing some other, I may shun you, ridicule you, mock you, advocate that you not be treated equally with the rest of us by the state, advocate that you have fewer civil rights than the rest of us, and the like. In not advocating that you be coerced I am putting up with your practice of your religion; in nonetheless mocking your religion I am not putting up with your practice of it. My behavior is a mixture of tolerance and intolerance.

Given that I disapprove of your practice of your religion, tolerance becomes a live option for me only if I believe that my own religion and morality permit it. Herein lies the greatest obstacle to tolerance: many religious people, down through the ages and yet today, believe that their religion obligates them not to tolerate the other. God demands that heresy be stamped out. Allah demands the elimination of the infidel. What made possible the emergence of widespread religious tolerance in the West was a deep theological alteration in the mentality of Western Christians.

And what is it that motivates people to go beyond believing that tolerance is permissible to actually tolerating the practice of a religion of which they disapprove? Sometimes what motivates them is consequentialist considerations: vivid awareness of the great personal and social evils that flow from intolerance coupled, perhaps, with the attraction of the personal and social goods that they think tolerance is likely to yield. It was the appalling bloodiness of the wars of religion in the seventeenth century that led European Christians to conclude that whatever was to be said for religious intolerance, it came at too high a price.

A consequentialist case for tolerance is unstable, however. Circumstances may change, such that the personal and social costs of intolerance no longer seem unacceptable. The more fundamental case for religious tolerance is that intolerance is unjust; it wrongs the person who is treated with intolerance. It wrongs her because qua human person she has dignity, worth. To be intolerant toward her practice of her religion is to violate that dignity, to treat her as if she did not have that worth. And that is to wrong her.

Thus a full case for religious tolerance that employed the resources of Christian scripture and the Christian theological tradition would argue, first, that Christian scripture and theology permit religious tolerance; from there it would go on to argue that human persons, one and all, have dignity, and it would conclude by arguing that religious intolerance is a violation of that dignity. In this essay I will assume that these three claims can be defended on the basis of Christian scripture and the Christian theological tradition. Rather than arguing for them here,[2] I will point to a theme in the Christian tradition concerning the import or significance of perpetrating on someone the injustice of religious intolerance—or of any other sort of injustice. To treat someone unjustly, to violate their worth or dignity, is not only to wrong them but is also to wrong God. To the best of my knowledge this theme was more prominent in the thought of John Calvin than in any other theologian from the tradition; for that reason, my development of the theme will take the form of an exposition of Calvin's theology of social injustice.[3]

The Augustinian Background

To fully understand the boldness of Calvin's thought on these matters we must be reminded of the pattern of thought on the place of suffering in human and divine life that was dominant in Calvin's predecessors. Obviously this is not the place to survey and summarize more than a thousand years of thought. So I shall confine myself to looking at Augustine, on the ground that his views on these matters both expressed a mentality that was already well entrenched in his day and that powerfully shaped the thought of his successors. The views of Augustine that I will summarize are those developed in the *Confessions* and in two other books that he wrote at approximately the same time, *Of True Religion* and *On Christian Doctrine*. Late in his life, when he wrote *The City of God*, his views had changed somewhat.[4]

In a passage from Book IV of the *Confessions*, Augustine exposes to full view the grief that overwhelmed him upon the death of a school friend from his home village of Tagaste in North Africa.

> My heart grew somber with grief, and wherever I looked I saw only death. My own country became a torment and my own home a grotesque abode of misery. All that we had done together was now a grim ordeal without him. My eyes searched everywhere for him, but he was not there to be seen. I hated all the places we had known together, because he was not in them and they could no longer whisper to me, "Here he comes!" as they would have done had he been alive but absent for a while. . . . My soul was a burden,

bruised and bleeding. It was tired of the man who carried it, but I found no place to set it down to rest. (IV, 4, 7)

The death of his friend occurred before Augustine's embrace of Christianity, the death of his mother, after. That embrace made his response to his mother's death profoundly different from that to his friend's death. "I closed her eyes," he says,

> and a great wave of sorrow surged into my heart. It would have overflowed in tears if I had not made a strong effort of will and stemmed the flow, so that the tears dried in my eyes. What a terrible struggle it was to hold them back! As she breathed her last, the boy Adeodatus [Augustine's son] began to wail aloud and only ceased his cries when we all checked him. I, too, felt that I wanted to cry like a child, but a more mature voice within me, the voice of my heart, bade me keep my sobs in check, and I remained silent. (*Confessions* IX, 12)

Augustine's struggle for self-control was not successful. He reports that after the burial, as he lay in bed thinking of his devoted mother, "The tears which I had been holding back streamed down, and I let them flow as freely as they would, making of them a pillow for my heart. On them it rested." So now, he says to God, "I make my confession. . . . Let any man read it who will. And if he finds that I sinned by weeping for my mother, even if only for a fraction of an hour, let him not mock at me . . . but weep himself, if his charity is great. Let him weep for my sins to you." The sin for which Augustine wants the person of charity to weep is not so much the sin of weeping over the death of his mother as the sin of which that weeping was a sign. "I was," he says, "guilty of too much worldly affection" (IX, 12).

How are we to understand the mentality coming to expression here? Along the following lines, I suggest. Augustine, with all the ancients, held that to be human is to be in search of happiness—*eudaimonia* in Greek, *beatitudo* in Latin. Furthermore, Augustine aligned himself with the Platonic tradition in his conviction that one's love is the fundamental determinant of one's happiness. Augustine never imagined that we human beings could root all love out of our lives.

It was as obvious to Augustine as it is to all of us that grief ensues when that which we love is destroyed or dies. In reflecting on his grief over the death of his friend, he says,

> I lived in misery like every man whose soul is tethered by the love of things that cannot last and then is agonized to lose them. . . . The grief I felt for the loss of my friend had struck so easily into my inmost heart simply because I had poured out my soul upon him, like water upon sand, loving a man who was mortal as though he were never to die. (*Confessions* IV, 6, 8)

The cure is to detach one's love from such objects and attach it to something immutable and indestructible. For Augustine, the only candidate was God. "Blessed are those who love you, O God. No one can lose you . . . unless he forsakes you" (*Confessions* IV, 9).

Augustine should not be interpreted as opposed to all enjoyment of earthly things: of food, of drink, of conversation, of visible beauty, of music. Suspicious and wary, yes; opposed, no. His point in the *Confessions* is only that we should root out all love for things whose death or destruction would cause us grief. To enjoy the taste of kiwi fruit is acceptable provided one's enjoyment is not such that should kiwi fruit prove unavailable one grieves. Though we must not love the world, we may enjoy it. Yet it must be admitted that Augustine says little or nothing by way of grounding the legitimacy of such enjoyment. In the famous passage in Book X of the *Confessions* where the things of creation speak, what they say is not "Receive us with enjoyment as God's blessing" but "Turn away from us to our maker." Further, Augustine was fond of saying that things of this world are to be used (*uti*) whereas God and God alone is to be enjoyed (*frui*).

Augustine held that the struggle to eliminate one's love for earthly things is never complete in this life; the newly oriented self never wholly wins out over the old. That introduces a new mode of grief into our lives—this a legitimate mode. We are to grieve over the repetitious reappearance of the old self—and correspondingly, to rejoice over the extent of its disappearance. And also—most extraordinary—we are to grieve over the sins of others and to rejoice over their repentance. Each of us is to be joined in a solidarity of rejoicing and grieving with all humanity—rejoicing and grieving over the *right* things, however, namely, over the religious condition of our souls.[5] I am to rejoice and grieve over the religious condition of my soul and, in the very same way, over the religious condition of your soul. This exception is important. Yet the general rule is that we are to struggle to eliminate grief from our lives by struggling to concentrate our love on God alone.

All this has been about us human beings. What Augustine says about God is the more or less obvious counterpart. God's life is through and through blissful. In God there is no emotional disturbance. Of sympathy, *Mitleiden*, with those who are suffering, God feels nothing, as also God feels no pain over the shortfall of godliness in God's errant creatures. God's state is what the Greeks called *apatheia*. God dwells eternally in blissful nonsuffering *apatheia*. Nothing that happens in the world alters God's unperturbed serenity. God is not oblivious to the world; there is in God a steady disposition of benevolence toward his human creatures. But this disposition to act benevolently proceeds on its uninterrupted successful course whatever transpires in the world.

For this understanding of God, Augustine and the other ancients had fundamentally two reasons. First, they were persuaded that God's existence is perfect existence, and they could not imagine perfect existence as anything other than undisturbed bliss through and through. And since they thought that God was changeless, they did not think that God's perfect existence was something God had to await; that would itself have been a mark of imperfection.

Second, they held that if God were to suffer and grieve, something outside God would have to bring that about in God—humanity's evildoing, for example. But God's changeless character and existence is not affected by anything outside Godself. God is the unconditioned condition of everything not identical with God. It was these two lines of thought, God's enjoying perfect existence and God's being the unconditioned condition, that led to the doctrine of the blissful apathy of God—or as it was traditionally called, God's impassibility.

Calvin on Injustice as Wronging God

Let us now turn to Calvin, beginning with a few statements by Calvin on his theology of social injustice and then tracing the path that led Calvin to his bold claims. In the course of carrying out his project of commenting on the books of the Bible, Calvin, in his *Commentary on Genesis*, was confronted with the following passage:

> I will demand an account of every man's life from his fellow man. He who sheds man's blood shall have his blood shed by man, for in the image of God man was made. (Gen. 9:5–6)

Calvin comments as follows:

> Men are indeed unworthy of God's care, if respect be had only to themselves; but since they bear the image of God engraven on them, he deems himself violated in their person. Thus, although they have nothing of their own by which they obtain the favor of God, he looks upon his own gifts in them, and is thereby excited to love and to care for them. This doctrine, however, is to be carefully observed, that no one can be injurious to his brother without wounding God himself. Were this doctrine deeply fixed in our minds, we should be much more reluctant than we are to inflict injuries.

The thought is striking. God "deems himself violated in their person," "no one can be injurious to his brother without wounding God himself." As if to make clear that speaking thus was not some fancy rhetorical flourish on his part, not to be taken seriously, Calvin adds that this doctrine "is to be carefully observed." It is to be "deeply fixed in our minds." To inflict injury on a fellow human being is to wound God. Behind and beneath the social misery of our world is the suffering of God. To pursue justice is to relieve God's suffering. If we really believed that, we would be much more reluctant than we are to inflict injuries.

A second passage worth having in hand before we trace out the path that led Calvin to these striking and provocative conclusions occurs in his *Commentary on Habakkuk*. The text on which he is commenting is this:

> The arrogant man shall not abide. His greed is as wide as Sheol, like death he never has enough. He gathers for himself all nations, and collects as his own all peoples. Shall not all these take up their taunt against him, in scoffing derision of him, and say, Woe to him who heaps up what is not his own—for how long?—and loads himself with pledges! (Hab. 2:5–6)

Commenting especially on the cry "How long?" Calvin says the following:

> This also is a dictate of nature. . . . When any one disturbs the whole world by his ambition and avarice, or everywhere commits plunder, or oppresses miserable nations—when he distresses the innocent, all cry out How long? And this cry, proceeding as it does from the feeling of nature and the dictate of justice, is at length heard by the Lord. For how comes it that all, being touched with weariness, cry out How long? except that they know that this confusion of order and equity is not to be endured? And this feeling, is it not implanted in us by the Lord? It is then the same as though God heard himself, when he hears the cries and groanings of those who cannot bear injustice.

Again the thought is striking. The cries of the victims of injustice are the cry of God. The lament of the victims as they cry out "How long?" is God giving voice to God's own lament.

Calvin's Anti-Augustinian Position on Enjoyment and Grief

What was the line of thought that led Calvin to such an extraordinarily bold theology of social injustice? A good place to begin is with his opposition to the Augustinian position on the place of grief in human life, namely, that we are to pursue the elimination of all grief by struggling to love God and God alone, with the exception that one is to grieve over one's own failure and that of one's fellows to accomplish this project. "Among the Christians," says Calvin, "there are also new Stoics, who count it depraved not only to groan and weep but also to be sad and care ridden" (*Institutes* III, viii, 9). Calvin affirms that on this they are quite wrong.

> [Our goal] is not to be utterly stupefied and to be deprived of all feeling of pain. Our ideal is not that of what the Stoics of old foolishly described [as] "the great-souled man," one who, having cast off all human qualities, was affected equally by adversity and prosperity, by sad times and happy ones—nay, who like a stone was not affected at all. (*Institutes* III, viii, 9)

One reason for repudiating the Stoic ideal is that it paints "a likeness of forbearance that has never been found among men, and can never be realized" (*Institutes* III, viii, 9). In setting before us this impossible ideal it distracts us from the attitude toward suffering that we ought in fact to cultivate.

> Thus afflicted by disease, we shall both groan and be uneasy and pant after health, thus pressed by poverty, we shall be pricked by the arrows of care and sorrow, thus we shall be smitten by the pain of disgrace, contempt, injustice, thus at the funerals of our dear ones we shall weep the tears that are owed to our nature. (*Institutes* III, viii, 10)

Calvin had a second reason for rejecting the Stoic ideal.

> Our Lord and Master has condemned [it] not only by his word, but also by his example. For he groaned and wept both over his own and others' misfortunes. And he taught his disciples in the same way. "The world," he says, "will rejoice, but you will be sorrowful and will weep" (John 16:20). And that no one might turn it into a vice he openly proclaimed, "Blessed are those who mourn" (Matt. 5:4). No wonder! For if all weeping is condemned, what shall we judge concerning the Lord himself, from whose body tears of blood trickled down (Luke 22:44)? If all fear is branded as unbelief, how shall we account for that dread with which, we read, he was heavily stricken (Matt 26:37, Mark 14:33)? If all sadness displeases us how will it please us that he confesses his soul "sorrowful even to death"(Matt. 26:38)? (*Institutes* III, viii, 9)

The discipline that we are to undertake in the face of sickness, death, poverty, disgrace, indignity, and injustice is not the discipline of no longer grieving over these, of becoming indifferent. Following the example of Christ, we are to let our God-given nature take its course, paying to justice the honor of grieving upon being treated unjustly, paying to life the honor of grieving upon the death of those we love. We are to let our wounds bleed, our eyes tear. The discipline we are to undertake is the discipline of becoming patient in suffering. I shall have something to say shortly about the nature of Calvinist patience and why Calvin thinks it appropriate.

Calvin's opposition to Stoicism and Augustinianism, then, was grounded in his conviction that they set for us an impossible and inappropriate ideal, contrary to our created nature, thus distracting us from the achievable and appropriate ideal of patience in suffering. But it is easy to see that his attitude toward grief also fits in with, and is supported by, his attitude toward enjoyment of the things of this world.

In a remarkable passage in the *Institutes* (III, x, 2) Calvin argues that of grasses, trees, and fruits we should appreciate not only their utility as nourishment but their beauty of appearance and pleasantness of odor and taste, of clothes we should appreciate not only their utility for keeping us warm but their comeliness, and of wine and oil we should appreciate not only that they are useful but that wine gladdens the heart and oil makes one's face shine. As if with his eye on Augustine's use/enjoyment distinction, he asks rhetorically whether God did "not, in short, render many things attractive to us, apart from their necessary use?" He answers that God did. So let this "be our principle, that the use of God's gifts is not wrongly directed when it is referred to that end to which the Author himself created and destined them for us, since he created them for our good, not for our ruin."

Augustine saw the things of the world almost exclusively as the works of God; hence he urges us to look away from them to their maker. They are to be seen as benefit only so far as they are useful for our continued existence and for our devotion to God. Pervasive in Calvin, by contrast, is the insistence that we are to see the things of the world not only as God's works but also as God's *gifts* to us, gifts in their utility as well as in their being enjoyable. "This life," says Calvin, "however crammed with infinite miseries it may be, is still rightly to be counted among those blessings of God which are not to be spurned. Therefore, if we recognize in it no divine benefit, we are already guilty of grave ingratitude toward God himself"(*Institutes* III, ix, 3).

One cannot overemphasize the pervasiveness of this theme in Calvin of the world as God's gift to us for use and enjoyment and of the counterpart theme of the propriety of gratitude. Never, in this regard, was there a more sacramental theologian than Calvin, one more imbued with the sense that in world, history, and self, we meet God. "Away, then, with that inhuman philosophy which, while conceding only a necessary use of creatures, not only malignantly deprives us of the lawful fruit of God's beneficence but cannot be practiced unless it rob a man of all his senses and degrade him to a block" (*Institutes* III, x, 3).

On Bearing the Image of God

I said that to understand Calvin's theology of social injustice and to appreciate its boldness we must discern his anti-Stoical and anti-Augustinian view as to the place of grief in human existence, and, correspondingly, his view as to the place of enjoyment. One does not say to the person suffering injustice that she should not care about justice so much that she grieves over its violation—that she should love only God. To the contrary, one encourages grief. But there is a second component as well in the path that led Calvin to his radical conclusions, namely, his thoughts on the image of God in human beings.

" 'So man was created in the image of God,' in him the Creator himself willed that his own glory be seen as in a mirror" (*Institutes* II, xii, 6). What Calvin means, of course, and what he says in his Latin, is not that male human beings were created in God's image but that male and female human beings alike were created in the image of God. "God looks upon Himself, as one might say, and beholds himself in men as in a mirror."[6] "God's children are pleasing and lovable to him, since he sees in them the marks and features of his own countenance. . . . Whenever God contemplates his own face, he both rightly loves it and holds it in honor." (*Institutes* III, xvii, 5).

God beholds what God has made. God observes that human beings are icons of Godself. God observes that they mirror God, that they image God, that they are likenesses of God. In this God delights. And this evokes God's love for them. God delights in all God's works. But human beings are singled out from other earthlings in that, in them, God finds God's perfections most clearly mirrored back to Godself.

A consequence of the fact that each human being mirrors God is that we as human beings exist in profound unity with each other: to see another human being is to see another creature who delights God by mirroring God. No more profound kinship among God's creatures can exist than this. Furthermore, each of us mirrors God in the same respects—though, as we shall see shortly, some do so more, some less. Thereby we also, in a derivative way, resemble each other. One could say that we mirror each other. In looking at you and me, God finds Godself mirrored. Accordingly, in my looking at you, I, too, discern, once my eyes have been opened, that you mirror God—and that you mirror me. I discern myself as in a mirror. I discern a family likeness. As Calvin puts it,

> We cannot but behold, as in a mirror, our own face in those who are poor and despised . . . though they are utter strangers to us. Even in dealing with a Moor or a Barbarian, from the very fact of his being a man, he carries about with him a looking-glass in which we can see that he is our brother and our neighbour.[7]

There were those who argued that the image of God in us can be, and in some cases has been, eliminated. Calvin disagreed.

Should anyone object, that this divine image has been obliterated, the solution is easy; first, there yet exists some remnant of it, so that man is possessed of no small dignity; and secondly, the Celestial Creator himself, however corrupted man may be, still keeps in view the end of his original creation; and according to his example, we ought to consider for what end he created men, and what excellence he has bestowed upon them above the rest of living things. (*Commentary on Genesis*, 9:6)

There is nothing that can happen to a human being, and nothing a human being can do, to bring it about that the image of God in that person is obliterated. Though a human being's mirroring of God can be painfully distorted, blurred, and diminished, it cannot be eliminated.

Naturally we want to know wherein lies our iconicity. In what respects do we mirror God back to Godself and then to each other? Calvin offers two rules of thumb for answering this question. First, our iconicity is to be discerned in what differentiates us from other earthlings: "The likeness of God extends to the whole excellence by which man's nature towers over all the kinds of living creatures" (*Institutes* I, xv, 4). Second, keeping in mind that our likeness to God can be increased and diminished, we must employ the rule that the fundamental goal of our human existence is to become as like unto God as possible—or to use the language of the Eastern Orthodox Church, to become as "divinized" as possible. And what would a human being's full likeness to God be like? We apprehend the answer to that question in Jesus Christ, who was "the express image of the Father."

When we follow these two rules of thumb, looking at our uniqueness and looking at Jesus Christ, one thing we learn is that those of us who are capable of functioning as persons are like God in being capable of understanding; and the more our understanding expands—especially our understanding of God—the more we become like God. We also learn that those of us who are capable of functioning as persons are like God in being capable of governing our affections and thereby our actions; and the more upright our heart is, the more like God we are. For Calvin, these two are the principal resemblances. But there are others as well. Our (mandated) governance of creation is a mirroring of God's governance, and our formation of communities is a mirroring of that perfect community which is the Trinity. No doubt some of us today would wish to add other themes—for example, that our creativity is a mirroring of God's creativity.

Love, Justice, and the Image of God

Calvin grounds the claims of love and justice in this phenomenon of our mirroring God. The standard picture of Calvin is that obligation, duty, responsibility, and the call to obedience loom large in his thought; and indeed they do. Yet for Calvin there is something deeper than these. All of us in our daily lives are confronted with other human beings. We find ourselves in the presence of an "other" who, by virtue of being an icon of God, makes claims on us. Moral reflection can begin either from the responsibility of the agent toward the other or from the moral claims of the other on the agent. The degree to which Calvin begins from the moral claims of the other is striking. The pattern is displayed with great insistence in this passage:

> The Lord commands all men without exception "to do good." Yet the great part of them are most unworthy if they be judged by their own merit. But here Scripture helps in the best way when it teaches that we are not to consider what men merit of themselves but to look upon the image of God in all men, to which we owe all honor and love. . . . Therefore whatever man you meet who needs your aid, you have no reason to refuse to help him. You say, "He is a stranger"; but the Lord has given him a mark that ought to be familiar to you, by virtue of the fact that he forbids you to despise your own flesh. You say, "He is contemptible and worthless"; but the Lord shows him to be one to whom he has deigned to give the beauty of his image. You say that you owe nothing for any service of his; but God, as it were, has put him in his own place in order that you may recognize toward him the many and great benefits with which God has bound you to him. You say that he does not deserve even your least effort for his sake; but the image of God, which recommends him to you, is worthy of your giving yourself and all your possessions. Now if he has not only deserved no good at your hand, but has also provoked you by unjust acts and curses, not even this is just reason why you should cease to embrace him in love and to perform the duties of love on his behalf. You say, "He has deserved something far different of me." Yet what has the Lord deserved? . . . It is that we remember not to consider men's evil intention but to look upon the image of God in them, which cancels and effaces their transgressions, and with its beauty and dignity allures us to love and embrace them. (*Institutes* III, vii, 6; translation slightly altered)

Several things in this passage are striking, in addition to the insistent grounding of the claims of love and justice in our ineradicable iconicity. One is Calvin's adamant insistence that, given that it is our iconicity that grounds these claims, the virtue or lack of virtue in the other person is irrelevant. Always the perpetrators of injustice want it otherwise. If the so-called blacks in South Africa just behaved, they would be given a voice in their governance.

If the Palestinians just behaved, the ending of the occupation of their land could be considered.

But how exactly does the fact that each of us is an image of God ground our claim to love and justice from our fellows? One would expect Calvin to say that it is the great *dignity* that supervenes on being an image of God that grounds the claim of the "other" on me. This dignity calls for respect; and there is no other way of showing the appropriate respect than by love and justice. Calvin does speak this way now and then. But his emphasis falls elsewhere. It falls, for one thing, on the fact that the other has claims on my love and justice because she and I are kinfolk in the deepest possible way, namely, by virtue of jointly imaging God. This comes out vividly in a passage from his *Commentary on Isaiah*. The passage on which he is commenting is this:

> Is not this the fast that I choose, to loose the bonds of injustice, to undo the thongs of the yoke, to let the oppressed go free, and to break every yoke? Is it not to share your bread with the hungry and bring the homeless poor into your house, when you see the naked, to cover them, and not to hide yourself from your own flesh? (Isa. 58:6–7)

Calvin's comment runs (in part) as follows (emphasis added):

> It is not enough to *abstain* from acts of injustice, if you refuse your assistance to the needy. . . . By commanding them to "break bread to the hungry," God intended to take away every excuse from covetous and greedy men, who allege that they have a right to keep possession of that which is their own. . . . And indeed, this is the dictate of common sense, that the hungry are deprived of their just right, if their hunger is not relieved. . . . At length he concludes—"and that you hide not yourself from your own flesh." Here we ought to observe the term "flesh," by which he means all men universally, not one of whom we can behold, without seeing, as in a mirror, "our own flesh." It is therefore a proof of the greatest inhumanity, to despise those in whom we are constrained to recognize our own likeness. (233–234)

In short, to fail to treat one's fellow human beings with love and justice is to fail in the duties of kinship and thereby to act with "the greatest inhumanity."

Injustice as Wronging God

There is a second way in which the iconicity of the other human being grounds her claim on me to love and justice, in addition to our being kin; it is toward this other way that our discussion has been moving. "God himself, looking on human beings as formed in his own image, regards them with such love and honor that he himself feels wounded and outraged in the persons of those who are the victims of human cruelty and wickedness."[8]

For Calvin, the demands of love and justice lie not first of all in the *will* of God, which is what much of the Christian tradition has held, nor in the *reason* of God, which is what most of the rest of the tradition has held. They lie in God's sorrow and in God's joy, in God's suffering and in God's delight. If I abuse something that you have made and that you love, then, at its deepest, what has gone wrong is not that I have violated *your* command not to abuse that object of your affection—though you may indeed have issued such a command, in which case I will have disobeyed it. What has gone wrong lies first in my having caused you sorrow by riding roughshod over your affections. The demands of love and justice are rooted, so Calvin suggests, in what Abraham Heschel in his book on the Hebrew prophets called the *pathos* of God.[9] To treat unjustly one of these human earthlings in whom God delights is to bring sorrow to God. To wound God's beloved is to wound God. The demands of justice are grounded in the fact that to commit injustice is to inflict suffering on God. They are grounded in the vulnerability of God's love for us, images of God. God is not *apathê*.

Though I do not propose developing it here, it is worth noting that this theme of the wounding of God is also given a specifically Christological and sacramental development in Calvin. At one point in his discussion of the Eucharist he says,

> We shall benefit very much from the sacrament if this thought is impressed and engraved upon our minds, that none of the brethren can be injured, despised, rejected, abused, or in any way offended by us, without at the same time injuring, despising, abusing Christ by the wrongs we do; . . . that we cannot love Christ without loving him in the brethren. (*Institutes* IV, xvii, 38)

Calvinist Patience

Before concluding, we must return to Calvin's doctrine of patience. Recall that Augustine said that we should struggle to withdraw all love for things whose death or destruction would cause us grief. Calvin's position was profoundly different. We should not try to alter our created nature; we should honor it. To indignity, death, injustice, and a multitude of other evils in this life, grief is not only the normal but the appropriate response. The discipline to be undertaken is not that of withdrawing all our attachments but that of being patient in our suffering. Patient grief is to be our stance.

When confronted with the prospect of the occurrence of some event likely to cause one grief, one can pursue the Augustinian course of struggling to alter one's nature so that, when the event occurs, one feels no grief. But one can also pursue the opposite course of trying to avert the occurrence of the event. Did Calvin, in commending patience, mean to recommend that we also renounce this latter course? Did he mean to say that we should no more seek to change the world than to change ourselves—that we should allow the threatening episodes to flow over us? Should we simply put up with religious intolerance, for example? Is Calvinist patience passive acceptance?

The suggestion lacks even initial plausibility. The Calvinist movement as a whole was characterized by its dynamic restlessness, this to be traced in good measure to Calvin himself—not only to his words but also to his actions in Geneva. It's true that when it came to the political realm, Calvin insisted that those not in positions of political authority were not to revolt. But not revolting is very different from passively accepting, as we all know and as the members of the Geneva city council experienced, to their dismay, in their conflicts with Calvin.

Calvin vigorously and unflinchingly denounced corruption in the church, tyranny in the polity, and inequity in the economy. And though it would not be inconsistent to denounce bishops, tyrants, and bosses while yet counseling passive acceptance of their orders and actions, Calvin regularly took the next steps of urging resistance to evil and struggle for reform and of himself practicing what he preached. Although not recommending revolt even as a last resort, in a famous passage from his *Commentary on Daniel*, Calvin unmistakably recommends defiant disobedience.

> Earthly princes lay aside all their power when they rise against God and are unworthy of being reckoned in the number of mankind. We ought rather strictly to defy them than to obey them whenever they are so restive and wish to spoil God of his rights and, as it were, to seize upon his throne and draw him down from heaven. (Dan. 6:22)

Given the situation depicted in the book of Daniel, one might wonder whether Calvin here has his eye exclusively on infringements on the free exercise of one's religion. When we are denied freedom of worship, we must disobey. But in his discussion of patience in the *Institutes*, Calvin puts the struggle for justice and the struggle for free exercise of religion on the same footing. We are called to both, and both may yield suffering and the honor of the martyr.

> To suffer persecution for righteousness' sake is a singular comfort. For it ought to occur to us how much honor God bestows upon us in thus furnishing us with the special badge of his soldiery. I say that not only they who labor for the defense of the gospel but they who in any way maintain the cause of righteousness suffer persecution for righteousness. (*Institutes* III, viii, 7)

In short, Calvinist patience is not the patience of passive acceptance but the patience of one who suffers as she struggles against the world's evils. It is the paradoxical unstable combination of patiently grieving over the deprivation and injustice that befalls us while struggling to alleviate that deprivation and undo that injustice.

In Conclusion

In this chapter I have taken for granted that intolerance toward a person's practice of his or her religion is an affront to that person's dignity and therefore unjust. Rather than employing the resources of Christian scripture and the Christian theological tradition in support of that claim, I have called attention to a theme in the tradition concerning the significance of the injustice of religious intolerance—and of any other form of injustice. To perpetrate the injustice of religious intolerance on a fellow human being is to wrong God; the cries of those who are persecuted or demeaned on account of their religion are giving voice to God's suffering.

The theme we have explored, of injustice as the wronging of God, does not by any means exhaust the significance of injustice. My discussion has assumed that injustice also, for example, bears the significance of being a violation of the victim's human dignity; and along the way Calvin has suggested that it bears the significance of being abuse of one's kin. The theme we have explored is one that is not prominent in the Christian theological tradition as a whole; its lack of prominence was one of my reasons for presenting it. Though not prominent in the tradition as a whole, it was prominent in the thought of John Calvin. It is for that reason that my presentation of the theme has taken the form of expounding Calvin.

No matter how much one may dislike the religion of the other person, she nonetheless bears the image of God and is on that account beloved of God. To treat her with intolerance is to wrong her. To wrong her is to wrong God. If we believed this, and believed it firmly, we would be much more reluctant than we are to treat someone with intolerance. And it makes no difference whether our intolerance is grounded in our religion or in something else.

Notes

1. Mark Braverman, himself Jewish, argues in his courageous book *Fatal Embrace* (Austin, TX: Synergy Books, 2010) that the root cause of Israel's discriminatory treatment of those who are not Jewish within the state of Israel and within the occupied territory is the conviction of Jewish exceptionalism that is lodged deep in the mentality of religious and nonreligious Jews alike.

2. I have done that in my essay "Do Christians Have Good Reasons for Supporting Liberal Democracy?" *The Modern Schoolman* LXXVIII (January–March 2001): 229–248.

3. What follows in this essay is substantially the same as my essay "The Wounds of God: Calvin's Theology of Social Injustice," *The Reformed Journal* 37, no. 6 (June 1987): 14–22.

4. On the change, see chapter 8 of my book *Justice: Rights and Wrongs* (Princeton, NJ: Princeton University Press, 2008).

5. In *The City of God*, Augustine holds that it is also appropriate to grieve over the misfortunes that befall ourselves and our fellows, the implication being that we are not to aim to achieve, here in this present life, full and complete happiness. As we shall see, Calvin is basically in agreement with late Augustine on this point.

6. From Calvin's sermon on Job 10:7, quoted in T. F. Torrance, *Calvin's Doctrine of Man* (Grand Rapids, MI: Wm. B. Eerdmans Publishing Company, 1957), 39.

7. From Calvin's sermon on Gal. 6:9–11, quoted in R. S. Wallace, *Calvin's Doctrine of the Christian Life* (Edinburgh and London: Oliver and Boyd, 1959), 150.

8. Ibid., 149, summarizing various passages from Calvin.

9. A. J. Heschel, *The Prophets* (New York: Harper and Row, 1962).

9

Caring for the "Other" as One of "Us": Religious Freedom for All

ZIYA MERAL

Ziya Meral is a Turkish Christian writer and researcher and a PhD candidate in political science at the University of Cambridge. He was trained as a sociologist at the London School of Economics and as a theologian at the London School of Theology, Brunel University. Meral has an extensive research and human rights advocacy record across the Middle East on religion and minority issues, and he regularly publishes academic essays and opinion editorials and comments in British and international media on Middle East and Turkish politics.

Introduction

The young man who was speaking boldly about standing for freedom, democracy, and a better future for his country had all of a sudden grown quiet and looked troubled. His posture, which had previously reflected the youthful courage and confidence captured in the iconic poster of Che Guevara hanging on the wall behind him, was now that of a vulnerable person, haunted by memories of his past and fears of tomorrow.

His posture changed as soon as I asked him about his detention. He had been arrested for converting from Islam to Christianity. He was never taken to a judge, and no formal charges were ever brought against him, but one night state security officers had broken into his home, forced him into a car, and driven him to a notorious prison in the desert. That night he was beaten, stripped naked, humiliated, insulted, and electrocuted in his genitals. He was kept in a dark cell for months with no window and with barely space enough to take a few steps. Like his arrest, his ordeal came to an abrupt end with no explanation.

With teary eyes, he said to me, "They thought that they broke me, but they were wrong! I am still here!" Although his body took months to recover, he maintained his public Christian stance. However, his ordeal left him with a suffering soul and deep wounds that have not healed. He still wakes regularly in the early hours of the morning, covered in sweat and strained with anxiety, reliving that dreadful night. Since then, he has not succeeded in developing friendships or romantic relations. He joked, "Who wants to buy damaged goods?" He continues to live in the same Middle Eastern country, in order to say, "I am still here!" to his torturers. I left him alone in his office with Che and walked the crowded, dusty streets with tears of rage streaming down my cheeks.

As a human rights researcher, I document and analyze the suffering of human beings. For me, intolerance is neither impersonal nor abstract. It has the real faces and names of individuals who suffer rape, beatings, indefinite detention, degrading treatment, forced migration, and denial of access to justice, health, education, employment, and housing simply because they believe in another religion or believe in none at all.

The cases that I personally encounter in the countries I monitor are only a small portion of a growing problem. Denial of religious freedom and persecution on the basis of religious affiliation are among the most widespread human rights abuses in the world today. Yet religious freedom is also one of the most overlooked and understudied aspects of human rights, even though freedom of thought, conscience, and belief are fundamental rights enshrined in virtually every human rights covenant.

There are multiple reasons for this. First of all, states, media, and even human rights organizations shun religious freedom issues lest the organization be branded as opposed to or supportive of a particular religion. In so doing, they fail to protect individuals from harm and they discourage human flourishing. Second, there is often ignorance among leaders about what religion is, why and how religious persecution happens, and why religious freedom matters. For most of the educated elite in Europe and North America, religion is simply a matter of private belief, and it does not have any place in the public square today. However, the vast majority of people, regardless of their education or income levels, hold religious beliefs that influence every aspect of their lives. Religious persecution, then, violates not just their private lives but also their socioeconomic and political lives as well.

If this ignorance about religious freedom is a blind spot for those who do not engage the issue, there is a growing blind spot for those of us who *do* engage the issue. Unless we address this blind spot, we contradict both the spirit behind human rights and our aims of advancing religious freedom.

The Blind Spot

The development of international human rights law is one of the few good things that came out of some of the darkest episodes of the twentieth century. Although controversies over cultural assumptions and lack of enforcement have continued, developing judicial and diplomatic mechanisms have enabled us to challenge powerful rulers and abusive regimes. International bodies, media, and nongovernmental organizations (NGOs) likewise provide us with platforms to raise our voices and take actions to protect individuals and minorities. We now have a never-ending flow of information available to us in the comfort of our homes that helps us learn what is happening around the world. Sovereign rulers can no longer simply hide the truth. Sooner or later, the truth comes out.

Yet few people realize that both the advancement and the implementation of human rights depend on the pressure we put on our own governments. Protests, votes, NGOs, and informal networks force them to take action. This is both a blessing and a curse. It is a blessing because it empowers us and serves as accountability to the powerful. It is a curse because if we do not do something about certain injustices, no one will.

Since no human being or community can address every ill in the world, we must choose issues that are close to our hearts and lives. I focus on human rights issues only in the Middle East and North Africa, not because I do not care about other regions or people but because, given my limitations, this is all I can do. Focusing on an area, a theme, or a concern enables one to advance that cause much more effectively than if one were to chase after every issue.

The vast majority of NGOs and campaigns that focus on religious freedom come out of faith groups. These groups, by and large, promote religious freedom only for believers of their religion. Christians set up organizations that document and raise awareness for the plight of their fellow believers. The Baha'i community does so for the Baha'is, Jewish groups for Jewish concerns, and Muslim groups for Muslims.

This is all too human. As a Christian, I feel a familial burden for the suffering of Christians. And if Christians in nonpersecuted settings do not work to alleviate the suffering of their fellow believers in other parts of the world, no one else will; if they ignore the fate of the ones suffering, they let down their own faith family.

However, this sort of sectarian and selective kindness is ultimately contrary to the spirit of human rights. In our efforts to defend ourselves, we ignore those who are "different" who face similar human rights abuses. Human rights advocacy becomes a game where everyone cheers only for their own team. The competition of this "game" often involves proving who suffers the most and is, therefore, most deserving of protection and special privileges.

It is ultimately not right to highlight the suffering of one particular group without also showing concern for groups who suffer a similar fate. By playing only for "our side," we unwittingly condemn other communities, and with our silence we condone their mistreatment. Thus, unknowingly, we are telling the world that only *our* community is worthy of protection and that we do not really care about the rights of others. Without realizing it, we undermine the very basis of human rights by selectively promoting religious freedom only for our fellow believers.

Three Reasons: Pragmatic, Ethical, and Theological

We *cannot* continue to speak only for fellow believers of our religion. There are three main reasons for this.

The first reason is pragmatic: ignoring the afflictions of others fails to address the root causes of persecution. In Iran, for example, the fate of Muslims who convert to the Christian faith is a serious human rights concern. Converts face intimidation, detention, physical abuse, and threats of capital punishment unless they return to Islam. The number of Christians from Muslim backgrounds in Iran has grown from a few hundred thirty years ago to at least 20,000 today. This has led to more persecution and, in return, more campaigns against Iran by Christians in the West.

Yet, in the same land, there are at least 300,000 Baha'is who suffer executions, lengthy jail terms, severe intimidation, and denial of access to education, justice, and economic opportunities. Thanks to the unceasing efforts of the international Baha'i community, the world has come to know about the heart-wrenching situation of Iranian Baha'is. Without these efforts, nothing would have been done to prevent the extinction of Baha'is in Iran.

However, the fate of Baha'is and the fate of Christian converts from Islam are linked. Both groups are seen as apostates, heretics, and subversives by the regime and clerics. They also share this fate with populations of other non-Muslims, such as Armenians, Assyrians, and non-Shiite Muslim groups, especially Sunni Arabs.

Iran's theo-political regime uses religion to legitimize its nation-making narrative. For them, to be an Iranian is to be Muslim—indeed, a Shiite Muslim, but not just any Shiite Muslim, a Shiite Muslim in agreement with the political, social, and religious vision of Ayatollah Khomeini. Whoever does not fit into this category is a threat and has to be assimilated or forced into submission.

Currently, Iranian jails are full of people from all of these "outside" groups. In a single prison cell, one can find a Baha'i, a Christian, and a Sunni. The reason they are there is the same. Raising only the case of the Christian, then, will not stop the threats to liberty. Unless the international community stands up and speaks for everybody's freedom, Iranian jails will continue to be filled with a host of religious believers.

Iran, of course, is not unique. What is true of Iran is true of all other countries where religious freedom is in jeopardy. Ultimately, unless faith-based groups unite and speak for people of other faiths, they will not be able to protect their own religious family. Christians will be secure and free to practice their faith in the Middle East only when their Jewish, Baha'i, and Muslim neighbors are free to do so as well. Christians cannot overlook the suffering of others, as this suffering is inherently interlinked with their own.

The second reason we cannot continue to speak only for our own religion is ethical: one should not ignore the sufferings of the "other." Imagine standing outside an Iranian prison cell that is full of people of all creeds, imprisoned for unjust reasons. Imagine that you have the power to release these prisoners. Suppose that every name you call out will be free. Which names would you call? Only those followers of your religion? Would you be morally praiseworthy if you wished for the release only for those of your kind?

Caring and working only for the rights of people who share our religious beliefs leaves others behind. If the core of human rights advocacy is the ethical imperative to prevent unjust suffering, then we cannot focus exclusively on our own.

Although we cannot alleviate every pain in the world, our limitations do not prevent us from caring for those who are not one of "us." It adds no additional burden to include the suffering of members of other groups to our cares and concerns. We simply cannot say, "Although we are sad to hear about the imprisonment of followers of other religions in a country where we work on behalf of our fellow believers, we cannot raise their concerns; however, our hearts are with them."

Ignoring the suffering of believers of other religions raises serious questions about the moral quality of our attitudes and work. This attitude turns our most noble efforts into mere partisanship. While professing "universal" human rights, we are actually far from them.

The third reason we cannot overlook the suffering of people who do not share our beliefs is theological. When Jesus was asked what the greatest commandment was, he answered, "You shall love the Lord your God with all your heart, and with all your soul, and with all your mind. This is the great and first commandment. And a second is like it. You shall love your neighbor as yourself. On these two commandments depend all the law and the prophets" (Matt. 22:37–40). According to Jesus, these two commandments are the cornerstone of all that we believe and have to live by. Clearly, for him, the love of God and personal dedication to follow his precepts is inseparable from the love of one's neighbor. In fact, one cannot claim to love God *without* loving his or her neighbor. The vast majority of the teachings of Christ focus on loving and restoring the dignity of those whom the religious shun. In eating with adulterers and tax collectors and in praising the goodness found in despised religious groups such as the Sadducees, Christ offered an example for his followers to see others as being equally as worthy of the love and blessings of God.

Christ identifies himself with whoever is unjustly excluded, mistreated, and left to suffer—not simply with those who are Christian. He goes further when he says that if any good thing is done for those who are suffering or in jail, it is as if it is done for him; and those who do not run to help the suffering are failing to run to help Christ (Matt. 25:31–46).

My faith in Christ challenges my natural inclination to esteem my own religion while denigrating the religion of others. My faith impels me to run to help those in dire situations, no matter their religious affiliation; their personal values and religious beliefs are irrelevant. They are my neighbors; without loving them as I love myself, I cannot claim to love God.

Loving Your Neighbor in the Twenty-First Century

Sadly, the blind spot under discussion is not limited to faith-based advocacy groups. The tendency to care only for our own at the expense of others lurks within all of us. It blinds even the most sensitive and good-hearted individuals. When I think about our tendency to selectively respond to those suffering from deprivation of religious liberty, three young women come to mind.

The first is a young Muslim woman in Turkey. I saw deep humiliation in her eyes as she was forced to remove her headscarf before entering a university campus. It broke my heart to see her forced to sacrifice her values because the rulers of the land had decided that she was not permitted to wear a visible symbol of her religious beliefs.

The second is a young woman in Iran. I watched her panic and cry for help as she was forced into a car by members of the quasi-religious militia Basij in Tehran. Her "crime" was that her headscarf, which is compulsory, revealed more hair than it should. I could not bear to see her abused and disrespected by bearded men, keen to stamp their brand of religion on her.

The third is a young woman in a Middle Eastern country. Her pastor told me that she was once a lively and bubbly Christian who played on her local church's worship team. Her spark was gone now. For her "crime" of leaving Islam for Christianity, a group of brutal men had violated her.

I get various reactions to these stories depending on the background of the listener. When I tell the first story of the young Muslim woman in Turkey to secular Turks, some of them explain that she deserved that treatment because she opposed the "secular" legacy of the founder of the Turkish republic. When I tell the story of the young woman in Iran, some of my Muslim friends tell me that although they do not condone such treatment, a woman in a Muslim society has to obey the rules. When I tell the story of the young woman in the Middle East, some of my European friends comment that this proves how oppressive Muslims are, and, therefore, European countries should ban minarets and take a harsher stance against Islam.

While some people claim that people who are *not* like them should face limitations, they get furious when they themselves or people like them face limitations; at that point, they demand that human rights be upheld. Yet a suffering Muslim is no different than an atheist or a Christian in the eyes of God. Nor is each different in the eyes of international human rights law. Injustices perpetuated against any of them can never be legitimized. Because *every* human being has the right to freedom of religion, *every* human being should live free from the fear of persecution—not just those who share my beliefs. Either all of us have these rights or none of us do.

We are dominated by voices trying to convince us that there are inherent and unavoidable clashes between different civilizations, different religions. The Internet, newspapers, and television overflow with messages that say that those who are not from our countries or religion or continent are evil and should be feared, excluded, and limited—maybe even conquered and vanquished.

The world desperately needs to hear the opposite message from those of us who hold very particular religious beliefs. We have to demonstrate and declare boldly that believing Christians, Muslims, Jews, and Baha'is should pray for and run to the aid of suffering members of other religious families and that, ultimately, we share a deep and common humanity with each other that can never—and should never—be done away with.

Conclusion

I must confess one thing. In the process of trying to draw attention to a blind spot that impairs those who are engaged in promoting religious liberty, I have not painted a complete picture. The beautiful truth is that the world is full of people who can and do regularly go beyond their religious allegiances and share the pain of others.

In 2007, the world was shaken by the brutal murders of two Turkish and one German Christian in Turkey. Five young men tied the Christians— Necati, Ugur, and Tilman—to chairs and tortured them for hours before slitting their throats. According to their own statements, the accused murderers (who were caught by the police at the scene of the crime) were trying to "get information" about the "secret aims and plans" of Christians to "destroy Turkey by converting Muslims."

These murders were only the latest in a growing number of attacks on non-Muslims in Turkey. The Turkish state offered dubious apologies and feeble efforts to stem this rising tide of violence. Public voices repeated that "they were sorry" and that "they do not condone violence." However, the public voices also said, "But missionaries are not innocent." To each expression of condolence was attached a "but" that granted some form of legitimacy to the violence against non-Muslims.

Although proselytizing is a violation of neither Turkish nor international human rights law, the Turkish state, to this day, sees the activities of non-Muslims as a security threat. Schoolchildren read about the "vicious historical agendas" of "missionaries" in their textbooks, which causes a wide-ranging negative attitude toward non-Muslims. For the fewer than 100,000 Christians left in this country of more than seventy million people, such attitudes elicit serious worries for their lives and the future of their dwindling communities.

This particular incident was personally difficult for me. One of the murdered Turks and his young family were longtime friends of mine from my home church in Izmir, Turkey. I still feel the pain I felt when I read detailed medical reports of their torture, and I endured long and restless nights afterward.

In the middle of this dark moment in my life, a simple email I received made all the difference. It was an email from a dear friend, Mustafa Akyol, a Muslim journalist and writer. Mustafa not only has written boldly against the persecution of non-Muslims, but, when the entire country seemed to be under a xenophobic neurosis, he even defended the right of people to convert to another religion and promote their own faith. His empathy for my community and for me was a strong beam of hope.

Fortunately, we regularly witness such beams of hope and courage, and they shine brighter when it is darker outside. History is full of accounts of neighbors who risked their own lives to protect and hide persecuted religious minorities. Such people have shown us in deed and truth what it means to love our neighbors, even when they are not "one of us."

10

A Minority with a Majority Opinion

HANNA SINIORA

Hanna Siniora is a Palestinian Christian living in East Jerusalem and the co-CEO of the Israel/Palestine Center for Research and Information. He has served as the editor-in-chief of Al-Fajr, *an East Jerusalem newspaper, and started the weekly English* Al-Fajr, *serving as its editor. In 2007, Siniora was awarded the Peace Prize of Honor from the Order of the Knights of Malta in recognition of his commitment to Palestinian-Israeli peace. He was also awarded the Papal Silver Olive Branch for Peace.*

A Minority Within a Minority

In Palestine, I am a minority within a minority. I am a Christian Arab in a primarily Muslim land. I am Roman Catholic within a Christian community that is overwhelmingly Greek, Syrian, and Armenian Orthodox, and I am within a community that has shrunk more than 80 percent in my lifetime. Yet my minority status has not given me, as some would surmise, the proverbial "chip" on the shoulder. Instead, I feel a greater sense of responsibility to serve justly the communities in which I have lived my life as well as the larger international communities with clear ties to my homeland.

I was born in Jerusalem in 1937, a year following the troubles of 1936 when British authorities hung from Damascus Gate Palestinian nationalists concerned with the unabated influx of European Jewry. The family pharmacy, run by my father, was and is just inside that Old City gate. As a boy I walked past it to school at École de Frères in New Gate of the Old City. By the time I was twelve, New Gate was the edge of the frontier called No Man's Land that separated Arab East Jerusalem from Jewish West Jerusalem.

From Prescription to Subscription

I chose to study pharmacology in Benares, India, graduating with a BS in 1969. My four years in India introduced me to the teachings of Mahatma Gandhi, which would impact my later personal and political life. I had been working as a pharmacist for my father barely five years when a cousin, Yusef Nasser, was kidnapped and presumed murdered. He was the publisher of an Arabic-language weekly he called *Al-Fajr (The Dawn)*. I remember it clearly because Yusef used to come over every night to our house to have a bite to eat before going home. He had published a caricature of the mayor of Hebron, Muhammad al-Ja'abari, with a shoe in his mouth, which is in Arab culture a grave insult. At the time, al-Ja'abari was pro-Jordanian and calling for a return to Jordanian rule in the West Bank. My cousin was a nationalist who wanted an independent Palestinian state.

Yusef knew the cartoon was a grave insult and also knew that the powerful mayor had what amounted to a clan mafia who wanted to kill him as a result. He hid for three days and then went to al-Ja'abari to apologize. Before returning to his own home, he came to our house and said he felt safe after his apology. That same night he was kidnapped, murdered, and believed buried in one of the graves of the al-Ja'abari clan. For years my wife and I, along with other family members, went regularly to search the caves around Hebron for clues as to Yusef's whereabouts. Since his disappearance in 1973, no trace of him has ever been found. That is how I became a journalist and the editor of a newspaper. It was under my management that *Al-Fajr* became a daily and that, in 1980, we launched the English weekly of the same name.

A Life in the Enemy's Hands

In the 1960s, my home in East Jerusalem came under the military occupation of and the attempted annexation by the state of Israel. Even so,

I had only forced contact with Israelis—soldiers at checkpoints, the military censor, and the like. But in 1979, a near-tragedy befell my family that changed everything.

My two-and-a-half-year-old son, Sama'an (Simon), fell gravely ill with meningitis. My wife and I took him to the local East Jerusalem Palestinian hospital, al-Makassed. The doctors there knew only one treatment—antibiotics and cortisone—and for nearly three months they experimented on him, pumping him full of cortisone to the point that he became a toddler balloon. He ate thirty eggs a day.

My wife, Norma, was frantic by the end of the three months. She was justifiably afraid that the hospital was killing our son. She screamed at me to put aside my nationalistic pride and take him to the Israeli hospital, Hadassah. In the face of such fury and anguish, I had no choice. Within forty-eight hours of his admission to Hadassah, the doctors found a small fistula in his spine that needed to be repaired. They explained that it would require an operation known as microsurgery. It was a very delicate procedure, they said, and if the scalpel moved only a hair in the wrong direction, it could result in Sama'an's paralysis.

I now faced the reality of placing my only son in the care of my enemy, who, with a possible misstep, could paralyze him or worse. The operation took ten hours and was a complete success. Three days after surgery he returned home. These people, who did in three days what Makassed had not done in three months, could not be all bad. They saved my son's life. I began to consider what that meant for our lives going forward.

I realized that my pride had been a factor in the three months of suffering I had allowed my son to endure. That humbled me. Pope John Paul II wrote: "There is a need to be humble so that divine grace may operate in us, transform our lives, and bring out fruits of goodness."[1] At that point, I was aware of divine grace and that it was somehow transforming. History will be the judge as to whether any fruits worth remembering were produced.

Over the next few years, my contacts with Israelis who were opposed to the continued occupation steadily increased. I have often wondered, why me? I believe my career as a "peace activist" evolved over time for several reasons. First, I was executive editor of *Al-Fajr*, which many, including the Israeli military censor, considered one of the voices of the Palestine Liberation Organization (PLO). That gave me a level of credibility that Israelis interested in peace wanted. Second, I not only had the ear of Yasser Arafat, but also, and more important, I was willing to put ideas out there in the public arena and allow Chairman Arafat to observe the response. Third, I was an independent in terms of factional identification. I was a known supporter of the PLO but without formal ties to any particular faction. This gave me a certain freedom of movement across the PLO political spectrum.

In the early 1980s, one of my most valued partnerships was with Israeli professor Moshe Amirav. He was a member of West Jerusalem's municipal council and worked closely with a number of Israeli mayors of West Jerusalem. As a lifelong resident of West Jerusalem, he was as concerned with the future of the city as I was. We both felt, and continue to feel, that Jerusalem is the key to a peaceful resolution of the Israeli-Palestinian conflict.

We met frequently and drew up a plan for the city that involved local sovereignty of each state in the areas in which they were the primary population and special, perhaps international, sovereignty over the holy places within the walls of the Old City. Each state would be allowed to declare their sovereign section of Jerusalem as their state capital. Jerusalem was then, and remains today, the flashpoint.

A Joint Jordanian-Palestinian Delegation

In 1985, the U.S. administration proposed a peace conference between Israel and a joint Jordanian-Palestinian delegation. At the time, the Americans refused to negotiate directly with the PLO and felt Palestinian rights should be addressed within the context of the Hashemite Kingdom of Jordan, the ruling power over East Jerusalem and the West Bank in the years between 1948 and 1967. Even after Israel's occupation of 1967, the Jordanian Religious Authority (al-Waqf) continued to govern the holy sites and imams of East Jerusalem. Two Palestinians were named to the joint delegation—my longtime friend Fayez Abu-Rahmeh, the former head of Gaza's Bar Association, and me.

As with all peace efforts in the Middle East, this one was not without controversy. It justifiably rankled Palestinian residents of the Occupied Territories and our representatives abroad to have our concerns submerged in a joint delegation as if the claims of Jordan's King Hussein to the West Bank, Gaza, and East Jerusalem were in any way equivalent to our own. Fayez and I were criticized a great deal for agreeing to be part of the delegation. However, we did not do so of our own accord. We were instructed to by Chairman Arafat, although we were not allowed to say so. He was already at that time seeking a solution that would give Palestinians a flag and a state to call their own. He was keenly aware that Israel and America routinely accused the Palestinian side of proposing no solutions. Although he had his doubts that the formula conceived by the Reagan administration would succeed, he made it clear that if it did fail, it could not be blamed on us. It was also a gesture to the Arab world that Palestinians, perhaps foremost among the Arabs, dreamed of a unified Arab confederation in which an independent Palestine could take her place alongside Jordan, Saudi Arabia, Kuwait, and so on.

Our immediate goal of talks within a joint delegation under the auspices of the Americans was to gain recognition of the PLO as the legitimate representative of the Palestinian people both under and outside of Israeli occupation. At that point, it was U.S. recognition of the PLO we wanted. Then we sought a feasible framework accepted by all for direct negotiations between Israelis and Palestinians. We saw the PLO-Jordanian agreement to jointly attend negotiations as a realization that each side needed the other and as a strong signal to the West that the Arabs were making sincere efforts to encourage the peace process.

Again, why me? Pope John Paul II, whom Fayez and I had the privilege of meeting in Rome two years later, said: "One must accept the call, one must listen, one must receive, one must measure one's strength, and answer 'Yes, yes.' Fear not." In the early 1980s, I accepted the call.

The joint delegation never got as far as actual talks. The partnership forged by Yasser Arafat and King Hussein proved to be incapable of overcoming the bad blood between the Hashemite Kingdom and the Palestinian leadership. In February 1986, Chairman Arafat asked Fayez and me to go to Amman to repair the damage done to the relationship. We met with King Hussein at his palace. He heard us out, but he refused to continue as part of the joint delegation. I believe there were two reasons for the king quitting the team. First, Syria was placing an undue amount of pressure on him to pull out of the peace talks because they were not included in the process. To illustrate their displeasure they planted bombs all over Amman. Second, the king used the hijacking of the *Achille Lauro* as an excuse, despite his knowledge that Arafat and the majority of the PLO had had nothing to do with the ship's hijacking or the murder of the elderly American.

By the time we returned to Jerusalem, the Israeli government had itself undergone a transformation that rendered moot all discussion of any direct talks at that time. When we left for Amman, Labor Party leader Shimon Peres was prime minister, and Likud Party leader Yitzhak Shamir was foreign minister. Upon our return from our meeting with King Hussein, Peres and Shamir had switched places.

Peres summoned the two of us and Palestinian professor Sari Nusseibeh to his office in Israel's Foreign Ministry. He told the three of us that Israel was ready to give Palestinians in the Occupied Territories autonomy if we three, and not the PLO, ran it. I laughed and told him he was talking to the wrong group and would have to talk to the PLO. We added that if he was willing to offer the three of us an independent Palestinian state, however, that we would take it. Obviously, he did not make the offer.

Brave New Ideas

One of the by-products of the joint delegation was that an atmosphere more conducive to unfettered thought was created, and some on both sides were brave enough to put forth proposals that were naturally shot down but had the weight of hanging around and quietly entering the subconscious of both populations. Sari, a member of one of the oldest and most influential Jerusalem families, suggested one of the most controversial.

By the late 1980s, Sari saw that Israel's military occupation of the West Bank and Gaza and its virtual annexation of East Jerusalem were nearing the twenty-year mark. In that time Israel had made occupied Palestinians totally dependent. We were not only Israel's number one market for its goods (to the near destruction of our own marketplace), but we were also a cheap labor force, with day labor in Israel accounting for more than a third of West Bank employment and for two-thirds of Gaza employment. All of our institutions, with the exception of the religious ones, were controlled by Israel. In short, the infrastructure of a Palestinian state either did not exist or was on life support in a maximum security prison hospital.

Sari proposed a backdoor approach to achieving Palestinian independence. It was a "get on the bus and then hijack it" kind of idea. He suggested that for the present, Palestinians stop calling for national rights and instead clamor loudly for civil rights within the Israeli state apparatus. That would embarrass Israel by showing it to be the apartheid state it was and, if successful, would allow Palestinians, as "citizens" of Israel, the chance to participate within and eventually take over the state, especially considering that the Palestinian birthrate was nearly five times that of the Israelis.

I was intrigued by the notion if for no other reason than the international public relations boon it could prove to be. It got me thinking about my home, Jerusalem, where 33 percent of the population was Arab Palestinian. We were given minimal rights as Jerusalem residents, and one of those was to vote in municipal elections. We had always considered participation in the elections to be treason by virtue of its being tantamount to recognition of Israeli sovereignty over the city. Nevertheless, in the light of Sari's proposal, I began to consider exercising this right.

While I continued thinking about it, I traveled the globe speaking everywhere about our struggle for an independent state within the 1967 borders.

The proposed joint Jordanian-Palestinian delegation had made me a recognizable figure. I spoke in forums as diverse as the Los Angeles World Affairs Council in February 1987, where the week before Prime Minister Shamir had appeared, and weeks later to a group of Italian Communist Party members in East Jerusalem. To each group my message was the same: recognize the Palestine Liberation Organization with its elected Palestine National Council (PNC) as our official representatives and allow them to negotiate an independent state with my hometown as its capital. I was aware, of course, that many in each audience saw me as an "acceptable alternative" to the PLO. Despite that misconception, I always made my position, which was that of the PLO, clear and hoped the sheer power of repetition would work in our favor.

Despite my family's fear for my safety and the risk of being further misunderstood, I continued to discuss with friends on both sides of the Mandelbaum Gate (the crossing point between East and West Jerusalem from 1948 to 1967) the prospect of fielding a Palestinian slate in the upcoming Jerusalem municipal elections. There were some, including Sari, who were opposed to it. Most felt it was too soon and that it was ceding an important weapon in the Palestinian arsenal with nothing in return. I felt then, as I often have since, that a quiver full of arrows is useless if the arrows are never placed to the taut string and fired; if the weapons one has cannot be used for whatever reason, choose another, as long as the ultimate goal remains the same.

On June 5, 1967, the twentieth anniversary of the Israeli occupation of East Jerusalem, the West Bank, and the Gaza Strip, I declared my willingness to put together an Arab ticket that would include myself to run in the upcoming municipal elections. I told the press that I wanted to show that Jerusalem was inhabited by real people, not ghosts, and that Israelis had to know there were two peoples living in this city. My platform was essentially the same as for the joint project I had with Moshe Amirav. It was based on the premise that the only way to resolve the Jerusalem issue is to give both peoples who reside in it sovereign rights, each on his own side of the city while municipal affairs could continue to be run jointly. I believe with all my heart that to find peace we must first find it in Jerusalem. I knew that this platform would kick up a political storm and was prepared for the torching of my cars and for the graffiti declaring Jerusalem the capital of only Palestine. I understood and even sympathized with the anger, but I was trying to protect what was left of our city and to protect the interests of its Arab minority.

The Danger of Being Misunderstood

Many of my fellow Palestinians misunderstood my role in our fight for independence. In March 1987, I met with Israel's Labor Party leader Abba Eban at the King David Hotel. We were there to approve a final draft of a joint statement declaring that peace could come only through an international peace conference to which each side freely chose their own delegation. Some presumed I was promoting myself as an alternative to the PLO. Although untrue, the false impression stuck fast in some quarters. Early in the morning following the signing, Norma woke me to say she smelled smoke. It took me a few minutes to awaken. When I did, I discovered both of our parked cars, which were in front of the house, ablaze.

In the six months between my elections announcement and the intifada (the 1987–1993 Palestinian uprising against Israeli rule), I traveled a great deal in an effort to explain my reasons for running. Publicly, I was on my own. The PLO both abroad and at home had denounced the plan. Some called it outright treason, others called it bad timing, others still thought the idea had merit but came too close to negating our claim to East Jerusalem. Privately Chairman Arafat worried that it would complicate the issue of national sovereignty and asked me to consult international lawyers. I agreed to consult, and I listened to each position, glad that the idea had at least been a conversation starter. Twenty years of occupation and no forward movement? Something had to be done.

With that announcement I was trying a new tactic, and, almost exactly six months later, Palestinian youth in the Jabalya Refugee Camp in Gaza chose a new weapon themselves.

On December 9, 1987, Palestinian youth picked up stones from the refugee camp's sandy floor and faced off against Israeli M16s and tanks. Thus began the intifada. The popular uprising swept like wildfire across the Occupied Territories. I was out of the country at the time but eagerly watched on hotel and airport televisions the young men confronting the might of the Israeli army. Someone else abroad was also watching. Shortly before my return home from Australia in time for Christmas, I received word that I should stop in Paris for a messenger from Tunis. An old friend from my early journalism days whom Israel had deported, Akram Haniyeh, was sent by Yasser Arafat to meet me. I was told that the chairman was thrilled with the intifada but fearful that it would not last long enough to make an impression on the world community. Within two weeks time, the PLO would be celebrating Fatah Day, on January 1, 1988, to commemorate the founding of the largest political party within the Palestine National Council. Arafat was concerned that the uprising last at least through the Fatah celebration. He asked me to think of something that would continue the momentum.

A Boycott Begins

It seemed only natural to me that a boycott of products that were either made or distributed through Israel and for which we had local equivalents was needed. Once home I contacted a fellow Palestinian who had experience with civil disobedience campaigns and had studied the works of Mahatma Gandhi and Martin Luther King, Jr. His name was Mubarak Awad. I determined that the only products completely replaceable in our market were cigarettes and soft drinks. I sent word to local leaders that we were launching a civil disobedience campaign and that the first action was a boycott of these two Israeli-distributed products.

In late January 1988, several activists joined me in signing a statement calling for a peaceful resolution to the conflict that would ensure both Israeli and Palestinian national rights. I went further and called for an association of Israel, Palestine, and Jordan patterned after the Benelux countries, and suggested that the West Bank and Gaza, like Luxembourg, could remain demilitarized. Although this was not a popular suggestion, our civil disobedience campaign really took off.

Each local community—neighborhood, village, refugee camp, town—organized every aspect of its life in an effort to declare not only independence from Israel but an ability to determine its own fate. Merchants went through their shelves and removed Israeli products. Young men organized watch groups to keep the military and settlers from sneaking in and wreaking havoc or assassinating leaders. Young women started planting gardens and growing communal food. Schools that were forced shut by Israel were opened in homes. Lists of medicines and provisions were made and distributed freely to those in need. Palestinians were learning how to build their own institutions and to govern themselves.

The signatories met in January and attempted to hold a press conference in which we not only explained our civil disobedience campaign, but also made fourteen demands of Israel, which Sari had authored, including a release of detainees and an end to Israeli taxation of the Occupied Territories. We also called on Palestinians to fly Palestinian flags, stop carrying their Israeli-issued identity cards, and stop paying taxes. Many of us were arrested at the press conference. The Shin Bet, Israel's security services, came to my home at dawn the next morning to arrest me before I had time to get out of the shower. Norma was surprised by the early knocking, but I told her I was expecting them. They waited in my living room while I got dressed, and Norma served them coffee and fielded crank calls from followers of the radical, racist Jewish leader Meir Kahane, who wanted me and the rest of my countrymen deported en masse across the Jordan River.

This was not the first time I had been detained, nor would it be the last. Six months after this arrest I would go on trial in Israel for publishing an interview in December 1986 with Yasser Arafat in *Al-Fajr*. I was charged with not having submitted it to the Israeli military censor.

First Palestinians to Meet U.S. Secretary of State

Six weeks after the intifada began, U.S. Secretary of State George Shultz was more open to meeting with elected members of the PNC despite their connection to the PLO. Chairman Arafat agreed to the meeting, and Fayez and I went to Washington, D.C. I told Secretary Shultz that Palestinians looked up to the American government and genuinely wanted a U.S.-led multinational peace force to protect us against the obvious brutality of the Israeli military. By that point the military were shooting and killing or injuring scores of Palestinian civilians every day.

We presented Shultz with a fourteen-point memorandum calling for an international conference as a forum for Israeli-Arab negotiations. We emphasized the Palestinian national right of self-determination and the establishment of an independent state on our national soil under the leadership of the PLO as our sole legitimate representative. He told us he would try to help. I was pleased with the outcome of this first meeting between members of the PNC and the U.S. administration. Even the Executive Committee of the PLO agreed with me, publishing a statement of their appreciation in the Arab press.

Secretary Shultz came to Jerusalem and wanted to meet with a number of us whom he mistakenly deemed independent of the PLO. The U.S. position was that they would meet with Palestine National Council members but not members of the PLO. Our position was that the PNC was the legislative body of the PLO in the same way that the U.S. Congress was the legislative body of the American government, and the two could not be separated. Thus, in October, we left him waiting at Jerusalem's American Colony Hotel.

A month later, in February 1988, Secretary Schultz told us that the Reagan administration accepted the idea of an international conference as a venue for direct Israeli-Palestinian talks. Prime Minister Shamir, to whom Secretary Shultz first told the new American position, immediately rejected it. By this time Chairman Arafat had decided to pull back so as not to appear too eager to accept American intervention. He decided to test U.S. resolve by insisting that PLO members from outside the Occupied Territories be allowed to meet with Shultz. This resulted in PNC members from the Diaspora, Edward Said and Ibrahim Abu Lughod, meeting with Shultz in Washington. Our January 1988 meeting did result in paving the way for American recognition of the PLO as the sole legitimate representative of the Palestinian people by the end of the Reagan administration. Of that, I am very proud.

Less than two years later, I became a member of the Palestinian National Council and remain a member to this day. As an official PNC member, I was nominated by the PLO to advise the Palestinian delegation to the international peace conference in Madrid in 1991. This conference laid the groundwork for the substantive Oslo Accords that began a year later in 1992.

I was almost a backup to the meetings in Oslo. Sari and I visited former Swedish foreign minister Sten Andersen in Stockholm just before the meetings and shortly after the Social Democratic Party of Sweden had been defeated. Minister Andersen told us that the Scandinavians felt a back channel was needed through which messages could be passed and ideas could be floated and that the two of us would fit the bill. Andersen suggested he talk to his counterpart in Norway, Foreign Minister Thorvald Stoltenberg. When he placed the call, however, he was told that Stoltenberg was in Bosnia-Herzegovina and would not be available for some time. Thus, we lost the chance to attend the Oslo Accords.

I find it ironic that in 1986, Sari, Fayez, and I turned down autonomy when offered to us by Shimon Peres. Six years later it was offered and accepted in Oslo, and we have been stuck in this autonomous purgatory ever since.

The next year, 1993, Arafat and Prime Minister Yitzhak Rabin, who had defeated Shamir in Israel's 1992 election, met twice in Washington, D.C.— once at the White House for the famous September 13 handshake and a second time at a museum. For the second meeting, Chairman Arafat invited me along. King Hassan of Morocco loaned us his 747 jet for the flight to Washington. There, before a very select audience, Yasser Arafat gave the best English-language speech I ever heard him give. Rabin was so impressed that he joked with him. "You must have Jewish blood in you," teased Rabin, "enabling you to speak so eloquently."

A Change of Roles

With Arafat recognized in Washington as the official spokesman of the Palestinian people, my role in the struggle changed significantly. I was no longer needed to float trial balloons or to meet with international officials as Arafat's proxy. I returned to Jerusalem and began working on ways in which the autonomy created in the Oslo Accords, which were ratified in 1994, would evolve into an independent Palestinian state.

The first significant change in my role involved my career. *Al-Fajr* ran out of money and closed its doors in 1993, after publishing as the unofficial voice of the PLO for nearly twenty-five years. In 1994, I started a weekly called *The Jerusalem Times*. Ten years later, when Chairman Arafat died, I closed the weekly but kept the name for an Internet newsletter published six days a week. But before that, I would serve the chairman once more—or at least try to. In 2002, he announced his intention to appoint me as Palestinian ambassador to the United States. I flew to Washington, only to be recalled almost immediately. It turns out that then Prime Minister Mahmoud al-Abbas felt he owed Hassan Abdel Rahman, the longtime PLO representative in Washington, a favor and lobbied for him to remain there. It was a political decision on the part of Arafat and I knew not to take it personally.

In the years since the Oslo Accords, I have concentrated my efforts across a wide range of business, social, and political forums. I am trying to build Palestinian infrastructure.

In 2005, I was asked to join the Israel-Palestine Center for Research and Information (IPCRI) as its Palestinian CEO. Its Israeli CEO is my friend and colleague Gershon Baskin. Through IPCRI we are able to work on a variety of projects, ranging from analysis of the second Camp David talks in 2000, whose failure coincided with the second intifada, to the need for and opportunity for renewable energy. At IPCRI we have several important departments that deal with final status issues, like the future of Jerusalem, the borders between Israel and Palestine, the right of return, the two-state solution, the future of Israeli settlements, and water and environment.

A number of positive things have happened regarding the peace process over the last decade. In 2002, and at every Arab Summit since, the Arab League proposed the Arab Peace Initiative offering Israel peace with all twenty-two Arab countries in return for the establishment of an independent Palestinian state on the 1967 borders. Of course, much has happened since then and much has not been said. Still, I remain optimistic.

Optimism is, after all, both a part of my nature and a part of my faith. From childhood I was taught to hope in Christ and to combine that hope with the good works a living faith demands, as cited in the book of James in the New Testament. It is as natural for me to keep hoping and actively pursuing the goal as it is to breathe. I will say that there is plenty of room for the church and other religious institutions to join me.

Religious Leaders Must Meet the Challenge

To date, religious leaders have preferred to remain on the sidelines. Previous timid attempts to deal with religious issues on a local and regional basis stemmed from a fear that religion would be exploited for political purposes in the context of the Israeli-Palestinian conflict. To use religion in a positive way in this conflict is essentially to tread on "virgin territory" (pun intended).

Religion constitutes a part of the problem in the Israeli-Palestinian conflict. And since it is a part of the problem, it also has to be a part of the solution. The concept of peaceful coexistence among Islamic, Judaic, and Christian peoples, if properly spread and taught by religious leaders of the three monotheistic faiths, is key to solving the conflict. It is of particular importance to solving the conflicts over holy places and can lead the way to an accommodation regarding the Jewish and Muslim sanctuaries in Jerusalem.

Pope John Paul II set a precedent in 2000 when he left the Holy Land bearing an olive branch to symbolize the need for peace in the Middle East and replanted it on the grounds of the Vatican. He repeatedly spoke about living in peace with one's neighbor. "Morality and law are the fundamental conditions for social order," he said. "States and nations are built upon law, without which they perish." He called upon us to be "active members of the people of God," to be "reconciled with each other and devoted to the work of justice, which will bring peace on Earth." One of the greatest honors I have ever received came in 2007 when a piece of the olive branch the Pope had replanted in the Vatican was taken, coated in silver, and presented to me for a "lifetime commitment to Palestinian-Israeli peace." With the silver olive branch came induction into the Order of the Knights of Malta.

I was raised to be a good Christian, but for me that does not mean simply to attend mass every Sunday. I believe that my deeds are my way of showing my adherence to my religion. I am tolerant. I try to understand the needs of both my side and the other side. I am not dogmatic. If someone convinces me that some of my decisions or ideas are not appropriate, I change them. I have always felt, in the context of the Israeli-Palestinian conflict, that there are possibilities of accomplishing the hopes and needs of both peoples who are fighting over the same homeland, and this is why I never stop trying to find a way out despite the ever-present deadlock. I have very close friends who are Christian, Muslim, and Jewish.

As a Christian Palestinian I have always advocated for the church to do much more to protect and provide better opportunity for the Christian community to stay in their homeland. I have repeatedly called for the church properties and their economic power to be used to build housing so that young couples especially have a home and a reasonable quality of life. The Catholic Church tries to provide some housing, but it is not enough. The Orthodox Church has totally neglected its responsibilities in this regard.

The churches have been active in private education for both Christians and Muslims in Palestine and for both Arabs and Jews in Israel. To some extent they are playing a mediating role in Muslim-Jewish relations, but they could do much more.

When Norma and I were preparing for marriage, the Catholic Church insisted that Norma, who is Greek Orthodox, convert. I felt uneasy about that demand because it should not matter which denomination one comes from. I feel comfortable going to an Anglican, Catholic, Lutheran, Orthodox, or Protestant church. This narrow-mindedness is no longer present within the Christian churches in Jerusalem. Ecumenical relationships have much more importance, as do interfaith relationships.

More than twenty years ago, a group of more than sixty laymen, both Christian and Muslim, myself included, began a dialogue as a way of handling problems before they got out of hand. For example, a number of years ago, a group of Muslim youth taunted Christian pilgrims during an Easter procession. Our Muslim partners in the dialogue visited the parents of these young people and extracted a promise, which has been kept, to respect Christians in the Holy Land. Before the dialogue, problems in the community tended to be ignored in an effort to appear in complete solidarity before the world. The reality is that no community, no matter how small or large, is 100 percent harmonious 100 percent of the time.

Christians Promoted, Not Persecuted

Contrary to reports being published that there is persecution of Christians in the Palestinian Authority, the exact opposite is true. That does not mean that there are not extremists who try to disrupt the excellent relations between the two communities that form one people. But the Palestinian government, since its beginning under Arafat's leadership, has tried to protect the tiny Palestinian Christian community that stayed in the country after a long, difficult period of occupation. Christian emigration is a direct result of the unstable situation in Palestine and not because of friction between the two communities.

President Arafat and the Palestine Legislative Council saw to it that Christians have over-representation proportional to their numbers, especially from Christian cities like Bethlehem, Jerusalem, and Ramallah. This shows there is no policy of discrimination against Christian Palestinians. In Bethlehem and Ramallah, where the population is overwhelmingly Muslim, it is Palestinian policy that the mayors and deputy mayors be Christian. The same is true in towns like Beit Jala and Beit Sahour, which have been historically Christian.

In Gaza there have been several attempts by extremist Islamic elements to disrupt the harmonious coexistence of Muslims and Christians, but even Hamas intervened and prevented discrimination against the Christian population. In Gaza there are still five Christian clans who continue to live there despite the difficulties.

I never felt discriminated against when I ran for the municipal council of Jerusalem. The PLO protected me from overzealous people who wanted me eliminated. The late deputy to Arafat, Khalil al-Wazir (Abu Jihad), told me to be careful because he was aware that some of the other PLO factions did not like my political initiatives. But their animosity had nothing to do with my faith.

When Fayez and I were appointed to the joint Jordanian-Palestinian delegation twenty-five years ago, we worked well together and developed a warm friendship that continues until today. It is difficult to meet face-to-face because he lives in Gaza and I live in Jerusalem, but every holiday—Christian or Muslim—we call one another. My daughter considers him a favorite relative. In fact, my family has far more close Muslim friends than close Christian ones. We have never seen a difference. We are all Arabs and all Palestinians.

I believe in the power of dialogue and in the search for common ground. This is why I feel that within the context of internal Palestinian differences— especially between Fatah and Hamas—both sides should try harder to find understanding because it will lead to a quicker Israeli-Palestinian solution and to a more harmonious life.

Jerusalem, the Center

The best place, in my opinion, to test this theory is still in the holy city of Jerusalem. The Old City of Jerusalem is the most important square kilometer in the world, and like everyone else—Arab, Palestinian, Israeli, Jew— I want it to be undivided and open, a city where people can move about freely and enter and enjoy their religious places. It requires a great deal of understanding and some faith to see this city as the city of peace, as a beacon of peace rather than of conflict.

I envision maintenance of the status quo with regard to the holy places. Currently the Israeli Ministry of Religious Affairs maintains its sites, the

Jordanian al-Waqf maintains Muslim sites, and the different Christian denominations maintain their own sites. I envision two sovereignties and two
capitals, and a super entity to deal with issues of joint governance. I would suggest that the Armenian community, unique among all of the disparate communities in the city, has excellent relations with and an excellent reputation
among both Palestinians and Israelis. Perhaps they would serve in the first
umbrella government.

With the city of Jerusalem holding forth as the city of peace, it would be
time to tackle the greater Palestinian-Israeli conflict. The obstacles preventing a lasting resolution seem to center on two important pressure groups—
refugees and settlers. From the Palestinian perspective, the right of return for
Palestinian refugees is sacred. No leader can resolve the conflict without a
satisfactory solution to this dilemma. It is a matter of common sense that Israel, with its aggressive right of return, or *aliya*, for any Jew anywhere, should
understand the importance of this to the Palestinians. We understand the importance of the settlers to the Israeli polity. They are an increasingly powerful
lobby within each successive Israeli administration, especially in the Netanyahu government, where they are actually an important part of the Israeli
cabinet.

My proposal, upon which both sides have already agreed, is to swap territory between Israel and Palestine along the Green Line, the demarcation line
of 1967. Both sides have agreed on the principle of a swap but not on the
extent of it. Our side says we will swap 1.9 percent of the West Bank for an
equivalent amount in Israel just over the Green Line and adjacent to the West
Bank. Israel wants 6.5 percent. Obviously, the final number lies somewhere
in between.

Palestinian residents of the West Bank (about two and a half million) currently live on only about 6 percent of the land. I propose that we resolve
both the refugee and settler problems by swapping 3 percent to 4 percent of
the West Bank for an equivalent amount in Israel, allowing us to absorb
those refugees who choose to return and those settlers who choose to remain. Settlers choosing to stay would become residents of Palestine and
subject to our laws but would remain citizens of Israel, much like millions of
ex-patriots worldwide. If there were Palestinians who chose to return to areas
to be swapped within Israel, they, too, would be residents of the Israeli state
but citizens of Palestine.

In this way, Israel could continue to see itself as a Jewish state with its
primary citizenry being Jewish, even if her total residency was not. It is my
hope that the Arabs of the Galilee and the Negev would find a fair and equitable resolution to their residency and/or citizenship aspirations. Although

they would be welcome in the Palestinian state, there is a need to maintain the nature of traditionally Arab areas such as Nazareth and Haifa. I feel we have in our area only two alternatives—either coexist and live together or commit mutual national suicide. I prefer the first option.

As a democrat, I believe people should have freedom of expression, of holding different political, religious, and cultural opinions, but that they should not use violence to get their way. To me, nonviolence is the best alternative, whether one is embroiled in an interpersonal or an international conflict. I take my cues on conflict resolution from my faith tradition and from my years in India and as a student of Mahatma Gandhi, Martin Luther King, Jr., and Nelson Mandela.

At age seventy-three, I am reminded of an old friend from Gaza, Zuheir al-Rayes, who was an ardent admirer of Gamal Abdel-Nasser in his youth. Zuheir used to talk about how close he was to Abdel-Nasser and tell stories about these momentous events of history he witnessed. I feel that way now—that history is somehow slipping by and that remaining optimistic in the face of overwhelming challenges is my greatest and sole surviving task.

Just into the new year of 2011, my granddaughter sat at our kitchen table working on a school report about American author and activist Maya Angelou. One of her quotations struck me as apropos. Angelou writes: "All my work, my life, everything I do is about survival, not just bare, awful, plodding survival, but survival with grace and faith. While one may encounter many defeats, one must not be defeated."[2]

At this stage of my life, what I can do is hope, propose, and advocate for solutions that I may never see come to light. But, I have faith that my four grandsons and two granddaughters will. My youngest, my namesake, is almost four years old. Surely if peace in the Middle East takes another sixty years to come true, at least there will still be a Hanna Siniora living in Jerusalem as a citizen of his capital city in the country of his birth. May he raise a glass to toast me in celebration.

Notes

1. Pope John Paul II, *Prayers and Devotions: 365 Daily Meditations*, ed. Peter Canisius Johannes van Lierde, trans. Firman O'Sullivan (New York: Penguin, 1998), quoted in the devotion for December 3, "The Grace of the Coming."

2. Quoted in Dolly A. McPherson, *Order Out of Chaos: The Autobiographical Works of Maya Angelou* (New York: Peter Lang Publishing, 1990), 10–11.

II

"Honor Everyone!" Christian Faith and the Culture of Universal Respect

MIROSLAV VOLF

Director of the Yale Center for Faith and Culture and the Henry B. Wright Professor of Theology at Yale Divinity School, Miroslav Volf is one of the most respected living Christian theologians. A native of war-torn Croatia, Volf's writing often draws on his own experience of war, injustice, and suffering to promote reconciliation and peace. Volf received a PhD in theology from the University of Tübingen in Germany and is the author of many scholarly articles and numerous books, including Exclusion and Embrace: A Theological Exploration of Identity, Otherness, and Reconciliation *and* Allah: A Christian Response.

Disclosure

I grew up under an antireligious regime of intolerance. Mild intolerance it was, compared with what many, especially religious groups, suffered in the twentieth century and continue to suffer in many places around the world today. But I know from firsthand experience what it means to live in bugged quarters, receive surreptitiously opened mail, and talk on tapped phone lines; "security agents" have threatened and interrogated me for months running.[1] I have also many times heard the story of my father's horrendous trials. An innocent man, he was, literally, nearly starved to death during months of detainment in a concentration-camp hell because the "powers that be" *assumed* his guilt without making even the slightest effort to check out his case—indeed, without even asking for his name.

At the level of my early and formative experiences, I associate irreligion with intolerance. But also in my experience, religion has not fared any better than irreligion. My grandfather was a Baptist minister and my father a Pentecostal one. They agreed that their communities had it easier under the rule of Communists than under the cultural and political dominance of Catholics and the Orthodox. My longing for the open horizon of respect grew in the constricted space of both religious and secular intolerance. The faith that my parents handed down to me (the faith that as a teenager I found too difficult a burden to bear) would not buckle under the pressure to abandon its own truth while it struggled against becoming infected by intolerance suffered at the hands of those who identified with the red star or with the cross.

But is the cross a symbol of an intolerant religion the same way the red star has become a symbol of an intolerant social and political project?

And the Intolerance Prize Goes to . . .

Imagine an international prize for the most intolerant religion. Which one would win? Also imagine a jury, made up of critics of religion, past and present. In the minds of the majority of such critics, *all* religions would be candidates for the prize because all are blindly irrational and, therefore, intolerant. Judaism, Christianity, and Islam—Abrahamic faiths that affirm the undisputed rule of one God and insist on one universal truth[2]—would likely emerge as the top contenders, embodying as they do what is sometimes called the "imperialism of the universal."[3] Christianity might be pronounced the winner for relentlessly seeking to impose itself on everyone under the guise of general benevolence. Or maybe the perverse prize might go to Islam, a religion that many of today's critics envisage as a blindfolded man with scimitar in hand.[4]

Religious people, prone to disparage their rivals, often join the critics. I have heard Christians insist that whereas Christianity is a religion of love, Islam is a religion of violence, with a fierce and irrational deity at its center demanding unconditional submission. And I have heard Muslims return the compliment. None less than the former president of Malaysia, Mahathir Mohamad, has said in my presence that, as the divinely commanded genocide of the ancient Canaanites attests, both Judaism and Christianity are clearly more violent than Islam.

If the critics (and rival advocates) of religion are correct about the intolerance of the Abrahamic faiths, a major storm looms on our horizon. First, ours is an interconnected and interdependent world in which many religions inhabit a common space within single states. Second, Christianity and Islam are the fastest-growing religions today and claim the greatest number of members; taken together, their adherents comprise more than half of living humanity. These two religions, in the critics' opinions, vie for first prize for intolerance. Third, because religious people, including Muslims, for the most part embrace democratic ideals, they will continue to push for their vision of the good life in the public square. Intertwined, growing, and assertive, religions will make life intolerable for millions—if the critics are correct.

But *are* the critics correct? In one respect, they are. Followers of all three Abrahamic faiths, especially of Christianity and Islam, have often been intolerant, even gruesomely violent. The history of their intolerance is long, and their path through time is littered with demeaned, displaced, and destroyed people. Perhaps surprisingly to some, many followers of these religions agree with critics on this point (though followers add that their religions have an even more impressive history of generosity and struggling for justice). So critics and advocates are united on this point: in practice, Abrahamic religions have often been and continue to be intolerant.[5] The dispute is primarily about whether intolerance is a defining characteristic of these faiths or a profound distortion of them.

Applied to the Christian faith, the faith that I embrace and about which I write here, the dispute is about what it means to be a consistent Christian—a Christian who lives in line with the letter and the spirit of basic Christian convictions. To take two contrasting examples: Is a Crusader exclaiming "Christ is the Lord" while cleaving the head of an infidel a consistent Christian?[6] Is a Trappist monk serving the Muslim poor while living under the threat of death from violent extremists a consistent Christian?[7] Is the Crusader misusing faith in his lust for economic, political, or cultural domination or is he unflinchingly enacting authentic Christian convictions? Is the Trappist monk moderating his fierce religion with common (secular) human kindness or is he consistently practicing the Christian faith? Put more generally, the dispute is this: Are intolerant Christians bastardizing their own religion or is the Christian faith itself an intolerant religion? Critics argue for the second position and insist that all impulses toward any toleration the Christian faith may contain must have come to it from secular sources and are in deep tension with the faith itself.

The issue is critical, and I do not mean just for the self-image and good reputation of Jews, Christians, and Muslims (though if the critics are correct, such people live in what is a religious equivalent of North Korea[8]). In a globalized world with resurgent religions, world peace itself greatly depends on religious tolerance. Religions are not going away. If intolerance is in their DNA, religiously inspired and legitimized conflicts are inevitable. In today's intermingled and interdependent world with vibrant and assertive religions, apart from genuinely religious motivation for tolerance, we can expect cold disrespect, zealous intolerance, and fierce violence to be the order of the day.

Are there genuinely religious reasons for tolerance? In this essay I will argue that authentic Christian convictions foster not just tolerance but genuine respect for all human beings. The idea of respect for all makes sense only if we distinguish between respect owed persons because of their achievements or status (as in, "I respect her for her integrity") and respect owed them simply because of their humanity (as in, "human beings must respect one another in all their diversity").[9] More on this fundamental distinction later.

Tolerance: The Chief Mark of the True Church

A specifically Christian argument for tolerance is not new. In what is likely the most influential text on tolerance ever written, *A Letter Concerning Toleration* (1689), John Locke, the progenitor of political liberalism, states in the very first sentence that toleration is "the chief characteristical mark of the true Church."[10] His argument in support of this claim rests mainly on two key Christian convictions.

TOLERANCE AND FREEDOM

The first conviction concerns the centrality of *freedom in coming to faith*. The nature of faith is such that no one can be forced to believe. To embrace (or reject) Christian faith is to reorient all the fundamental commitments of one's life. If we are forced to believe, we will believe insincerely and thereby both dishonor God[11] and violate our own conscience.[12] "True and saving religion," writes Locke, "consists in the inward persuasion of the mind, without which nothing can be acceptable to God."[13] Such faith can grow only in the soil of freedom.

A critic may raise an eyebrow out of suspicion that Locke might be importing "inward persuasion" into the Christian faith from outside, from his modern sensibilities. Locke has in mind a lone individual, before God, heeding the voice of his conscience alone. But such a person, a critic might contend, is a product of an individualistic age whose ways of understanding the human person and social relations have been brought about by secular developments. After all, the argument about freedom in coming to faith flows from the pen of a philosopher dubbed the progenitor of Western "possessive individualism."[14]

The eyebrow can safely come down. Cultural novelty and the character of Locke's own individualism need not concern us here. From the very beginning, Christians have insisted on the need to embrace faith freely. The apostle Paul wrote that "one believes with the heart," which is to say not by mere outward conformity to surrounding influences or explicit dictates, but with the very core of one's being (Rom. 10:10). Similarly, around A.D. 300, during the Diocletian persecution, Christian apologist Lactantius insisted that "nothing is so much a matter of free-will as religion; . . . if the mind of the worshipper is disciplined to it, religion is at once taken away, and ceases to exist."[15] A century earlier, Tertullian made the same point: "It is unjust to compel freemen against their will" to engage in religious rituals, for the gods "can have no desire of offerings from the unwilling."[16] Faith is essentially a free and personal act. Coerced faith is no faith at all. Both early and contemporary Christians agree on this point.[17]

TOLERANCE AND LOVE

The second reason Locke thinks that tolerance is a chief mark of the true church concerns the centrality of *love in the exercise of the Christian faith*. The apostle Paul wrote famously that no matter how deep is my knowledge of the tenets of my faith, no matter how impressive are my moral achievements, if I "do not have love, I am nothing" (1 Cor. 13:2). Echoing Paul, Locke argues that even if a person has a true claim to orthodoxy, to moral excellence, or to liturgical correctness, "yet if he be destitute of charity, meekness, and goodwill in general towards all mankind, even to those that are not Christians, he is certainly yet short of being a true Christian himself."[18] Intolerance is incompatible with genuine love because it is implausible that "infliction of torments and exercise of all manner of cruelties" is an expression of love[19]—a stance that advocates of fierce love from Augustine on have disputed. For Locke, intolerance is therefore incongruous with authentic faith. An intolerant faith is a seriously compromised faith.

Locke's two Christian arguments for tolerance—how one comes to faith and how one should live as a person of faith—are compelling.[20] The first is an argument for specifically religious toleration, Locke's primary concern; the second is comprehensive and grounds all other kinds of toleration. A consistent Christian is a tolerant Christian, Locke argues.

We can strengthen his case. We could argue that all Christian convictions about the self, social relations, and the good are governed by the claim that God, far from being a domineering despot, is self-giving love (as I have done in *Free of Charge*).[21] We could demonstrate that Christians should love their neighbors and honor their personal and communal integrity precisely in circumstances rife with potential for intolerance—when they face "others" who are different and whose behavior they disapprove of, or at whose hands they have suffered violence (as I have done in *Exclusion and Embrace*).[22] We could show that the neighbors whom Christians should love and respect include their chief religious rivals—Muslims. We could also make the case for a Christian's public engagement being guided by the Golden Rule, which obliges us to grant to others the same rights we seek for ourselves (as I have done in *A Public Faith*).[23] All these would be important, specifically religious arguments for tolerance and respect.

But in the present essay, I will take a different approach. I will zero in on the grounds for respect found in the Christian Holy Scriptures. In fact, I will concentrate on a single command. It is found in 1 Peter, a text that speaks more explicitly and comprehensively than any other in the New Testament on how Christians ought to live in socially pluralistic settings laden with tensions. The command is terse and direct: "Honor everyone" (1 Pet. 2:17).[24] For Christians who consider the Holy Scriptures to be the word of God, to honor everyone is not a mere suggestion or a counsel of prudence, but a strictly religious duty. In what does this duty consist?

Honoring

Let us first take up the idea of "honoring" and then turn to the more surprising, even radical, part of this command, namely, that Christians should honor *everyone*. I will use "honoring" and "respect" as synonyms.

HONOR, PERIOD!

In discussing toleration, philosophers sometimes speak of the "circumstances of toleration." They describe conditions under which we are called to show tolerance. Three such conditions are crucial: (1) diversity, (2) disapproval, and (3) disparity in power.[25] The letter of 1 Peter addresses Christian communities living in a setting in which all three of these conditions obtain. First, these communities embarked on a way of life markedly different from the surrounding culture and even different from their ancestors; these Christians saw themselves as "a chosen race" and "a holy nation" (2:9). Second, they felt "maligned" as "evildoers" (2:12), and they in turn believed that their compatriots' lives were marked by "futility" (1:18). Finally, they were a small and powerless minority, a network of insignificant communities scattered throughout the Roman Empire (1:1–2). Different, disliked, and marginalized, they faced abuse and mild persecution (1:6, 3:9). These are exactly the circumstances that cry out for toleration.

Surprisingly, 1 Peter contains no demand—not even a plea—for Christians to be tolerated. Later Christian writers, starting with Tertullian (b. A.D. 160), will issue such demands. And before Tertullian, theologians had argued for toleration without demanding it: Justin Martyr (A.D. 100–165) noted in his *Apology* that people of diverse religions "all are profane in the judgment of one another, on account of their not worshipping the same objects."[26] He argues if Rome tolerates such religions, it should tolerate Christians as well, rather than putting them "to death as sinners" even though they "do no wrong."[27] Being religiously different, Justin Martyr argued, is no ground for intolerance.

Tertullian's and Justin Martyr's stances are what we would expect: the weak and marginal preach tolerance to the strong and dominant who oppress them. 1 Peter is different. This text does not address the strong and dominant at all. It demands nothing of others but much of the Christian communities themselves. Instead of insisting that the persecuting non-Christians tolerate Christians, it commands the persecuted Christians to honor non-Christians!

If we focus on the *regime of intolerance* under which Christians were suffering, such a command makes little sense and might reek of internalized oppression and servility. It seems strangely misdirected—addressed to those who suffer intolerance rather than directed against social arrangements that foster intolerance and the individuals who perpetrate it. But if we shift attention to the *mindset of intolerance*,[28] then the command that they "honor everyone" makes sense—a more profound sense than would their legitimate demand to be tolerated. For intolerance suffered engenders intolerance perpetrated. Intolerance suffered seeks to infect the mind of the persecuted, as I know from firsthand experience and as studies in social psychology attest.

The command to honor everyone stops people from perpetrating the kind of intolerance they themselves are forced to endure. Even more, it emphasizes that respecting a person is not a matter of the reciprocal exchange of equivalents: I will respect you if you respect me, and I will respect you to the extent that you respect me. Instead, respecting a person is a matter of a moral stance, an unconditional imperative:[29] I will respect you whether you respect me or not. The command is not "Honor, if you are honored" or "Honor, if you want to be honored." The command is, "Honor, period." The hope is, of course, that others will do the same and that the respect will be mutual. But that outcome is neither the reason nor the condition of my honoring.

As a moral stance and a command of the one God of all people, the injunction to honor everyone has universal validity. It is not simply what Christians ought to do; it is what everyone ought to do. And so the command issued to weak and persecuted Christian communities is, implicitly, a demand—a moral demand—binding on their abusers as well: They, too, ought to honor everyone, including Christians. The text has planted a seed from which the explicit demand for tolerance will sprout. It has also countered a prevalent tendency of victims of intolerance (a tendency to which the ancient Christians themselves will succumb after Christianity has been established as the religion of the empire): the weak issue demands to the strong but conveniently forget those demands when they themselves achieve a position of power.[30] "Honor everyone" is valid for all, the marginalized and not just the dominant, and maybe especially for the marginal once they have become the dominant.

HONOR, NOT TOLERATE!

The command is to honor or respect, not merely to tolerate. I write, "*merely* to tolerate," knowing well that for many, mere tolerance would mean life rather than death, or at least a sheltered space to live without exclusion and abuse. So it was for me, growing up as a minister's kid in a country ruled by Communists committed to atheism as a social good. "You tall one! Get out of the classroom, and never show up again with that thing around your neck!" This was my biology teacher bellowing. She disliked the cross I was wearing. A fierce atheist, she could not abide the display of religious symbols in the classroom. I would have been grateful for mere tolerance—a resigned acceptance that a student deluded enough to commit himself openly to a religious faith has a right to learn biology in a public school. Respect would have been too much to ask for.

Tolerance may be our best hope in some situations, but there is still something "mere" about it. "To tolerate someone else is an act of power," writes Michael Walzer in *On Toleration*. He continues: "To be tolerated is an acceptance of weakness."[31] Moreover, toleration can go hand in hand with a stance of affective and moral exclusion. After the Communist regime has been toppled, I can commit myself to tolerate old-style Marxist teachers intolerant of me and my faith while projecting utter disdain and disgust every time I encounter them or speak of them.

No such power dynamic is implied in "honoring," at least not in the way 1 Peter employs the term, and, obviously, disdain is excluded. I can honor my superiors ("the king" [2:17], in the monarchical political order of 1 Peter); I can honor my subordinates ("wives" [3:7], in the patriarchal cultural setting of 1 Peter); and I can honor my equals (the majority included in "everyone"). The outsiders, all of them, writes one commentator, "are not to be despised because they are not believers, nor hated because they are persecutors, nor treated with contempt because they are of lower rank or status, but treated with honor."[32]

But what does honoring a person, every person, consist of? 1 Peter is silent on the matter. The text implies that honor is owed people because of their social station ("the king," "wives"), as well as that honor is owed all ("everyone"), presumably because of their humanity. But what precisely *is* the honoring owed all? We will not go wrong if we assume that to honor persons as human beings (as distinct from honoring them for status or achievement) means to treat them as beings created and loved by God. Since they are created by God, we need to refrain from violating their integrity as human beings; since they are loved by God, we need to help nurture their capacities and powers.[33]

One way to articulate a Christian account of respect is to compare it with that of Immanuel Kant, a German philosopher pivotal in developing the Western concept of respect. He famously distinguished between "respect" and "love." To "respect" means not to debase a person as a mere means to one's own subjective ends; to "love" means to make the ends of another person my own ends.[34] Understood Christianly, in honoring or respecting people we, in a sense, combine Kant's respecting and loving without completely identifying them: we do not treat people as a means to our own ends, and we do seek to further other people's ability to pursue their own ends. Respect, then, is a mode of love. That is different from tolerance, though not less than tolerance.

HONOR, EVEN WHILE DISAPPROVING!

Tolerance, it is sometimes said, is close to blithe indifference, even casual acceptance. Respect, it is claimed, is virtually identical with full approval, even strong endorsement. If that were true, 1 Peter would be a text of intolerance and disrespect because a note of strong disapproval runs through it—disapproval not only of the abuse Christian communities were suffering, but also of the outsiders' very way of life. True, 1 Peter establishes a difference between insiders and outsiders not by primarily rejecting what is outside, but rather by affirming the communities' core convictions. ("Soft difference" is what I have called this stance elsewhere.[35]) Still, the text draws bold boundary lines between Christian and non-Christian ways of living and does so in religious and moral terms. Is that very act of critical demarcation a mode of intolerance and disrespect?

It is not. If we were unable to tolerate and respect notwithstanding disapproval, the consequences would be grave. Here is what follows from two premises I believe are uncontested.

Premise One: Differences in ways of life among religions and secular world-
views run deep and stubbornly endure; chances of erasing them are slim.

Premise Two: People consistently (and rightly) refuse to accept what they
find unacceptable.

Conclusion: If acceptance were required for tolerance, the pervasive
mindset of intolerance would endure as well.

Consequence: To prevent the world from sinking into intractable conflicts,
we would need to counter pervasive mindsets of intolerance with regimes
of intolerance. Some form of totalitarianism is the inevitable consequence
of the inability to tolerate while disapproving.

Summary: If tolerance means acceptance, intolerance rules.

As it turns out, the idea of tolerating despite disapproving is built into the
very logic of tolerance. Tolerance would undo itself if it were incompatible
with disapproval. For, by definition, tolerance is needed in situations of disapproval, when we judge a person or a group to be morally wrong.[36] Take
disapproval away, and tolerance disappears as well because there is nothing
to tolerate.

It is similar with respect. What would happen if, out of respect for someone whose views or behavior I disapprove of, I changed my opinion? Respect would turn into a condescending lie and cancel itself out. For I
cannot change my considered opinions at will.[37] Respect requires judgment
rendered truthfully, whether that judgment is positive or negative. Commitment to truthfulness—and therefore to standing by one's considered
negative judgment—is a condition of the possibility of both tolerance and
respect.

HONOR, AND CALL IT AS YOU SEE IT!

"Every man has commission to admonish, exhort, convince another of
error, and, by reasoning draw him to truth," wrote Locke in *A Letter Concerning Toleration*.[38] He did not dwell much on how to respect people as one
draws them to truth. It sufficed for him to note: "It is one thing to persuade,
another to command; one thing to press with arguments, another with penalties."[39] His topic was tolerance. If you persuade and press with arguments,
you tolerate; if you command and press with penalties, you do not. But 1
Peter calls for respect, not mere tolerance. How then do you engage respect-
fully those with whom you disagree, those whose views you disapprove of?

In describing how Christians should commend their way of life to non-
Christians—how they should give "an accounting for the hope" they have—1
Peter uses two nouns: "gentleness" and "respect" (3:15–16).[40] Gentleness is a
servant of respect. A gentle person forgoes aggressiveness, open or hidden,

and grants others time to come to their own judgment. When truth is at stake, respecting others requires more than simply not violating the integrity of their search for truth. Respecting them means (1) we do not distort our impression of them. Instead, we take pains to get to know them accurately, also including how they understand and experience themselves and how they understand and experience us.[41] Respecting them means (2) we treat them as possible sources of insight, not merely as "beneficiaries" of our instruction. Facing them, we are aware of our likely lack of understanding and remain open to be surprised by who they are and what insights their convictions may contain.[42]

Friedrich Nietzsche's philosophy is as far from the way of Jesus Christ as Dionysus, god of libidinal revelry, is from the Crucified, the God of sacrificial love.[43] When I taught the course "Nietzsche for Theologians" at an evangelical institution, I laid down a rule: In the class we were not allowed to tear down Nietzsche's philosophy but only to discuss what is right about it. Most students were predisposed to think that Nietzsche was utterly wrong, and the rule was designed to help them learn from him; if they attacked too soon, they would close themselves off from his insights.

But the rule was not merely a pedagogical tool. Its goal was also to facilitate respect. I granted from the start that Christians find much to disagree with in Nietzsche's philosophy. For instance, I myself disagreed even with his setting libidinal revelry in complete opposition to sacrificial love, let alone with his celebration of "hard" power[44] and his unqualified denial of God.[45] But disagreeing with persons, even arguing with them strenuously, is not a form of disrespect; treating them from the start as either benign simpletons or sly purveyors of error from whom no insight can come *is* a form of disrespect. Notwithstanding his heavy-handed, anti-Christian polemics—especially in his late book *The Anti-Christ*[46]—Nietzsche deserves respect, including the respect of treating him as a potential source of insight.[47]

And so does everyone else.

Everyone

Everyone? Really everyone? Even those who, unlike Nietzsche at the height of his powers, cannot formulate a single, half-baked thought? Even those who, very much unlike Christ, crucify others on the cross of crucifiers' own utter selfishness?

INDISCRIMINATE RESPECT

After Jared Lee Loughner shot at point-blank range U.S. Representative Gabrielle Giffords, killed six people, and wounded nineteen, I posted on my Facebook wall: "1 Peter says: 'Honor everyone.' 'Honor'—not merely 'don't demean' or 'tolerate,' but honor. And 'everyone'—not only 'those in our political camp' or 'with our moral persuasions,' but everyone." I meant the comment as a reminder that in a polarized and vociferous political and cultural climate, we ought to respect our opponents. To me, the shooting was a warning, an enactment of the inhumane depth to which we may sink if we fail to sustain a culture of respect even for those with whom we profoundly disagree.

One of my Facebook friends pushed the comment to its conclusion. He asked: "Does this also mean: 'honor' the shooter?" "Yes, honor the shooter as well," I responded without flinching. "We should honor all folks whom God loves and for whom Christ died, and who, whatever else they are, are neighbors we are commanded to love as we love ourselves." The reach of God's love is the scope of our respect. As the first is universal, the second must be as well. Just as God's love is utterly indiscriminate, embracing people of all colors, creeds, and credentials whether they are the most admirable saints or the most deplorable evildoers, so also our respect should be indiscriminate.

This seems a radical stance—and from one angle it is. We should respect absolutely everyone on account of nothing else but the mere reality of their humanity! When it comes to respect, the only relevant question is: "Is this a human being?" If the answer is "Yes," then respect is owed.[48] From another angle, the idea that we should respect everyone seems almost trite. It is so much a self-evident truth in contemporary modern culture that it feels more like a tacit cultural-background assumption—more like the cultural air we breathe—rather than an explicit moral conviction. But when a killer puts a bullet through the head of a citizen who belongs to a different political party, embraces a different religion, or lives by a different moral code, we realize how fragile that assumption is. Why *should* we respect the killer? How *can* we respect him? Even more radically, how can we claim that the worst human being has the same dignity and demands the same respect as the noblest one?[49] For this is what the belief in equal dignity entails.

PERSON AND WORK

Christian theologians distinguish between "persons" and their "deeds," or between "person" and "work." We ought to respect all persons, but not necessarily all their deeds; some of their convictions, actions, or practices may deserve the very opposite of respect. But they themselves still deserve undiminished respect.

Advocates of the "politics of equal dignity" make a similar distinction. Kant, who gave the idea of human dignity its "most impressive and systematic expression,"[50] is a good example. He says that all human beings have equal dignity and therefore deserve equal respect because they all are capable of directing their lives guided by rational principles. He did not mean that they have dignity because they *actually make* rational choices. Instead, they have dignity because of their capacity for doing so. "This potential," writes Charles Taylor, explicating Kant, "rather than anything a person may have made of it, is what ensures that each person deserves respect."[51] With regard to the capacity for rational action ("person," in my sense), devils and deacons, the vicious and the virtuous have equal dignity and deserve equal respect. With regard to the *exercise* of this capacity ("work," in my sense), they do not deserve equal respect; I must not respect a vicious man as a moral agent though I continue to respect him as a human being.

Many people feel that there is something artificial and strained—something "academic" and "philosophical," in a derogatory sense—about the distinction between person and work. Persons are responsible for their deeds. Deeds—especially misdeeds—are not like water that slides off a duck's back without leaving a trace; instead, they "stick" to the doers and qualify their identities. Equally significantly, deeds shape the character of doers; repeated deeds create habits, and habits form character.

With this kind of reasoning, a friend of mine resolutely resisted the idea of respecting the "shooter." She could not see how Mr. Loughner's deed could rightly elicit our disgust and merit utter condemnation while Mr. Loughner as a person would deserve respect. His deed, she sensed, somehow *is* his person. A noble or successful person could be respected; respect for her moral or professional achievements redounds to her, and we respect the person because of her achievements. Correspondingly, it would seem, we should despise an ignoble person because of her despicable deeds; a person who commits evil deeds is an evildoer (even if it is true that she is also more than merely an evildoer).

Though the distinction between person and work sits uneasily with us, most of us, in fact, make this distinction, and we do so in the case of those we love. In Shakespeare's *Measure for Measure*, Isabella pleads before the judge for the life of Claudio, her brother, by urging the judge to condemn Claudio's fault but not Claudio himself.[52] She wants clemency, and to grant it is to separate the doer from the deed, the person from the work. Similarly, all those who want to be truly loved make the distinction as well. When my older son was three, he expected (and told me so in unmistakable terms) that I would love him even if he were to become a donkey, let alone if he misbehaved! Love is love, he insisted rightly, and if the father loves, he will love irrespective of what the son does. My son separated the doer from the deed.

This basic insight about the nature of love lies at the heart of the general distinction in Christian theology between "person"—any person—and his "work." Martin Luther, a fierce German Protestant reformer, believed that it would be unworthy of God to love us because of our noble deeds or fail to love us because of our dastardly ones. God loves and, therefore, creates human beings; God loves created human beings just because they exist. At the same time, just because God loves each human being unconditionally, God cannot love that which harms human beings. Hence God condemns sin and does so because of love for all human beings—saints and sinners alike.[53]

That God's love grounds the distinction between person and work makes it possible for Christians to respect every*one* without thereby committing themselves to respecting every*thing*. Without belief in the God who loves, is it plausible, on purely secular grounds, to distinguish between person and work and, therefore, to prescribe respect for everyone, no matter how evil their deeds? Maybe. But regardless, this distinction is one important way in which the Christian faith underwrites respect for everyone. While condemning Mr. Loughner's deed, we ought to respect him as a person. We should abstain from violating his integrity as a human being and seek to nurture his capacities and powers.[54]

RESPECTING WHAT WE DISAGREE WITH?

I respect a person because of her humanity, but I respect her work because of its excellence. Or, to rephrase it in reference to myself as a recipient rather than as a giver of respect: I can simply *claim* respect for my self, but I must *earn* respect for my work. Clearly I, as an imperfect human being, cannot expect respect for everything that I believe or do, especially not in a world of pervasive differences in convictions and values, nor can I give respect for everything another flawed person believes or does. So we seem to have arrived at a "rule of respect" analogous to the well-known, though disputed "rule of love": "Love the sinner, but hate the sin!"[55] The "rule of respect" is then "Respect the person, but do not respect his mistaken convictions or misguided behavior!"

Might it be possible, however, to respect not just the person whose convictions we reject, but, in some cases, those mistaken convictions themselves? Cases in which respect for convictions is *not* appropriate are easy to find. If Mr. Loughner thought that his shooting rampage was justified, we could hardly respect his "moral stance." Similarly, most of us agree that we ought to despise rather than respect the views of those who, like the Gaddafi regime in February 2011, believe that it is justifiable to shoot and bomb peaceful demonstrators. So it is with many moral stances of which we highly disapprove—we judge the character of the deed as evil, and we withdraw respect.

Should we do the same with overarching interpretations of life that differ markedly from ours? The issue is acute in relations between religions, especially when monotheists are involved.[56] To believe in one God is to affirm a single religious truth, and, therefore, to reject all other religions as at least in some significant way false.[57] If we apply the person versus work distinction to the world of monotheistic religions, it seems that a monotheist would respect all adherents of other religions, but not the religions themselves because he would consider the religions significantly mistaken. We could then believe, as some Christians do, that Muhammad was demonically inspired and that Islam is an evil religion while still respecting individual Muslims. Not surprisingly, most Muslims do not feel that such Christians respect them even when those Christians are committed to tolerating them. Neither do Christians, when the roles are reversed. For religious beliefs are ultimate; they are the most basic convictions a person can hold. Most people crave being respected not just for their bare humanity, but also in the fundamental orientation of their being.

There is no compelling reason why monotheists must withdraw respect from religions with which they disagree. In fact, it is likely that it would be a mistake not to respect these religions. Recall my earlier discussion of teaching Nietzsche, a thinker whose overarching interpretation of reality is, from a Christian standpoint, markedly more mistaken than a religion such as Islam. I asked my students—with the help of a rule!—to respect Nietzsche by treating him as a potential source of insight. But long before teaching that class, I myself actually came to respect his work. His philosophy was imaginative, his thinking stringent, his writing rhetorically powerful, some of his insights deep, and his overall position seductively compelling—all extraordinary achievements demanding respect. For a while, one of his books was on my nightstand; I was reading him before turning off the light, as a spiritual exercise of sorts.

I respect Nietzsche's thought, not just Nietzsche as a person, and I do so while continuing to embrace, happily and fully, all the major Christian convictions that Nietzsche set out to annihilate. I respect, in a similar way, the interpretations of reality put forward by Socrates, Buddha, and Muhammad—all seminal visionaries who advocated less radical alternatives to the Christian faith than did Nietzsche. My conviction that God is one, that truth is one, and that religions make truth claims in no way hinders me from respecting either the philosophies of Nietzsche and Buddha (who did not believe in

God) or the thought of Socrates and Muhammad (who believed in God, though each in his own way and differently from my way).

I imply that the attitude toward the visions of the founders of religions (Buddha, Muhammad) should be similar to the attitude toward the thought of major philosophers (Nietzsche, Socrates). However, is the comparison between the two—founders of religions and philosophers—fair? It is.

How did I come to respect Nietzsche's work? The process had three elements: openness, presumption, and judgment. First, I was open to Nietzsche as a source of insight—a consequence of respecting him as a person, as I have argued earlier. Second, I was nudged to take him seriously by having a presumption that Nietzsche's work in fact does contain important insights—a presumption I adopted because he is considered a major thinker in the Western intellectual tradition. Finally, I studied his writings and formed a judgment that his thought warrants respect even though I profoundly disagree with him.

I suggest that we come to respect (or not to respect) the vision of a founder of a religion in a similar way: we assume a stance of openness to insights, we grant the presumption of worth, and we make a judgment that either results in respect or does not. With regard to the presumption of worth, Charles Taylor writes:

> It is reasonable to suppose that cultures [and religions] that have provided the horizon of meaning for large numbers of human beings, of diverse characters and temperaments, over a long period of time—that have, in other words, articulated their sense of the good, the holy, the admirable—are almost certain to have something that deserves our admiration and respect, even if it is accompanied by much that we have to abhor and reject . . . it would take a supreme arrogance to discount this possibility a priori.[58]

Just because so many diverse people have found different world religions compelling, we should presume that they deserve respect. Now, presumption is not yet a considered judgment that respect is in fact due. But such a judgment is, I believe, likely to follow.

However, what if a person's considered judgment does *not* result in respect for other religions? For example, the person finds the treatment of women in a particular religion deplorable, and she cannot respect a religion that abuses women so egregiously. If that conclusion were an informed and considered judgment rather than a merely negative reaction, she would find herself back to respecting persons—all persons—without respecting their beliefs or practices. She would be acting no differently from robust atheists, committed to equal dignity and respect for all—including for those who hold what they consider to be archaic and dangerous beliefs that merit only ridicule and reprimand.

In sum:

> Respect for all people? That's an unconditional moral obligation.
> Respect for world religions? That's a likely result of a considered judgment, notwithstanding deep disagreements.

The Christian faith, with its belief in the one God of love, demands the first attitude and is compatible with the second. When it comes to respect, that is the upside of embracing the Christian faith.

God, Dignity, and Respect

There is more to the upside. To examine it, I return to the respect for persons as distinct from their views and inquire about the spaciousness of the "circle of respect."

Absent the God of love, I wondered previously whether we would have sufficient grounds to respect those whose deeds we seriously condemn—evildoers. Absent the God of love, there is a category of people who would most certainly fall out of the circle of respect.

Once again, recall Kant on dignity and respect (respect being the appropriate response to a person's dignity). He grounded human dignity on a particular capacity of human beings: their ability to set ends and direct their lives through reason. For Kant this capacity, and nothing else, gives human beings dignity.[59] Like Kant's account, secular accounts of human dignity and respect are all built on a foundation of some human capacity. But what about human beings who are incapable of rationally directing their lives? Taylor describes what we tend to do in such cases:

> Our sense of the importance of potentiality reaches so far that we extend this protection [that is, the claim that they have dignity and deserve respect] even to people who through some circumstance that has befallen them are incapable of realizing their potential in the normal way—handicapped people, or those in a coma, for instance.[60]

This is what we tend to do. But can we adequately justify such expansion of the "circle of dignity"?[61] What if someone were to argue, adhering to Kant strictly, that a person with Alzheimer's disease (or an infant) does not have dignity since she lacks the capacity of directing her life rationally? She then would not deserve respect. If you ground human dignity in a capacity, those with the relevant capacity will deserve respect and those without it will not.

You can affirm equal respect for those who have the capacity, but not equal respect for everyone. No *capacity* of human beings can ground universal human dignity. Absent God, some human beings inevitably fall out of "the circle of respect."

What difference does God make? If God created all human beings and loves each one of them, then *all* human beings—all those who have been born of a human being[62]—have dignity and deserve respect. God's relation to them as the Creator who loves *them*, not any of their capacities, grounds their dignity.[63] Affirmation of the existence of the one God of all people, critics argue, leads inevitably to intolerance. Affirmation of the existence of the one Creator who loves each human being, I contend, is not only compatible with universal respect but provides the only compelling reason for such respect.

The Prize for Intolerance

Which religion gets the intolerance prize? In a sense, this chapter does not help answer this broad question. First, I have written here only about the Christian faith, and exclusively about authentically Christian convictions rather than about actual practices of flesh-and-blood Christians. Second, I have made no comparative judgments, no claims regarding either the superiority or inferiority of Christianity with regard to tolerance and respect. In its march through history, has Christianity been more intolerant than other religions (and secular philosophies of life), as some have argued?[64] I do not know what the answer is. I do not even know how I would go about finding the answer, what the proper method of assessing the relative intolerance of various religions might be. I would never accept the dubious honor of sitting on a jury whose task it was to decide the prizewinner.

But I did try to answer a related and more important question: Is the Christian faith itself intolerant or are intolerant Christians bastardizing their own religion? I have argued that the practice of intolerance and disrespect strains against fundamental Christian convictions and violates an explicit Christian command. And I have argued that the Christian faith offers significant resources to foster a culture of universal respect. This culture, I believe, is what we need in today's intermingled and interdependent world, all awhirl with rapid change and alive with vibrant and assertive religions.

Notes

1. For an autobiographical account, see Miroslav Volf, *The End of Memory* (Grand Rapids, MI: Eerdmans, 2006).

2. See the relation between monotheism, exclusivism, and intolerance in Jan Assmann, *Moses the Egyptian: The Memory of Egypt in Western Monotheism* (Cambridge, MA: Harvard University Press, 1997); and Assmann, *Die Mosaische Unterscheidung, Oder der Preis des Monotheismus* (Munich: Carl Hanser, 2003).

3. This phrase is from Pierre Bourdieu. See *Firing Back: Against the Tyranny of the Market* 2 (London: Verso, 2003), 86; *Pascalian Meditations* (Stanford, CA: Stanford University Press, 2000), 71.

4. One of the twelve famous Danish cartoons portrayed Muhammad in this way.

5. By "practice" here I mean not just intolerance in the violent action of Christians but also intolerance in the very way they have formulated Christian convictions, intolerance in "deed" and in "word."

6. The example comes from George Lindbeck, *The Nature of Doctrine* (Louisville, KY: Westminster John Knox, 1984), 64.

7. For an account of seven Trappist monks who were beheaded in Algeria in 1996, see the movie *Of Gods and Men*.

8. See Christopher Hitchens in a debate with Tony Blair about whether or not religion is a force for good ("Is Religion a Force for Good in the World?" Munk Debates, November 26, 2010, video, www.c-spanvideo.org/program/Blairan).

9. "United Nations Millennium Declaration," no. 6 (www2.ohchr.org/english/law /millennium.htm).

10. John Locke, *A Letter Concerning Toleration*, in *Two Treatises of Government and a Letter Concerning Toleration*, ed. Ian Shapiro (New Haven, CT: Yale University Press, 2003), 215.

11. "Whatsoever is not done with that assurance of faith is neither well in itself, nor can it be acceptable to God. To impose such things, therefore, upon any people, contrary to their own judgment, is, in effect, to command them to offend God; which, considering that the end of all religion is to please him, and that liberty is essentially necessary to that end, appears to be absurd beyond expression" (ibid., 233).

12. "No way whatsoever that I shall walk in against the dictates of my conscience will ever bring me to the mansions of the blessed" (ibid.).

13. Ibid., 219.

14. See C. B. Macpherson, *The Political Theory of Possessive Individualism: Hobbes to Locke* (Oxford: Clarendon, 1962).

15. Lactantius, *Divine Institutes*, vol. 20 (as quoted by John R. Bowlin, "Tolerance Among the Fathers," *Journal of the Society of Christian Ethics* 26, no. 1 [2006]: 27).

16. Tertullian, *Ad Scapulum*, vol. II (as quoted in Bowlin, "Tolerance Among the Fathers," 18). How Augustine, with his own interpretation of "Compel people to come in" (Luke 14:23; see "Concerning the Correction of the Donatists," in *St. Augustine: Letters 156–210*, trans. Roland Teske [Hyde Park, NY: New City, 2004], 185) and the whole tradition that followed him comport with this account of faith must remain unexamined in this short essay (see Bowlin, "Tolerance Among the Fathers," 28–31).

17. This was one of the main points of Pope Benedict XVI's remarks on Islam and violence in his infamous Regensburg address. Significantly, he makes his point by quoting a Byzantine emperor, who argued that "faith is born in the soul, not the body. Whoever would lead someone to faith needs the ability to speak well and to reason properly,

without violence and threats" (see "Faith, Reason, and the University—Memories and Reflections," *The Holy See*, September 12, 2006, www.vatican.va/holy_father/benedict _xvi/speeches/2006/september/documents/hf_ben-xvi_spe_20060912_university -regensburg_en.html; for the discussion, including Muslim reactions, see Volf, *Allah: A Christian Response* [San Francisco, CA: HarperOne, 2011], 19–39).

18. Locke, *A Letter Concerning Toleration*, 215.

19. Ibid., 216.

20. For a comprehensive discussion of the whole range of Locke's arguments for tolerance, see Susan Mendus, *Toleration and the Limits of Liberalism* (Atlantic Highlands, NJ: Humanities Press International, 1989), 22–43.

21. Volf, *Free of Charge: Giving and Forgiving in a Culture Stripped of Grace* (Grand Rapids, MI: Zondervan, 2006).

22. Volf, *Exclusion and Embrace: Theological Exploration of Identity, Otherness, and Reconciliation* (Nashville, TN: Abingdon, 1996).

23. Volf, *A Public Faith: How Followers of Christ Should Serve the Common Good* (Grand Rapids, MI: Brazos, 2011).

24. As I expound the command here, I will not be able to relate it to biblical texts in which it seems that Jesus and Christians are described as doing exactly the opposite of what obeying this command seems to require, such as when Jesus tells "the Jews" who seek to kill him, "your father is the devil" (John 8:44). On this issue see Volf, *Captive to the Word of God: Engaging the Scriptures for Contemporary Theological Reflection* (Grand Rapids, MI: Eerdmans, 2010), 105–110.

25. For a discussion of "the circumstances of toleration," see Mendus, *Toleration*, 8–9.

26. Justin Martyr, *Apology*, I, 24 (www.earlychristianwritings.com/text/justinmartyr -firstapology.html).

27. Ibid.

28. For the distinction between "regimes of intolerance" and the "mindset of intolerance" see Michael Walzer, *On Toleration* (New Haven: Yale University Press, 1997), 8–13.

29. Socrates was famous for having advocated the unconditional validity of moral commands: when injured, we should not "injure in return, as many imagine; for we must injure no one at all," it being the case that "injustice is always an evil" (Plato, *Crito* 49b).

30. John Locke has commented on the tendency for persecution and tolerance to become a function of relative power: "Where they have not the power to carry on persecution and to become master, there they desire to live upon fair terms and preach toleration" (Locke, *A Letter Concerning Toleration*, 217).

31. Walzer, *On Toleration*, 52. He references Stephan Carter's claim that "the language of tolerance is the language of power" (*The Culture of Disbelief* [New York: Basic Books, 1993], 96).

32. I. Howard Marshall, *I Peter* (Downer's Grove, IL: Intervarsity Press, 1991), 85. See also Leonard Goppelt, *A Commentary on 1 Peter*, trans. John E. Alsup (Grand Rapids, MI: Eerdmans, 1993), 190; Joel B. Green, *I Peter* (Grand Rapids, MI: Eerdmans, 2007), 76.

33. I draw here on David Kelsey, *Eccentric Existence: A Theological Anthropology* (Louisville, KY: Westminster John Knox Press, 2009), 279–280.

34. See Immanuel Kant, *The Metaphysics of Morals*, ed. Mary Gregor (Cambridge: Cambridge University Press, 1996), 155–156 [6:393–394]. On respect in Kant, see Gene Outka, "Respect for Persons," *Westminster Dictionary of Christian Ethics*, ed. James F. Childress and John MacQuarrie (Philadelphia: Westminster Press, 1986), 540–545.

35. On the difference between insiders' and outsiders' being "soft" in 1 Peter, see Volf, *Captive to the Word of God*, 65–90.

36. What is sometimes called "the paradox of toleration" involves explaining "how the tolerator might think it good to tolerate that which is morally wrong" (Mendus, *Toleration*, 20).

37. See on this point (in the context of the discussion of the equal worth of diverse cultures), Charles Taylor, "The Politics of Recognition," *Multiculturalism and the Politics of Recognition*, ed. Amy Gutmann (Princeton, NJ: Princeton University Press, 1994), 68–72.

38. Locke, *A Letter Concerning Toleration*, 219.

39. Ibid.

40. The word for "respect" is literally "fear." Scholars debate whether it refers to reverence for God (see Goppelt, *I Peter* [German edition, *Der erste Petrusbrief*, (Göttingen: Vandenhoeck & Ruprecht, 1977), 237]) or respect for people (see Norbert Brox, *Der erste Petrusbrief* [Zürich/Neukirchen-Vluyn: Benzinger/Neukirchener, 1979], 160). The use of "fear" elsewhere in the epistle suggests reverence for God (1:17; 2:18; 3:2), but the present context favors respect for people.

41. On combating prejudice as discussed in this section, see Volf, *Allah*, 203–207.

42. On this point, see the reflections on evangelism in Volf, *Allah*, 207–213; on witness, see Volf, *A Public Faith* (chapter 6).

43. The last line of Nietzsche's autobiography, *Ecce Homo* (an allusion to Pilate's words of Christ at the end of John's Gospel) reads, "Have I been understood?—*Dionysus against the Crucified*" (Friedrich Nietzsche, *Ecce Homo: How One Becomes What One Is*, trans. R. H. Hollingdale [London: Penguin, 1992], 104 [emphasis in original]).

44. See Nietzsche, *Thus Spoke Zarathustra*, ed. Adrian Del Caro and Robert Pippin (Cambridge: Cambridge University Press, 2006), 172.

45. See Nietzsche, *The Gay Science*, trans. Walter Kaufmann (New York: Vintage, 1974), 108, 125, 343.

46. Nietzsche, *Twilight of Idols/The Anti-Christ*, trans. R. J. Hollingdale (London: Penguin, 1990).

47. Shortly after he completed *The Anti-Christ*, Nietzsche fell into permanent insanity. In that state also, he deserved respect. But of course at that point, by definition, he ceased to be a potential source of insight; and treating him as a potential source of insight *then* would have, in a condescending sort of way, been to disrespect him as a person.

48. A form of respect can also be owed beings other than humans. But I am here referring to the particular kind of respect owed human beings.

49. Explicating Kant's position on human dignity, Allen Wood writes: ". . . the worst human being (in any respect you can possibly name) has the same dignity or absolute worth as the best rational being in that respect (or any other)" (*Kant's Ethical Thought* [Cambridge: Cambridge University Press, 1999], 132).

50. Steven Lukes, *Individualism* (Oxford: Blackwell, 1973), 45.

51. Taylor, "The Politics of Recognition," 41.

52. William Shakespeare, *Measure for Measure*, in *Riverside Shakespeare*, ed. G. Blakemore Evans (Boston: Houghton Mifflin, 1974), 560.

53. On the distinction between person and work in Luther, see Gerhard Ebeling, *Luther: An Introduction to His Thought*, trans. R. A. Wilson (Philadelphia: Fortress, 1970), 148–158.

54. Clearly, "respect" in my sense of the term is compatible with punishing the offender. Indeed, under certain circumstances, punishment may be a way to respect the person as the doer of a morally abhorrent deed.

55. Some object to the rule, but most who do so merely dispute the sinfulness of a given act for which respect is withheld rather than rejecting the rule itself. When there is agreement that the behavior in question is sinful or evil, most Christians at least accept the rule.

56. I make an assumption for which I am unable to argue here: all religions are not fundamentally the same. In this I differ from many contemporaries, scholars and laypeople alike, who unthinkingly embrace the idea of the basic sameness of all major religions, so that the choice between them is a matter of an accident of birth or of a preference for a certain way of life, but not a matter of *truth*. In contrast, I believe that religions, among the other things they do, make claims to truth and that these claims sometimes overlap among religions (as when both Jews and Muslims say that they believe in one God), but sometimes also contradict one another (as when Christians claim that Jesus Christ was God incarnate and Muslims claim that he was a special prophet).

57. For a discussion of this issue, see Volf, *Allah*, 221–224.

58. Taylor, "The Politics of Recognition," 72–73.

59. See Wood, *Kant's Ethical Thought*, 132–133.

60. Taylor, "The Politics of Recognition," 41–42.

61. For the phrase, see Nicholas Wolterstorff, *Justice: Rights and Wrongs* (Princeton, NJ: Princeton University Press, 2008), 333.

62. German theologian Dietrich Bonhoeffer, who worked in the time of Nazi disregard for human life (especially damaged human life), suggested this "definition" of a human being. He writes: "The question of whether life, in the case of persons severely retarded from birth, is really *human* life at all is so naïve that it hardly needs to be answered. It is disabled life, born of human parents, which can be nothing else than *human life*" (*Dietrich Bonhoeffer Works*, vol. 6, *Ethics*, ed. Clifford J. Green [Minneapolis: Fortress, 2005], 195 [emphasis in original]).

63. In different ways, both Wolterstorff (*Justice*, 323–361) and Kelsey (*Eccentric Existence*, 276–279) make that argument.

64. See Naveed Sheikh, *Body Count: A Quantitative Review of Political Violence Across World Civilizations* (Amman: Royal Islamic Strategic Studies Centre, 2009).

Abraham's Muslim Children

12

God Needs No Defense

ABDURRAHMAN WAHID

Kyai Haji Abdurrahman Wahid was Indonesia's first democratically elected president and served as chairman of the world's largest Muslim organization, the Nahdlatul Ulama, from 1984 to 1999. He is widely recognized as one of the twentieth century's leading Islamic intellectuals and is renowned for his defense of religious and ethnic minorities, as well as freedom of thought, expression, and conscience. President Wahid received the Friends of the United Nations Global Tolerance Award in 2003 and the Simon Wiesenthal Center's Medal of Valor in 2008. Among his many affiliations, Kyai Haji Abdurrahman Wahid was co-founder, patron, and senior advisor of LibForAll Foundation and its International Institute of Qur'anic Studies, which generously provided permission to reprint this essay.

As K. H. Mustofa Bisri[1] wrote in his poem *Allahu Akbar*: "If all of the 6 billion human inhabitants of this earth, which is no greater than a speck of dust, were blasphemous . . . or pious . . . it would not have the slightest effect upon His greatness."

Omnipotent, and existing as absolute and eternal Truth, nothing could possibly threaten God. And as ar-Rahman (the Merciful) and ar-Rahim (the

Compassionate), God has no enemies. Those who claim to defend God, Islam, or the Prophet are thus either deluding themselves or manipulating religion for their own mundane and political purposes, as we witnessed in the carefully manufactured outrage that swept the Muslim world several years ago, claiming hundreds of lives, in response to cartoons published in Denmark. Those who presume to fully grasp God's will and dare to impose their own limited understanding of this upon others are essentially equating themselves with God and are unwittingly engaged in blasphemy.

As Muslims, rather than harshly condemning others' speech or beliefs and employing threats or violence to constrain these, we should ask: why is there so little freedom of expression and religion in the so-called Muslim world? Exactly whose interests are served by laws such as Section 295-C of the Pakistani legal code, "Defiling the Name of Muhammad," which mandates the death penalty for "blasphemy," which Pakistan's Federal Shari'a Court has effectively defined as:

> Reviling or insulting the Prophet in writing or speech; speaking profanely or contemptuously about him or his family; attacking the Prophet's dignity and honor in an abusive manner; vilifying him or making an ugly face when his name is mentioned; showing enmity or hatred towards him, his family, his companions, and the Muslims; accusing, or slandering the Prophet and his family, including spreading evil reports about him or his family; defaming the Prophet; refusing the Prophet's jurisdiction or judgment in any manner; rejecting the Sunnah; showing disrespect, contempt for or rejection of the rights of Allah and His Prophet or rebelling against Allah and His Prophet.[2]

Rather than serve to protect God, Islam, or Muhammad, such deliberately vague and repressive laws merely empower those with a worldly (that is, political) agenda and act as a "sword of Damocles," threatening not only religious minorities, but the right of mainstream Muslims to speak freely about their own religion without being threatened by the wrath of fundamentalists—exercised through the power of government or mobs—whose claims of "defending religion" are little more than a pretext for self-aggrandizement.

No objective observer can deny that Pakistani society—like so many others in the Muslim world—has undergone a process of coarsening under the influence of such laws, as well as by the rise of religious extremism and the loss of true spirituality. Therefore, the profound meaning and purpose of Islam remain veiled from human understanding.

The renowned Qur'anic injunction "Let there be no compulsion in religion" (2:256), anticipated Article 18 of the Universal Declaration of Human Rights[3] by more than thirteen centuries and should serve as an inspiration to

Muslim societies today, guiding them on the path to religious freedom and tolerance.

In its original Qur'anic sense, the word *shari'a* refers to "the way," the path to God, and not to formally codified Islamic law, which only emerged in the centuries following Muhammad's death. In examining the issue of blasphemy and apostasy laws, it is thus vital that we differentiate between the Qur'an—from which much of the raw material for producing Islamic law is derived—and the law itself. For although its revelatory inspiration is divine, Islamic law is man-made and thus subject to human interpretation and revision.

For example, punishment for apostasy is merely the legacy of historical circumstances and political calculations stretching back to the early days of Islam, when apostasy generally coincided with desertion from the caliph's army and/or rejection of his authority and thus constituted treason or rebellion. The embedding (that is, codification) of harsh punishments for apostasy into Islamic law must be recognized as a historical and political by-product of these circumstances framed in accordance with human calculations and expediency, rather than assuming that Islam, and shari'a, must forever dictate punishment for changing one's religion.

The historical development and use of the term *shari'a* to refer to Islamic law often leads those unfamiliar with this history to conflate man-made law with its revelatory inspiration and to thereby elevate the products of human understanding—which are necessarily conditioned by space and time—to the status of divine.

Shari'a, properly understood, expresses and embodies perennial values. Islamic law, by contrast, is the product of *ijtihad* (interpretation), which depends on circumstances (*al-hukm yadur ma'a al-'illah wujudan wa 'adaman*) and needs to be continuously reviewed in accordance with ever-changing circumstances, to prevent Islamic law from becoming out of date, rigid, and noncorrelative—not only with Muslims' contemporary lives and conditions, but also with the underlying perennial values of shari'a itself.

Throughout Islamic history, many of the greatest *fiqh* (Islamic jurisprudence) scholars have also been deeply grounded in the traditions of *tassawuf*, or Islamic mysticism, and recognized the need to balance the letter with the spirit of the law. The profoundly humanistic and spiritual nature of Sufi Islam facilitated the accommodation of different social and cultural practices as Islam spread from its birthplace in the Arabian Peninsula to the Levant, North Africa, the Sahel and Sub-Saharan Africa, Persia, Central and South Asia, and the East Indies archipelago. By many estimates, a majority of the Muslim population in most of these regions still practice a form of religious piety either directly or indirectly derived from Sufism. And the greatness of traditional Islamic art and architecture—from the wonders of Fes and Grenada to Istanbul, Isfahan, Samarkand, and Agra—bears testimony to the long line of Sufi masters, guilds, and individual artists who strove to ennoble matter, so as to transform our man-made environment into "the veritable counterpart of nature, a mosaic of 'Divine portents' revealing everywhere the handiwork of man as God's vice-regent."[4]

Indeed, the greatness of classical Islamic civilization—which incorporated a humane and cosmopolitan universalism—stemmed largely from the intellectual and spiritual maturity that grew from the amalgamation of Arab, Greek, Jewish, Christian, and Persian influences. That is why I wept upon seeing Ibn Rushd's commentary on the *Nicomachean Ethics*, lovingly preserved and displayed, during a visit some years ago to Fes, Morocco. For if not for Aristotle and his great treatise, I might have become a Muslim fundamentalist myself.

Among the various factors that have contributed to the long decline of Arab and Muslim civilizations in general, and greatly hindered their participation in the development of the modern world, was the triumph of normative religious constraints, which ultimately defeated the classical tradition of Islamic humanism. Absorption of "alien" influences—particularly in the realm of speculative thought, and the creation of individual, rational, and independent sciences not constrained by religious scholasticism—was defeated by internal control mechanisms exercised by religious and governmental authorities, thus paralyzing Muslim societies.

These same tendencies are still on display in our contemporary world, not least in the form of severe blasphemy and apostasy laws that narrow the bounds of acceptable discourse in the Islamic world and prevent most Muslims from thinking "outside the box," not only about religion but also about vast spheres of life, literature, science, and culture in general.

Religious Understanding Is a Process

Anyone who is sincere in understanding his or her faith necessarily undergoes a process of constant evolution in that understanding, as experience and insights give rise to new perceptions of the truth. For as God states in the Qur'an: "We will display Our Signs upon the horizon, and within themselves (humanity), until it is clear to them that God is the Truth (*al-Haqq*)" (41:53).

Nothing that exists is self-sufficient, other than God. All living things are interdependent and owe their very existence to God. Yet because God's creatures exist within time and space, their perceptions of truth and reality differ from one to the next, conditioned by their personal knowledge and experience.

As referenced above, Islam views the world and whatever information we may obtain from it as signs leading to knowledge of God. Muslim scholars (*ulama*) traditionally classify three stages of knowledge: first, the science of certainty (*'ilm al-yaqin*), which is inferential and concerns knowledge commonly held to be true, whether by scientists, intellectuals, or *ulama* themselves. Second, the vision of certainty (*'ain al-yaqin*) represents a higher level of truth than the first. At this stage, one directly witnesses that information about an objective phenomenon is indeed true and accurate. Third is the truth or reality of certainty (*haqq al-yaqin*), that is, truth that reaches the level of perfection through direct personal experience, as exemplified by a saint's mystical communion with God.

The fact that the Qur'an refers to God as "the Truth" is highly significant. If human knowledge is to attain this level of Truth, religious freedom is vital. Indeed, the search for Truth (that is, the search for God)—whether employing the intellect, emotions, or various forms of spiritual practice—should be allowed a free and broad range. For without freedom, the individual soul cannot attain absolute Truth, which is, by its very nature, unconditional freedom itself.

Intellectual and emotional efforts are mere preludes in the search for Truth. One's goal as a Muslim should be to completely surrender oneself (*islâm*) to the absolute Truth and Reality of God, rather than to accept mere intellectual or emotional concepts regarding the ultimate Truth. Without freedom, humans can only attain a self-satisfied and illusory grasp of the truth, rather than genuine Truth itself (*haqq al-haqiqi*).

The spiritual aptitude of any given individual necessarily plays a key role in his or her ability to attain the Truth, and the particular expression of Truth apprehended by one person may differ from that of the next. Islam honors and values these differences, as well as religious freedom itself, recognizing that each human being comprehends God in accord with his or her own native abilities and propensities, as expressed in the *Hadith Qudsi*:[5] "*Ana 'inda zann 'abdi bi*"—"I am as my servant thinks I am." Of course, one's efforts to know God (*mujahadah*, from the same root as the word *jihad*) should be genuine and sincere (*ikhlas*), leading to a state of self-transcendence. In such a state, humans experience God's ineffable presence and their own annihilation. Muslim fundamentalists often reject this notion, because of their shallow grasp of religion and lack of spiritual experience. For them, God must be understood as completely transcendent (*tanzih*) and far beyond the reach of humanity, with no hope for anyone to experience God's presence.

Such views are mistaken, for as the Qur'an itself states: "Whichever way you turn, there is the face of God" (2:115).

Nothing can restrict the absolute Truth. Sufism—whose purpose is to bring Muslims to the third stage of knowledge, that is, the truth and reality of certainty—emphasizes the value of freedom and diversity, both as reflections of God's will and purpose and to prevent the inadvertent or deliberate conflation of human understanding (which is inherently limited and subject to error) with the Divine. Faith (*îmân*) and surrender to God on a purely intellectual level are not enough. Rather, a Muslim should continuously strive to experience the actual presence of God (*ihsan*). For without experiencing God's presence, a Muslim's religious practice remains on a purely theoretical level; *islâm* has not yet become an experiential reality.

Sanctions against freedom of religious inquiry and expression act to halt the developmental process of religious understanding dead in its tracks—conflating the sanctioning authority's current, limited grasp of the truth with ultimate Truth itself and thereby transforming religion from a path to the Divine into a "divinized" goal, whose features and confines are generally dictated by those with an all-too-human agenda of earthly power and control.

We can see this process at work in attempts by the Organization of Islamic Conferences, the UN General Assembly, and the UN Council on Human Rights to restrict freedom of expression and institute a legally binding global ban on any perceived criticism of Islam, to prevent so-called defamation of religion. Whether motivated by sincere concern for humanity or political calculation, such efforts are woefully misguided and play directly into the hands of fundamentalists, who wish to avoid all criticism of their attempts to narrow the scope of discourse regarding Islam and to inter 1.3 billion Muslims in a narrow, suffocating chamber of dogmatism.

Although hostility toward Islam and Muslims is a legitimate and vital concern, we must recognize that a major cause of such hostility is the behavior of certain Muslims. These Muslims propagate a harsh, repressive, supremacist, and often violent understanding of Islam, which tends to aggravate and confirm non-Muslims' worst fears and prejudices about Islam and Muslims in general.

Rather than legally stifle criticism and debate—which will only encourage Muslim fundamentalists in their efforts to impose a spiritually void, harsh, and monolithic understanding of Islam upon all the world—Western authorities should instead firmly defend freedom of expression, not only in their own nations, but globally, as enshrined in Article 19 of the Universal Declaration of Human Rights.[6]

Those who are humble and strive to live in genuine submission to God—*islâm*—do not claim to be perfect in their understanding of the Truth. Rather, they are content to live in peace with others, whose paths and views may differ.

Defending freedom of expression is by no means synonymous with personally countenancing or encouraging disrespect toward others' religious beliefs, but it does imply greater faith in the judgment of God than in the judgment of man. Beyond the daily headlines of chaos and violence, the vast majority of the world's Muslims continue to express their admiration of Muhammad by seeking to emulate the peaceful and tolerant example of his life that they have been taught, without behaving violently in response to those who despise the Prophet or proclaim the supremacy of their own limited understanding of the Truth. Such Muslims live in accordance with the Qur'anic verse that states, "And the servants of (Allah) the Most Gracious are those who walk in humility, and when the ignorant address them, they say 'Peace' " (25:63).

Notes

1. Descended from a long line of charismatic religious leaders, Kyai Haji Mustofa Bisri heads the Raudlatuth Tholibin Islamic boarding school in Rembang, Central Java. Widely revered as a religious scholar, poet, novelist, painter, and Muslim intellectual, K.H. Mustofa Bisri has strongly influenced the Nahdlatul Ulama's social, educational, and religious development over the past thirty years.

2. Mohammad Asrar Madani, *Verdict of Islamic Law on Blasphemy and Apostasy* (Lahore, Pakistan: Idara-e-Islamiat, 1994).

3. "Everyone has the right to freedom of thought, conscience, and religion; this right includes freedom to change his religion or belief, and freedom, either alone or in community with others and in public or private, to manifest his religion or belief in teaching, practice, worship, and observance."

4. Roloff Beny, Seyyed Hossein Nasr, and Mitchell Crites, *Persia: Bridge of Turquoise* (New York: New York Graphic Society, 1975).

5. Muslims regard *Hadith Qudsi* as the words of God, repeated by Muhammad and recorded on the condition of an *isnad* (chain of verification by witness[es] who heard Muhammad say the hadith).

6. "Everyone has the right to freedom of opinion and expression; this right includes freedom to hold opinions without interference and to seek, receive, and impart information and ideas through any media and regardless of frontiers."

13

The Middle Way

HEDIEH MIRAHMADI

*Hedieh Mirahmadi is an attorney, author, and founder and president
of the World Organization for Resource Development & Education
(WORDE). WORDE works to improve communication between Muslim and non-Muslim communities in order to reduce social conflict and
political instability. Mirahmadi is the editor of several books, including*
Islam and Civil Society *and* In the Shadow of Saints.

Sharing a Meal

When I think about the universal principle of "accepting the other," I
am reminded of a story we are taught in Islam about Prophet Abraham and
the Zoroastrian. It is a wonderful example of how faith teaches us to love
one another, regardless of our individual religious paths.

> The Prophet Abraham never liked to eat alone. He felt that food was a divine
> blessing and, as such, should be shared with others, particularly those in
> need. Therefore, he made it his constant practice that before a meal he would
> invite someone to eat with him. One day, Abraham invited a fire worshiper
> to have a meal with him. On sitting down to eat, Abraham asked him to
> begin in God's name and to recite, "In the Name of God, the Beneficent, the

Merciful." The Zoroastrian said, "You want to buy my religion with your one meal? I am a fire worshiper. Why must I take God's name?"

This shocked Abraham, who preached of the One God, the Creator, while this person wanted to eat in the name of his fire. Unable to tolerate this idolatry, Abraham asked the man to leave his table. The Lord immediately sent a revelation to Abraham: "For the past ninety years this person has not taken My Name at all, in spite of which I have been feeding him without fail, while you found it difficult to feed him just this one meal. Regardless of whether he takes My Name or not, you cannot eat until you bring him back and make him happy. If you do not, I will remove you from the roster of My prophets."

Abraham immediately went in search of the man. When Abraham saw the man, he began to chase him; the man became so frightened that he started to run away. Prophet Abraham called to him to stop, as he meant him no harm. Upon reaching him, Abraham told him, "My Lord has reprimanded me on your behalf," and he explained what had happened. The man was surprised and said, "O Abraham, if your Lord is such that He would rebuke you on my behalf, then surely He is One worthy of worship."

I like this story because it highlights so much of what I find true and beautiful in my faith, Islam. In portraying Abraham as an exemplar of good behavior, it connects Islam to the teachings of previous prophets and religions. I find that much of Islam's teachings are like this, incorporating the stories of earlier prophets, messengers, and saintly figures wherever they highlight a religious teaching, moral lesson, or solution to an ethical dilemma.

This story also demonstrates the importance of generosity, humility, hospitality, and, most important, the ideal of self-sacrifice in Islam. Few of us today would consider inviting a stranger to share a meal, much less to enter our home; yet Abraham refused to partake in a meal without finding someone to share it with.

But the most significant part of this story is its emphasis on going beyond *tolerance* in our everyday ethical behaviors and striving to reach *acceptance* of the other—a distinction that I will discuss in greater detail below. As the story so aptly portrays, God, in his divine wisdom, created all kinds of people. Some worship him, some worship others, and some do not worship at all. However, God does not withhold his divine gifts and mercy from any of them. The Lord does not demand all of creation to accept only one faith, so why do we?

Although it is true that Islam has its own set of required beliefs, this story aptly illustrates the guiding principle that "there is no compulsion in religion."[1]

At the same time this story demonstrates the importance God places on practicing goodness and charity with everyone, regardless of whether or not they accept him. In the Holy Qur'an, God has said about human beings, "I have created them with both My hands."[2] If he created us from clay and imbued us with his divine light and love, who then are we to reject anyone?

Unfortunately, the core values of this example (which every schoolchild used to learn in Muslim communities around the world) are drowned out by extremists on the fringes of Muslim society. These radicals have waged a propaganda campaign to shape the discourse that defines the relationship Muslims have with the rest of civilization. They view the world in an ancient and outmoded paradigm in which the world is bifurcated into the Muslim "Land of Islam" and the non-Muslim "Land of War."

In many Western countries, extremists have taken advantage of undereducated Muslims that face cultural and linguistic barriers to perpetuate the belief that Muslims are better off further isolating their communities than integrating into the Land of War. I was once surprised to find literature in a mosque in Washington, D.C., that advocated the creation of Muslim hospitals, judicial courts, and schools as part of a larger scheme to sequester Muslims from the broader American community. Unfortunately, these tactics build hatred and mistrust of non-Muslims over time. They also create a siege mentality within the Muslim community in which dialogue and interfaith engagement are readily discouraged. In this way, extremists have supplanted classical Islamic values of tolerance and social harmony with violence and insurrection. This is a horrendous development not only for me, but also for the vast majority of Muslims throughout the world who reject extremism and seek to live harmoniously with our non-Muslim neighbors.

Classical Islam calls people to the middle way in all things: in belief, worship, ethics, morality, behavior, individual interactions, social interactions, and intellectual understanding. The Holy Qur'an states: "Thus, We have appointed you a middle nation, that you may be witnesses over mankind, and that the messenger may be a witness over you."[3] The "middle way" means a way that does not exaggerate, that avoids the extremes of being either too strict or too lenient. The middle way is not harsh, but it does not allow the ego free rein. It is a way that all should strive for.

The Prophet—whom all sincere Muslims strive to emulate—rejected extremism. About himself and his way, the Prophet said, "God did not send me to be harsh, but He sent me to teach in a gentle and easy manner."[4] Ayesha, the wife of Prophet Muhammad said, "If the Prophet was given the choice between two options, he would always choose the easier one."

Principles of Tolerance and the Unity of Humanity

Modern-day Muslim scholars often repeat the catchphrase "Islam tolerates other religions." I believe, however, that this is an inadequate representation of the faith. *Tolerate*, as defined in *Merriam-Webster's Dictionary*, is to "endure, put up with, to bear." According to this definition, tolerance allows one to develop only superficial or shallow relationships devoid of compassion, empathy, and mutual understanding. In Islam it is not sufficient to simply tolerate others. Rather, Islam encourages Muslims to listen to and observe others so that we may truly understand them and accept them as part of God's creation. Acceptance—more so than tolerance—breathes life into social structures, potentially shifting them from a stance of conflict to one of mutual respect.

The injunction for acceptance was established when God said in the Holy Qur'an: "O mankind! We created you from a single (pair) of a male and a female, and made you into nations and tribes, that ye may know each other, not that ye may despise (each other). Verily the most honored of you in the sight of God is (he who is) the most righteous of you."[5] This verse is generally the strongest affirmation of Islam's belief in the unity of mankind and the equality of each soul, applying to both men and women, as well as to every race, tribe, and ethnicity. It emphasizes that the true measure of value is not a person's wealth or status, but rather his or her moral character, or "righteousness."

The principle of human dignity and unity is emphasized repeatedly in the Holy Qur'an: "Now indeed, We have honored the children of Adam, and borne them over land and sea, and provided for them sustenance out of the good things of life, and favored them far above most of Our creation."[6] Humankind, having been descended from one father and one mother, is unified at the root of the tree of human existence. For that reason, Muslims believe that all of humanity are brothers and sisters and that this familial relationship holds priority despite any material differences that may exist.

Hajj, Islam's annual pilgrimage to Mecca, Saudi Arabia, is a unique and unparalleled demonstration of humanity's unity. There is nothing like it in the world. By official count, millions of people attend this event each year from around the globe. All come together to worship in one place, from every race, culture, nation, and tribe, without discrimination. The Prophet of Islam emphasized this principle when he said: "There is no difference between an Arab or a non-Arab, except through righteousness."[7]

During Hajj, all pilgrims stand together in identical garb, covered only with unstitched sheets of white cloth, dressed as ascetics. In hajj clothes you cannot differentiate between the leader of a nation and a simple street-sweeper. On the last day of the pilgrimage everyone comes together on the Plain of Arafat imploring God in one voice, in unity. This demonstration of humanity's common origins and oneness has taken place every single year for over 1,400 years as living proof of the well-known prophetic principle "Mankind are equal just as the teeth of a comb are equal."[8]

According to Islamic law professor Dr. Khaled Abou al-Fadl, "One can easily locate an ethical discourse within the Islamic tradition that is . . . tolerant toward the other and mindful of the dignity and worth of all human beings."[9] Among the basics of this relationship is mutual, general well-being (or welfare) of a society and cooperative relationships. Therefore, it is clear that Islam did not intend to ban friendships with people of other faiths, despite misinterpretations by those who seek to isolate Muslims. On the contrary, there are countless stories of Muslims and non-Muslims living together peacefully side by side. For example, Dr. Ahmad Mohamed El Tayeb, the current head of the world's foremost Islamic educational institution, Al Azhar, narrates:

> Muslims have always coexisted with other religions—with Christians and Jews in the western flank of Islamic dominions and with Hindus and Buddhists in the eastern flank. One can always find examples, in this context, for a bonding of people that springs from the inner gestures of a humanity deeply enriched by its life of faith. This has indeed been my own personal experience, in Upper Egypt, where Muslims have lived side by side, for centuries, with their Coptic Christian brethren.[10]

The relationship between Muslims and their non-Muslim neighbors and fellow citizens must be one of courtesy, friendly social intercourse, mutual welfare, and cooperation for the sake of righteousness; this is what true Islam calls for. Friendship should be afforded to even those who fought the Muslims, despite their enmity. God says in the Holy Qur'an: "It may be that God will grant love (and friendship) between you and those whom you (now) hold as enemies. For God has power (over all things); And God is Oft-Forgiving, Most Merciful."[11]

Because the Prophet Muhammad is the exemplar of conduct for Muslims, it is important to consider his relationship with people of other faiths. Dr. Tayeb provides another example:

> One day a funeral of a Jew passed by, and the Prophet Muhammad stood up for it, out of respect. Some of those present expressed surprise, since it was not one who believed in Islam or acknowledged it as a religion. The answer of the Prophet was this: "But is it not a human soul?" This practical

demonstration on the part of the Prophet of Islam consecrates the equality of human beings as such, in both rights and duties.[12]

As this story illustrates, right from beginning the Prophet did not treat the Jews as the "religious other." He tried to integrate them in a political community through what is known as the Mithaq-i-Madinah (Pact of Medina). This agreement was between the nascent Muslim community, the various Jewish tribes, and the pagan tribes. It should be noted that even the tribal "other" remained an important constituent.[13]

The Pact of Medina, drawn up by the Prophet himself, demonstrates his ethical norms, his spirit of inclusiveness, and his innovative approach to a modern, complex society. He described this community as *ummah wahidah*, that is, "one community." Whereas in other empires of the world, religious minorities were tolerated but not given any political rights, in the community of the Prophet the non-Muslims were given security rights, political rights, and cultural rights equal to the Muslims. Religious freedom was guaranteed, and all groups were accorded rights to self-governance and autonomy. However, it was also required that Muslims and non-Muslims share the military burden against the enemies of the new state and share the cost of war. There was no state taxation system, so each tribal community had to provide arms, horses, and camels for war preparations.[14]

Although some Muslim leaders deviated from the Prophet's example over time, rulers of the Umayyad Dynasty of Greater Syria and the Abbasid Era in Baghdad and Cairo, the Mughals in Greater India, and the sultanates of the Far East serve as excellent examples of leaders who successfully governed diverse peoples, who had separate languages, cultures, and doctrinal beliefs. Their success lay in their commitment to learn from the nations over which Muslims held influence, and various cultures were adapted and adopted instead of being destroyed.[15]

Respecting and accepting other faiths does not mean we will not disagree about matters of faith and society. However, traditional Islamic law and the Qur'an reinforce the belief that such disagreement should not lead to violence. Traditionally, Muslims believe that it is better for mankind to pursue good deeds, to submit ourselves to the will of God, and to abide by the moral boundaries of social justice—and to let God decide on matters of faith. There is a passage in the Holy Qur'an where the Prophet said: "I believe what Allah has revealed of the Book, and I am commanded to do justice between you. Allah is our Lord and your Lord. For us are our deeds; and for you your deeds. There is no contention between us and you. Allah will gather us together and to Him is the eventual return."[16] Therefore, the commandment to avoid hostility and disagreement in faith is extremely clear. The real message of the Qur'an is what it calls *istibaq al-khayrat* (excelling each other in good deeds).[17] Unfortunately, people waste too much time disputing with each other about beliefs rather than competing with each other in doing good deeds.[18]

Principle of Diversity and Plurality

God says in the Holy Qur'an:

Verily the ends you strive for are diverse.[19]

And if God had so willed, He could surely have made all mankind one single community: but [He willed it otherwise, and so] they continue to hold divergent views.[20]

And if God had so willed, He could surely have made you all one single community: but [He willed it otherwise] in order to test you by means of what He has permitted for you. Compete, then, with one another in doing good works![21]

Of all the religious traditions, Islam is unique in that it states that God did not intend for all mankind to be a single faith. It is upon this principle that Islam was instituted, not upon the principle of homogeneity, which we often see imposed on Muslims today by groups, scholars, and governments who adhere to very strict, literalist, and simplistic understandings of the faith. These groups do Islam a great disservice, showing it as primitive in its approach, medieval in attitude, and unable to adapt to the changes inherent in the social and cultural fabric of a "new world culture," which has come about with the advent of globalizing technology.

Early in Islamic history, a heretical group of Muslims, known as the Khawarij, asserted that they alone possessed the "true" understanding of the religion and that all who disagreed with them were unbelievers, despite their profession of the Islamic faith. Ali, the son-in-law and cousin of the Prophet and the fourth caliph of the early Muslim community, considered this extremist aberration so dangerous and contrary to Islamic teachings that he made it a crime for anyone to preach such tenets. However, he predicted that modern forms of this heresy would plague the Muslim nation throughout its existence.

Whoever thinks that human beings must be identical, all adhering to one system and one way, is in fact an enemy of freedom and diversity and believes in a totalitarian ideal that is impossible to fulfill and contrary to Qur'anic teachings. It is contrary to the original spirit of discourse in Islam both to stifle intellectual freedom and to stifle debate about the varied approaches to law and society. Stifling debate is like imposing a dictatorship on religion, utterly confining its scope. The Prophet said to his companions, "The differences among you are a blessing."[22] Saying "no" to differences only limits the flourishing of creative geniuses. Islam views diversity as one of God's patterns of creation. No two snowflakes are the same, for the Creator of snowflakes is named the Unique One, al-Ahad, and, therefore, each one of his creations are unique. How could one expect that humans would break from this divine pattern?

God says in the Holy Qur'an, "Verily the ends ye strive for are diverse,"[23] "... and they [human beings] shall continue to differ,"[24] and "To each among you have we prescribed a law and an open way. If Allah had so willed, He would have made you a single people."[25] Again, he reminds us that diversity and multiplicity are God's pattern: "And among His Signs are the variations in your languages and your colors."[26]

Absolute oneness applies to God alone. For those other than God, diversity is the primary condition: human or angel, inanimate or animate, solid or liquid or gas. Therefore, the existence of differences is not an aberration (as some retrogressive Muslims maintain), but is, in fact, to be expected, given our varying natures.

It is only through our diversity that we are able to learn; for without diversity in thinking, competition is eliminated, and humanity would fall to the lowest common denominator. Intellectuality requires competing stimuli and the exchange of ideas in order to function. The appearance of varied approaches is the fruit of mental and spiritual labor. Thus, we see that rather than restricting Muslims to keep to themselves, the Prophet encouraged them to learn from others. This is clear from the famous hadith "Seek knowledge even if it is in China." This hadith and many like it—for example, "Be learners from the cradle to the grave"—endowed the Muslim nation with a drive to learn and seek knowledge even if it was "not invented here." Thus, we see the Muslims were the conveyors of knowledge and the brilliant lighthouse of advancement for many centuries and were the transmitters of the learning that fostered the Renaissance in medieval Christendom. If the Muslims had not delved deeply into all sciences and generated vast amounts of new knowledge, as well as studied and conveyed to the West the knowledge of the ancient Greeks, Romans, Phoenicians, Indians, and Persians, there may never have been the impetus for the deep and insightful thought processes that were essential to the transformation of Europe.

Principles of Religious Freedom

Based on the principle of diversity, one finds its corollary in freedom of religion. God said, "There should be no compulsion in the matter of faith."[27] This principle is so important in Islam that if a person is coerced to become a Muslim, his acceptance of Islam is considered legally invalid. Even Ibn Taymiya, founder of the Salafi school—considered to be one of the more extreme sects in Islam today—explained that unbelievers who made no attempt to encroach upon Islam's homeland would not have Islam imposed upon them by force. "If the unbeliever were to be killed unless he becomes a Muslim, such an action would constitute the greatest compulsion in religion," which would run contrary to the Qur'anic rule that "no compulsion is prescribed in religion."[28]

As an Abrahamic faith, Islam embraces Christians and Jews as monotheists and believers in one God. In the Holy Qur'an, God praises their prophets: "Say: 'Who then sent down the Book which Moses brought? A light and guidance to man.' . . . We sent Jesus the son of Mary, confirming the Law that had come before him: We sent him the Gospel: therein was guidance and light, and confirmation of the Law that had come before him."[29] The Qur'an further recognizes their holy books, the Torah and Bible, as Divine revelations to mankind and honors Christians and Jews as "People of the Book."

The People of the Book were afforded not only the freedom of belief, but they were allowed to maintain their own religious law and practices—even those that conflicted with the teachings of Islam. Over time, additional religious groups were afforded similar rights. One of the major jurists of Islam, Imam Malik ibn Anas, opined that Zorastrians should be treated the same as the People of the Book by the Prophet and his successors.[30] In the early eighth century, the first Muslim prince to rule India, Muhammad bin Qasim, vowed to protect not only Muslim mosques and shrines, but also Hindu places of worship. During the Arab rule of Sindh from the eighth to the tenth centuries, Islamic law was adapted to include Buddhists as People of the Book.[31]

During the Muslim empires of the past, People of the Book were able to administer their own laws in lieu of shari'a. For example, they were allowed to consume the food "of their religion," including items that were prohibited by Islam, such as pork and wine. Even in social affairs, such as marriage, divorce, and charity, non-Muslims had the freedom to govern their community as they wished, without conditions or limits.

The Prophet Muhammad himself respected the prophets who came before him. When he and his companions victoriously entered the Arabian city of Makkah, he ordered the destruction of all the idols inside the Ka'bah, with the exception of one image, which he covered with both his hands in a gesture of protection. When they had finished removing the other images, the Prophet took away his hands, revealing the image he had carefully hidden: the child Jesus with his mother Mary. This image, on an interior column, was the only image that remained inside the Ka'bah.[32] Similarly, after the Ottomans conquered Constantinople and converted the huge cathedral Aya Sofia (or Hagia Sofia) into a mosque, they left icons of Jesus and Mary intact on the ceiling, despite the prohibition of images in a mosque.

In addition to the Prophet's example, the Holy Qur'an commands Muslims to afford autonomy and respect for world religions and their practices. In chapter six, verse 106, God commands, "Do not abuse those they appeal to besides God. If it had been God's plan, they would not have taken false gods: but We made you (O Muhammad) not one to watch over their doings, nor are you set over them to dispose of their affairs." Similarly, in chapter 109, verse six, God states, "Unto you your religion, and unto me my religion." Based on these verses, Muslim jurists have concluded that religious freedom is a core principle in Islam.

Historical Examples of Religious Freedom

It is important to highlight some historical examples of religious tolerance and support for non-Muslim communities after the time of the Prophet Muhammad in order to demonstrate that some of the current interactions between Muslims and non-Muslims have greatly diverged from their historical roots.

Whether it is the destruction of Christian holy sites in Egypt, the demolition of Buddhist statues in Afghanistan, or the mass exodus of Christians from Iraq, the despicable violence against these communities is antithetical to the legacy of previous Muslim societies. Unfortunately, some Muslim leaders and fringe groups are doing a great disservice to the reputation of Islam and to the way the world perceives Islamic law and our notions of justice. Historical examples of social cohesion, compassion, and justice can provide Muslims with the evidence they need to reverse the tide of interreligious enmity and malevolence. It also provides non-Muslims with the hope and reassurance that such balance and harmony could someday return.

CHARTER OF PRIVILEGES TO THE MONKS OF ST. CATHERINE'S
MONASTERY ON MOUNT SINAI

In A.D. 628, the Prophet Muhammad wrote a letter granting a "Charter of Privileges" to the monks of St. Catherine's Monastery on Mount Sinai. An early example of religious freedom and tolerance toward Christians, the charter ensures several human rights, such as the freedom of worship and movement, freedom for Christians to appoint their own judges and to maintain their own property, exemption from military service, and the right of protection in war. The entire text of the letter follows:

> This is a message from Muhammad ibn Abdullah, as a covenant to those who adopt Christianity, near and far, we are with them. Verily I, the servants, the helpers, and my followers defend them, because Christians are my citizens; and by Allah! I hold out against anything that displeases them.
>
> No compulsion is to be on them. Neither are their judges to be removed from their jobs nor their monks from their monasteries. No one is to destroy a house of their religion, to damage it, or to carry anything from it to the Muslims' houses. Should anyone take any of these, he would spoil God's covenant and disobey His Prophet. Verily, they are my allies and have my secure charter against all that they hate. No one is to force them to travel or to oblige them to fight. The Muslims are to fight for them.
>
> If a female Christian is married to a Muslim, it is not to take place without her approval. She is not to be prevented from visiting her church to pray. Their churches are to be respected. They are neither to be prevented from repairing them nor the sacredness of their covenants. No one of the nation (Muslims) is to disobey the covenant till the Last Day (end of the world).[33]

COVENANT OF CALIPH OMAR, OR THE CODE OF OMAR

Caliph Omar often visited Jewish and Christian holy sites. Once when he went to the Jewish temple, he was disturbed to find that the Romans had stored their refuse there, and he immediately began to clear the trash with his hands. Afterward, the caliph went to the Church of the Holy Sepulcher. When prayer time arrived, he was offered a place to pray inside the church, but he refused to do so, knowing that if he were to pray inside the building, the church would be transformed into a mosque. Instead, he honored the Christians' sacred building by praying on the steps outside, thereby allowing the church to remain a Christian holy place. He then offered the people of Jerusalem a covenant of peace and protection of their holy places, such as the Church of the Holy Sepulcher and the old Jewish temple.

INCLUSION OF THE HINDUS OF INDIA

When Muhammad bin Qasim introduced Islamic rule to the Indian sub-continent in the early eighth century, Hindus were treated as People of the Book. In addition, both Hindus and Buddhists were invited to serve in the administration as trusted advisors and governors. The tradition of inclusion was further strengthened by the Sufis, particularly of the Chistiya order, who had assimilated a number of local customs and traditions.[34] Over time, Indian scholars such as the renowned Mazhar Jan-i-Janan also accepted the Divine origin of the Vedas, the Hindu sacred texts and further suggested that the Hindu Krishna and Rama Chandra were both prophets who preached the oneness of God.[35]

LETTER FROM CALIPH ALI TO MALIK AL-ASHTAR,
THE GOVERNOR OF EGYPT

Caliph Ali wrote to his companion Malik Al-Ashtar about governing with compassion Muslims and non-Muslims alike:

> Remember, Malik, that amongst your subjects there are two kinds of people: those who have the same religion as you have, they are brothers to you; and those who have religions other than that of yours, they are human beings like you. Men of either category suffer from the same weaknesses and disabilities that human beings are inclined to, they commit sins, indulge in vices either intentionally or foolishly and unintentionally without realizing the enormity of their deeds. Let your mercy and compassion come to their rescue and help in the same way and to the same extent that you expect Allah to show mercy and forgiveness to you. You must always appreciate and adopt a policy which is neither too severe nor too lenient; a policy which is based upon equity will be largely appreciated.[36]

This letter was used in the 2002 United Nations Development Programme's Arab Human Development Report as an example of good governance for the Arab world.

LETTER FROM CALIPH OMAR TO GOVERNOR ADI IBN ARTAT

This letter, from Caliph Omar to Governor Adi ibn Artat, instructs Muslims to care for elderly non-Muslims:

> With the name of God, the Most Merciful, the All Merciful. From the Servant of God, Commander of the Faithful, 'Omar (ibn 'abd al-'Aziz) to (the governor) 'Adi ibn Artat and to the believing Muslims in his company: Peace be with you. Whereafter I send you praise of God, beside Whom there is no God. Thereafter: Pay attention to the condition of the Protected (non-Muslims),

treat them tenderly. If any of them reaches old age and has no resources, it is you who should spend on him. If he has contractual brethren, demand these latter to spend on him. Apply retaliation if anybody commits tort against him. . . . Peace be with you.[37] [emphasis added]

PEACEFUL COEXISTENCE IN ISLAMIC SPAIN (AL-ANDALUS)

Under the Ummayad Caliphate in the ninth century, the heartland of the Muslim empire was southern Spain, or Andalusia. This region played an active role in promoting multicultural learning and religious tolerance. Christians, Jews, and Muslims lived in peaceful coexistence, and Christians and Muslims used to pray together in the Great Mosque of Cordoba (today, the Cordoba Cathedral). It was at this time that the writings of ancient Greek philosophers were preserved and translated by Muslim scholars. Non-Muslims living in Andalusia were not forced to live in ghettoes or other segregated places; they were not forced to be slaves; they were not prevented from practicing their faith; they were not forced to convert or die under Muslim rule; nor were they banned from any particular ways of earning a living. Not only were Jews and Christians able to contribute to society and culture, but they could also work in all branches of civil service.

EDICT FROM THE SULTAN OF MOROCCO

The Sultan of Morocco, Muhammad ibn Abdullah, issued the following edict on February 5, 1864, to advise Moroccan governors how to treat their Jewish populations:

> To our civil servants and agents who perform their duties as authorized representatives in our territories, we issue the following edict:
> They must deal with the Jewish residents of our territories according to the absolute standard of justice established by God. The Jews must be dealt with by the law on an equal basis with others so that none suffers the least injustice, oppression, or abuse. Nobody from their own community or outside shall be permitted to commit any offense against them or their property. Their artisans and craftsmen may not be scripted into service against their will, and must be paid full wages for serving the state. Any oppression will cause the oppressor to be in darkness on Judgment Day and we will not approve of any such wrongdoing. Everyone is equal in the sight of our law, and we will punish anyone who wrongs or commits aggression against the Jews with divine aid. This order which we have stated here is the same law that has always been known, established, and stated. We have issued this edict simply to affirm and warn anyone who may wish to wrong them, so the Jews

may have a greater sense of security and those intending harm may be deterred by greater sense of fear.[38]

These edicts and practices are part of the real legacy of Prophet Muhammad to civilization. From these examples, it is evident that hard-line Islamists today are making up their own faith. Moreover, their calls to revert back to Islamic practices of the seventh century are misleading because they have no intention of following the early Muslim communities' examples of interfaith tolerance, acceptance, and peaceful coexistence. It is also significant to note that many of the worst examples of Muslim/non-Muslim tensions are occurring in modern times—after the advent of militant Islamist doctrine.

Historical Examples of the Exchange of Knowledge Across Different Faiths

We also see that there was a great interchange of ideas and ideals between Christian and Islamic domains. For example, Islamic religious studies took some of its methodology from Christians, such as John Philoponus (whom Muslims refer to as Yahya al-Nahwi). Similarly, at important moments in its own history, Christian Europe has been strengthened by the study of Islamic thinkers. In an interfaith forum, Islamic scholar Abdal Hakim Murad highlighted some of the major sources of Islamic influence on the West:

> Who can deny the impact of Ibn Rushd, the shari'a judge of Cordoba, on Europe in the age of St. Thomas Aquinas? Or the importance of Ghazali, known to the Latins as Algazel, in his rigorous refutation of the misplaced and sometimes subpagan metaphysics of Avicenna? Or the *mutakallimun*, the Muslim theologians known as "Loquentes" in the West, whose rigor in the use of reason made them ideal interlocutors, albeit at the distance required by the culture of the time, for the most rigorous of Christian thinkers?[39]

Even within the sensitive field of Islamic law, Muslim jurists had an openness to learn from Christian and Jewish counterparts. The Qur'anic exegesis known as the Isra'īliyāt emerged from such conversations. The experience of being around knowledgeable Christian and Jewish scholars who debated, analyzed, and rigorously critiqued the laws of religion helped the Muslims develop their own theology (*kalām*) by which they were able to answer theological questions and counter theological attacks. This led the Muslims to develop the classical systems of Islamic jurisprudence that have influenced Islamic theology and law ever since.[40]

In short, Muslims historically found themselves immeasurably enriched by the knowledge, experience, and wisdom of other communities and traditions; and the greatness of the civilization they built was very much influenced by that sharing. In a way, then, we can see Muslims actively manifesting the Qur'anic command to come to know the "other" and to "compete" in the pious race to do good works.

Historical Examples of Gender Equity

In sharp contrast to the negative images that we see today,[41] Islam has a rich tradition of gender equality. In the context of faith, there is no distinction between a Muslim man and a Muslim woman: both have the same rights and obligations and are promised equal rewards in heaven. Even though the principle of equality is illuminated throughout the Qur'an, the wife of the Prophet Muhammad, Umm Salamah, once asked him why women were not specifically mentioned by God in the Qur'an.[42] Soon after, the following verses were revealed to the Prophet Muhammad:

> Verily, for all men and women who have surrendered themselves unto God, and all believing men and believing women, and all truly devout men and truly devout women, and all men and women who are true to their word, and all men and women who are patient in adversity, and all men and women who humble themselves [before God], and all men and women who give in charity, and all self-denying men and self-denying women, and all men and women who are mindful of their chastity, and all men and women who remember God unceasingly: for [all of] them has God readied forgiveness of sins and a tremendous reward.[43]

Although Prophet Muhammad taught his community by example to respect and honor women, this verse formalized the principle of gender equality and guaranteed several rights in a time and place where women were often considered nothing but chattel. As prominent scholars, businesswomen, and activists, many women in the Prophet's family epitomized the symbols of moral excellence. Unlike the situation in many Muslim-majority countries today,[44] these women were prominent figures in the public sphere. Moreover, they were strong pillars in early Islamic society and served as role models for both men and women. Much has been written on their illustrious contributions from which we can learn.[45]

Although we often have a different impression of Muslim women, Islam gave women rights and freedoms that were not realized in the West until the women's movements of the twentieth century. These rights included the right to life free from female infanticide; the right to an education; the right to choose, reject, or divorce a husband; the right to own personal property exclusive of anyone else; the right to a dowry; the right to keep her family name after marriage; the right to run a business, engage in a trade, and employ men; the right to reserve and manage her own wealth; and the right to obtain legal and religious counsel without coercion. They even had the right 1,400 years ago to teach the highest knowledge—the religious sciences—on equal terms with men.

The moderate majority of Muslims believe these rights help communities grow. Certainly we can agree these rights are inalienable, much like Thomas Jefferson's assertion of the human being's inalienable rights to life, liberty, and the pursuit of happiness. And yet in some parts of the world, these God-given rights have been systematically denied to women by religious fanatics.[46]

Afghanistan, under the Taliban's rule, is one of the worst recent examples of abuses of women's rights. Prior to the Taliban coming to power, women were active members of the educational system as students and teachers, representing 70 percent of teachers in the capital of Kabul in 1996.[47] However, when the Taliban took over, they not only revoked women's rights to public education, but they restricted women's right to work, freedom of movement, and women's access to health care. Within five years, Afghanistan had the second highest maternal mortality rate in the world, and female literacy fell to about 13 percent of the population.[48] Although the Taliban continue to burn girls' schools today, men and women are working hard to provide education for girls.

In 2009 Sakeena Yaqoubi, founder of the Afghan Institute of Learning (AIL), an institute dedicated to reconstructing education and health systems for women and children in Afghanistan, spoke at the annual Sacred Circles conference in the National Cathedral about her efforts to provide girls education. She told a striking story about her work. One day, after visiting one of the learning centers her organization had built, a group of armed men stopped her car. Having received death threats for her work, she expected to be kidnapped. But the men asked her to build a school in their village for their girls. AIL has since expanded to providing education for more than 300,000 students and has trained more than 7,000 female primary school teachers. They offer women literacy classes as well as classes in Qur'anic interpretations that substantiate the rights of women under Islam.

I consider myself blessed to have been classically trained in Islamic doctrine by one of those Muslim leaders who embodies the true spirit of the Prophet Muhammad's egalitarianism toward women. Shaykh Hisham Kabbani, the world-renowned Sufi scholar and cleric, has always afforded the women in his tutelage the same rights and privileges as his male students. He emphasizes the principle that women and men are equal in the sight of God and that both have equal opportunity to excel in the religious, business, or political sectors. It is so important for people in positions of authority to lead by example rather than just words, and Shaykh Kabbani manages to do just that.

Conclusion

Historically, Islam has not only established and supported universal principles of human rights, but also fostered tolerance and acceptance of different religions and cultures. Unfortunately, the Islam I am describing—which is based on the example of the Prophet Muhammad—although practiced widely today, is under virulent attack.

One of the greatest threats to the practice and understanding of Islam today are religious extremists who have misinterpreted its foundational principles. Although they constitute a very small minority of Muslims, they are actively framing the narrative of Islam as a religion of hatred, religious intolerance, and violence. Online, as well as in the real world, it is difficult to separate fact from fiction; the inordinate attention extremists receive from the media has made them appear as if they are the predominate voice of Islam. Unfortunately many moderate Muslims are afraid to challenge extremists.[49] As a result, the mainstream majority has all but lost its voice to a rabid minority who use their draconian version of Islamic doctrine as an instrument of oppression and war for their own political purposes.

There is a grassroots effort in Muslim communities around the world to reclaim the image of Islam as a religion that is equitable, just, and socially responsible. This is truly a struggle within the Islamic world for the very soul of Islam. However, we should be mindful that it is part of a long process that will take generations to unfold, just as the West took centuries to progress from the world of Dante's Christianity to that of Martin Luther King and Desmond Tutu. The Islamic world is in the midst of its own transformation. Real social growth and development take time, and for this process to be truly organic, we must understand and accept that.

I hope that in the course of time, the democratic reality of classical Islam—as it was practiced for centuries—will assert itself and the middle way will prevail. It is interesting to note that today the most widely read poet in America is the great Sufi saint Jalaluddin Rumi. He was and remains a perfect exemplar of the Islam that we have been pointing to, an Islam that apparently finds sympathetic reverberations in the hearts of many.

What can I do, Muslims? I do not know myself. I am neither Christian nor Jew, neither Magian nor Muslim, I am not from east or west, not from land or sea, not from the shafts of nature nor from the spheres of the firmament, not of the earth, not of water, not of air, not of fire. I am not from the highest heaven, not from this world, not from existence, not from being. I am not from India, not from China, not from Bulgar, not from Saqsin, not from the realm of the two Iraqs, not from the land of Khurasan. I am not from the world, not from beyond, not from heaven and not from hell. I am not from Adam, not from Eve, not from paradise and not from Ridwan. My place is placeless, my trace is traceless, no body, no soul, I am from the soul of souls. I have chased out duality, lived the two worlds as one. One I seek, one I know, one I see, one I call. He is the first, he is the last, he is the outer, he is the inner. Beyond He and He is I know no other.

Notes

1. Holy Qur'an 2:256.
2. Holy Qur'an 38:75.
3. Holy Qur'an 2:143.
4. Hadith narrated by An-Nasa'i.
5. Holy Qur'an 49:13.
6. Holy Qur'an 17:70.
7. Hadith narrated by Ahmad ibn Hanbal.
8. Hadith narrated by Bukhari.
9. Khaled Abou El Fadl, "Islam and the Theology of Power: Supremacist Puritanism in Contemporary Islam Is Dismissive of All Moral Norms or Ethical Values," *Middle East Report* 221 (Winter 2001). Available at www.islamfortoday.com/elfadl01.htm.
10. Ahmad Mohamed El Tayeb, "Islam and the Other Religions" (submission from the participants prior to the Christian-Muslim Summit, Washington Cathedral, Washington, DC, March 1, 2010).
11. Holy Qur'an 60:7.
12. Tayeb, "Islam and the Other Religions" (address).
13. Asghar 'Ali Engineer, "The Concept of 'Other' in Islam," *Islam and Modern Age* 4, no. 9 (September 2001): 6.
14. Dr. Vincent J. Cornell, "Islam: Theological Hostility and the Problem of Difference" (paper presented at the Elijah Interfaith Academy Meeting of Board of World Religious Leaders, Seville, Spain, December 15, 2003). It is interesting to note that leading Islamic scholars of India quoted this political pact drawn up by the Prophet to oppose the separation of Pakistan from India. According to Dr. Cornell, they maintained that because the Prophet created a singular political entity for the heterogeneous community, the same should apply to an Indian Muslim state.
15. Timothy J. Gianotti, "Sharing Wisdom: A Muslim Perspective" (paper presented in preparation for the meeting of World Religious Leaders, Amritsar, India, November 26–30, 2007). http://elijah-interfaith.org/uploads/media/BP_Islam.doc.
16. Holy Qur'an 42:15.
17. Holy Qur'an 5:48, 2:148.
18. Engineer, "The Concept of 'Other' in Islam."

19. Holy Qur'an 92:4.

20. Holy Qur'an 11:118.

21. Holy Qur'an 5:48.

22. Hadith narrated by Abdullah ibn 'Umar and 'Abdullah ibn 'Abbas.

23. Holy Qur'an 92:4.

24. Holy Qur'an 11:118.

25. Holy Qur'an 5:48.

26. Holy Qur'an 30:22.

27. Holy Qur'an 2:256.

28. Shaykh Muhammad Al Hasan Al Shaybani, *Siyar: The Shorter Book on Muslim International Law*, trans. Mahmood Ahmad Gazi (Islamabad, Pakistan: Islamic Research Institute, 2005), 59.

29. Holy Qur'an 5:44–46.

30. Imam Malik ibn Anas, *Muwatta,* Volume: Zakat, trans. A'isha 'Abdarahman at-Tarjumana and Ya'qub Johnson. Center for Muslim-Jewish Engagement, USC. Online edition available at http://www.cmje.org/religious-texts/hadith/muwatta/.

31. Alexander Berzin, "Islamic-Buddhist Dialogue" (November 1995, revised November 2006). Available at www.berzinarchives.com/web/en/archives/study/islam/general/islamic_buddhist_dialog.html.

32. Tayeb, "Islam and the Other Religions."

33. In Dr. Akram Zahoor and Dr. Z. Haq, *Muslim History: 570–1950* C.E. (Gaithersburg, MD: AZP, 2000), 167.

34. Ali Asghar Engineer, *Islam in Contemporary World* (New Delhi: Sterling Publishers Pvt. Ltd., 2007).

35. Yohanan Friedman, "Medieval Muslim Views of Indian Religions," *Journal of the American Oriental Society* 95, no. 2 (1975): 214–221.

36. "An Order to Maalik al-Ashtar." Available at www.al-islam.org/nahjul/letters/letter53.htm.

37. Muhammad Hamidullah, *Introduction to Islam* (Beirut, Lebanon: Holy Koran Publishing House, 1977).

38. In Yusuf Qaradawi, *al-Aqaliyyat ad-Diniyya wa-Hal al-Islami* [Religious minorities and their solution in Islam] (Al-Qāhirah: Maktabat Wahbah, 1996), 58–59.

39. Abdal Hakim Murad, "Human Dignity and Mutual Respect" (address, First Catholic-Muslim Forum, Rome, November 5, 2008). Available at http://acommonword.com/en/a-common-word/16-conferences/297-human-dignity-and-mutual-respect.html.

40. Gianotti, "Sharing Wisdom: A Muslim Perspective."

41. See Amira el-Azhary Sonbol, ed., *Women, the Family, and Divorce Laws in Islamic History* (Syracuse, NY: Syracuse University Press, 1997).

42. Narrated by Imam Ahmad.

43. Holy Qur'an 33:35.

44. See Fatima Mernissi, *Dreams of Trespass: Tales of a Harem Girlhood* (Boston: Addison-Wesley Publishing, 1995).

45. See Shaykh Muhammad Hisham Kabbani and Laleh Bakhtiar, *Encyclopedia of Muhammad's Women Companions and the Traditions They Related* (Chicago: Kazi Publications, 1998).

46. See Kecia Ali, *Sexual Ethics and Islam: Feminist Reflections on Quran, Hadith, and Jurisprudence* (London: One World, 2006); Leila Ahmed, *Women and Gender in Islam: Historical Roots of a Modern Debate* (New Haven, CT: Yale University Press, 1993).

47. Eva Mulvad, filmmaker, "A Woman Among Warlords: Women's Rights in the Taliban and Post-Taliban Eras," PBS's *Wide Angle* (aired September 11, 2007). Video and additional information available at www.pbs.org/wnet/wideangle/episodes/a-woman -among-warlords/womens-rights-in-the-taliban-and-post-taliban-eras/66/.

48. CIA World Factbook, "Afghanistan" (last updated September 27, 2011) (population literacy data established 2000). Available at www.cia.gov/library/publications/the -world-factbook/geos/af.html.

49. Akbar Ahmad, *Journey into America: The Challenge of Islam* (Washington, DC: Brookings Institution Press, 2010), 5, 254.

14

Islam as the Embodiment of Divine Mercy and Tolerance

M. FETHULLAH GÜLEN

M. Fethullah Gülen is a Turkish Muslim scholar with millions of follow-ers. An inspirational leader who encourages a life guided by Islamic principles, Gülen was ranked the most important public intellectual in the world in a Prospect Magazine/Foreign Policy poll. He is the author of many books, including Toward a Global Civilization of Love and Tolerance, The Essentials of the Islamic Faith, *and* Emerald Hills of the Heart *(four volumes).*

A Brief Introduction to Islam

A religion, philosophy, or ideology should be viewed from the perspec-tive of its sources, basic nature, and principles. Just as it is not possible to understand Marxism without knowing Karl Marx or Hinduism without knowing the Vedas and Upanishads, neither can any Divine religion— whether it be Judaism, Christianity, or Islam—be known without knowing its basic sources and foundations: God, the reality of Divine revelation, and the sacred books, such as the Torah, the Gospel, and the Qur'an, which were formed from Divine revelations. The main source of Judaism and the Torah is God, the main source of Christianity and the Gospel is God, and the main source of Islam and the Qur'an is also God.

God created humankind as His vice regent on earth, honoring humanity with the mission of acting and improving the earth on His behalf and revealing what He wants to be done and not done by means of Moses and the Torah, Jesus and the Gospel, and, finally, Muhammad, upon him be peace and blessings, and the Qur'an. The differences between Judaism, Christianity, and Islam are not with respect to their origins; they are only in the way their followers have historically developed the secondary principles of each religion. If there are irreconcilable differences between the doctrines or practices of these religions, they are not because of the religions themselves but because of their followers.

Islam's Inclusiveness and Rejection of Separatism

The first, most important point to be considered in viewing Islam is that it does not restrict God's message to a certain people or geography or generation or race. According to the Qur'an, God addresses all of humankind; therefore, Islam recognizes all the Divine religions previous to it, with their prophets and sacred books. Believing in all of the previous books and prophets is an essential principle of Islamic belief. The denial of a prophet or sacred book is tantamount to disbelief and rejection of Islam. A Muslim, including the Prophet Muhammad, upon him be peace and blessings, himself and any other Muslim, is a true follower of Abraham, Moses, David, Jesus, and all other Hebrew prophets, as well as a follower of the Torah, the Psalms, and the Gospel at the same time he or she follows Prophet Muhammad, upon him be peace and blessings, and the Qur'an. The Qur'an says explicitly:

> The Messenger believes in what has been sent down to him from his Lord, and so do the believers; each one believes in God, and His angels, and His Books, and His Messengers: "We make no distinction between any of His Messengers (in believing in them)." And they say: "We have heard (the call to faith) and obeyed. Our Lord, grant us Your forgiveness, and to You is the homecoming." (*Surah al-Baqarah* 2:285)

Islam does not advocate separatism; it embraces all races and colors. The only honor in Islam lies in piety, in fulfilling, in the best way, the laws that have been manifested in God's religion and His universe. In addition, Islam's universality, which is based on giving equal value to everyone as servants of God and accepting them as brothers or sisters, rejects any differences based on color, race, language, and geography. The Qur'an declares:

> O humankind! Surely We have created you from a single (pair of) male and female, and made you into tribes and families so that you may know (and

help) one another. Surely the noblest, most honorable of you in God's sight is the one best in piety, righteousness, and reverence for God. Surely God is All-Knowing, All-Aware. (*Surah al-Hujurat* 49:13)

The Meaning and Basic Aim of Islam

The word *islam* means submission to God, as well as the ensuing peace, contentment, and salvation. Therefore, Islam's essence, nature, and aim are the achievement of balance, order, unity, peace, and togetherness in the lives of human beings as well as all creatures in the world. God says to Prophet Muhammad, upon him be peace and blessings, in the Qur'an: "We have not sent you (O Muhammad) but as an unequalled mercy for all the worlds" (*Surah al-Anbiya* 21:107). This means that the aim of Islam is to embrace all people and things within mercy, which is the source of order, balance, peace, and contentment. Likewise, in the *Basmala* ("In the Name of God, the All-Merciful, the All-Compassionate"), the formula of Islam, which is regarded as the seed that contains Islam in its entirety in the most condensed form, God introduces Himself as *ar-Rahman* (the All-Merciful) and *ar-Rahim* (the All-Compassionate). God has universal, all-embracing mercy for all beings as *ar-Rahman* and particular mercy for each and every being as *ar-Rahim*. All of His other attributes and names, including those that call for the punishment of evildoers, take their sources in His being the All-Merciful and the All-Compassionate.

In another verse that defines the nature and basic aim of Islam, God Almighty declares: "I have not created the jinn and humankind but to (know and) worship Me (exclusively)" (*Surah adh-Dhariyat* 51:56). When we look at differences in the human and animal kingdoms, we see that animals come into the world with all the information they will need in life and adapt to life easily, immediately or shortly after birth. However, it takes approximately one year for human beings to learn to walk, and many years for them to learn and adapt to the conditions of life. In order to realize their goal of existence, animals have no need to learn. In addition, since animals have no willpower as distinct and determined as that of human beings, their whole life passes along the line that God Almighty decreed for them. However, human beings are created to progress and become perfected through constant learning and worshipping God.

A human being is a complete being formed of a body, mind, and spirit. In addition, a human being has been endowed with conscience, a conscious nature. Conscience, or the conscious nature, is one of the most important faculties of a human being. It distinguishes between what is good and evil, feels pleasure and exhilaration in what is good, and suffers from and is grieved by what is evil. It consists of four basic elements: the spiritual intellect (or heart), willpower, the mind, and the power of perceptiveness (or the mechanism of feelings). These four elements are also regarded as the senses of the spirit. In addition to their different duties and functions, each of these senses has an ultimate purpose for its existence. The ultimate purpose of the mind is to have knowledge of God (*ma 'rifetu'llah*), recognizing or having knowledge of God through traveling from His works to His acts, to His names and to His attributes, and to His Essence. The ultimate purpose of the heart, or spiritual intellect, is to have a vision of God or to reach a certain degree of consciousness of God, through which one feels as if one "sees" God or, at least, is constantly aware of God's omnipresence. The ultimate purpose of willpower is to worship God, and the power of perceptiveness is to love God. The perfect form or degree of worship, which Islam calls *taqwa*, is the result of the functions of all these four senses. The functions of these four elements of conscience also mark degrees of certainty in belief. The degree of belief that is based on established or verified knowledge and acquired with the mind is called *certainty of knowledge*. The degree of belief that is based on vision of the heart is *certainty of vision*. And the highest degree of belief, which is based on or arises from the experience of the truth of religion with one's whole being is *certainty of experience*. Thus, the ultimate purpose for the creation of human beings is that they know and worship God with all the dimensions of their existence. And thus, belief in God is creation's highest aim and most sublime result; humanity's most exalted rank is knowledge of Him that is contained in this belief. The greatest happiness of humanity lies in love of God contained within knowledge of God. The purest joy of the human spirit and heart is the spiritual ecstasy contained within the love of God. All true happiness, pure joy, and unclouded pleasures are contained within knowledge and love of God.

Islam has the material for the realization of the Divine purpose for the creation of humanity. Another significant point that helps us to understand this is the appointment of humanity as vice regent on the earth by God, as it is pointed out in different places in the Qur'an (for example, 2:30–34). That is, God Almighty set humanity on the earth so that humanity might know and work and improve the earth. Before He set humanity on the earth, He taught the father of humanity, Adam, the "names"—that is, He showed Adam the archetypes of all things on the earth, and He equipped all human beings with the capacity to know and employ things. The angels, who are the inhabitants of the heavens, worship God and carry out His orders without the least degree of disobedience. Although humanity is fallible and is given the ability to disobey and rebel, God made the angels prostrate before Adam to show respect, not vice versa, because humanity had been endowed with the potential to learn and to improve the earth and because humanity has the capacity to be perfected through knowledge. Thus, if the Divine purpose of the creation of humanity is, as stated in the verse above (51:56), to know and worship God, one of the most important dimensions of worship is knowledge and progressing through this knowledge.

Three Aspects of the Prophetic Mission

Scientific knowledge is unable to lead human beings to good on its own, for human beings are fallible, and they tend to follow their carnal desires. Therefore, in addition to scientific knowledge, every human being needs spiritual education. The first and foremost education necessary for human beings is that their carnal soul should be trained and educated to acquire high moral qualities. Among the most important and influential means of this education are acts of worship, such as prayers, fasting, charity, remembrance of God, and pilgrimage, which also lead believers to due recognition of God and help to transform certainty of knowledge to certainty of vision. These and similar acts of worship or devotion train and educate human beings both individually and as members of a community. The following verse, which describes the duties of Prophet Muhammad, upon him be peace and blessings, or the three basic aspects of his prophetic mission and, therefore, the essence and fundamentals of Islam, expresses these realities:

> We have sent among you a Messenger of your own, reciting to you Our signs and Revelations (ayah), and purifying you (of false beliefs and doctrines, and sins, and all kinds of uncleanness), and instructing you in the Book and the Wisdom, and instructing you in whatever you (must but) do not know. (2:151)

The verse explains that, like all other prophets, Prophet Muhammad, upon him be peace and blessings, and, therefore, the Divine religion, has three basic duties or missions. One of them is reciting God's signs and revelations to people. The original word that we have translated as God's signs and revelations is ayah. The Qur'an uses the term ayah for both the verses of the Qur'an and for all the phenomena in the universe. Ayah literally means "sign," meaning that each verse of the Qur'an and each phenomenon in the universe is a sign of God and other truths of the Divine religion. Muslim scholars view both the universe (macrocosm) and humanity (microcosm), and even history, as books like the Qur'an and call the Qur'an the "revealed universe" and the universe and humanity the "created Qur'an." Whereas the Qur'an is the source of the religious sciences, the universe, humanity, and history are the sources of human sciences. Studying these two kinds of sciences, which are equally sacred, are means of realizing the Divine purpose for the creation of humanity and for appointing humanity as God's vice regent on the earth. Thus, the first and foremost mission of our Prophet, and therefore the basis of Islam, is instructing people in the Divine Scripture and the books of the universe, humanity, and history. The Divine Scripture is the translation of these other books, and these other books are the physical manifestations of the Divine Scripture.

The second duty of Prophet Muhammad, upon him be peace and blessings, was to purify people. He was to purify their minds of wrong information, false beliefs, and false doctrines and purify their hearts of sins and evil qualities. The first of these two aspects of purification occurs through scientific, true knowledge, and the other through worship, prayer, reflection, and struggling against sins and carnality. The third duty of Prophet Muhammad, upon him be peace and blessings, and, therefore, the third basic mission of Islam, is to teach purified, learned minds and to establish in purified hearts the Qur'an, religious knowledge based on the Qur'an, wisdom, and whatever people need for their happiness in both worlds. "Wisdom" means to know the meaning of natural and historical phenomena, the Divine purposes for the existence of the universe and humanity and for the events in human life, and the ways to apply or practice the Qur'an in life. The Prophet, upon him be peace and blessings, practiced the Qur'an both individually and in the life of his community and so laid down the principles of understanding and practicing it. With the many logical, scientific, and legal principles that the Qur'an and the practice of the Prophet gave rise to, such as consensus of scholars, *ijtihad* (deduction of new laws from the basic principles of Islam and Islamic life), analogy or syllogism, public benefit, and blocking harm, Islam has opened a practical way and a propitious ground for human intellect.

Islam as Manifestation of Divine Mercy

To conclude, Islam aims at the realization of the three basic missions discussed and must be viewed from this perspective. However, today the material is given priority over the spiritual, the body over the spirit, the worldly over the afterlife. Politics directs and governs human activities and thought, so Islam is mainly viewed from the temporal perspective of the world and global politics and, therefore, cannot be seen in its essential nature and is unjustly made the victim of many misunderstandings.

244 M. Fethullah Gülen

Thus, the most important points are that Islam is based on belief, worship, knowledge, and purification of minds and hearts and that it has its source in God's all-embracing mercy. As mentioned above, God Almighty introduces Himself in the *Basmala*, which is the seed or formula of Islam, as the All-Merciful and the All-Compassionate and states in the Qur'an that He sent Prophet Muhammad, upon him be peace and blessings, as an exceptional, unparalleled mercy for all beings. He also mentions, in the initial verses of the Qur'anic chapter called *ar-Rahman* (the All-Merciful), creating humanity and endowing it with the capacity of speech as the first and foremost manifestation of His being the All-Merciful: "The All-Merciful. He has taught the Qur'an; He has created humankind; He has taught him speech" (55:1–4).

All this means that God's manifestation of Himself with the Qur'an, Islam, and His last prophet, Prophet Muhammad, upon him be peace and blessings, is a complete manifestation of mercy. This realization of mercy does not include only human beings but all of creation. Do we not see that out of His mercy, God Almighty has created the whole universe, as well as organisms, as a symphony of mutual helping and solidarity, making each part needy of the whole and the whole needy of each part. Just as the whole body of a human being cooperates in the recovery from any hurt or disease, so, too, does almost the whole universe in the production of, say, a single cherry or an apple or for the germination and growth of a seed into a tree. For human beings to be able to produce a single apple or make a loaf of bread, almost all the elements of the universe cooperate: seeds with their capacity for germination and growth, soil, the sun with its light and heat, water or rain, and the earth, with its daily and yearly movements. Days and years and seasons cooperate in extremely sensitive measures and perfectly balanced proportions. In the end, a stalk of wheat or a tree presents grains or apples to human beings in the name of Divine mercy. Islam, as the translation of God's creation and administration of the universe, is also the title of this cooperation.

Behaviors Hateful in God's Sight

Given that Islam is the embodiment of Divine mercy and that the whole universe, which is the physical manifestation of Islam, is an organism where all parts help each other, what is most hateful in God's sight is hatred and enmity, shedding blood, and the destruction of order, peace, cooperation, and harmony. In many of its verses, the Qur'an severely condemns and prohibits what it calls disorder and corruption, which are the causes of this destruction:

Disorder (rooted in rebellion to God and recognizing no laws) is even far
graver and more sinful than killing. (2:191, 2:217)

Do not cause disorder and corruption in the land, seeing that it has been so
well-ordered. (7:85)

Do good to others as God has done good to you (out of His pure Mercy and
Grace), and do not seek corruption and mischief in the land, for God does
not love those who cause corruption and make mischief. (28:77)

Do not go about acting wickedly on earth, causing disorder and corruption.
(2:60, 7:74, 11:85, 26:183)

The Qur'an, which prohibits disorder and corruption, also prohibits behaviors that cause them. As it orders doing good to others, it also orders mutual
helping in virtue and goodness and prohibits mutual helping in sinful, iniqui-
tous acts and hostility (5:3). It also declares: "Never let your detestation for
a people or a people's detestation for you move you to commit violations
(acts of aggression and injustice)" (5:3). The Qur'an is so insistent on doing
good, on seeking justice and righteousness, on observing every person's rights,
and on global peace and order that it even has rules for secret conversations
and meetings: "No good is there in most of their secret counsels except for
him who exhorts to a deed of charity, or kind, equitable dealings and honest
affairs, or setting things right between people" (4:114–115).

A Monument of Mercy and Goodness

Islam and its Prophet, as well as all other prophets, upon them be
peace, are monuments of mercy, affection, and goodness. The Qur'an tells
that Prophet Jesus, upon him be peace, will turn to God on Judgment Day on
behalf of those who associated partners with God among His people, saying:
"If You punish them, they are Your servants; and if You forgive them, You
are the All-Glorious and Mighty, the All-Wise" (5:118). Of Muhammad,
upon him be peace and blessings, and his position among humankind, God
says in the Qur'an: "But God will not punish them so long as you are among
them" (8:33). God Almighty means that the existence of Prophet Muhammad, upon him be peace and blessings, and Islam, when accurately practiced,
are barriers before Divine punishment and certain calamities in the form of
which Divine punishment sometimes comes. The Prophet himself, who declares, "I have not been sent to call down curses on people, but as a mercy,"[1]
and "I am a Prophet of forgiveness and mercy,"[2] showed in practice that Islam, which is a universal manifestation of God's mercy, which embraces all
things (7:156), is a mercy not only for human beings, especially children,
women, the elderly, the diseased, orphans, the helpless, and the destitute, but

also for all of creation, including animals and vegetation. He wept together with a child who was weeping, and once said: "I stand in prayer and wish to prolong it, but I hear a child cry and shorten the prayer considering his/her mother's anxiety."[3] Thus, he stated his exceptional compassion and pity for children and mothers. He once accompanied a half-crazy woman who took him by the hand to do her work, and he did it. He forgave a Jewish woman who put poison in his food to kill him; he never repelled any evil done to him with evil; and he embraced all animals in his mercy and forbade killing even snakes. Once he told that out of compassion, a fallen woman gave a thirsty dog water that she took out of a well and finally went to Paradise, whereas another woman went to hell because she left a cat hungry and caused its death.[4]

God's Messenger, upon him be peace and blessings, planted 500 date palms at once[5] and encouraged planting trees, saying: "If a Muslim plants a tree and if any domestic or wild animal or a bird eats of its fruit, it will bring him a merit of charity;"[6] and "Even if one has a sapling in his hand when he sees the world being destroyed should plant it."[7] He also warned one who was beating down leaves for his flock, saying, "Beat down leaves gently; do not break the boughs and branches of the tree!"[8] He said that the whole earth was a place of worship for him, and Muslims could perform their prayers wherever they wanted on the earth, provided the place was clean. He declared Makka and Madina and their vicinities to be sacred; their animals cannot be killed and their vegetation cannot be cut.

Essential Principles of Behavior

Prophet Muhammad, upon him be peace and blessings, was the "walking Qur'an"; he was the full embodiment of the Holy Scripture. He acted so because the Qur'an orders mildness, gentleness, modesty, humility, helping others, living for the welfare of others, forgiveness, repelling an evil with what is good, affection, love, and mercy as the essential principles of behavior. This commandment is not only toward Muslims, but toward all things. Islam aims to develop human beings from being potentially human to being truly human. It develops the human character in the best way. The Qur'anic verses 22–39 in Surah al-Isra' (17) promulgate some of the essential principles of behavior as follows:

Do not associate any partners with God.[9]
Worship none but God alone.
Treat parents as kindly and generously as possible.
Give their due to your relatives, to the needy and the wayfarer.
Do not be miserly, nor waste your wealth.

Do not kill your children for fear of poverty (either before or after their birth).

Do not approach any unlawful sexual intercourse.

Do not kill any soul, which God has banned, save in just cause.

Do not approach the property of an orphan, except purely for their good.

Give full measure when you measure, and weigh with an accurate balance.

Do not follow anything about which you have no certain knowledge.

Do not strut about the earth in haughtiness or self-conceit.

Do not set up any rivals with God.

Forgiveness and Doing Good to All

The following verses establish some other elements of building a Muslim character:

> Do not forget magnanimity among yourselves. Whatever you do, surely God sees it well. (2:237)
>
> Whoever acts wrongfully through enmity (toward others) and by way of deliberate transgression and wronging, We will surely land him in a Fire to roast therein; that indeed is easy for God. (4:30)
>
> Goodness and evil can never be equal. Repel evil with what is better (or best). Then see: the one between whom and you there was enmity has become a bosom friend. (41:34)
>
> The recompense of an evil deed can only be an evil equal to it; but whoever pardons and makes reconciliation, his reward is due from God. Surely He does not love the wrongdoers. (42:40)
>
> But, indeed, whoever shows patience and forgives (the wrong done to him), surely that is among meritorious things requiring great resolution to fulfill. (42:43)

The Qur'an orders Muslims to treat kindly and do good to all those who do not fight against them:

> God does not forbid you, as regards those who do not make war against you on account of your religion, nor drive you away from your homes, to be kindly to them, and act towards them with equity. God surely loves the scrupulously equitable. (60:8)

No Religious Compulsion

During the last two centuries, it wrongly has been claimed that, according to Islam, the world is divided into two: the home of Islam and the home of war. This wrong conception treats Islam as on par with warfare, whereas the truth is completely the reverse. First of all, Islam decisively bans compulsion in religion: "There is no compulsion in the religion. The right way stands there clearly distinguished from the false. Hence, he who rejects false deities and believes in God has indeed taken hold of the firm, unbreakable handle; and God is All-Hearing, All-Knowing" (2:256). This verse was revealed for the following reason.

The pagan Arabs of Madina had special respect toward the Jews and Christians as they had God-revealed books. Those among them who had no children surviving vowed that if they had surviving children they would raise them in Judaism or Christianity. When Islam entered Madina, there were many Arabs who had been converted into one of the two religions, and their parents, who had accepted Islam, began to use force to convert them to Islam. The verse under discussion came and prohibited compulsion. In interpreting this verse, the late Hamdi Yazir, a contemporary eminent Turkish interpreter of the Qur'an, writes as follows.

> Religion does not include, nor admit, any acts done through compulsion, for it is based on voluntary action. For this reason, compulsion is forbidden by Islam. That is, anything involving force or compulsion in the name of religion is outside the field of religion. Even though others use force or compel people to do or not to do something, religion never admits compulsion. Religion is a testing and people will be judged in the other world according to their voluntary acts. Any religious act done through compulsion does not bring any reward; and an act of worship which is not done through free will is not counted as worship.[10]

Calling with Wisdom and Exhortation

Islam has forbidden compelling people to accept the religion. Islam treats people as the addressees of God's call. It calls people to God but never exerts force in its call, nor does it permit punishment of those who reject its call: "Call to the way of your Lord with wisdom and fair exhortation, and argue with them in the best way possible" (16:125). "And say to My servants that they should always speak (even when disputing with others) that which is the best. Satan is ever ready to sow discord among them. For Satan indeed is a manifest enemy for humankind" (17:53).

While sending Prophets Moses and Aaron, upon them be peace, to the Pharaoh, who was one of the most pitiless tyrants of human history, God Almighty ordered them to speak to him gently: "Go, both of you, to the Pharaoh for he has exceedingly rebelled. But speak to him with gentle words, so that he might reflect and be mindful or feel some awe (of Me, and behave with humility)" (20:43–44).

People of the Book

It is worth discussing how the Qur'an orders Muslims to behave toward Jews and Christians, whom it calls the People of the Book:

> Do not argue with those who were given the Book save in the best way, unless it be those of them who are given to wrongdoing (and, therefore, not accessible to courteous argument). Say (to them): "We believe in what has been sent down to us and what was sent down to you, and your God and our God is one and the same. We are Muslims wholly submitted to Him." (29:46)

This manner is in fact the general way in which the Muslims must behave in their relationship with the followers of other faiths. They must speak to them with gentle words and behave toward all in a mild manner. If, however, those addressed show a harsh reaction, then the Muslims must avoid disputation with them, because the Qur'an also bans harsh treatment and disputation:

> The (true) servants of the All-Merciful are they who move on the earth gently and humbly, and when the ignorant, foolish ones address them (with insolence or vulgarity, as befits their ignorance and foolishness), they respond with (words of) peace (without engaging in hostility with them). (25:63)

As a matter of fact, the Qur'an orders gentleness, kindness, and fair exhortation in dealings with everyone who is not intent on aggression. This kind of behavior builds bridges among people where they can meet and shake hands. A Muslim following this command can draw attention to common points between People of the Book and Muslims. In addition, this command says to call on the People of the Book with a warm style, which today we call dialogue, a call which has been resonating for fourteen centuries:

> Say (to them, O Messenger): "O People of the Book, come to a word common between us and you, that we worship none but God, and associate none as partners with Him, and that none of us take others for Lords, apart from God." If they (still) turn away, then say: "Bear witness that we are Muslims (submitted to Him exclusively)." (3:64)

If the call of Islam is not accepted, Muslims should say: "Bear witness that we are Muslims (submitted to God exclusively)," and "You have your religion (with whatever it will bring you), and I have my religion (with whatever it will bring me)" (109:6). Concerning the verse 3:64 quoted above, Hamdi Yazir comments:

> The verse has shown how various consciences, nations, religions, and books can unite in one essential conscience and word of truth, and how Islam has instructed the human realm in such a wide, open, and true path of salvation and law of freedom. It has been shown fully that this is not limited to Arab or non-Arab people. Religious progress is possible not by narrow consciences or by being separate from one another, but by being universal and broad.[11]

Islam and Pluralism

For the present world, which searches for pluralism or ways for the followers of different religions to be able to live together in peace, Islam has a bright, fourteen-century-long experience of peaceful coexistence. Fourteen hundred years ago, Islam established interfaith dialogue and tolerance, which the Papacy later launched toward Muslims and Jews in 1963 as a way of living together in peaceful coexistence with the followers of other faiths. In Makka, where they were subjected to cruel persecution, Muslims adopted as a principle "being handless toward those who beat and tongueless toward those who curse." When they had to emigrate to Madina in order to be able to live according to their faith, God's Messenger first signed a pact with the Jewish and pagan Arab tribes, which some modern scholars and historians regard as a written constitution. According to this pact, Muslims, Jews, and pagan Arabs were free to live each according to their faith and would cooperate to protect the city against outside attacks.[12] Citing all examples of the Muslim experience of living together with followers of other faiths in peace and brotherhood would cover volumes. A few examples will be enough to show modern people how to live with "others" in peace.

EXAMPLES OF LIVING IN PEACE

Before the demise of our Prophet, upon him be peace and blessing, a sixty-person Najran Christian delegation came to Madina. They discussed Islam and Christianity with the Prophet and ultimately insisted on their faith. They were allowed to stay and perform their devotions in the Prophet's mosque. In the end, an agreement was made with them. The gist of this agreement, which was made with the Najran Christians within the borders of the Islamic government, was as follows:

> All the people of Najran and their dependencies are under the protection of God and Muhammad, upon him be peace and blessings, all their lives,

properties, religious beliefs and practices, families, and places of worship are under protection. No bishops or priests or monks can be deported from their places of duty. All the people of Najran and their dependencies will neither be wronged nor wrong others. None of them will be punished because of a crime committed by others.[13]

A historical episode, which is told by Balazuri, a famous Muslim historian, and describes how pleased the native peoples were with their Muslim administration, is of great significance:

> Muslims conquered Hims in 635 during the Caliphate of 'Umar. The next year, when Heraclius, the Byzantine emperor, marched against the Muslims with massive troops, and the Muslims, who decided to evacuate the city, refunded the inhabitants of Hims the tribute they had taken from them, saying: "We received this tribute from you in return for protecting you. But now we are unable to protect you." But the people of Hims replied: "We like your rule and justice far better than the state of oppression and tyranny in which we were. We can repulse the army of Heraclius from the city with your help." The Jews rose and said: "We swear by the Torah, no governor of Heraclius shall enter the city unless we are first conquered and exhausted." Saying this, they closed the gates of the city and guarded it. The inhabitants of other cities, Christians and Jews, who had been capitulated did the same. When by God's help the Byzantines were defeated and Muslims won, they opened the gates of their cities, went out with the singers and players of music, and paid the tribute.[14]

After Sultan Mehmet II conquered İstanbul in 1453, he allowed Jews to settle in İstanbul. He even encouraged Jews to emigrate to the Ottoman lands, and many Jews moved to the Ottoman lands from many European countries. Rabbi Isaac Tzarfati wrote to the Jews in Germany the following letter inviting them to Turkey:

> Listen my brethren, to the counsel I will give you. I, too, was born in Germany and studied Torah with the German rabbis. I was driven out of my native country and came into the Turkish land, which is blessed by God and filled with all good things. Here I found rest and happiness. Turkey can also become for you the land of peace. If you who live in Germany knew even a tenth of what God has blessed us with in this land, you would not consider any difficulties, you would set out to come to us. . . . Here in the land of the Turks we have nothing to complain of. We possess great fortunes; much gold and silver are in our hands. We are not oppressed with heavy taxes, and our commerce is free and unhindered. Rich are the fruits of the earth. Everything is cheap, and every one of us lives in peace and freedom. Here the Jews are not compelled to wear a yellow hat as a badge of shame, as is the case in

Germany. . . . Arise my brethren, give up your lands, collect your forces, and come to us. Here you will be free of your enemies, here you will find rest.[15]

In addition to permitting the followers of other faiths to live according to their faith freely, Muslims have not objected to mosques, churches, and synagogues being built side by side. More than that, it has been witnessed many times that while Muslims perform their worship in a mosque, Jews and Christians fulfill their religious devotions in other parts of the same mosque at the same time.[16] The religious tolerance of the mosques, churches, and synagogues existing side by side in several cities of Turkey has its source in the very essence of Islam.

Acting Sensitively Toward Followers of Other Faiths

The legal injunctions of Islam aim for the realization of five basic human rights or freedoms: the right to or freedom of faith and living according to one's faith, the right to or freedom of life, the right to have or freedom of having personal property, the right to have or freedom of having a family, and the right to or freedom of mental and physical health. Not only Muslims but all people, regardless of faith, color, or race, enjoy these rights.

It can even be said that Muslim authorities historically have been more sensitive to protecting the rights of non-Muslims than Muslims under their government, because Prophet Muhammad, upon him be peace and blessings, said: "Whoever transgresses against the rights of the non-Muslims under their administration, I will be his enemy. Whomever I am an enemy to, I will settle accounts with them on Judgment Day."[17] Both the Prophet himself and his successors like 'Umar, the Second Caliph, emphatically advised the fulfillment of the prescribed prayers and observation of the rights of non-Muslims on their deathbeds. Islam also brought about pluralism in the legal system and allowed the Jews and Christians to apply their civil laws in their lives and be judged according to their own laws (Qur'an, 5:43–48).

Muslim Penal Law and Islam's Stance on War

In our day, some elements of Muslim penal law and Islam's stance on war can be put forward to criticize Islam. Those critics of Islam claim that Islam encourages violence and can provide an excuse for certain acts of terrorism. We should immediately point out that Islam can never provide an excuse for either violence or terrorism. There is not a single Qur'anic verse, nor a Prophetic tradition to justify such a claim. How can a religion that orders excellence or perfect goodness (*ihsan*) as the essence of any action, a religion that forbids even handing a knife to another person by its sharp blade, provide an excuse for violence or terrorism?

The Qur'an never criticizes people by name; while it mentions examples of virtue such as the Prophets by name, it condemns and censures evil attributes and acts, without specifying or exposing people guilty of them by name. It does not even mention the most infamous, sinful, and cruel people of history by name. Instead, it mentions titles, such as the Pharaoh. With the exception of Abu Lahab, an uncle of the Prophet who inflicted on him the most pitiless of torments and tortures, we cannot find the name of even one who pitilessly persecuted the Muslims in Makka for thirteen years or of those hypocrites who continuously plotted against God's Messenger and Muslims in Madina. Also, the Qur'an does not consider and attaches no value to being called a Muslim or a Christian or a Jew in order to deserve salvation. Rather, it considers and draws the attention to attributes and acts, saying:

> (The truth is not as they claim, but this:) Those who believe (that is, professing to be Muslims), or those who declare Judaism, or the Christians or the Sabaeans (or those of some other faith)—whoever truly believes in God and the Last Day and does good, righteous deeds, surely their reward is with their Lord, and they will have no fear, nor will they grieve. (2:63)

This verse categorically rejects the illusion cherished by some that by virtue of being called Muslims or Jews or Christians, one can have a monopoly over salvation. Salvation depends on true belief and good deeds.

Again, the Qur'an orders good deeds and kind treatment to everyone, without discriminating based on faith, color, or race, unless they wage war on Muslims, prevent them from practicing their faith, or drive them out from their lands because of their faith:

> God does not forbid you, as regards those who do not make war against you on account of your religion, nor drive you away from your homes, to be kindly to them, and act towards them with equity. God surely loves the scrupulously equitable. (60:8)

The primary verse that the critics of Islam cite as a basis for their claim that Islam makes room and provides an excuse for violence is 9:5:

> Then, when the (four) sacred months (of respite, during which fighting with those who violate their treaties was prohibited to you) are over, then (declare war on them and) kill them wherever you may come upon them, and seize

them, and confine them, and lie in wait for them at every conceivable place. Yet if they repent and (mending their ways) establish the prayer (as a mark of showing their sincerity in repentance) and pay the prescribed purifying alms (their prescribed taxes), let them go their way. Surely God is All-Forgiving, All-Compassionate.

This verse, in addition to being so clear in meaning as to refute the claims that it provides a basis for violence, is not an independent one in establishing an injunction and should therefore be evaluated in the general context where it is. When we review this verse both independently and within the general context where it is (9:1–6), there is only one conclusion to draw.

Prophet Muhammad, upon him be peace and blessings, signed treaties with neighboring pagan and polytheistic tribes. Being a God-revealed religion "that regards the killing of one innocent person as equal to killing all of humanity, and the saving of one life as equal to saving the lives of all humanity" (5:329), therefore attaching the greatest value to life, Islam orders a Muslim authority to remain faithful to any treaty it has made until the end of its term. More than that, as a principle that does not even exist today among the laws of the most democratic countries of the modern world, Islam orders a Muslim authority that if the other side betrays the agreement, the Muslim authority must publicly and officially declare to the other side that the agreement is no longer valid. If it has to declare war after the agreement loses its validity, it should grant them respite so that a new evaluation of the situation can be made. Islam does not permit preemptive strikes. "If you have strong reason to fear treachery from a people (with whom you have a treaty), return it to them (that is, publicly declare to them, before embarking on any action against them, that you have dissolved the treaty), so that both parties should be informed of its termination. Surely God does not love the treacherous" (8:58). God's Messenger also says: "Whoever is bound in a treaty with a people cannot dissolve this treaty until either the term is up or until he publicly declares that it has been annulled."[18] In another saying, he declares: "Do not be treacherous, even to him who is treacherous to you."[19] Even today's most civilized nations do not comply with this principle, established fourteen centuries ago by Islam.

Thus, some of the tribes with whom God's Messenger had made pacts did not observe the conditions of the treaties. They began attacking Muslims without warning, preventing safety of travel and killing Muslims wherever they found them. As sufficiently explicit in the verses under discussion, the Qur'an ordered the Messenger to prevent those aggressing tribes from their atrocities in violation of the agreement they had made with the Muslims. However, the Qur'an also ordered that if they gave up their atrocities and demanded a new treaty, God's Messenger should make peace with them: "But if you repent and give up hostilities, this will be for your good" (9:3). "Yet if they repent and (mending their ways) establish the prayer (as a mark of showing their sincerity in repentance) and pay the prescribed purifying alms (their prescribed taxes), let them go their way" (9:5). All this shows that even in warfare, Islam is ready to make peace and enter into a treaty with the opposing side. More than that, if anyone from the opposing, warring side seeks asylum from the Muslim authority, the latter is obliged to give it: "And if any of those who associate partners with God (and are at war with you) seeks asylum of you (O Messenger), grant him asylum, so that he may hear the Word of God, and then convey him to his place of security. That (is how you should act) because they are a people who have no knowledge (of the truth)" (9:6).

In addition to all these principles, the Qur'an orders the Muslim authority to fulfill its obligations to the other side with whom it made a treaty: "Those among the people who associate partners with God with whom you made a treaty, and who have not thereafter failed to fulfill their obligations toward you (required by the treaty), nor have backed anyone against you. Observe, then, your treaty with them until the end of the term (that you agreed with them). Surely God loves the God-revering, pious (who keep their duties to Him)" (9:4).

Islam has also set limitations and strict rules on the conduct of the Muslims at war; for example, they cannot betray any agreements that they entered into. They cannot plunder and commit any injustices or use torture. They cannot hurt children, women, the elderly, or other noncombatants on the enemy side. They cannot destroy orchards and tillage, nor kill livestock. They must treat with respect the religious persons who live in hermitages and convents and spare their edifices.[20]

War and Penal Law Are Not Essential

We should point out that war and penal law have no essential place in the general fabric of Islam. To explain more clearly, God Almighty uses the term "evil" for any punishment and the recompense of any evil committed: "The recompense of an evil deed can only be an evil equal to it; but whoever pardons and makes reconciliation, his reward is due from God. Surely He does not love the wrongdoers" (42:40). That is, both war and punishing are evil in essence or in themselves, and as a principle, the Qur'an urges repelling any evil with what is good and praises those who act so: "And those who . . . repel the evil with what is good: Such are those for whom is the everlasting abode (of happiness)" (13:22, 28:54). "Repel the evil (committed against you and your mission) with the best (of what you can do)" (23:96). "Repel evil with what is the best" (41:34). However, it sometimes requires that an evil that cannot be repelled or prevented with what is good should be repelled or prevented with evil. For example, what is essential for human life is health, and therefore any medical treatment applied to a healthy body in the name of recovery would end in a bad result. Any treatment must only be applied to an ill body. The treatment may be a certain medicine, a period of bed rest, or an operation. In and of themselves, these treatments are not good and should not be applied to a healthy body. Though they are an evil, they are good with respect to their results when they are applied to an ill body. Cutting off a limb would never be good in itself, but when a gangrenous limb is cut off for the sake of the general health of the body, the person can recover. Thus, war and penal law, like serious medical treatments, are not good in themselves and are necessary only to repel greater evils or to restore the health of an individual or a society. Islam views both war and penal law in this way. Just as an operation cannot always be avoided for the recovery of a patient, sometimes war or penal punishment cannot be avoided. They can be necessary in order to restore individual or societal health. Islam aims at the mental, spiritual, and bodily health of people and the absolute justice, equity, and order of society. Therefore, it allows war or penal punishment only in case of "diseases" that must be eliminated for the ultimate good of individuals and society.

Conclusion

Islam is the religion of mercy, salvation, peace, order, safety, dialogue, and tolerance. It aims at the happiness of people in both this world and the next. Without excluding any people and regardless of the differences of faith, color, sex, and race, all of its injunctions aim to secure the basic rights and freedoms of people: the right to or freedom of faith and living according to one's faith, the right to or freedom of life, the right to have or freedom of having personal property, the right to have or freedom of having a family and reproduction, and the right to or freedom of mental and physical health. Islam is pure justice and mercy for the whole of creation. It regards the killing of one innocent person as equal to killing all of humanity and the saving of one life as equal to saving the lives of all humanity. It decisively forbids compulsion in the name of religion and builds bridges where the followers of all faiths can come together and shake hands. It has a fourteen-century-long history of pluralism and securing a peaceful coexistence for the followers of different faiths, which the modern world direly needs. It approaches certain realities of human history and life, such as war and punishments, from the perspective of ideals—health, peace, order, harmony, mutual helping and social solidarity, peaceful coexistence, justice, mercy, and salvation—and therefore has used these realities like antidotes or medicines. Finally, humanity is fallible by nature, and just as it is an injustice to blame Christianity and Judaism or any other religion because of the faults of some of their followers, so also is it an injustice and unfairness to criticize Islam because of the faults of some Muslims.

Notes

1. Abu al-Husayn Muslim ibn al-Hajjaj, *al-Jami' as-Sahih* (*Sahihu Muslim*), Vol. I–III, "Birr," 87, Çağrı Yayınları, İstanbul 1992.

2. Ibid., "Fadail," 557; Ahmad ibn Hanbal, *al-Musnad*, Vol. I–VI, Çağrı Yayınları, İstanbul 1992, 4:395.

3. Abu 'Abdullah Muhammad ibn Isma'il al-Bukhari, *al-Jami' as-Sahih* (*Sahih al-Bukhari*), Vol. I–VIII, "Adhan," 65, Çağrı Yayınları, Istanbul, 1992; *Muslim*, "Salah," 192.

4. *al-Bukhari*, "Anbiya," 54, "Musaqat," 9; *Muslim*, "Salam," 153–155, "Fadail," 76.

5. Ahmad ibn Husayn ibn 'Ali ibn Musa Abu Bakr al-Bayhaqi, *as-Sunan al-Kubra*, Vol. I–X, Maktabat ad-Dar al-Baz, Makka 1414/1994, 10:312.

6. *al-Bukhari*, "Adab," 27; *Muslim*, "Musaqat," 10.

7. Ahmad ibn Hanbal, *al-Musnad*, 3:191.

8. Ibn al-Athir, 'Izz al-Din Abi al-Hasan, *Usd al-Ghaba fi Ma'rifa as-Sahaba*, Beirut, 3:276.

9. The word *partners* here means any person, thing, idol, or force that would replace a part of God's lordship, divinity, or creation.

10. Elmalılı Hamdi Yazır, *Hak Dini Kur'an Dili*, Eser Neşriyat, İstanbul, 2:860–861.

11. Ibid., 2:1131–1132.

12. Ibn Hisham, *as-Sirat an-Nabawiyya*, Maktaba al-Kulliyat al-Azhariyya, Egypt, 2:106; Abu 'Ubayd, *Kitab al-Amval*, Egypt (Turkish trans: C. Saylık, Istanbul, 1981), 235.

13. Ibn Hisham, *as-Sirat an-Nabawiyya*, 1–2: 574, Ibn Sa'd, *at-Tabaqat al-Kubra*, Beirut, 1:357–358.

14. Abu al-Abbas Ahmad ibn Yahya al-Balazuri, *Futuh al-Buldan* (Trans: K. Z. Ugan), Istanbul, 1955, 1:219–220.

15. S. J. Shaw, *The Jews of the Ottoman Empire and the Turkish Republic* (New York: Macmillan, 1991), 11–33. Quoted by F. Apaydın, P. Alister, "Blissful Years of the Jews," *The Fountain Magazine* 7:9–10. http://www.fountainmagazine.com/article.php?ARTICLEID=521.

16. Shams al-Aimma as-Sarakhsi, *Kitabu Siyar al-Kabir*, Ankara, 1989, 1:90–91; al-Balazuri, ibid., 187.

17. Yusuf an-Nabhani, *al-Fath al-Kabir*, Beirut, 3:144; 'Ala al-Din 'Ali Muttaqi al-Hindi, *Kanz al-Ummal fi Sunan al-Aqwal wa al-Af'al*, Vol. I–VIII, HN (Hadith number): 10909, Beirut, 1985.

18. Sulayman ibn Ash'as as-Sijistani Abu Davud, *Sunan Abu Dawud*, Vol. 1–4, "Jihad," 152, Çağrı Yayınları, İstanbul 1992.

19. Ibid., "al-Buyu'," 79.

20. Ibn al-Athir, *al-Kamil fi al-Tarikh*, Beirut, 1979, 3:227.

15

The Historical and Religious Seeds of "Honor"

RANA HUSSEINI

Award-winning journalist, human rights defender, and author of Murder in the Name of Honor, *Rana Husseini has focused on the brutal crimes that are committed against Jordanian women in the name of family honor. Husseini has earned nine local and international awards, including a medal from Jordan's King Abdullah II in 2007, for reporting on such crimes. Her work has resulted in the formation of the National Jordanian Committee to Eliminate So-called Crimes of Honor.*

"Honor" Murders

When I began advocating against the brutal murder of women in the name of "honor" almost seventeen years ago in Jordan, I never imagined that this cause, among many other causes, would be used by the West to attack the Islamic religion. Of course, the abuse and the use of Islam increased following 9/11. All of a sudden, I sensed that it was an issue of East versus West and that the West believed that only "evil Muslims and Arabs" were responsible for the bad things that happen in the world, and specifically in "our" part of the world. One bad thing that the West believed Muslims and Arabs were responsible for are so-called "honor" murders that target women who violate their family's honor, its reputation, and the code of chastity they are expected to abide by. I have also noticed the bias in the Western media's coverage of certain domestic violence events, including labeling and clearly identifying the religion and name of the perpetrator if he is a Muslim—a practice I did not find when I read of murder and abuse targeting women and children by, let us say, non-Muslims and non-Arabs.

Much of the international attention on the so-called honor crimes has suggested that Islam, or strict interpretations of Islam, are to blame. I believe this is because of a general ignorance of Islam as a religion and its position on so-called honor crimes and women. Moreover, so-called honor crimes occur widely throughout the world; these crimes occur in countries such as Bangladesh, Brazil, Ecuador, Egypt, Great Britain, India, Israel, Italy, Morocco, Pakistan, Palestine, Sweden, Turkey, Yemen, and Uganda—far from the exclusively Islamic "club" of countries.

Sadly, much of the blame for this misconception lies at the door of the Western media. Often out of misunderstanding rather than malice, these media outlets expose so-called honor crimes in a way that fuels further misconceptions of Islam and shores up the divisions between the two worlds, rather than fostering greater understanding. The fact is, in Islamic countries the religious laws are very clear against relying on hearsay "evidence" and are also very strict about what is required to prove adultery. This means that it is nearly impossible to prove adultery in Islam, and adultery is considered a private and personal issue.

Islam is against the murder of civilians; Muslims believe the soul is God's property and humans cannot take it away. However, misconceptions about Islam and its laws persist and are unfortunately abused both internationally and locally to serve political interests and to exploit power.

Although much has been written by Western scholars on this issue from their perspectives, I felt it was crucial for someone from this part of the world to describe the problem from within our own communities while outlining Christianity's and Judaism's positions on issues related to adultery and women's chastity.

For readers who do not know what a so-called honor crime is, it is a crime that is usually committed against women who sully their family's "honor" and reputation by becoming a victim of rumor, suspicion, rape, or incest. Other "crimes" based on cultural and traditional beliefs that entail violations of the family's "honor" include being pregnant out of wedlock, engaging in extramarital affairs, going missing from the family's home, and choosing to marry a man against the family's wishes or (sometimes) from a different religion.

The Case of Surjit Athwal

A widely reported international case from a few years ago involved Surjit Athwal, a twenty-seven-year-old of the Sikh faith and a married mother of two, from India. Surjit worked as a customs officer at Heathrow Airport and lived in west London. In 1998, she was having an affair with a co-worker and planned to divorce her husband of ten years, Sukhdave Athwal, thirty-four. The marriage had been arranged by their parents.

When Surjit's mother-in-law, Bachan Athwal, heard this, she convinced her son that Surjit deserved to die for shaming him and the family. In addition to having an affair, Surjit also smoked, drank alcohol, and wore her hair short. That year, Surjit traveled to India with her mother-in-law, thinking they would be attending a family wedding. (On the day Surjit left, her husband took out a £100,000 insurance policy on her.) When she did not return, her husband told her children that she had abandoned them.[1]

While on a visit to India, Surjit's brother, Jagdeesh Singh, learned some details about her death from two relatives. He says that he was told that Surjit "was driven off in a car and taken to the banks of a nearby river. She was pulled out of the car, strangled, suffocated to death, and then her body was thrown into the river" in the hopes that it would be lost forever.

Jagdeesh spearheaded a campaign to investigate her murder. British police traveled to India to investigate but found no information; even a reward of £10,000 failed to produce results. "With greatest of respect to them," Jagdeesh said, "all the leading police investigators at the beginning were white, English officers who did not quite appreciate the subtleties and the unseen aspects of honor violence, the details around honor and family and practices within a Punjabi family culture." Jagdeesh criticized the British Foreign Ministry for failing to exert pressure on the Indian government to intensify its investigations. He said that during this same period, a British woman who had vanished in Japan received a great deal of attention from Foreign Secretary Robin Cook (who refused to meet with Jagdeesh and his family) and Prime Minister Tony Blair. In 2003, five years after the murder, Jagdeesh finally met with (the new) Foreign Secretary Jack Straw who promised to seriously investigate the case.[2]

In 2007, Surjit's husband and mother-in-law were tried in London. Her mother-in-law (aged seventy at the time of the trial) claimed innocence throughout the trial but was nonetheless sentenced to a minimum term of twenty years. Surjit's husband (aged forty-three at the time of the trial) was sentenced to life, with a minimum term of twenty-seven years. The judge, Giles Forrester, told the pair,

How you could commit this unspeakable act I do not know. There was no motive worthy of the name. You did it because you perceived she had brought shame on the family name. In reality you murdered her for no better reason than the existence of matrimonial difficulties and the likely break-down of the marriage. You decided the so-called honor of your family name was worth more than the life of this young woman.[3]

Surjit's daughter, Pavan, did not learn the truth about what had happened until August 2008, when she turned seventeen. She had accepted that her grandmother's and father's convictions were a mistake and that her mother had simply abandoned her. Pavan said, "For years I was told that my mum didn't love us anymore and that we should just forget about her. My brother and I grew up hating her because we thought she'd just left us; why would we doubt our dad?"[4]

The Case of Du'a Khalil Aswad

In 2007, Du'a Khalil Aswad, a seventeen-year-old northern Iraqi tried to convince her boyfriend, Muhannad, a Sunni Muslim, to elope, saying she would convert from her family's religion, Yazidism, to Islam. Her boyfriend hesitated, insisting that her family approve their marriage.

Yazidism is a small branch of Yazdanism, a religion with ancient Indo-European roots. Although Yazidism draws on elements of other religions, including Christianity and Islam, it is a unique religion whose followers venerate a blue peacock "angel" known as Malak Taus. As a religious minority, they have often been persecuted. Yazidis are primarily Kurdish speaking, and most of them live in the Mosul region of northern Iraq. The tightly knit group rarely accepts converts to their religion, and they strongly oppose marriage to non-Yazidis.

Du'a was a second-year student at the Fine Arts Institute in Bashiqa, Iraq (a town that is 80 percent Yazidi[5]), when she informed her parents of her decision to elope. They were not pleased with her plans to marry a Muslim, but they did not try to stop her. Later, worried for her safety from male members of the family, her father took her to a cleric for protection, where she lived for a number of months.

On April 7, 2007, some family members arrived at the cleric's home to tell Du'a that her family had forgiven her and that they now welcomed her home. Du'a believed they were telling her the truth, but the cleric was suspicious. Next, the men stormed the house and dragged Du'a outside.

Waiting for her were at least a dozen male family members who started kicking and hitting her. They pulled her hair and pushed her to the ground.

The men tore her skirt, exposing her legs—a shameful image representing her shaming of the family. One man kicked her between the legs.

In the crowd of onlookers, a number of people filmed this attack with their mobile telephones. These videos show Du'a screaming for help, trying to cover her legs with her arms. They also show a number of police officers standing nearby, doing nothing to stop the attack.

As the men started throwing larger and larger stones at Du'a, she used her arms to cover her head instead of her legs. When a large brick struck the back of her head, she stopped moving for a few moments. The attackers chanted, "Kill her, kill her," during the thirty-minute stoning.

Finally, one of her cousins picked up a huge rock and dropped it on her forehead. The mob continued kicking her.

After she was dead, her cousins took her body to the outskirts of Bashiqa where they burned her remains with a dog, symbolizing her worthlessness.

An autopsy showed that she died of a fractured skull and spine.

According to the police chief in Mosul, most of the killers were cousins of Du'a and their friends. Journalists were told that the police did not intervene in the stoning because they believed Du'a was guilty of "immoral behavior . . . [for] breaking a taboo prescribed by social tradition, rather than [for] changing faith."[6]

It was only when police learned that Du'a may have been killed for attempting to convert from Yazidism that they chose to issue warrants for the arrest of her killers. The religious leader of the Yazidis, Tahsin Saeed Ali, publicly condemned the stoning as "a heinous crime." In trying to downplay the religious motivation of the killers, he said that they acted out of "old traditions," implying that their motivation was based on cultural values not religious ones.[7]

So was Du'a murdered because she attempted to convert to Islam or because she lost her virginity before marriage? Sources close to her family claim that she did not actually convert to Islam and that it was her desire to run away with Muhannad that provoked her cousins.

The hospital autopsy confirmed that she was a virgin.

The History of So-Called Honor Killings

United Nations figures for the year 2000 indicate that 5,000 women around the world are killed every year for reasons related to family honor. Experts believe that the real figure is much higher.

The unfair and systematic labeling of these murders being based on only Islamic practices and life habits pushed me to try to gain a better understanding of the roots of so-called honor crimes. I did not have to read long to learn that this practice, as well as other forms of abuse of women, has precedents throughout history in both the East and the West. The origin of honor-based violence against woman and issues such as female chastity and virginity are not exclusive to any ethnicity, religion, or geography.

Starting with those ancient civilizations that have left us a record of their laws and social customs, there is a consistent pattern of "blame" in cases of sexual misdeed, adultery, and betrayal—and this blame rests with the woman. Rome, Assyria, India, and the ancient American cultures have consistently depicted women as the original source of wrongdoing and even of evil. Many historians, sociologists, and anthropologists have written at length about this.

One of the earliest of all recorded sets of laws, found among the Sumerians in ancient Mesopotamia, the Code of Hammurabi (ca. 1800 B.C.) stipulated that if a woman displays immoral behavior, runs away from the marital home, neglects her husband, or embezzles money, then she should be drowned.[8] Wives convicted of adultery were drowned.[9] This code served as the basis of law for the Babylonians, Assyrians, and, eventually, the Hebrews. In Assyria, the law gave men the power to punish their wives for adultery as they saw fit, whether it be execution, mutilation, or forgiveness.[10] The Sumerian code did not contain a single law to punish a man who betrays his wife.

Matthew A. Goldstein, who has studied honor killings in the Roman Empire, observed that the status of women in ancient Rome depended mostly on their male relatives. Fathers were given the power of life and death over their daughters. For starters, he wielded absolute power over newborns; he could decide to kill any newborn male if the baby had been born handicapped and any newborn female if he thought he already had enough daughters.[11] Once a woman married, her father's authority was transferred to her husband.[12] Female adultery was considered a crime under Roman law; if a husband discovered his wife in a compromising position, he had a legal right to kill her without fear of prosecution or punishment.[13]

In addition, family members could be prosecuted for not taking action against an adulterous female.[14] Such legislation was intended to preserve the rights of married Roman soldiers who spent many long years abroad propagating the expansion of the Roman Empire. Of course, the soldiers were not expected to remain chaste on these campaigns.[15]

In India, ancient Hindu law was very harsh in dealing with women. Women were seen as a necessary evil; they were needed to produce children, but at the same time they were believed to be a never-ending source of shame and disgrace and were always considered the root of marital discord.[16]

On the other side of the world, Aztec laws (put into place between 150 B.C. and A.D. 1521) punished female adulterers with death by strangulation or stoning. However, the husband, according to Aztec law, was required to provide proof and was forbidden, on pain of execution, from killing his wife, even if he caught her in the act.[17]

In Peru, between 1200 B.C. and A.D. 532, Incas punished both male and female adulterers by tying their hands and feet to a wall and leaving them to die. Claiming the crime was committed in the heat of the moment was an acceptable defense for men who killed their wives on the suspicion of adultery, but wives who killed their husbands were hung by their feet until they died.[18]

In ancient Egypt, a woman who committed adultery was burned to death, whereas her partner was thrown into the Nile River to drown.[19]

Much of the current commentary on so-called honor crimes focuses on the religious element, sometimes implying that it is religion itself that is to blame. Sin is a central preoccupation for all the major religions, and some in the Judeo-Christian tradition believe that Eve was fully responsible for the first sin. When God confronted Adam with his sin, he—seeking to deflect blame—replied, "The woman whom You gave to be with me, she gave me from the tree, and I ate."[20] The human race as a whole, according to this view, was damned for her mistake.

Judaism, Christianity, and Islam all punish adultery severely. In Judaism, adultery is forbidden by the seventh commandment of the Decalogue, but only the act of a married woman engaging in sexual intercourse with another man counts as adultery. In this case, both the woman and the man are considered guilty. This does not apply to a married man having relations with an unmarried woman.

In the book of Leviticus in the Old Testament, the death penalty was imposed on a man who committed adultery with a married woman.

The issue of virginity is stressed in Deuteronomy 22:13–21, where the text suggests that in the event the husband of a bride claims that his wife was not a virgin on the marriage day, the bride's parents would be summoned by a judge to show that the linen from the marriage bed was stained with blood to prove their daughter was a virgin.[21]

The punishment for a woman losing her virginity while still single in her father's home is death by stoning (Deut. 22:13–21). And a raped virgin woman must marry her attacker regardless of her feelings toward the person who raped her (Deut. 22:28–29).

The Black Jews, who fled Palestine for different parts of Africa in A.D. 70 following the destruction of Herod's Temple, also put great emphasis on women's chastity, and if a husband "received damaged goods, his guilty wife was unsexed and her left breast was cut off by a priest." The Black Jews kept all the Jewish traditions, including practicing polygamy, circumcision, and the hierarchal rule of rabbis.[22]

Highlighting the importance of virginity, preacher John Chrysostom (A.D. 349–407) attempted to convince young widowed women not to remarry, saying, "We men . . . love most what no one else has used or taken advantage of before us, so that we are the first and only masters."[23]

The Christian religion in the eleventh century also placed great emphasis on women's virginity; it was valued above marriage. Moreover, it was taught that virgin women received better rewards in heaven than married women.[24] Female children were brought up learning that virginity was both a social and religious value and that the honor of the family depended on it; girls were taught to guard "their treasure with their lives."[25] Christian societies treated virgin women as creatures whose innocence needed to be cultivated and protected. In other words, the "intact seal" of a woman became her essence.[26]

In Europe during the early ages, the importance of chastity, virginity, and the good behavior of women was clearly emphasized. In the first century, German adulteresses were flogged and buried alive.[27] It was common throughout Europe for men to murder their wives because they suspected infidelity and to kill their daughters because they eloped. It was also common for brothers to kill their sisters because they refused to marry the man their family had chosen for them.[28]

Turning to Europe during the Middle Ages, incidents of murdering and burning women for adultery were commonplace and have been documented extensively. Feminist and sociologist Dr. Nawal Saadawi mentions in her book *Woman Is the Origin* that in fourteenth-century Europe "wise and smart women" were considered sorceresses by the church, often so designated because of their use of herbs to cure illnesses. They were killed, burned, or locked in hospitals for the mentally ill, both in the name of religion and to preserve the values of the society.[29] The real reason for this, she writes, was that male priests were afraid of losing power because they were supposedly the sole authority when it came to healing sick people. Anything else was ungodly.[30]

In Renaissance Italy, women were executed for adultery.[31] Historian Keith Thomas says that in the sixteenth century, chastity was considered the essence of female virtue and that women were expected to be a virgin on their wedding night.[32] In her book on adultery and inquisition in early modern Spain, professor of Spanish and Portuguese languages and literatures Georgina Dopico Black said that in the sixteenth and seventeenth centuries, the body and soul of married women "became a site subject to scrutiny of a remarkable array of gazes: inquisitors, theologians, religious reformers, confessors, poets, playwrights, and, not least among them, husbands."[33] Married women were simply entities that provided men with legitimate children. Women carried the burden of their family's honor and were responsible for protecting their family's reputation.[34] Again, with striking similarity to the cases I have investigated in Jordan, the mere suspicion of adulterous desire routinely legitimized the brutal murder of women by their husbands.[35]

In her book *The Second Sex*, French philosopher, novelist, and essayist Simone de Beauvoir described many plays and operas written during the 1880s in Europe that portrayed women as sinners and evil creatures. In these plays it was clear that punishing "evil women" was not left to the husband; it was the responsibility of the community because the woman's misbehavior offended the whole of society. Stories in Spanish literature of the Middle Ages often tell of a king or a baron who wantonly murdered women. Knights often valued their horses more than their women, whom they chastised, beat, and dragged by the hair.[36]

In France, the Napoleonic Code, hastily drafted by four jurists in 1804, has a great deal to answer for. Incredibly, it is still applied in many Arab countries today. It placed married women entirely under male guardianship (often interpreted as ownership). The wife had to obey her husband, and the husband had the power to condemn her to solitary confinement for adultery, and to divorce her (but not the other way round). If he caught her in the act of adultery and killed her, he was excused by law.[37]

Coming closer to our own times, any reader of Victorian literature will be able to cite endless examples of women as weak and dependent creatures. Charlotte Brontë's Mr. Rochester (*Jane Eyre*) kept his first, deranged wife in the attic. Thomas Hardy's novels are peppered with dramatic scenes hinging on "ownership" of women and even their sale. Judy Mabro writes in her book *Veiled Half-Truths: Western Travellers' Perceptions of Middle Eastern Women* that the act of wife-selling took place in England in the nineteenth century, "frequently in the cattle markets, and popular custom often demanded that the woman be led there in a halter."[38]

The Value of Virginity

Coming closer to the twenty-first century, obsession with virginity and virtue remains an important factor for many. According to a study conducted by researcher Mohamed Awad, 99.2 percent of women interviewed in Egypt believed that a woman's honor lies in her virginity, and only 0.8 percent said that it is based on her principles and values.[39]

In a special report for the *New York Times*, journalist Douglas Jehl wrote: "What is honor? Abeer Allam, a young Egyptian journalist, remembered how it was explained by a high-school biology teacher as he sketched the female reproductive system and pointed out the entrance to the vagina. 'This is where the family honor lies!' the teacher declared."[40]

In China, a Chinese billionaire placed an ad in a newspaper in Shanghai in January 2006 seeking a virgin to marry.[41] He received 600 applications. He interviewed twenty before finally choosing the "lucky" bride. The *New York Times* noted in its January 2006 report that these kinds of ads have been common since 2004, and it is usually rich Chinese men seeking virgin brides.[42] The ads and a report by a Chinese newspaper drew mixed reactions from the Chinese community, from one woman saying she was saving her virginity for a good price to others who described the practice as selling themselves as cheap merchandise. The obsession with female virgins in China prompted a forty-three-year-old man to purchase the virginity of seventeen schoolgirls in Nanyang, Henan Province, according to a report in the *Shanghai Daily* in May 2006.[43]

Indicating that chastity is still a serious concern in Italy, the country's highest court ruled in 2006 that it was a less serious crime to sexually abuse a teenager if she was not a virgin. The court ruled in favor of a man who appealed his forty-month-old verdict after being found guilty for forcing oral sex on his fourteen-year-old stepdaughter. His mitigating circumstance was that the victim was not a virgin; he ended up receiving a lower sentence, according to a short report that appeared in *Ms. Magazine* in the summer of 2006.[44] And in Sicily, there exists a minimum penalty of three years in prison for murders of "honor."[45]

Female Genital Mutilation

According to the World Health Organization, the genitals of 130 million women worldwide have been mutilated in the practice known as female circumcision. Two million women are subjected to this practice yearly.[46] The United Nations states that fifteen of twenty-eight African states where female genital mutilation (FGM) is prevalent have enacted laws criminalizing the practice, and five other African states are considering drafting legislation on FGM. Two of the nine countries in Asia and ten nation-states in other parts of the world have enacted legal measures prohibiting and criminalizing FGM.[47]

Despite the common information that is repeated by the United Nations, governments, and activists that FGM is a practice found in Africa and some countries in the Middle East, some U.S. writers have recently revealed that FGM had been practiced in the United Kingdom during the Victorian era and in the United States in the early 1990s.[48]

The United Kingdom and the United States were obsessed during the era at the end of the eighteenth century and the early 1990s with women's masturbation. Physicians tried various methods to stop women from masturbating, including applying caustic substances to the clitoris and vulva to produce a chronic sore and the complete excision of the clitoris with scissors. According to Martha Coventry, a Minneapolis writer, she had a clitoridectomy when she was six after her family noticed that her clitoris looked two or three times bigger than the normal size.[49]

Coventry refers to Isaac Baker Brown, a famous gynecologist in the United Kingdom during the 1850s who had a theory that all women's diseases "could be attributed to overexcitement of the nervous system; and the pudic [*sic*] nerve, which runs into the clitoris, is particularly powerful. When aggravated by habitual stimulation, this nerve puts undue stress on the health of women."[50] He lists what he described were the eight stages of progressive diseases triggered by masturbation. He said first comes hysteria, followed by spinal irritation, hysterical epilepsy, cataleptic fits, epileptic fits, idiocy, mania, and, finally, death.[51]

Coventry said Baker Brown believed that eradicating the clitoris made intractable women happy women and made rebellious teenage girls settle back into the bosom of their families while married women formerly averse to sexual duties became pregnant.[52] Baker Brown's theories of female clitoridectomy, according to Coventry, influenced U.S. doctors who discussed his procedure in medical journals in 1866. In 1894, a U.S. surgeon reported that he excised the clitoris of a 30-month-old child to "stop her from masturbating and slipping into insanity."[53]

Macquarrie University anthropologist Dr. Kirsten Bell wrote an essay stating that clitoridectomies were occasionally endorsed in Australia and the United States well into the 1960s as a cure for excessive masturbation. Bell referred to the popular Christian coming-of-age manual *On Becoming a Woman*, first published in 1951 and reprinted in 1968, in which Dr. Harold Shryock writes:

> There are teenage girls who, impelled by an unwholesome curiosity or by the example of unscrupulous girl friends, have fallen into the habit of manipulating these sensitive tissues as a means of excitement. This habit is spoken of

as masturbation. . . . There is an anatomical factor that sometimes causes irritation about the clitoris and thus encourages a manipulation of the delicate reproductive organs. . . . Oftentimes the remedy for this situation consists of a minor surgical operation spoken of as circumcision. This operation is not hazardous and is much to be preferred to allowing the condition of irritation to continue.[54]

Positive Religious Stances Toward Women

Religion, as it evolved, has not always maintained hostility to women. It is one of the defining characteristics of the New Testament that Jesus treated women with dignity, even women who might be regarded as outcasts: "He blessed their children, raised their dead, forgave their sins and restored their virtue and honor. Thus, he exalted the position of womanhood himself."[55]

A common story, often used to describe the Christian stance on adultery, is that of the adulterous woman brought to the Mount of Olives to receive her punishment. Jesus was already there. He was preaching and was surrounded by a large audience. The men who had brought the woman made her stand before the group and said to Jesus, "Teacher, this woman was caught in the act of adultery." There was no mention of her male partner or partners. "In the Law, Moses commanded us to stone such women. Now what do you say?" Jesus replied: "He who is without sin among you, let him cast the first stone." Nobody was willing to do this, and the crowd departed, leaving the woman alone with Jesus. He asked her, "Has no one condemned you?" "No one, sir," she replied. "Then neither do I condemn you," Jesus declared. "Go now and leave your life of sin."

William E. Phipps, who wrote a book on Muhammad and Jesus in which he compared the two prophets and their teachings, explained Jesus' stand: "Jesus was indignant that those men had apprehended only one member of the liaison. . . . Obviously, the accusing men had indulgently winked at the male participant."[56]

Archimandrite Christoforos Atallah, the representative of the Greek Orthodox patriarchate for North Jordan and vice president of the ecclesiastical court, confirmed to me during an interview that there are no stories in the New Testament that mention the male accomplice in any adultery case. He argues that the point of this story is to show how Jesus Christ used his wisdom and the true meaning of his religion to show his followers that dealing with any mistake is done through love and forgiveness.

A parallel story is often told in relation to the position of Islam regarding adultery. A woman adulteress told Prophet Muhammad (Peace Be Upon Him) that she was pregnant out of wedlock and wanted to be stoned for her sin. The Prophet (PBUH) told her to return after she had delivered the baby. After delivering the baby, the woman returned to Prophet Muhammad (PBUH), but he asked her to return after she had finished weaning the baby. When she returned, she was stoned. No mention is made of her male partner. It is clear from both of these stories that within these cultures men bear no responsibility for the act of adultery.

The Islamic scholar Dr. Hamdi Murad explained to me that in the second story, the woman pointed to the man (allegedly) responsible for the pregnancy. The man, however, denied any wrongdoing. Therefore, Prophet Muhammad (PBUH) did not order any punishment for him. From an Islamic perspective, Dr. Murad says, the punishment for adultery is inflicted only if an individual confesses or if there were four witnesses who could testify against the accused.

Dr. Murad also spoke about another, less-familiar story, in which a man named Maez went to the Prophet (PBUH) to confess to adultery. The Prophet (PBUH) ignored the confession, but the man was insistent, so the Prophet (PBUH) ordered that he be punished by stoning. Meanwhile, the woman involved in this instance, according to Dr. Murad, did not confess, and so received no punishment.

Prophet Muhammad (PBUH) stated in one of his sayings that came in Sahih al-Muslim (Book 032, Number 6362): "He who is involved in bringing up daughters, and is benevolent towards them, will have his benevolence a shield for him against Hell-Fire."

The Holy Qur'an also calls upon parents to accept newborn baby girls with the same joy they would receive a baby boy: "And whenever one of them receives tidings that a female has been born for him, his face remains darkened, and he is filled with suppressed rage! He hides himself from people because of the bad news he has received. (He asks himself) whether he should keep it (the baby) with disgrace, or bury it in the dust? Verily, their judgment is evil" (Surah Al-Nahl 58–59).

King Abdullah's former advisor on Islamic affairs, the late Sheikh Izzedin Al-Khatib Al-Tamimi, emphasized that these verses played an important role in saving female babies from being murdered at birth.[57]

The Qur'an is very strict when it comes to the offense of damaging a woman's reputation by spreading unfounded rumors of adultery or bad behavior. Islam specifically forbids spying on people and revealing people's secrets with the aim of harming them or causing them punishment:

> And for those who accuse their wives (with adultery) but they have no witnesses except themselves; let them testify four times; (swearing by Allah) that they are telling the truth. And (they swear) a fifth time, invoking the Curse of Allah upon themselves if they are telling lies. (Surah Al-Nur 6–7)

Another verse stipulates: "Those who slander chaste, careless, and believing women are cursed in this world and in the Hereafter, and for them there will be a great punishment" (Surah Al-Nur 23). Furthermore, "O you who believe! Avoid much suspicion, because some suspicion may be a sin" (Surah Al Hujurat 12).

As Dr. Murad explains, the Qur'an states: "And those who accuse chaste women with adultery and do not bring four witnesses, flog each one of them (with) eighty strips and afterwards do not accept their testimony at all. They are indeed evil liars" (Surah Al-Nur 4), and:

> Those who spread that slander are a gang among you. Do not consider it a bad thing for you. Nay, it is good for you. For every one of them is his share of sin; and for him among them, who had the greater share of it, will be a great punishment. When you heed it, why did not the believers—men and women— think well of their own people, and say: "This is an evident falsehood?" Why did they not bring four witnesses to prove it? But, because they did not bring four witnesses, they are the liars in the sight of Allah. (Surah Al-Nur 11–13)

The punishment for adultery is addressed to both the male and female adulterer equally:

> The adulterer and the adulteress, lash each one of them a hundred stripes. And do not let pity for the twain prevent you from obeying Allah, if you believe in Allah and the Last Day. And let a group of the believers witness their punishment. (Surah Al-Nur 2)

Dr. Murad also refers to a story where a man asked the Prophet (PBUH) what kind of punishment should be given if he found his wife committing adultery with another man and killed them both. The Prophet (PBUH) replied that either he must bring four witnesses of good reputation or he, the accuser, would be killed.

Conclusion

Unfortunately, I only have room to sketch out the bare minimum of the historical and religious seeds of dishonor here, but I hope this chapter serves well enough to make the point that so-called honor crimes stem from a long and complicated sociopolitical and religious history, stretching back to ancient times. Because of these deep historical roots, so-called honor killings are not going to disappear overnight, no matter how much campaigning and will for political change there is. Having said that, I believe there is cause for optimism as more people speak out against so-called honor crimes.

For example, British police officers are now being educated to recognize the signs of "honor" violence, and they are directed to treat these crimes as seriously as they treat racial violence.[58]

In 2002, Diana Nammi started the Iranian and Kurdish Women's Rights Organisation to serve Kurdish-, Farsi-, and Arabic-speaking women in London. In 2010, the organization took 1,500 calls on its advice line,[59] and they are currently advocating for a national strategy on "honor"-based violence.[60] Nammi says that "care workers, teachers, general practitioners, hospitals, and welfare officers should all be trained to recognize when someone is in danger of becoming a victim of an honor killing and help them."[61]

In 2008, laws to prevent forced marriages and to help those already in forced marriages were introduced in England, Wales, and Northern Ireland.[62]

In Turkey, so-called honor killings used to be considered crimes of "extreme provocation," and Turkish penal code allowed the time in prison of the killer to be significantly reduced "when a killing was carried out immediately before, during, or immediately after a situation of anticipated adultery or fornication."[63] In a new law, which took effect in 2005, honor killings are now considered a form of voluntary homicide, and the killer can be sentenced to life in prison with no reduction of sentence. In addition, family members who encourage the killing can be charged with a crime.[64]

Therapist and advocate Aruna Papp stresses that the issue of so-called honor crimes is not limited to Muslim communities: "Unchallenged violence against women, including honor killing, is also a distressing feature of Sikh, Hindu, and South Asian Christian communities."[65] Papp was raised in India in a Christian home; however, the central Christian values of individual worth were subjugated by a culture that reinforces the worthlessness of women: "From an early age, I, like millions of other females, knew that girls were dispensable. We suffered from . . . a brutal brainwashing technique that internalizes the idea in both men and women that women are unworthy creatures."[66] Papp now lives in Canada and is active as a consultant, counselor, and writer on topics of cultural violence. She wrote a public policy report on culturally driven violence in Canada's immigrant communities, released in 2010, with the goal of "blunt[ing] the effect of these detrimental and destructive cultural traditions" and encouraging immigrant communities to value gender equality.[67]

Jagdeesh Singh, the brother of Surjit Athwal, who was murdered in 1998 by her husband and mother-in-law for seeking a divorce, continues to speak out against so-called honor crimes. He says that successfully prosecuting these criminals will help bring down the "very obstinate power structure which oppresses women and young people."[68] But he adds that the ethnic and religious communities themselves must publicly condemn these types of crimes: "It is incumbent upon us as individuals, families, and groups to raise our voices over this. If we don't, then we are just as guilty as the perpetrators."[69]

I believe that great strides will be made as more and more people speak out against the crimes and educate others. More important, with uniformed denunciation of so-called honor crimes worldwide, people will become more aware of religious stands on women's issues without prejudice or discrimination toward the noble religions of the world.

Notes

1. *Daily Mail*, "Grandmother Jailed for Life over Honour Killing of 'Cheating' Daughter-in-Law," September 19, 2007. Available at www.dailymail.co.uk/pages/live /articles/news/news.html?in_article_id=482669&in_page_id=1770.

2. Jane Hutcheon, "In the Name of Honour," ABC News, September 19, 2007. Available at www.abc.net.au/news/stories/2007/09/19/2037201.htm.

3. *Daily Mail*, "Grandmother Jailed for Life."

4. Joanne [pseud.], "Pavan Athwal: Keeping Her Mother's Memory Alive," December 15, 2008. Available at www.stophonourkillings.com/?q=node/3263.

5. Jesse Nunes, "Iraq's Sectarian Strife Engulfs Minority Yazidis," *Christian Science Monitor*, April 24, 2007. Available at www.csmonitor.com/2007/0424/p99s01-duts .html.

6. Institute for War and Peace Reporting, "'Honour Killing' Sparks Fears of New Iraqi Conflict," May 14, 2007. Available at www.ekurd.net/mismas/articles/misc2007/5 /kurdlocal356.htm.

7. Ibid.

8. Paul Frischauer, *Sex in the Ancient World*, translated into Arabic by Faeq Dahdouh (Ninaoi Press, 1999), 92.

9. Ibid., 77.

10. Russian Information Network, "Crime and Punishment in the Ancient World of the Bible." Available at http://istina.rin.ru/eng/ufo/text/299.html.

11. Frischauer, *Sex in the Ancient World*, 400.

12. Matthew A. Goldstein, "The Biological Roots of Heat-of-Passion Crimes and Honour Killings," *Politics and the Life Sciences* 21, no. 2 (September 2002): 28–37.

13. Frischauer, *Sex in the Ancient World*, 428.

14. Goldstein, "The Biological Roots of Heat-of-Passion Crimes and Honour Killings," 29.

15. Frischauer, *Sex in the Ancient World*, 428.

16. Ibid., 176.

17. Goldstein, "The Biological Roots of Heat-of-Passion Crimes and Honour Killings," 29.

18. Ibid.

19. Adel Azzam Al Hait, "Femicide in Defense of Honour in Jordan: Theoretical Analysis and Current Practices" (diss., University of Warwick [United Kingdom], September 2001), 5.

20. It is not clear if Adam was blaming Eve or God. In either case, God would have none of it and attributed full responsibility to Adam.

21. Pauline Schmitt Pantel, Georges Duby, and Michelle Perrot, eds., *A History of Women in the West I: From Ancient Goddess to Christian Saints* (Cambridge, MA: Belknap Press, 2002), 304.

22. Paul Tabori, *Taken in Adultery: A Short History of Woman's Infidelity Throughout the Ages, Its Reward, and Its Punishment* (London: Aldus Publications, 1949), 20.

23. Pantel, Duby, and Perrot, *A History of Women in the West I*, 306.

24. Christiane Klapisch-Zuber, Georges Duby, and Michelle Perrot, eds., *A History of Women in the West II: Silences of the Middle Ages* (Cambridge, MA: Belknap Press, 1998), 212.

25. Ibid., 213.

26. Ibid.

27. Ibid., 171.

28. Jacob Burckhardt, *The Civilisation of the Renaissance in Italy* (London: Penguin Books, 1990), 48.

29. Dr. Nawal Saadawi, *Woman Is the Origin: Studies on Women and Men in the Arab Society* (Beirut, Lebanon: Arab Institute for Studies and Publication, 1990), 160, 167.

30. Ibid.

31. Burckhardt, *The Civilisation of the Renaissance in Italy*, 48.

32. Keith Thomas, "The Double Standard," *Journal of the History of Ideas* 20 (April 1959): 200.

33. Georgina Dopico Black, *Perfect Wives, Other Women: Adultery and Inquisition in Early Modern Spain* (Durham, NC: Duke University Press, 2001), xiv.

34. Natalie Zemon Davis, Arlette Farg, Georges Duby, and Michelle Perrot, eds., *A History of Women in the West III: Renaissance and Enlightenment Paradoxes* (Cambridge, MA: Belknap Press, 2003), 476.

35. Black, *Perfect Wives, Other Women*, 12.

36. Simone de Beauvoir, *The Second Sex*, trans. and ed. H. M. Parshley (New York: Vintage Books, 1989), 100, 190.

37. Black, *Perfect Wives, Other Women*, 111.

38. Judy Mabro, *Veiled Half-Truths: Western Travellers' Perceptions of Middle Eastern Women* (London: I. B. Tauris, 1996), 21–22.

39. Mariz Tadros, "Like a Match Stick," Al-Ahram Weekly Online, no. 573 (February 14–20, 2002). Available at http://weekly.ahram.org.eg/2002/573/li1.htm.

40. Douglas Jehl, "For Shame: A Special Report—Arab Honor's Price: A Woman's Blood," *New York Times*, June 20, 1999. Available at www.nytimes.com/1999/06/20/world/for-shame-a-special-report-arab-honor-s-price-a-woman-s-blood.html.

41. Howard W. French, "Rich Guy Seeks Girl, Must Be Virgin: Read This Ad," *New York Times*, January 14, 2006. Available at www.chinadaily.com.cn/english/doc/2006-01/24/content_515001.htm.

42. Ibid.

43. Zhang Liuhao, "Man Purchases 17 Girls' Virginity," *Shanghai Daily*, May 25, 2006.

44. *Ms. Magazine*, Global Section, Short Takes (Summer 2006): 33.

45. Germaine Tillion, *The Republic of Cousins: Women's Oppression in Mediterranean Society*, trans. Quintin Hoare (London: Al Saqi Books, 1983), 34.

46. Anna Karamanou, "Women: The Target of Fundamentalists," *Al Raida* XIX, nos. 97–98 (Spring–Summer 2002): 4.

47. Document no. A/61/122/Add.1, "In-Depth Study on All Forms of Violence Against Women," Item 60 on Advancement of Women, Report of the Secretary-General for the 61st Session of the General Assembly (July 6, 2006). Available at http://www.un.org/ga/61/third/item61summary.shtml.

48. Martha Coventry, "Making the Cut: It's a Girl . . . or Is It? When There's Doubt, Why Are Surgeons Calling the Shots?" *Ms. Magazine* X, no. 6 (October–November 2000): 54.

49. Ibid., 54.

50. Ibid.

51. Ibid.

52. Ibid.

53. Ibid.

54. As quoted in Kirsten Bell, "Genital Cutting and Western Discourses on Sexuality," *Medical Anthropology Quarterly* 19, no. 2 (June 2005): 125–148. Available at www.cirp.org/library/anthropology/bell1/.

55. John MacArthur, *Twelve Extraordinary Women: How God Shaped Women of the Bible and What He Wants to Do with You* (Nashville, TN: Nelson Books, 2005), xiv.

56. William E. Phipps, *Muhammad and Jesus: A Comparison of the Prophets and Their Teachings* (New York: Continuum, 2003), 135.

57. Sheikh Izzedin Al Khatib Al Tamimi, "Women and Children's Rights Between the Islamic Sharia and the International Conventions" (paper presented at a UNICEF conference on merging the Convention on the Elimination of Discrimination Against Women (CEDAW) and the Child Conventions in the Law Colleges Curricular, June 14, 2000), 14.

58. Jerome Taylor, "My People Refuse to Talk About Honour Killings," *Independent*, December 19, 2009. Available at www.independent.co.uk/news/uk/crime/article1845103.ece.

59. Joanne [pseud.], "'Honour' Killings Plan Does Not Go Far Enough, Says Women's Rights Group," March 8, 2011. Available at www.stophonourkillings.com/?q=node/5301.

60. See the Iranian and Kurdish Women's Rights Organisation website (www.ikwro.org.uk).

61. Diana Nammi, "Training Is Needed to Recognise Dangers," *Independent*, June 29, 2007. Available at www.independent.co.uk/opinion/commentators/diana-nammi-training-is-needed-to-recognise-dangers-455141.html.

62. Divya Talwar, "Forced Marriage Helpline to Close," BBC News, November 18, 2009. Available at http://news.bbc.co.uk/2/hi/uk_news/england/8365066.stm.

63. Zulfu Livaneli, "Honor Killings and Violence Against Women in Turkey," Turkish Cultural Foundation (summarized from an April 2006 address by Livaneli at New York University, New York City). Available at www.turkishculture.org/lifestyles/lifestyle/the -women/honor-killings-426.htm.

64. Ibid.

65. Aruna Papp, "Canada Must Come to Grips with 'Culturally Approved Violence' Against Women," *National Post*, August 14, 2009.

66. Ibid.

67. Barbara Kay, "Honor Killings Must Be Confronted Here at Home," *National Post*, July 7, 2010. Available at http://fullcomment.nationalpost.com/2010/07/07/5957 /#more-5957.

68. Taylor, "My People Refuse to Talk About Honour Killings."

69. Ibid.

16

An Islamic Treatise on Tolerance

ABDOLKARIM SOROUSH

Translated by Nilou Mobasser

Abdolkarim Soroush is an Iranian philosopher, a devout Muslim, and one of the leading intellectual forces behind the Islamic republic's pro-democracy movement. A Muslim activist during the 1979 revolution in Iran, Soroush has since braved death threats to argue for Islamic plural-ism and challenge the notion that religion should not be open to differ-ent interpretations. The author of many books, including many about Islam and democracy, Soroush has taught at the University of Tehran, Harvard, Princeton, and Yale. In 2005, Time listed him as one of the world's 100 most influential people.

Defending Tolerance in Iran

When my book *Tolerance and Governance* was being put forward for publication (1995), Iran was experiencing its most severe period of political asphyxiation since the revolution. I was forced to leave the country, having been subjected to savage physical assaults at universities and public venues, as well as fierce written attacks in newspapers. I lost my job and security and—far away from my family—spent my time fleeing from country to country (Germany to Britain to Canada). The Iranian Culture Ministry had fallen into the hands of a minister who came from the ranks of extremist conservatives—a minister who would not allow the publication of even a shred of "un-Islamic" material. The newspaper and book market was undergoing an unparalleled slump, and I was not offered the chance to defend myself against the insults and calumnies directed at me. My students also had been banned from writing or explaining anything.

Under these oppressive conditions, one of my audacious students (a friend who is now serving a six-year prison term because of his courage in revealing secrets behind the killing of a number of writers) had the courage to push through the publication of my book. The book was a collection of my writings, but it also included scholarly critiques of my work, written by others, that had appeared in various publications. This approach was almost unprecedented in the history of Iran's book industry, but a subsequent development was to make it truly unprecedented. The Culture Ministry was preventing the publication of the book as it stood; the ministry required that we include a long, critical piece written by one of the agents behind the regime's policy of cultural repression (he happened to be a leading member of the Ansar-e Hezbollah vigilante group). The book now bears within it that unwanted article like an illegitimate child. But without that bastard article, the book never would have been published. The bittersweet irony is that this illegitimate element was the cause of the book's legitimacy.

My aim in this chapter is to persuade Muslims that it is possible for them both to safeguard their Muslim values and norms *and* to live in a democratic society; one need not acquire one at the cost of the other. Muslim values include not only tolerance but also the responsibility to criticize officials and hold them accountable; both of these notions—tolerance and public accountability—are firm pillars of democracy. At this point, we need to focus on giving precedence to rights over duties and substituting interpretive pluralism for an interpretive monopoly (that is, the official interpretation of religion by rulers). Tolerance, of which we are in great need in the larger Muslim world today, is by no means alien to our Iranian culture and Islamic creed. Two of Iran's greatest poets and thinkers—Hafez and Rumi—reveal in their work that tolerance has been a part of our culture and the Islamic creed for centuries.

Pluralism in the Qur'an

Let us first turn to the Qur'an. In chapter 60, verses 8–9, we read:

Allah does not forbid you in regard to those who did not make war against you on account of religion and did not expel you from your homes that you may deal with them with kindness and justice. Indeed Allah loves the just. Allah forbids you only in regard to those who made wars against you on account of religion and expelled you from your homes and supported others in your expulsion, that you may make friends with them.

This categorical and lucid statement concerns relationships between Muslims and non-Muslims. These verses were revealed to Muhammad during the second phase of his mission, when he was living in Medina as the powerful head of the first Islamic state. How, then, should the now dominant Muslims treat their non-Muslim neighbors? Although not straightforwardly written, the verses commend without reservation the showing of kindness and justice toward non-Muslims neighbors. These verses are significant because the kindness toward neighbors they enjoin is not an arbitrary and unexpected recommendation on the part of Allah but is rather a reasoned conclusion stemming from a principle of justice. This is precisely what makes it universal and categorical.

To be sure, a few verses in the Qur'an ostensibly enjoin Muslims to wage war (jihad) against infidels. The first thing to realize is that the word *jihad* does not mean "holy war," it means "striving," for personal betterment and for the betterment of society (which, admittedly, means the spread of Islam). But these verses should be read and interpreted in the light of and under the guidance of the verses from chapter 60. Chapter 60 has "guardianship" over the jihad verses because they are reasoned, whereas the others are merely recommendations. There is therefore no incompatibility between these two apparently contradictory verses. Moreover, on closer inspection most of these verses commend peaceful or defensive jihad.

Another relevant verse dealing with the same subject is the celebrated verse 13 from chapter 49:

> O mankind! We created you from a single (pair)
> of a male and a female
> And made you into Nations and Tribes that
> Ye may know each other
> (Not that ye may despise each other)
> Verily, the most honored of you
> In the sight of Allah
> Is (he who is) the most righteous of you.

Now consider chapter 10, verse 99: "And had your Lord willed, those on earth would have believed—all of them entirely. Then, [O Muhammad], would you compel the people in order that they become believers?" Not everybody is conditioned or expected to believe; nor has God willed or wished them to do so. So we are then forbidden to usurp God's authority and force others to believe.

When all of these verses are conjoined, with many others, the Qur'an offers a realistic picture of the pluralistic nature of the human condition (religion, culture, language, and so on) endorsed by Allah and preached by his apostle.

Therefore, neither the Prophet nor his followers can or should force people to become believers; on the contrary, since a world teeming with difference and disagreement is willed and welcomed by God, his sincere servants are to welcome it or, at least, tolerate it. Here again we find ourselves in front of a fundamental principle that deduces tolerance from the fact that God ordained differences among people.

Finally, in the first verse of chapter 49 we find a warning: "O who you have faith, do not venture ahead of Allah and his apostle." This warning is directed at those who do not come to terms with cultural and religious pluralism, who have not managed to understand the design of the Creation and the will of the Creator. Anyone struggling to do the impossible job of reducing the many and diverse God-created shades and colors to a single monolithic color is contradicting his will and venturing ahead of him.

Hafez

Hafez, the renowned Iranian poet of the fourteenth century, exalted the virtue of tolerance. He wrote:

> In these two expressions lies peace in this world and the next
> With friends, magnanimity; with enemies, tolerance.

Hafez penned these words a century after the Mongol invasion of Iran when Iranians, with the horror and distress of that invasion still etched on their minds, were struck by the Timurid thunderbolt. The flames of insecurity, injustice, and destruction seared the land, and not only were local rulers and politicians incapable of tolerating one another, but religious and sectarian leaders, too, were engaged in unending feuds, each one considering the other to have been duped by Satan and destined for hell. In Hafez's words, "the orb was in a grim temper" and society in need of "a sage proposition." The sage proposition, which could provide felicity and peace both in this world and the next, was, to Hafez's mind, nothing other than the two noble and lofty notions of magnanimity and tolerance; the first toward friends and the second toward enemies. If I were in Hafez's place, I would add a concluding phrase to his verse as follows: with friends, magnanimity; with enemies, tolerance, but not with the enemies of tolerance.

Hafez knew well that inviting people in a religious society to exercise tolerance would fail to have any impact or captivate hearts unless it was accompanied by an insightful theory of human nature and religion. This is why he astutely tried throughout his works to use the language of poetry and allusion to elucidate a theory of this kind and to persuade his audience that magnanimity and tolerance were sound philosophical notions that rested on solid foundations.

Human fallibility, both in the realm of theory and in the realm of practice, was something that was never far from Hafez's mind, and he tried to use religious mythology to highlight it and lay it bare. According to Islamic accounts, the presence of humans on earth was the result of two original sins: one committed by Satan and the other committed by Adam. God commanded all the angels to bow down before Adam; only Satan disobeyed, and his punishment was that he was banished from heaven by God and so had the opportunity until the end of time to deceive and lead astray Adam's offspring and to try to lure them away from God. (This myth does not appear in the same form in the Jewish and Christian scriptures).

The second sin was that Adam, tempted by Satan, ate the forbidden fruit. No sooner had he tasted the fruit than he became aware of his own nakedness and sexuality. The punishment for this sin was that Adam and Eve were banished from heaven and descended to earth, where they married and became the founders of humankind and human history.

On Hafez's reading, then, individual humans, who are the products of sin and are never immune from Satan's temptations, can neither stake a claim to infallibility themselves nor expect others to behave perfectly nor treat harshly those who err. Flawless behavior is compatible with neither human nature nor the genesis of human existence. Hafez expresses this idea in gracious terms:

> Who are we to profess innocence?
> When saintly Adam was stung by sin.

As far as Hafez is concerned, sin is a defining, ineluctable feature of human nature and conduct, and intelligent people must take this into account in their conception of the world and human life. They must not disregard its vital role even though it is morally reprehensible.

Hafez goes even further and, in one of his works, qualifies humans with the two adjectives *somnolent* and *wine-tainted*. "Somnolence" refers to theoretical fallibility, and "wine-tainted" refers to our transgressions. (Bear in mind that in Islamic law drinking wine is considered a sin.) Hafez is saying, we humans see truths with half-open eyes or in a dream-like state; hence, we do not have a totally clear conception of truth. No one possesses the truth because everyone is somnolent. No one has absolute vision; hence, no one can call another blind and treat him or her with violence. We are all half-blind, half-aware creatures, and we have to lend one another a hand. The practical outcome that emerges from this image is tolerance and patience—not just with friends but also with enemies, because we are all humans; we are all somnolent and wine-tainted.

Even more explicit and precise conclusions can be drawn from this mythology-based reading: for example, we can infer that truth and religiosity must never be used as weapons. For they are of the nature of language, not claws. Rather than encouraging arrogance and imperiousness, truth and religiosity should foster humility and forbearance. Someone who is closer to the truth should be more humble and more tolerant toward others than someone who is deluded about possessing the truth and becomes self-righteous and imagines that everyone else is deprived of the truth.

Hafez even drew on the troubling notion of determinism (predestination, fatalism) to reinforce his tolerance-inclined thinking. He says that we are all prisoners of destiny; a Muslim person is Muslim by virtue of geography and history, just as a Christian is a Christian on the same grounds. If Iranians were born in the Netherlands and the Dutch in Iran, then the latter would be Muslims and the former, Christians. How, then, can we prisoners of history and geography put on airs and claim to be superior to others, or, even worse, resort to weapons and wage war on one another? Prisons should make people humble and prisoners kinder to one another in the light of their shared fate. We are the prisoners of our history, geography, learning, and beliefs, and once the veil has fallen away, we will see with what fallacies and superstitions we were afflicted.

Hafez, who lived in a religious society filled with Sufi[1] sentiments, whilst being a serious critic of this society concurred with a determinist position of this kind and wrote:

> Rob me not of hope in eternal grace
> How can you know who is truly favored and who disgraced?
> Not only I happened to lose piety
> My Father also opted for losing the eternal heaven.

Hafez accepted his fallibility as a descendent of Adam but did not accept that his transgression removed the possibility of benefiting from God's mercy and grace. He believed that good people and bad people were destined to lead a life of felicity or villainy. And more delicately and profoundly, he wrote:

Are the chaste and the unchaste not both from the same tribe?
Which one do I choose to fall for? What choice?

In other words, when the saint and the sinner are in the same position in terms of their divinely decreed destinies, which one do we freely choose?

Is it meaningful to speak of choice and will? We can see what dubious underpinnings Hafez is prepared to call upon to bolster his belief in tolerance. To borrow an analogy from Mowlana Jalal-al-Din Rumi, we can see how Hafez turns dust into gold with the magic of his words in order to empower and enrich society with the resulting treasures.

From this panoply of views, epistemological doubt because of our half-open eyes is the most important and the most acceptable.

Rumi

Let us turn to the great poet Rumi (1207–1273), who lived a century before Hafez. He came from Balkh (in modern-day Afghanistan), and his travels took him to Iran, Iraq, and Hijaz. Finally, he came to reside in Konya (in modern-day Turkey) and was buried there. But his teachings captivated the entire Islamic world—and, in our times, also enraptured the West—and inspired many ardent hearts and lovers of God.

In order to demonstrate the extent to which human knowledge is incomplete and relative, he recounts an Indian fable to us in verse. The Indians had put an elephant on display in a dark chamber, and in order to see it, the people had to file past it in the dark. Since they could not see in the dark, they felt the elephant with their hands. On leaving the chamber, they told others about their experience. The ones who had touched the elephant's feet said, "I saw a column." The ones who had touched the elephant's back said, "I saw a plank." The ones who had touched its trunk said, "I saw a pipe," and so on.

Rumi tells us that if these people had had candles in their hands, their differences would have disappeared. But, alas, in the dark chamber of nature, our knowledge of the truth (which is symbolized by the elephant) is fragmented. We each hold a portion of the truth and no one has all of it (apart from, he believed, mystics, who possess special, kohl-lined eyes). This understanding of the deficiency of knowledge should make us more humble, and patience and tolerance are nothing other than the fruits of the tree of humility.

Rumi held that prophets played two major roles: teacher and healer. He even attached more importance to their role as healers than as teachers. The main purpose of prophets and religions is to cultivate people's spirits and heal their souls, not to fill their minds with learning, but to fill their hearts with the love of God and love for one another and to cleanse them of sickness and hatred. The mind, too, when liberated from vice, can find its way more nimbly to the hidden chamber of the world's secrets; a mind that is in chains is a prisoner of nature.

Rumi told theologians that God had given them reason purely to recognize the truth, and he had sent religion for people to worship the Creator; woe betide them if they used it to other ends and for other purposes. The mind is like a guiding cane in the hands of the blind, not a weapon in the hands of antagonists with which they can beat each other:

> When the cane becomes an instrument for clamor and war
> smash it into a thousand pieces, O blind one!

There can be no better argument than this for exercising tolerance. When something is misapplied and used for the opposite purpose from the one for which it was intended, it must be discarded, even if it is the "cane" of reason and religion. If religions and ideologies turn into instruments of animosity and if they sow hatred, vindictiveness, and arrogance instead of filling hearts with love and magnanimity and inclining hearts toward the Creator, they must be abandoned.

Were prophets not physicians and healers? Are religions not servants of morality and the virtues? What sort of religiosity is it that increases sickness and sets people against each other and assigns people to heaven and hell? Read the stirring words of Muhyi al-Din Ibn-Arabi, the great Islamic mystic and Rumi's contemporary:

> I'm a disciple of the religion of love
> wherever the convoy of love goes, my religion and faith follow.

Mystically, Rumi takes things even further; he says that religion is neither a sword nor a cane, but a rope, a rope that the individual must grasp autonomously, with a longing to ascend, in order to climb out of the well of ignorance and conceit and glimpse the light of knowledge, magnanimity, and kindness. Many are the people who have been deceived by the Qur'an and the Bible (and by religion, in general) because it is not enough for a book to be a book of guidance; the reader must want to be guided; otherwise, a totally humane creed can produce totally inhumane results in corrupt and sullied hands. Rumi used the very evocative and expressive term "an upward yen." Beseech God continually that you may not stumble over these deep sayings and that you may arrive at the journey's end.

> For many have been led astray by the Qur'an:
> by clinging to that rope a multitude have fallen into the well.
> There is no fault in the rope,
> for you had no desire to reach the top.
> (*Mathnawi*, Book III, 4207–4209)[2]

Rumi says to the individual, "The rope is in your hands, but you do not wish to climb out of the well. You descend into the well instead. You do not have 'an upward passion.'" This is why rectifying the direction and the objective takes priority over the means and the instruments. There are people who turn religions into the instruments of animosity, and there are people who turn them into the instruments of kindness and coexistence. It depends on their "passion," which comes before religion and sits outside of it.

Sufism's Upward Yen

When we speak of the intolerance of believers toward one another, we must not forget nonbelievers. Just as we can have religious fundamentalism, so, too, can we have secular fundamentalism. Intolerance is a plague that both the believer and the unbeliever can be afflicted with, and if attention is not paid to the biological origin of it, its mental structure, and the inherent deficiency of human knowledge and if there is no "upward yen," we can all sink into pride and narrow, rigid prejudices, which produce the fruit of hatred, violence, elimination, folly, and decline. Before anything else, we must rectify our passion.

Anyone who thinks that he or she has special qualities or especially clear eyesight so that he or she can view humanity and history from a greater height and has discovered the hidden and ultimate secret of humanity's existence and history's destination, anyone who imagines that politics and statesmanship are the realization of a divine or historical (religious or secular) promise, anyone who believes that he or she has a superior and different standing from everyone else, anyone who treats others in a way that he or she would not want to be treated can easily succumb to destructive violence and intolerance and even consider this violence sacrosanct. This kind of intolerance is the worst kind because it is seen by the perpetrator not only as his or her right but also as his or her divine or historical "duty." Is it interesting to note that mystics and prophets were of the opinion that, despite possessing special forces and qualities, they had a mission to behave toward the masses as if they were one of them and that they even believed that the unkindness of the masses toward them was an intrinsic hardship of the spiritual path that they had to endure.

Islamic Sufism, despite its shortcomings, is the bearer and teacher of values that we are in great need of today if we are to foster tolerance. Sufis used to teach people to view power and wealth with the utmost suspicion, to be extremely wary of the afflictions that they could give rise to, and to know what mortifications their emergence, growth, and unchecked existence could bring. We can even use the denigration of power and wealth to strengthen—from a moral perspective—the fair distribution of power and wealth, which are among the pillars of liberal democracy or social democracy.

By teaching humility and rejecting avarice (even excessive avarice for knowledge) and by restraining the quest for pleasure and bolstering the quest for virtue, Sufis guided people in a direction that reduced tension and conflict amongst them, thereby encouraging coexistence and moderation. Sufis always asked God to grant them the ability to do two things: battle against the self and behave benevolently toward others; they believe that the latter was a product of the former. They maintained that a person has to be hard on himself in order to be magnanimous toward others; a person has to refuse to forgive herself in order to be forgiving toward others.

It is sad to say that in our world the internal moral elements of seeking virtue and trying to perfect oneself have become so weak that external measures cannot easily instill patience, magnanimity, and humility in people. One of the reasons humility has been considered the greatest virtue and arrogance the greatest vice is that humility breeds tolerance and arrogance breeds violence. Sufis hold love in high esteem precisely because love makes the lover humble. They, therefore, considered conceit to be the slayer of love. The people who turn religiosity into a factor that feeds selfishness and a sense of superiority—and are arrogant and self-righteous because they claim to be pious and obedient to religious law—truly commit the greatest injustice against celestial creeds. Erasmus was a committed Christian and, at the same time, a humble and tolerant humanist. His "desire for the top" prevented him from falling into the trap of ostentatious, degenerate piety. In the words of Sa'di, the illustrious Iranian poet of the thirteenth century: "The fruit-laden branch bends to the ground." In other words, the more fecund a person is, the more humble he is. It is people who are vacuous and inwardly impoverished who fail to be humble and tolerant toward others.

Tolerance and Love

In my country, Iran—a religious state—tolerance has reached its nadir today; I will go so far as to say that today in Iran tolerance is seen as a vice rather than a virtue. Before, when we lived under a secular, undemocratic state, it was also intolerant. Today, we endure an intolerant, *religious* state. (Hence, religiosity is not a necessary condition of intolerance, nor is secularity a sufficient condition for tolerance.) Today, not just unbelievers but even believers are not tolerated by the state in Iran. And there is no other reason for this than that the rulers see themselves as the measure of what is true and what is moral. And the rulers are bent on taking people to heaven even if they have to drag them there in chains. The concept of *duty* has left so little room for *rights* that even when the people want to criticize their rulers, they have to ask them for permission.

Newspapers tremble and are easily banned with the mere stroke of a pen because their variety and plurality is itself a call to tolerance and pluralism. Conversely, semiarmed groups of hooligans can operate with impunity and insolence and appear at public gatherings in order to break them up and beat up opponents. They are left free to behave in this way because they are the living embodiment of the absence of magnanimity and tolerance. The country's officials view these incidents with total indifference because this is what their brand of religiosity, or better put, their "downward yen," decrees.

Our statesmen have taken the rope of religion and are taking the people deep down into the well of obscurantism. There are only two reasons for this: first, their own downward passion and second, vacuity (their own lack of ideas). If they had an upward passion and were rich in learning and spirituality, the fate of religion and religiosity would undoubtedly have turned out better, and they would have adopted as their slogan: "magnanimity toward friends and tolerance toward enemies."

The conclusion I wish to emphasize is that tolerance is an extra-religious (and certainly not an anti-religious) virtue, exactly like love, which, in the words of the great Rumi, "lies beyond all religions." Religions have asked humans to obey God and to refrain from sin. But love (and love of God, at that) is not a religious duty; it is an extra-religious, moral virtue, which, of course, also enriches and lends meaning to religion. Tolerance, too, must be viewed in this same light. It is a virtue that we are all in great need of, whether we are believers or unbelievers. The enemies of tolerance—in whatever guise, religious or secular—are enemies of both humanity and religion. We must guide them. And it is only by teaching tolerance that we can, in Hafez's words, ensure peace in this world and the next.

Notes

1. A mystical form of Islam that seeks union with the All-Merciful.
2. Alternative translation:

> Many have been led astray by the Qur'an:
> by clinging to that rope many have fallen into the well.
> There is no fault in the rope, O perverse man,
> for it was you who had no desire to reach the top. (II, 4210–4211)

Index